Register for Free Membership to

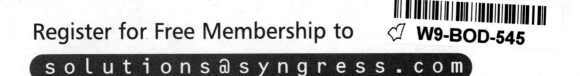

W9-BOD-545

IT Ethics Handbook

Right and Wrong for IT Professionals

Stephen Northcutt

KEY	SERIAL NUMBER
001	HJ4GEW4E39
002	PO98FGKL99
003	82H2728GNK
004	CVPLQ6WQ23
005	RTY872KM8N
006	VBTT5HJ834
007	HJJD3EGHBC
008	29MK45MN8N
009	62JTVB762M
010	IM6T56GNCF

PUBLISHED BY
Syngress Publishing, Inc.
800 Hingham Street
Rockland, MA 02370

IT Ethics Handbook: Right and Wrong for IT Professionals

Printed in the United States of America
1 2 3 4 5 6 7 8 9 0
ISBN: 1-931836-14-0

Acquisitions Editor: Christine Kloiber   Cover Designer: Michael Kavish
Technical Editor: Stephen Northcutt   Copy Editor: Judy Eby
                                                Page Layout and Art: Patricia Lupien

Distributed by O'Reilly & Associates in the United States and Canada.

Acknowledgments

We would like to acknowledge the following people for their kindness and support in making this book possible.

A special thanks to Stephen Northcutt, Brian Correia, Lynn Lewis, Lara Corcoran, and Suzy Northcutt at the SANS Institute for being so easy to work with.

Syngress books are now distributed in the United States and Canada by O'Reilly & Associates, Inc. The enthusiasm and work ethic at ORA is incredible and we would like to thank everyone there for their time and efforts to bring Syngress books to market: Tim O'Reilly, Laura Baldwin, Mark Brokering, Mike Leonard, Donna Selenko, Bonnie Sheehan, Cindy Davis, Grant Kikkert, Opol Matsutaro, Lynn Schwartz, Steve Hazelwood, Mark Wilson, Rick Brown, Leslie Becker, Jill Lothrop, Tim Hinton, Kyle Hart, Sara Winge, C. J. Rayhill, Peter Pardo, Leslie Crandell, Valerie Dow, Regina Aggio, Pascal Honscher, Preston Paull, Susan Thompson, Bruce Stewart, Laura Schmier, Sue Willing, Mark Jacobsen, Betsy Waliszewski, Dawn Mann, Kathryn Barrett, John Chodacki, and Rob Bullington.

The incredibly hard working team at Elsevier Science, including Jonathan Bunkell, Ian Seager, Duncan Enright, David Burton, Rosanna Ramacciotti, Robert Fairbrother, Miguel Sanchez, Klaus Beran, Emma Wyatt, Rosie Moss, Chris Hossack, and Krista Leppiko, for making certain that our vision remains worldwide in scope.

David Buckland, Daniel Loh, Marie Chieng, Lucy Chong, Leslie Lim, Audrey Gan, Pang Ai Hua, and Joseph Chan of STP Distributors for the enthusiasm with which they receive our books.

Kwon Sung June at Acorn Publishing for his support.

David Scott, Tricia Wilden, Marilla Burgess, Annette Scott, Geoff Ebbs, Hedley Partis, Bec Lowe, and Mark Langley of Woodslane for distributing our books throughout Australia, New Zealand, Papua New Guinea, Fiji Tonga, Solomon Islands, and the Cook Islands.

Winston Lim of Global Publishing for his help and support with distribution of Syngress books in the Philippines.

Technical Editor & Author

Stephen Northcutt, Director of Training and Certification for the SANS Institute, is a graduate of Mary Washington College. Before entering the computer security field he had a varied career as a Navy helicopter search and rescue crewman, white water rafting guide, culinary chef, martial arts instructor, cartographer, and network designer. He is the author or co-author of various publications including: *Incident Handling Step-by-Step, Intrusion Signatures and Analysis, Inside Network Perimeter Security, SANS Security Essentials, Network Intrusion Detection, 3RD edition* and now *IT Ethics Handbook: Right and Wrong for IT Professionals*. He was also the original author of the Shadow Intrusion Detection system and first DoD Shadow team leader before becoming the Chief for Information Warfare at the Ballistic Missile Defense Organization.

Special Contributors

Bryce Alexander, Network Engineer, The Vanguard Group

Kevin Behr, CTO IP Services, President, ITPI

Susan Bradley

Chris Brenton, SANS Instructor and Private Consultant

Guy Bruneau B.A. GSEC, GCIA, GCUX, Senior Security Consultant, InfoPeople Security Solutions Inc.

Paul Craig, CEO, Pimp Industries

William H. Curd, Ph.D., Ltd.

John W. Dozier, Jr., Esq., Internet and E-commerce Law

Jeremy Faircloth, Systems Engineer and Author

John Fielding, Software Engineer

Stephen Fried, Lucent Technologies, Director, Security Architecture

Jess Garcia, Security Engineer, National Institute for Aerospace Technology (INTA) – Spain

Joe Grand, President & CEO, Grand Idea Studio, Inc.

Ron Gula, CTO, Tenable Network Security

Jens Haeusser, Manager, Information Security Office, University of British Columbia

Laura Hunter, Network Engineer and Technical Trainer

Chris Hurley

Algis Kibirkstis, System Designer (Security), Ericsson Canada

Randy Marchany, SANS Instructor

Mark Markevitch, Independent Consultant

Greg Miles, Ph.D., CISSP, CISM, Security Horizon

Derek Milroy, GSEC, CISSP, MCSE, CCNA, Consultant

Sumanth Naropanth, Systems Engineer, Wipro Technologies, Bangalore, India

Ima Nauditor, Fortune 1000 company

William Occam

Angela Orebaugh, Security Consultant

Tom Parker, NetSec Inc., "Managed Security – Business Relevance"

Jerry Patterson, Senior Security Engineer, Tarpat Network Consulting

Jeff Payne, GIAC Certified, IA Analyst Inc.

Rex "Red" Rabinski

Russ Rogers, CISSP, Security Horizon

Marcus H. Sachs, The SANS Institute

Rob Shein, EDS, Washington, D.C.

Ed Skoudis, SANS Instructor

Robert M. Slade, Author of "Software Forensics"

John Stewart, Independent Researcher

Jason Soverland, System Administrator

Frank Thornton, Technology Consultant, Blackthorn Systems

Barbara Weil Laff, Director, Ireland, Stapleton, Pryor & Pascoe, P.C.

Benjamin Wright, Chief Legal Counsel, PestPatrol.com

Author Acknowledgements

In business it is so easy to take the most expedient path. A business person is faced with ethical choices many times every single day and sometimes the way that seems right to a person, isn't truly right; we have an incredible capacity to delude ourselves. One of the most useful things to do when faced with a hard choice is to discuss it with another person of integrity. During the writing of this book I faced as many ethical issues in a short number of days as I have at any time of my life. And so I want to thank the many patient people that have been willing to help me to ponder the path of wisdom:

My wife, Kathy Northcutt, who is willing to debrief me on every issue of the day during our afternoon swim.

Zoe Dias, Faculty Director, SANS, who helps me make the hard decisions every day. As part of our problem solving process we ask, "Is this ethical?"

Lynn Lewis, trusted assistant in the SANS executive office, who has to bear with me as I face these ethical issues.

Nancy Pierce, trusted assistant in the SANS executive office, spent her first week with SANS helping spot and remove the typographical errors and clumsy wording from the manuscript.

Alan and Marsha Paller, Director of Research, Director of Finance, SANS, who are my sounding boards on the hardest and thorniest issues.

Thanks to Gal Shpantzer and Andrea Hoy for their help on the E-mail Chapter and Roland Grefer for the assistance on the Privacy Chapter.

In addition, I would like to acknowledge Cynthia Madden and Cynthia Welti, who helped me with the bulk of the heavy lift of the initial writing of the book. It is regretful that they were not involved at the end of the work, but it will be true for all time and space that we could not have done this without them.

A thousand thanks to Christine Kloiber and the rest of the edit team at Syngress. Thanks to Andrew Williams for the help in getting additional soap box opinions and war stories. I really appreciate your support (and the three extra days for a final edit pass).

Dedication

This has been a much tougher task than writing about firewalls, VPN or intrusion detection systems, but worth the effort many times over if it gives the reader pause for thought. If this book helps you that is wonderful, but any credit for that is not mine, but rather the Lord Jesus Christ, for as the good book says in James 1:5 If any of you lacks wisdom, he should ask God, who gives generously to all without finding fault, and it will be given to him.

A Word About Icons

Throughout this book, two different icons will be used at the beginning of each shaded sidebar. These icons are representative of a "Soapbox", where the writer is stating their viewpoint on a specific issue or dilemma, and an "Anecdote" (cartoon bubble) where a personal story is related. These sidebars have been provided by Stephen Northcutt, as well as a number of Special Contributors who have voiced their opinion on the various topics covered by this book. At times the sidebars may agree with the text, at times they may not, but each one will have their own unique, ethical standpoint for the reader to consider.

Contents

Introduction

The purpose of this introductory chapter is to lay the foundation for the rest of this book. This chapter is a bit more academic than the rest of the book, but it is important that we all use a common language when discussing terms such as moral, ethical, culture, law, and policy. These concepts are crucial to being able to assess right, wrong, and due diligence. A quote from the movie Ghostbusters is an excellent introduction to ethics in information technology (IT):

Dr. Egon Spengler: Don't cross the streams.

Dr. Peter Venkman: Why?

Dr. Egon Spengler: It would be bad.

Dr. Peter Venkman: I'm fuzzy on the whole good/bad thing. What do you mean "bad"?

Dr. Egon Spengler: Try to imagine all life as you know it stopping instantaneously, and every molecule in your body exploding at the speed of light.

Bill Murray's character, Dr. Venkman, is fuzzy on the whole good/bad thing and thus is in good company with most workers in information technology. Or is that wrong?

There was a movement towards "moral relativism" in the late 1990s (i.e., you do what is right for you and I will do what is right for me). Moral relativism is still taught in colleges and universities, but it will rapidly get you fired in the workplace. The most important thing we learned as we worked on this book was that people and organizations have a strong sense of right and wrong. This is not to say they will not do wrong, but that they know they are doing wrong. The most striking thing about the real-life issues discussed in this book is how many of the people were fired or disciplined when they were caught.

Information technology, computers, and networks do not raise new ethical issues; stealing is still stealing and stalking is still stalking. However, the Internet does contribute a fascinating sense of anonymity; the notion that no one can see or find out what we are doing.

When people think of ethics, they often think of *personal values*. While they are a large part of ethics, because of the rapid advancement of information technology, a redefinition of ethics must occur that includes the non-human element and what it represents—the computer. The purpose of ethics in information security is not just philosophically important, it can mean the survival of a business or an industry. Dr. Venkman may have been fuzzy on the whole good bad thing, but after Dr. Spengler explained the effects of protonic reversal, Dr. Venkman was able to mentally file crossing the streams in the "bad" category. The principle of deterrence is applicable to the workplace (i.e., repercussions have an impact on our sense of ethics).

Our actions and choices regarding computers will probably not result in all life as we know it stopping instantaneously, but ethical lapses can still have a disastrous effect. A perfect example of this is Enron. Enron went from being a visionary corporation to the butt of jokes throughout corporate America.

The ethical failure of Enron and their auditors' ethics created such a disaster that the damage extended far beyond the demise of Enron and Andersen. Consider the following quote.

> "My name is Frank Nusspickel and I'm a New York, CPA, an audit partner with the New York City office of Andersen, LLP, and a former President of the New York Society of CPA's. I am here today because faith in my firm and the accounting profession, and in the integrity of the capital markets system has been shaken."

*TESTIMONY OF ANDERSEN, LLP BEFORE THE NEW YORK STATE
SENATE HIGHER EDUCATION COMMITTEE KENNETH P. LaVALLE,
CHAIRMAN*

In the end, the auditors lost respect, prestige, money, and business opportunities. Those of us in IT and, even more importantly, in information security, should learn volumes from that event. However, even though we as a community have some deep uneasy feeling that all is not well, we, like Dr. Venkman, are fuzzy on that whole good/bad thing. This book's goal is to take the fuzz out of good and bad across hundreds of IT- related issues. We do it with many people's opinions and stories. We approach most issues with both a conservative and a liberal view and summarize by showing the path of wisdom. This will help you in your management decisions and policy development so you can identify the times to go against what is expedient or expected in order to maintain your core values. A strong ethical environment is part of the formula for corporate success; ethics is business smarts.

Before diving into the countless interesting and diverse ethical issues that arise in the workplace, we must first discuss five related concepts that come to play in determining one's action in response to any situation. These concepts are *ethics*, *morals*, *policy*, *law*, and *culture*.

At the individual level, our ethics are based on our personally accepted principles. There is also the notion of a corporate set of ethics. A company has a general sense of ethics that drives the policies it sets. This ethics stems from the company founders and develops over time. Companies have a reputation in the industry for being loose and fast or old and stodgy, a reputation that corresponds to their sense of corporate ethics.

Morals are accepted from an authority, usually cultural or religious. Today, morals are conceived around six dominant religious thoughts: Buddhism, Christianity, Hindu, Islam, Judaism, and Moral Relativism. However, there are a thousand shades of grey for each of these primary categories.

Corporate policy provides the framework in which a company's employees are to act in response to various situations. Ideally, policies are derived from the corporate *Mission Statement*. The company then creates a top-level policy that is broad but sets the tone for issue-specific policies. In addition to the several written policies companies have, such as a Non-Compete Agreement and Standards of Business Conduct, there are the conventions and modes of behavior often referred to as the *Corporate Culture*.

Companies and organizations operate under a variety of local and national laws. Law is a separate matter from ethics; however, the two often overlap. Some laws are so widely agreed upon that they reflect sound ethics, such as the law against child pornography. At the other end of the spectrum there are laws that are routinely ignored such as speed limits on freeways where ethics are not compromised by not obeying the law.

Sometimes law and ethics are in opposition. Two examples from U.S. history are the Black Codes that defined the freed African Americans as legally subordinate, and the Jim Crow laws that imposed racial segregation primarily in the southeast. They were laws, but there is no way they can be considered ethical. Further, if one could save a life by breaking a law, one might be morally justified to do so.

When we consider great ethical lapses (Enron or the Klu Klux Klan), we realize that it requires an enormous investment to believe that something so wrong is okay. These obviously wrong belief systems make an impact that lasts generations and are always negative and always result in lost productivity and profit.

Stealing is generally considered morally wrong; the Bible, Koran, and Torah all agree on this. It is typically against the law and considered unethical. So how can peer-to-peer networking for downloading copyrighted music, movies, and books be okay?

@#&!?!

I Was a Victim

Sometimes there is a tendency to consider this type of theft a victimless crime. The day I found Network Intrusion Detection 3rd Edition available on the Internet I was just sick to my stomach. Judy Novak and I worked for months on that book. If you have ever come back home to your apartment or home and found it robbed, then you know exactly how I felt. I hope two people read this book: the employee at Pearson Publishing who committed the error of judgment that allowed a .pdf of our book to end up in the wild, and the low life that is serving it up for others to steal.

Stephen Northcutt

The law can provide deterrence against abandoning a reasonable sense of ethics or morals and simply choosing to do whatever we please. People may consider downloading music to be their right; however, it is an illegal act. The law is being enforced and for some, the penalty costs are too high. In this case, the law would validly supercede the ethics. The recording industry is doing a very credible job of using the law as a deterrence.

Finally, we consider culture; a mixture of norms, standards, and expectations for members of a community. In terms of ethics in IT, we have four types of cultures to consider: *corporate culture*, *nations or people groups*, *globalization*, and *Internet culture*.

Corporate culture is a result of expectations and standards that reflect the ethics of an organization and is often reflected in corporate policy. To evaluate the ethics of an organization we look for three things: *formal ethics*, *informal ethics*, and *ethics leadership*.

Formal ethics opinions or perceptions are often published. They include items such as a code of ethics or an ethics policy, as well as issue-specific guidance. If you were to enter "formal ethics opinions" into google, you would find examples especially for trusted professionals such as lawyers or certified public accountants (CPAs). Most organizations have not completed a formal ethics statement or policy, though it is certainly a good idea. We have included a sample one as a sidebar in this chapter that you can download an electronic version from: www.sans.org/resources/policies/

In the spirit of "tastes great, less filling," different camps have different views about the exact definition of informal ethics guidance or perceptions. One explanation is material that has not received the same level of consensus or rigorous testing as formal ethics. The Sidebar "Dispensing Legal Advice over the Internet" gives you the feeling of a published informal ethic.

Legal Advice over the Internet

Is it proper to deliver professional advice directly to consumers via the Internet?

A number of legal help services have sprouted on the World Wide Web, where a consumer can ask a general question of a lawyer. Sometimes fees are charged and sometimes the advice is free. An example is: www.freeadvice.com.

Oftentimes the people operating these sites do not wish for their content to constitute specific legal advice in an attorney-client relationship for any of three reasons:

1. An attorney dispensing legal advice to true legal clients owes ethical duties of confidentiality, loyalty, and diligence, and the presence of those duties would make the Web service more rigid and expensive.

2. Often, these Web sites are owned and operated at least in part by non-lawyers, and any lawyers who are contributing to the sites will have an ethical duty not to split legal fees with non-lawyers.

3. Sometimes the people operating or providing content through the sites are non-lawyers and state ethics laws prohibit non-lawyers from practicing law. The laws behind each of these three reasons are intended to protect consumers of legal services.

In order to avoid classifying their content as specific legal advice creating an attorney-client relationship, the Q&A Web sites usually post disclaimers and try to make their answers generic.

Interestingly, when legal question and answer shows were first broadcast over radio in the 1930s, local bar associations took action, in the name of professional ethics, to shut the shows down, claiming they were a threat to unsophisticated consumers. The fear was that consumers would not understand the information delivered through the shows and mistakenly believe their legal problems were simpler than was actually the case.

The modern version of the Q&A radio show is the Q&A Web site. But today is not the 1930s. Even though the Q&A Web phenomenon has been the subject of considerable discussion by bar associations, no one is taking action against the Web sites. An important reason is that people

Continued

> perceive the profession would lose if it tried to shut down the sites today. That perception is supported by the recent experience in Texas, where the profession tried to drive out publishers of legal how-to manuals and software, but was roundly rebuffed by the legislature.
>
> The trend in this area of law seems to be leniency and support for innovative sources of legal information for consumers.
>
> *Benjamin Wright*
> *Chief Legal Counsel*
> *PestPatrol.com*

Another explanation for an informal ethic would be to describe a body of information that is either not written down or poorly documented, but that nevertheless is consistently and powerfully held in an organization. We will try to illustrate this concept with an anecdote.

@#&!?!

We don't Party Hearty

When I attended my first SANS conference in 1995, there was a tendency for some people to treat it as a party experience. There were only two SANS conferences a year and it was a chance to meet long lost friends. There were activities like "beer brewing BOFs." There were some great stories, especially from New Orleans, about flamboyant discretions committed by the top names in technical information security. In 2000 as the GIAC Certification series was unveiled and the level of technical intensity started to climb, the culture began to rapidly change. No written memo was ever issued that stated drinking your brains out was against the rules, but the old party hearty instructors began to disappear at an amazing rate. Today only two of the instructors from before year 2000 survive and continue to teach and they fully understand the importance of discretion.

Stephen Northcutt

This anecdote is an example of an informal ethic as it seems to apply in the IT world. In the 1990s, a behavior was considered cool and part of being accepted by the culture. In the year 2000 and beyond, it was a ticket to termination. The period of change was very painful for a number of people.

Discrepancy is Expensive

Anytime there is a difference between a formerly perceived and under-stood informal ethic there will be costs to the organization in terms of job turnover, job satisfaction and commitment decrease. Anytime there is a difference between a formal ethic, and a corresponding informal ethic, the same problems will occur.

Stephen Northcutt

We have discussed formal and informal ethics; we should now consider eth-ical leadership. Just because you are a vice president or a CEO does not mean you are a leader in terms of either positive or negative ethics in your organiza-tion. This is a very important concept. To understand the concept fully, we ask people to think back on their high school experience. You were probably pri-marily associated with a group that mostly could be defined by either positive or negative ethics.

If the people you spent the majority of your time with drove cars very fast, were fixated on getting someone to buy them beer, were into drugs, were focused on sex even at the risk of pregnancy or disease, then that might show a negative ethical bent. There were a number of examples of ethical leadership in such a group. One or two people were the top dog. There was the pretty girl that kept falling for Mr. Wrong, a bad individual and a negative ethical leader. If you fast-forward to the maturity level of today from high school, you have a pretty good idea of the profile negative ethical leaders exhibit.

If the people you spent the majority of your time with were in service clubs, were fixated on grades, were into student government if they could take the time away from being an Eagle scout, were focused on sex ,but virginity was a legiti-mate option, then that might be an indicator of a positive ethical bent. There were a number of examples of ethical leadership in such a group. One or two people in such a group typically are accepted to an Ivy League school and achieve significant success.

Most of us fall between the extremes. We hope the proceeding two para-graphs help you begin to think about the positive and negative ethical leaders in your organization. Of course, these two examples are simplistic. They do not take into account gossip, intentional dissention, race, creed, and culture issues, financial status, the evil clerk syndrome, or the overbearing or obnoxious boss. When we evaluate organizations, we find that if we can identify the major players in terms of the formal and informal ethical position of the organization, and then interview those players about their high school experience and how they presently view the world, it gives us a powerful model to understand the forces they exert on the organization.

In addition to the actual human leaders, there is a thought leadership component to ethical leadership. Ben and Jerry's is a good example. The company leaders have a positive ethical leadership style and the company, especially five years or so ago, reflected this leadership style right down to the mission statement element of informed prosperity. In general, an organization with positive ethical leadership both at the senior management and second level management will prosper.

In contrast, there is the example of Foundstone and NT Objectives. Only the sources close to both companies will ever know for sure what went on, but from the reports in the trade press there were numerous examples of negative ethical leadership. After a breakup between the two companies, a number of press articles claimed widespread copyright infringement at Foundstone. The leaders of both companies were dragged through the mud with claims that they were dishonest and difficult to deal with. We have met and done business with both individuals and find it hard to believe any of the claims. However, one thing is certain, there were leaders of negative ethics somewhere in both groups.

One link that discusses the situation in a fairly balanced fashion is found at: www.varbusiness.com/components/Nl/Insider/article.asp?ArticleID=43015

Formal Ethics Statement
<Company Name> Ethics Policy

1. **Overview** <Company Name> purpose for this ethics policy is to establish a culture of openness, trust, and integrity in business practices. Effective ethics is a team effort involving the participation and support of every <Company Name> employee. All employees should familiarize themselves with the ethics guidelines that follow this introduction.

   <Company Name> is committed to protecting employees, partners, vendors, and the company from illegal or damaging actions by individuals, either knowingly or unknowingly. When

Continued

<Company Name> addresses issues proactively and uses correct judgment, it will help set us apart from competitors.

<Company Name> will not tolerate any wrongdoing or impropriety at anytime. <Company name> will take the appropriate measures and act quickly in correcting the issue if the ethical code is broken. Any infractions of this code of ethics will not be tolerated.

2. **Purpose** Our purpose for authoring a publication on ethics is to emphasize the employee's and consumer's expectation to be treated to fair business practices. This policy will serve to guide business behavior to ensure ethical conduct.

3. **Scope** This policy applies to employees, contractors, consultants, temporaries, and other workers at <Company Name>, including all personnel affiliated with third parties.

4. **Policy**

  ■ Executive Commitment to Ethics

    ■ Top brass within <Company Name> must set a prime example. In any business practice, honesty and integrity must be top priority for executives.

    ■ Executives must have an open door policy and welcome suggestions and concerns from employees. This will allow employees to feel comfortable discussing any issues and will alert executives to concerns within the work force.

    ■ Executives must disclose any conflicts of interest regarding their position within <Company Name>.

  ■ Employee Commitment to Ethics

  ■ <Company Name> employees will treat everyone fairly, have mutual respect, promote a team environment, and avoid the intent and appearance of unethical or compromising practices.

    ■ Every employee needs to apply effort and intelligence in maintaining ethics value.

    ■ Employees must disclose any conflict of interests regarding their position within <Company Name>.

    ■ Employees will help <Company Name> to increase customer and vendor satisfaction by providing quality products and timely responses to inquiries.

Continued

- Company Awareness

- Promotion of ethical conduct within interpersonal communications of employees will be rewarded.

- <Company Name> will promote a trustworthy and honest atmosphere to reinforce the vision of ethics within the company.

- Maintaining Ethical Practices

- <Company Name> will reinforce the importance of the integrity message and the tone will start at the top. Every employee, manager, and director needs to consistently maintain an ethical stance and support ethical behavior.

- Employees at <Company Name> should encourage open dialogue, get honest feedback, and treat everyone fairly, with honesty and objectivity.

- <Company Name> has established a best practice disclosure committee to make sure the ethical code is delivered to all employees and that concerns regarding the code can be addressed.

- Unethical Behavior

- <Company Name> will avoid the intent and appearance of unethical or compromising practice in relationships, actions, and communications.

- <Company Name> will not tolerate harassment or discrimination.

- Unauthorized use of company trade secrets and marketing, operational, personnel, financial, source code, and technical information integral to the success of our company will not be tolerated.

- <Company Name> will not permit impropriety at any time and we will act ethically and responsibly in accordance with laws.

- <Company Name> employees will not use corporate assets or business relationships for personal use or gain.

5. Enforcement

- Any infractions of this code of ethics will not be tolerated and <Company Name> will act quickly in correcting the issue if the ethical code is broken.

Continued

> - Any employee found to have violated this policy may be subject to disciplinary action, up to and including termination of employment

The difference in culture between two organizations can be startling. Imagine leaving government service after 25 years to take a job at a major Wall Street player. All of a sudden you would be expected to move much faster than before, dress better, be alert, quick on the uptake, fast on your feet, and hungry to take advantage of an opportunity. After 25 years of being told to slow down, you would suddenly be aware of a need to go faster. Most people cannot handle a shift in culture that significant.

@#&!?!

Cisco and Drug Tests

Note: This is a third-hand story and I only know the government side of it. If you have first-hand information and are willing to share documented information for this example, that would be wonderful!

Corporate culture literally drives the critical policy decisions an organization makes. When I was a researcher at a U.S. Navy lab, there was an interaction between the U.S. government and Cisco. The government was arguing that if they were going to buy Cisco routers, then Cisco needed to implement drug testing. Cisco declined. I was speaking with a senior government official who was implying that Cisco would not implement the drug tests because they had something to hide. Fortunately, the government wisely backed down or they would have been forced to do without Sun Microsystems as well, which has also never done drug testing. Cisco's decision had nothing to do with a pro-drug use attitude. Cisco employees at this stage of company growth were highly motivated, almost to a maniacal degree. The company simply eschewed any unnecessary intrusion which might cause employees to take their eye off the ball. The policy decision was congruent with the management style and culture of Cisco at the time. They stuck to their guns and it was the government that blinked.

Stephen Northcutt
www.workforce.com/section/06/feature/23/53/63/

We have focused most of the culture discussion on corporate culture, since this book is focused on ethics in IT organizations. However, the culture of a nation or people group also affects ethics. This goes beyond the typical "ugly American" lack of politeness such as trying to establish service level agreements within a company or taking a business card with one hand in Japan. We will try to illustrate how differences in culture can actually make someone appear untrustworthy with an anecdote.

@#&!?!

Preachers in London

A California based conservative church named Calvary Chapel was expanding into the UK. A bunch of pastors from the U.S. flew to meet their counterparts in London, they met on a Sunday afternoon and went to lunch. The Brits ordered beer with lunch and the conservative Christians immediately began to have doubts they should be in their denomination. They had ordered coffee and the Brits were wondering the same thing about them as they reckoned Sunday was supposed to be a day of rest for that denomination.

Stephen Northcutt

Globalization is also a cultural force. Change tends to increase stress, hamper communication, and confuse organizational relationships. Clearly we are in a time of unparalleled change. People groups that have lived with a stable culture for hundreds of years or more are changing. The United Nations Education Scientific and Cultural Organization (UNESCO) is pursuing the notion of universal ethics, or more simply, the globalization of ethics. As we become more interconnected, this becomes more important.

The Internet is a major driver for globalization of culture, and we briefly consider it in terms of its own culture. In e-mail, there are expected norms, standards, and expectations. If you do not believe us, write ten friends with your cap key set on. You will be told you were shouting. Chat rooms have a particular set of expectations and even their own language. And we can easily make a case that this unique culture has ethical ramifications; how do you feel about spam? Would you feel that posting a personal e-mail expressing your love for a young male friend on a public newsgroup would be a violation of trust?

We have explained how we are using the terms ethics, morals, policy, law, and culture in this book. We discuss a wide variety of issues; many that actually happened to someone who felt the need to respond to the situation ethically. We explain the issue and then give a classic conservative and liberal response to it. Liberal and conservative do not imply a right way of thinking, nor do they correspond to political views. The best way to think of them is as guardrails to help keep you focused on the issue in light of your corporate culture. For example, a conservative corporate culture might assert an employee has no presumption of privacy. In such a conservative corporate culture, your e-mail or other transmissions might be monitored. A more liberal culture might choose to trust the employees and grant them a presumption to privacy.

Since the key is your own corporate culture, you will not always accept our summary answer. Also, please keep in mind that the Soapbox and Anecdote features were contributed by many people and may not represent the ethical positions of the author team.

The best way to use a book like this is to remember the *watermelon principle*. Eat the fruit, spit out the seeds, swallow what works for you in the context of your organization's culture, and move on. If an issue really makes you hot under the collar and you just have to speak to someone, contact the lead author, Stephen Northcutt, at Stephen@sans.org. You can be sure that while he may not agree with you, he will treasure your opinion as well as read and respond to your note.

Chapter 1

System Administration and Operations

Ethical Dilemmas in this Chapter:

- **General Ethics Responsibility for Architects**

- **Ethics Responsibilities for System Implementers**

- **Day-to-day System Administration**

- **Administrative Spying**

- **Inappropriate System Use**

- **Networking**

Introduction

In this chapter, we discuss system administration and operational ethics in relation to computer network architecture and the technical organizational infrastructure of corporate resources. Overall system administration and operational responsibility incorporates daily operations, infrastructure security, and networking.

We cover system architecture and implementation issues, system administration, administrative spying, inappropriate system use, and the ethical dilemmas of network administrators such as handling mass e-mails and insecure wireless connections.

Within each primary section mentioned above, we delve into specific issues concerning system administration. For example, in the "Inappropriate System Use" section, ethical issues concerning allowing the use of networked computer games are illustrated.

The system administrator holds the keys to most of the technological resources of a corporation. With this kind of power comes great ethical responsibility.

Separation of Duties

Everyone that has taken a course in information security knows what "separation of duties" is and that we are supposed to implement it. It is obvious that in order to help prevent abuse of power the people you have watching for attacks against your environment must not also be the people who have complete access and control over your environment. This is understood in other places where people are given power to help or harm; the U.S. government was designed to keep each part in check by having the other parts watching and monitoring. In banks or stock brokerages and other financial institutions, the person responsible for watching for inappropriate behavior is completely separate from the person who makes a trade or performs a transaction of any sort. This is also why the police are monitored by their Internal Affairs Division, or why an Independent Counsel is supposed to be appointed when the President does something wrong. If your system administrator goes bad and decides to attack you they will almost certainly succeed. However, by separating functions and by not giving the administrators unlimited power, you improve the chances that your organization will survive and detect

Continued

> the attack and its source. I'd say if you don't pay attention to separation of duties you show a lack of professional ethics.
>
> *William Occam*

General Ethics Responsibility for Architects

The ethical expectations of computer architects are similar to that of physical architects who design houses. For example, if you paid someone to design a house in Hawaii, you would expect them to have an ethical responsibility to address threats relating to the geographical area such as termites and hurricanes. In system architecture, the same expectations apply. The following two sections, "Building the System" and "Designing the System," address two key ethical dilemmas that system architects face on the job.

Don't Believe Everything You Hear

"Just trust us, it's secure." Famous last words.

Specifying and purchasing products based on your security needs is not a "one size fits all" decision. Most organizations end up implementing a product or technology because their clients use it or they've heard good things about it. That is an unethical and unprofessional choice.

Before specifying or purchasing a technology for your network, always ask technical questions to the people that designed the product, not the people who sell the product (unless, of course, they are one in the same). Be cautious of dealing with companies who will not let you interface directly with the engineers. Ask them why they think the product is secure, ask how it was designed, ask how it was tested, ask how they can back up their claims, ask about their security policies and procedures. If they can't explain any of that, become suspicious.

Product vendors sometimes use "security through obscurity" to claim that their security is unbreakable. Due to a general lack of understanding of secure design practices, they actually believe it. "The attacker will never be able to figure out how we encrypt the data," they say. "Our scientists have created an unbreakable code." However, security through obscurity

Continued

does not work, as once the obscurity has been discovered, the security is moot. This has been shown by numerous security vulnerabilities in the past decades.

When choosing products or technology to incorporate into your network, do not be afraid to ask questions. The key is to not just blindly trust the glossy marketing material. Don't believe everything you hear. Challenge the claims. You don't want to lead your company into a false sense of security.

Nothing is 100% secure, and if someone says their product is, proceed with caution.

Joe Grand, President & CEO, Grand Idea Studio, Inc.

Building a System – Is it Secure Enough?

You are an administrator hired to design and build a new system. Is it appropriate to build a system within the requirements defined that may not necessarily be able to withstand a virus attack?

Conservative A system architect must possess the ability to monitor the system and design procedures with the strength to withstand a malicious attack and not crumble when the first worm hits. If the architectural design fails, the system architect did not do the job. Management then has the responsibility to replace them with someone qualified for the work at hand.

Liberal In reality, a new worm or virus often holds an arsenal of unexpected and unanticipated forms of attack that most system architects cannot prepare for in advance. This is not the fault of the architect. However, if a known virus or worm takes down the system, the architect is at fault.

SUMMARY

Determining if a system administrator built a strong system depends upon the type of attack that took it out. In most cases, a properly designed system should be able to withstand a malicious attack. However, some attacks can be devastating regardless of the preparation. Consider the type of attack and benchmark it against how effective it was at other organizations when making a determination if the system architect is at fault.

Designing a Secure System – What about Legacy Applications?

You are building a new system that is completely solid; however, you have not taken into account an old legacy system that communicates with your new system, which is weak in security. Is it appropriate to design a strong system that does not take into account the entire picture and add necessary security to weaker legacy systems associated with the new strong system?

Conservative A system architect must take into account the existing infrastructure in its entirety, including an old legacy system that is weak at operating system level. The system architect holds the responsibility to build in layers of protection into the architecture that supports such systems. This is the foundation expectation of system architecture.

Liberal This issue depends entirely on the time allocated to the new system design and the specifications issued up front. If no such expectations exist prior to the design and the budget and time allocated are limited, it is not the responsibility of the system architect to go beyond the scope of the project to ensure enterprise-level security.

SUMMARY

In general, overall system security should take priority. If a project's scope does not allow for adequate security, the system administrator should bring this to the attention of senior management. Who is at fault ethically may be the system administrator, senior management, or possibly all of the parties involved.

Ethics Responsibilities for System Implementers

The area of system implementation for administrators carries with it an incredible level of ethical responsibility. When implementing a new system, the foundation is set. That foundation will dictate all future technology efforts. Careful consideration and planning must go into implementing a new system.

Architecture and Communication – Whose Problem is It?

Management requires the system implementer to carry out the system design presented to them. If they do not think it will work, is it their responsibility to communicate their assessment of the proposed architecture or simply go ahead with the project and attempt to implement it anyway?

Conservative   The system implementer should immediately communicate to management that the architecture is poor and therefore will not work once it is goes live. A system implementer should not waste the time and money of the company by going ahead anyway. It is their ethical responsibility to communicate their assessment to senior management.

Liberal   Management hires system implementers to do just that—implement. It is not within the scope of the job to question the system architect's job.

SUMMARY

When management issues technical projects, they do not always meet the mark since they specialize in management and not necessarily technology. Management and technical experts need to work closely together when implementing a system so that they consider all aspects.

Underpaid Systems/Database Admins

It bothers me to no end that we pay for high-end developers, write security policies for applications, and spend a great deal of money and energy on 'defense in depth.' After all that, we look for a low-cost resource pool to administer the system we have just built and give them full blown access rights to add, delete, change, and view the very data we're trying to protect. In short, we give the keys to the kingdom to junior-level people and somehow still think we're approaching information security safely.

John Stewart, Independent Researcher

Performing Shortcuts – When is it Okay?

If the system implementer is a under a very tight deadline, is it acceptable for them to perform shortcuts to get the job done?

Conservative The system implementer should request an extension on the deadline and certainly not perform shortcuts. This will only cost the company more money in the end and make the system vulnerable to attack.

Liberal There are certain levels of shortcuts that are acceptable. If information technology professionals did not take shortcuts, nothing would ever happen in the industry. Perfect development efforts take a lifetime to build. The system implementer should calculate the risk associated with the shortcuts and only implement ones that do not put the system at risk of attack.

SUMMARY

Performing shortcuts when implementing a new system is not always a good idea but unfortunately sometimes it is necessary in order to meet aggressive time constraints. The best way to avoid disaster is to have a well-balanced team consider the outcome. This team, which consists of both managers and technologists, considers the necessary short cuts and determines how they will affect both the business and the system security. Communication is the key.

Using Design Tools – Can You use Your Own Tools?

You are an administrator building a new system. You personally own a great architecture tool, which maps out the network infrastructure for you. Is it appropriate to use an architecture design as the base for your new system architecture obtained from a software tool that the company does not own or is using in a trial manner?

Conservative It is not appropriate to utilize an architecture design tool that is not formally under a software license agreement with the company for which you are doing the work. Obtain proper legal licensing for the tool and verify that you have permission to implement the new system architecture obtained from the tool.

Liberal If you, as the system implementer, personally own the tool then you have the right to use the architecture designs contained within that tool as long as you are adhering to your license agreement.

SUMMARY

Using an illegally owned or pirated tool is against the law and a bad choice plain and simple. Using a network design from a tool you have for a trial basis is in the gray area of ethical behavior. Using a tool that you personally own for a job is a personal or policy choice, not an ethical one.

FTP Servers – What about Access Control?

You have set your file transfer protocol (FTP) server up in a manner that allows anonymous users to view the files. This is true for a lot of companies and their FTP servers. Is there a problem with this?

Conservative Setting up the FTP server in a manner in which anonymous users can view files on it is certainly an ethical and information security problem. This is a security risk to the information technology infrastructure and you as the system administrator know that. Fix this problem immediately.

Liberal It is better to disallow anonymous users from viewing files on the FTP server, but in some cases it is relatively harmless. Just take into account the types of files shown and the security risk involved.

SUMMARY

It is up to every system administrator and corporate information security policy to determine the acceptable risk for their company. Acceptable risk has many factors including the type of data exposed, the level of the resources exposed, and the security threat. This ethical determination must be weighed and considered carefully.

Responsibility of Hardware and Operating System Vendors – Can They be Held Accountable?

You purchased an operating system upgrade, which consequently crashes your system. Since you signed an agreement that you assume all risk when performing the upgrade, are you just out of luck now?

Conservative Immediately get in contact with the corporate legal department and have them issue a formal complaint to the vendor indicating the details of what happened when you installed the product upgrade purchased from them. Make sure you have everything legally documented in case the upgrade results in a negative impact on the business as a whole and you must take the vendor to court for damages.

Liberal Get in contact with the vendor that issued the operating system upgrade and explain your situation. They must maintain a reasonable level of responsibility for their product even if you signed an agreement to take full responsibility. You and the vendor should be able to work together on this problem and solve it.

SUMMARY

Determining fault in the software industry is significantly trickier then in other industries. Unfortunately, sufficient laws are not in place at this time to cover the intricacies of technology. Feeling out what is ethical and what is legally acceptable may be harder then one might think.

Day-to-day System Administration

System administration is defined as the daily responsibilities of the administrator such as monitoring the system, managing users and passwords, allocating system resources, and installations.

In this section, we discuss the administrative aspects of ethically handling the daily routine responsibilities of the system administrator, which include e-mail, passwords, patches, hardware, installations, access paths, and log files.

Using Alternate E-mail Programs – Is it Okay?

The company's e-mail product is terribly slow. Is it acceptable for you as the administrator to use a different one for your e-mail?

Conservative As the system administrator, you know the security consequences concerning the use of external mail applications. They are simply dangerous. Answer this question with a resounding "No!" Do not put the system at risk in this manner for any reason including speed. Your computer is the must valuable one of all of the computers for hackers.

Liberal Since you know what you are doing there really is not a big deal in using an external e-mail program. Just install it on a machine that does not have administrative privileges and set up a user account for yourself on that computer so you do not unnecessarily put the primary box at risk.

SUMMARY

Making personal judgment calls for yourself or others is an interesting ethical situation. Sometimes policy can slow you down too much, especially if it is boilerplate policy that is not customized to the needs and environment of your organization. Knowing when to break the rules and when not to, often falls in the hands of the system administrator.

PASSFLT and Password Policy – Should You Bypass It?

You have a password policy within your organization utilizing PASSFLT. PASSFLT is a windows security measure, which requires secure passwords and will not accept a password unless it meets certain requirements such as a mix of alphanumeric and numeric values. As the system administrator, you can go around PASSFLT and occasionally do. Is this okay?

Conservative You must set the example for policy as the system administrator. Do not go around PASSFLT. Your machine requires greater security then any other machine at the company.

Liberal In most cases, this is not a very good idea. However, if you have to set up a temporary password that will have a very short life span this is acceptable. There may be some additional similar situations in which going around PASSFLT are within reason as well.

SUMMARY

As the system administrator do you break the rules to make your job easier, or do you stick to the rules and toe the line. That is for you to decide.

Testing Patches – Is it Necessary?

Your organization has a policy of testing all patches before installing them. SQL Slammer hits and essentially takes your entire network offline. Do you install the patch without testing it?

Conservative No. You must find a way to test the patch in your testing environment even if it takes significantly longer to fix the system. Never go against policy, for its existence is to protect the system.

Liberal Heck yeah! Install that patch ASAP. You would be crazy not to. This is one of those circumstances where you must go strait to the patch installation because the system is already in a compromised position and the longer you wait the more the damage will incur.

SUMMARY

As a systems administrator, you may sometimes find yourself in circumstances where you must break policy to save the system itself. Like in warfare, triage is necessary at times.

Logon and Logoff Process – How Important is It?

You are working late one evening when your boss suggests a bite of dinner. Aware of your grumbling tummy, you join your boss and forget to logoff your administrative account on the company computer. Is this a problem?

Conservative   Forgetting to log off your company computer when you are the systems administrator is a terrible mistake. You should immediately return to the office and properly log off the machine. It is currently completely vulnerable!

Liberal   Since you were working late, there is probably no one else in the office or very few people. This is an error and you should make certain you never do it again. After you return from dinner, check to see if anyone has used the computer by looking at the log files. If everything is fine, properly log off the machine when you complete your work for the night.

SUMMARY

Failing to log off the administrative machine is always an error on the part of the system administrator. Leaving the machine open to anyone who passes by is extremely dangerous for the security of the entire network.

@#&!?!

Don't Claim to Write Backdoors in Nuclear Plant Software

During the Y2K frenzy of the late 90s, I was working at an electric utility. I managed a team that was installing the utility's software on Y2K-compliant platforms and writing scripts that would automate parts of the installations. The scripts ran with workstation administrator-level privileges so that they could update operating system files, configuration settings, and permissions. One afternoon, a few of our contractors came to me and said that another contractor told them that he had been inserting backdoors into the scripts he had been writing. What made this particularly troubling was that his recent scripts had been for software for our nuclear power plants. We tended to believe that he was joking about the backdoors, especially because all script code was reviewed before it was put into production. However, we all had the same reaction: this should be treated as if he'd joked about having a bomb on an airplane or in a

Continued

crowded theater. There are some things that you just don't joke about. As soon as we confirmed that the contractor had made the backdoor claims, he was immediately let go. My manager had the unenviable task of telling the nuclear plant's IT management about the issue, while my staff and I performed thorough reviews of all the scripts that the contractor had written, as well as other scripts and programs that he had access to. Although we confirmed that there were no backdoors, we found password cracking software on the contractor's workstation!

Rex "Red" Rabinski

Shoulder Surfers – Change the Password?

You are logging onto your computer and a coworker is watching over your shoulder. Should you revise your password or are you just being overly paranoid?

Conservative If a coworker is watching you log on to the administrative machine, the odds are good that they want to obtain the password for malicious means. Immediately change the password for protection purposes.

Liberal Changing the administrative password every time there is a coworker at your desk while you are logging in is quite tedious and unnecessary. If you know the person well and cannot actually verify that they know the password and intend harm, simply do not worry about it.

SUMMARY

Administrator passwords require protection and secrecy from all including senior management and technical staff. Suspicion of someone else knowing the system administration password is cause enough to change it immediately.

Default Installations – Who's Fault is It?

You set up an operating system with defaults to save time. You later discover that this has left your system vulnerable to attack. Who is at fault: the vendor or you the administrator?

Conservative　You and the vendor are at fault. You are at fault because you did not do your homework and verify that the defaults were secure. The vendor is at fault for creating system defaults that are grossly insecure.

Liberal　You are not really at fault here. When you purchase an operating system, it should be secure with the factory defaults set. This is negligence on the part of the vendor.

SUMMARY

Take your time when installing new vendor solutions, especially operating systems. Review the user manuals and supporting documentation. This will prevent the above issue from happening to you. Make sure you know exactly what you are getting yourself into and always test a new tool, operating system, or upgrade on a test machine first.

Establishment of Access Paths – Should You Refuse?

Your boss' son is in the office and your boss has asked you to provide him with access to the Internet on one of the office computers so that he can do his homework. Providing access to the Internet means creating an access path on the corporate network. Is it ever appropriate to set an access path for an unauthorized user?

Conservative　You must refuse the request of your boss. It is never appropriate to allow access to the corporate network to an unauthorized user. He very well may be a hacker like many young people these days.

Liberal　Your boss' son is hardly a threat to the security of the corporation and besides, if your boss made the call to provide his son with access it is his responsibility if there is a problem. Just give him the minimum possible access required to access the Internet.

SUMMARY

Balancing office politics and security procedures frequently places the system administrator in a precarious position. If you refuse your boss' son access, in most cases, the boss will hold that against you. However, if you give him access and he wreaks havoc on the system, you are in the wrong again and will be the one to take the heat. This is a no-win situation.

Server Logs Security Tools – Should You Alter Them?

Your coworker who is also a close friend has been using his company computer to surf inappropriate Web sites. Is it okay to alter the logs containing these entries in order to protect your friend's actions?

Conservative Altering system logs is a serious offense and not allowable, especially in the above-mentioned circumstance. You could be facing legal issues as well as the ethical one you face now.

Liberal Protecting your friends is a tricky issue. This is a case of the ethics of friendship versus corporate ethics. Your friend has made a terrible error by using company resources to surf inappropriate Web sites on the Internet. This one time you may consider removing or altering the logs and tell him not to do it again because you will not remove the logs a second time.

SUMMARY

At times in our lives, we find ourselves in circumstances where we are asked to ignore our own personal ethics, corporate policy, or even the law, to help out someone close to us in need. Consider all of the repercussions carefully before making your decision because you will have to live with them whatever choice you make.

Altering Logs – Is it a Bad Idea?

The hard drive space on the server is getting full so you decide that you need to delete some old log files. Is it okay to alter or delete logs that contain significant security events such as attempts to guess passwords or using privileges not authorized, and so on?

Conservative Never alter or delete log files that contain security events. This is evidence in case an arrest is required for hacking the system. Under no circumstances should you remove this information.

Liberal Even the liberals agree that removing significant security events from the log files is not smart. If you do not have enough physical, hard drive space then create redundant backups of the log files and properly store them for easy retrieval.

SUMMARY

Altering logs with significant security events from a conservative and liberal point of view is just a bad idea. The only reason why someone would do this without creating backups of them is to cover their own tracks.

Administrative Spying

System administrators possess great power in the corporate world—they have the ability to spy on fellow employees. They can see the Web sites employees are visiting, monitor employee e-mails and on-line chats, view data on personal computers connected to the corporate network, and much more. This section addresses what is acceptable on the part of the system administrator in terms of spying or monitoring other employees of the company. In some cases, spying may be necessary in order to determine illegal or inappropriate activity; in other cases, it is stalking.

This section focuses on the primary issues: direct spying on employees while they are performing on-line chats, monitoring internal activities such as e-mail, and sniffing personal computers while connected to the corporate network.

@#&!?!

Ethics and Legalities of Spying on Employees

Consider the issue of corporate "spying" on employees by installing software on their computer to capture all work and communications. I think that the current practices are highly unethical, although seemingly legal. For instance, I consider it unethical to not apprise a new employee of such a policy until after he comes to work for your company, particularly when it is understood that personal communications through e-mail and chat will occur.

John W. Dozier, Jr., Esq.
Internet and E-commerce Law

Spying on Employees – Is it ever Acceptable?

The system administrator is known to spy on employees while they are chatting online. Is this acceptable?

Conservative It is not appropriate to impinge on the privacy of others even if you are the system administrator. There is no good reason why a system administrator should be spying on employees unless they are performing activity that is putting the computing resources at risk.

Liberal The system administrator has the responsibility to monitor and administrate system use and access. They should know what is happening online for security purposes. It is their responsibility to determine if people are properly using system resources for business purposes or for personal purposes. They also need to be aware of potential security risks. Administrators may pay close attention to the activities of individuals that are higher risk to system security. This type of monitoring is within reason.

SUMMARY

Issues of spying, ethically speaking, come down to intent. Intent is the force or reason by which we are doing something. If your intent is not personal but strictly out of concern for the security of the system, you may be ethically correct in using your administrative access to spy on someone. However, some people would argue that under no circum-

www.syngress.com

stances should you ever spy on anyone regardless of the suspicions you may have in their use of the system. They argue that personal privacy is a fundamental right. Finally, spying on employees to gain private information is just plain wrong.

@#&!?!

Who Watches the Watchers?

Network intrusion detection systems (NIDS) are deployed so they see a majority of the network traffic, including all of the e-mail, chats, file transfers, and Web browsing which occurs. Any NIDS that has a programmable signature language can be easily modified to capture all of the traffic from a particular person and then later viewed. Some security administrators find this access way to tempting and have used NIDS to monitor their romantic interests, political adversaries, or even senior management. This represents a huge liability to government and enterprise organizations. To avoid this, security groups should start with their people and make sure they are of high moral character and are not likely to abuse the information they have. But since we all trust "the guy next store," we need to regularly audit the configuration of our NIDS devices and what is being done with the data it has collected.

Ron Gula, CTO
Tenable Network Security

Monitoring of Internal Activities – Audit Archived E-mail?

Although not engaged in blanket monitoring, you occasionally examine archived e-mail. On one occasion, you find a string of e-mails where an employee has sent out confidential data. Was it appropriate for you as the system administrator to monitor e-mail? In addition, will it be appropriate for you to address the employee who has distributed confidential information via e-mail?

Conservative You were in the right to randomly monitor the archived e-mail. You should immediately address the individual who sent out the confidential information via e-mail and their manager. You can explain that this type of information draws attention to itself, which is why you noticed it even though you do not perform blanket electronic mail monitoring. It is appropriate for the system administrator to monitor e-mail activity. However, it is not appropriate for the system administrator to monitor e-mail and read it because they are nosey.

Liberal You want to be careful here because you do not necessarily have the right to monitor e-mail unless it is specifically outlined in your job description. Make a mental note and let this one slide. Purchase some software that has e-mail auditing capabilities that can detect this type of information. If it happens again, bring the problem up to the employee and senior management. Be sure to document everything carefully.

SUMMARY

When in doubt of your responsibility as the system administrator, refer back to your job description. Do a little homework and know what senior management's expectations of you are in relation to e-mail monitoring. Then determine what is inappropriate. Once you know what you can comfortably do to protect the company you will be stronger in dealing with inappropriate behavior on the part of the employees.

Ethical Use of Remote Desktop Management Software

Remote desktop management software like RealVNC is a boon to system administrators who can configure and/or troubleshoot users' systems without being physically present at the location. This saves a lot of time and money, especially in large IT organizations. However, this software demands strong ethical responsibilities on part of both the system administrators and the users (or clients). System administrators, powered with superuser privileges to access the client systems, must not peek into confidential or personal information that may reside on the client machine. At the same time, the clients must take care to see that this software is either disabled or closed completely whenever they are not at their ter-

Continued

minals. Even if system administrators could be trustworthy, these client systems could run the risk of remote access to their machines via the Internet by malicious elements who can track the client's long periods of inactivity before striking. Damages caused during these incidents could be unfathomable.

Sumanth Naropanth,
Systems Engineer, Wipro Technologies, Bangalore - India

Sniffing – An Invasion of Privacy?

Some developers use their personal laptops to develop code from home, which they then plug into the network when they come in during the day. Is it appropriate to look at what is on their computer when they are in the office?

Conservative Sniffing is not appropriate and is an invasion of personal privacy. Under no circumstances is this type of behavior acceptable in the corporate environment. In the case of government and military personnel, sniffing may be appropriate and employees are forewarned that their computers and person may be searched.

Liberal What the employee does not know will not hurt them. Maybe you will find some hacking tools on their machine, which will help you to determine if they have been accessing the system inappropriately. When they connect their laptop to the corporate network, they must presume their information is then made available to the system administrator.

SUMMARY

When you consider sniffing an employee's personal computer logged into the network, think about the old social wisdom: would you want someone to do that to you? Try to apply that principle to others.

Inappropriate System Use

System administrators have the responsibility to enforce proper system use. Inappropriate system use falls into several categories including access, machines, games and music, e-mail, and Internet distribution.

The access issues discussed below include incorrect access, sharing of privileges with unauthorized users, and sharing of expanded system access with other employees. There are several issues concerning computer games and music, among them variations on using computer games at work and downloading MP3 music files with company resources on company time. Finally, we cover inappropriate e-mail and Internet use such as personal e-mail lists, mass e-mails, and using the Internet when its access is prohibited.

System Administration and Information Security in Opposition – Override Security System Requirements?

You are a system administrator and have been pressured to provide access for a corporate VIP, which overrides the information security officer's system requirements. Do you do it?

Conservative You should never provide access to someone that overrides the information security officer's system requirements regardless of who they are. Explain the importance of this to the VIP. If they insist on the access, contact the information security officer for permission.

Liberal As the system administrator you know who is okay with system access and who is not. It is okay to make judgment calls from time to time when necessary, even if those judgment calls do not correspond directly to the information security officer's system requirements.

SUMMARY

Overriding generic policy may be acceptable in some circumstances, but you should not challenge the authority of the information security officer. They put the system requirements in place for a reason.

Sharing System Privileges – Should You Provide Access?

A system administrator from the European office is visiting you to discuss the overall administrative aspects of the corporate business continuity plan. She asks if she can log into your administrative machine to check out how you have set up the system. She has requested your administrative password. She is not an authorized user at your New York location. Is it ever appropriate to share your administrative system privileges with an unauthorized user?

Conservative Even when dealing with other system administrators, providing an unauthorized user access is not acceptable. In this circumstance, you should log on yourself without her seeing the password, and personally show her the system setup you have in New York so that she may duplicate it in Europe. Do not provide the administrative password.

Liberal Since your coworker is a system administrator at the European office, and the purpose of her visit is to work with you in creating an overall business continuity plan globally, you should not deny her access to the system and administrative privileges. Some rules actually hinder the job at hand.

SUMMARY

In most cases, you should never provide access to an unauthorized user. The above situation is a little gray because of the circumstances, but even so, a conservative administrator is more positively looked upon than a liberal one because of the responsibility they have and how much danger is invoked if the system were breached at the administrative level.

Sharing System Privileges with Your Boss – When is it Necessary?

You are lying in bed barely recovering from a long night of the Hong Kong Flu. Your boss needs a file on your computer and calls you at home. Feeling like death, you give your boss your password over the phone even though you know it is against company policy to share passwords. Was this a bad decision?

Conservative Divulging your personal password over the phone is a major breach of security. You can never be certain that no one else is listening in on the call. For that matter, you cannot be absolutely certain it is your boss you are speaking with on the phone. Do not provide the requested information at any cost.

Liberal Although it is never a good idea to give your administrative password on the phone to anyone else, even if it is your boss, sometimes it is required to circumvent a serious disruption to the business. In this circumstance, you have to take a calculated risk and provide the requested information.

SUMMARY

Access to the administrative password requires diligent protection under all circumstances. You must use your best judgment in a circumstance such as this one. By failing to provide your password, the business may suffer significantly. However, you will put the systems at risk by revealing your password over the phone and providing it to anyone regardless of who they are.

Lending the System Administration Machine – Is it ever a Good Idea?

You have the quickest computer in the company since you perform system administration. One of the programmers asks to use your machine for 20 minutes in order to run a portion of their code that needs a fast operating speed. Do you give up your machine to the programmer?

Conservative The administrative machine is for administrative purposes. No exceptions to this rule are acceptable. What if there was a bug in their code that rendered the machine inoperable? Bad idea!

Liberal It is probably not a good idea to offer up the administration machine to anyone, even a seasoned computer programmer. However, in this circumstance you may choose to run the code yourself to test it for them on a higher speed machine if that is what their work requires and there are no other resources available.

SUMMARY

The administrative computer is more dangerous to lend than the administrative password. When someone has access to that machine, they obtain access to all system resources. The destructive power is great.

Computer Games – Remove from the Network?

You notice that every day after lunch the entire programming team is taking up network resources to play a computer game. Do you talk to them, report them to management, kick them off the game, or join them?

> **Conservative** You should remove the game from the network so that the programmers cannot play, because the game takes up valuable system resources and negatively affects the performance of network operations.
>
> **Liberal** You should talk to the programming team and explain that when they use the game it significantly impacts the performance of the network and therefore they cannot play it during normal working hours. If this does not work you may need to escalate the matter to senior management.

SUMMARY

The issue of allowing games on the network appears cut and dry from an administrative point of view—it is not appropriate and is an abuse of the network. However, politically speaking, alienating yourself from the rest of the technical team can put you in hot water very fast. Whatever you decide to do in this situation, make sure your communication is sensitive and well thought out. You have to make difficult decisions that may cause animosity towards you personally.

Justifying Game Use – Sending Mixed Messages?

Your U.S. government agency allows employees to play computer games during the holiday season; afterward the system administrator is required to delete all of the games on the network. Why was it okay during the holiday season and not after?

> **Conservative** If senior management approves the use of a game during the holiday season, that is their prerogative and should be taken as a bonus not a given. There is no justification for using the game beyond the allocated time period, especially in the case of a government agency.

Liberal Allowing the use of network computer games during certain times of the year sends mixed messages to employees. This would indicate that computer games do not have a negative impact on computing resources, which is not true. Since you as the administrator can no longer enforce the right use of system resources, it makes it difficult to justify to the employees why they cannot use the game at other times. Therefore, you may be tempted to leave the game on the network for those who were hooked during the holiday season and want to play again after normal working hours.

SUMMARY

It is not uncommon to see system administrators break the rules in areas such as computer games. Often it is not just the technical team but also the administrator who likes to play during down time. Making the determination to delete the files correctly aligns you with senior management.

Music Downloads – Should you Allow It?

You notice that some members of the technical database team are downloading massive amounts of MP3 (electronic music) files from Internet music download sites. Some of these sites are legal and others are not. You yourself have downloaded a couple on your home computer. Would you feel like a hypocrite turning the people at work in?

Conservative Work is different from home use. What people do at home is on their own time at their own risk. What the company's personnel do at work puts the business at risk. You should turn in the individuals who are downloading electronic music files onto their corporate computers, whether they are accessing the MP3 files from legal or illegal distribution Internet sites.

Liberal Verify if the employees are accessing illegal music distribution sites and determine the volume of downloading that is occurring. If personnel access legal music distribution sites in a small quantity leave it alone. However, if they are downloading from illegal sites in massive quantity give them a warning. If they do not adhere to the warning, report them to senior management as they are putting the company at risk legally and abusing company resources technically.

SUMMARY

Downloading MP3 files onto corporate machines is not just an ethical issue; it is a legal one as well. When dealing with computer games you must make an ethical choice. When dealing with large quantities of MP3 files from illegal sites you are venturing out of the area of ethical into legal. Use caution and due diligence regarding the jeopardy placed on the corporation through this type of activity. As the systems administrator you may also be guilty if you knowingly allow the activity. In the case of small downloads of MP3 files from legal sites, you must make an ethical choice to allow this type of activity or not.

E-mail to Company List – Should You Block Access?

Many employees use the corporate e-mail package to send mass e-mails regarding personal garage sales, birth announcements, party invitations, and so on, to a company list. Is this okay?

Conservative   It is never appropriate to utilize any corporate resources including corporate e-mail for personal means. As the system administrator, you need to issue a memorandum indicating that employees must understand that this type of activity is not acceptable. You should also block access to distribution lists to everyone except those who require the lists for business reasons.

Liberal   An occasional e-mail to a large e-mail list is fine. If you completely remove all personal aspects of working on a team, you end up with a very dry work environment that no one enjoys, which will in turn cause heavy turnover in personnel. Finding a balance is required for successful information technology teams. Consider what an acceptable use of corporate e-mail is and what it is not. Try not to be so stringent that no one wants to work for the company because it feels too impersonal.

SUMMARY

Part of the role of the system administrator is to control the flow of network traffic, e-mail resources, and system abuse. Mass e-mails can clog up the e-mail server and in some extreme cases the network. It is your job to assess the appropriateness of this type of network use and respond accordingly.

@#&!?!

Overly Aggressive Anti-spam

Everyone's favorite e-mail topic is spam. The fight against spam in some ways has become downright scary. I posted to a list recently (NANOG) and had my perimeter slammed by port scans and relay checks. It lit up my alerting system like a Christmas tree. Apparently, this is someone's idea of a "feature" in that they probe the hell out of you before accepting your e-mail. So maybe they get less spam, but everyone else's incident handlers stay pretty busy. The operator feels totally justified in this activity.

   When I asked about this I was basically told, "Well, you would not have this problem if you were not anal about checking your logs." Go figure.

Chris Brenton , Independent Consultant

Personal E-mail Lists – Are they Acceptable?

An employee has created their own e-mail distribution list within the company mail program and sends daily jokes to their friends at work. Is this type of e-mail use abuse of company resources or within the acceptable range of behavior?

Conservative Since heavy e-mail volume clogs up the e-mail server and potentially other system resources, this type of behavior is unacceptable. Prohibit e-mail list mass mailing use for that particular user.

Liberal Daily joke e-mails may be fun and lighten the workplace but they do cross over into system abuse. Speak with the employee and explain how they affect the network and e-mail server. In most cases, the e-mail joke lists will not be that large as to warrant a technical response from systems administration. However, if the e-mail distribution is large, ask them to terminate sending daily joke to such a large group of people.

SUMMARY

This is one issue that you may consider bumping up to senior management and let them make their own decision regarding the ethical behavior of e-mailing jokes to personal distribution lists.

General Mass E-mail – Should You "Reply All?"

A sales agent indiscriminately sent some marketing material that was not of general interest to the company mailing list at your large company. The list was unusable for the next three days because of the number of people who hit "reply all" and wrote, "Take me off this list." Is it ethical to hit "reply all" when you are only responding to one person, the sender?

Conservative It is obnoxious when you reply all to a large distribution list, which wreaks havoc on the e-mail server and network resources. This is unethical behavior if the user knows they are sending their reply to everyone on the distribution list.

Liberal Sometimes hitting "reply all" is the only way of getting the attention of others to indicate an inappropriate e-mail was sent. It applies pressure on the sender of the mass e-mail. It creates a disturbance and negatively affects the mail server.

SUMMARY

As the system administrator, you would never want people to "reply all" on a mass e-mailing for the reasons mentioned above. Some people are ignorant of the fact that the list may become unusable and, therefore, are not ethically accountable in comparison to those that know what it will do to the system and do it anyway.

Using the Web when it is Not Allowed – When Do You Allow Access?

Web access is blocked from the computers where you work and you are responsible for keeping it blocked. One of the programmers comes up to you and says that they work much better if they can take a break every couple of hours and surf the Web for 15 minutes. Do you provide them the access on this basis?

Conservative Policy is policy and providing unauthorized access to corporate resources is in direct breach of these protective measures put in place to ensure system integrity and protect the company from attack. In addition, if you bypass corporate policy and provide access to this one programmer, you can be certain that the entire programming department will demand access as will the rest of the company. Stick to the rules. That is why they were created in the first place. Information security rules are non-negotiable.

Liberal In some cases, such as in the case of an exceptional programmer who needs to rest their mind from time to time, you may want to make a request to senior management to allow them access to the Internet. The entire purpose of the policy is to keep production up since not everyone can responsibly handle access to the Internet without significantly affecting their work. Management may allow access on a case-by-case basis.

SUMMARY

System administrators must decide how they will operate in relation to the employees at a given company. Handling privileges and access on a case-by-case basis is one option; however, some employees may not find this option ethically fair. Another way to handle privileges and access is by imparting by-the-book fairness to all; people will not feel slighted if you do things this way.

Networking

One aspect that falls under the general category of system administration is network administration. Networking involves controlling an integrated computer system and maximizing performance and productivity of that system. Network management has five categories according to the International Organization for Standardization (ISO): fault management, accounting management, configuration management, security management, and performance management.

In this section, we discuss the ethical issues that arise for network administrators. These ethical dilemmas include but are not limited to selling corporate bandwidth and the use and abuse of wireless systems.

Selling Bandwidth – Is it ever Appropriate?

Your company has more bandwidth than it needs, and an employee is selling it to another company for a profit. Do you report them or let them make an extra buck? Would your answer to this question be different if they were using the money they made from selling the extra bandwidth to buy network equipment for the information technology that the company needs?

> **Conservative** Whether the money goes into the employee's pocket or the company's pocket, selling bandwidth without complete approval from senior management is completely inappropriate. Report this type of behavior to senior management immediately upon discovery.
>
> **Liberal** If the employee is keeping the money for personal purposes, speak directly to them and try to encourage them to stop this type of transaction right away. If they refuse, report them to senior management. However, if the employee is being resourceful and making money for the company to better run the information technology department and expand the budget, praise them for their ingenuity.

SUMMARY

It is dangerous business when employees go outside of the company to gain profits from company resources for either themselves or the department. Try to keep yourself clean of side deals such as this one, because the ethical repercussions are high.

Wireless Systems – Should You Take Advantage?

A company that shares the same building as the one you work in uses a wireless network that is not very secure. Since wireless systems are available if you are in range of the signal, is it inappropriate to tap into the neighboring company's wireless network?

Conservative It is never appropriate to tap into another company's network under any circumstances. This is invasion of privacy, even if they have not secured the network properly. You should inform the company of the vulnerability of their wireless network.

Liberal If the business next door to you is irresponsible enough to have a wireless network that is not secure, out of curiosity you may check out their network. However, any form of malicious attack is inappropriate.

SUMMARY

If someone left a one-hundred dollar bill in a lost jacket and you found the jacket, would you keep it or return it? Taking advantage of the weaknesses of others highlights who you are as a human being.

There is No Ethical War Driving

Hacking is often defined as "a form of malicious attack" whereby a person known as a Hacker breaks into a computer system that they are not authorized to use. This includes attempts to bypass the security mechanisms of an information system or network for the purposes of obtaining or damaging information. I could not disagree more with that definition. This is a definition that has been pushed upon the general public by media outlets and fear-mongers that have no idea what a "Hacker" or "Hacking" really is.

Hackers make life better. I don't mean my own life because I am an information security professional that would be out of work if people

Continued

weren't trying to break into networks. I mean everyone's life. I can see the wheels turning now. "Has Chris lost his mind? Hackers aren't good. Hackers are evil." Wrong. I once read an outstanding article by Ming of Mongo that stated that the Wright Brothers were Hackers. They took things that had one intended purpose, bicycle parts, and used them for another, to build the first airplane. What a great analogy. Hackers take things apart. Hackers break things, find out how they work, and put them back together in a way that makes them work better. Hackers make computers faster. Hackers figure out how to make your car's engine run cleaner and more efficient so that you only have to get your oil changed every 5000 miles instead of every 3000. Hackers just saved you money. Thank a Hacker. Hackers are your friends.

Okay, so now you are saying, "All right Chris, I get it. Hackers are good people. But what does that have to do with your title 'There is No Ethical War Driving'?" Excellent question; glad to see you are paying attention. War Driving is the act of moving around a specific area and mapping the population of wireless access points for statistical purposes. These statistics are then used to raise awareness of the security problems associated with these types of networks. War Driving does not utilize the resources of any wireless access point or network that is discovered without prior authorization of the owner. There is nothing unethical about this. Therefore, by definition, there can be no "unethical" War Driving. If there can't be unethical War Driving, it stands to reason that there can be no "ethical" War Driving. There is just War Driving.

Once again, a term has been desecrated by overzealous reporters that are determined to shock you with scary words. Words like War Driver, wireless Hackers armed with laptops, whackers (an oh so clever media shortening of wireless hackers); words designed to make you fear something you don't understand.

Gaining access to networks, (wired or wireless) without authorization is a crime. Individuals that access networks without authorization are criminals. Once a person crosses this line, he has stopped War Driving and started practicing criminal activity. The War Driving was neither "ethical" nor "unethical." It was just War Driving. The crime was, of course, unethical. Some people will point out that the criminal used data collected in a War Drive to commit his crime. I concede this point. I also point out that if a person drives to the bank so that he can rob it, he isn't practicing "unethical driving." He is just driving. Robbing the bank is of course unethical, the way he arrived there is immaterial.

War Drivers take their own time to analyze wireless network security, without causing harm, without accessing networks, without utilizing

Continued

resources that don't belong to them. War Drivers promote wireless network security. War Drivers pay their own way to security conferences and spread the word. War Drivers, like Hackers, are your friend. They aren't "ethical" War Drivers. They're just War Drivers.

Finally, you may be asking yourself why the words Hacker and War Driver are capitalized throughout this article. They are capitalized to finally give these people, the War Driver and the Hacker, the respect they deserve.

Chris Hurley

Chapter Summary

In this chapter, we discussed the ethical considerations of system administrators and operations management. We defined this role as a person who is responsible for overall system administration and the corresponding responsibilities in daily operations, infrastructure security, and network management. We delved into the specific aspects of the general administrative role. Several people within an organization often perform the role of systems administrator with different specializations. We tossed around ethical matters such as integrating security with design, right password use, and proper utilization of system resources.

In this ethical discussion, we reviewed when it is appropriate for a development system administrator to perform shortcuts in order to get the job done, and when it is unethical to do so because it jeopardizes overall system security.

You learned about how to establish and enforce appropriate access to the appropriate people and stay within corporate policy and ethical boundaries. This means not giving your private administrative password to anyone regardless of their position in company.

This chapter also included the common administrative ethical dilemma of spying on other employees. We considered in what cases spying is appropriate behavior and under what circumstances it is unethical.

Following administrative spying you learned how to set up boundaries for appropriate system use. You now know when it is necessary to bump a problem up to senior management and when you should handle it yourself through communication or technical means.

At this point, you should be aware of the incredible ethical scope and responsibility of the system administrator. System administrators and operational managers need to use their power carefully in the interest of the company.

Frequently Asked Questions

The following Frequently Asked Questions, answered by the authors of this book, are designed to get you thinking about the ethical circumstances you may face when pursuing a career as a system administrator. Remember, unless legal issues are involved, there is no right answer to any of the material in this chapter. Some answers may be more ethical then others but the true response is up to you.

Q: If a system administrator is required to complete an administrative redesign under a very tight deadline, is it acceptable for them to perform shortcuts, which will affect the security of the system to get the job done on time?

A: Never perform shortcuts that make a computer system vulnerable to a malicious attack. There are acceptable shortcuts; however, this is not one of them.

Q: Is it ever appropriate to alter system log files?

A: System log files are necessary to track potential hackers, viruses, and daily activities. A system administrator should never alter the logs.

Q: Is it ever appropriate ethically speaking for someone with system administration privileges to spy on a fellow employee by viewing their chats, e-mail, or computer files?

A: The only case when this type of behavior is appropriate is when you as the administrator suspect the employee of malicious intent to the system.

Q: Is it ever appropriate to give someone else the system administrator user ID and password.

A: You should never provide the system administrator user ID and password to anyone regardless of their role in the company. If necessary, set up a new account for them to use that grants them more privileges then they normally require.

Q: Are mass e-mails using corporate computing resources for personal reasons acceptable?

A: In some minor and infrequent cases it may not be a problem to send mass e-mails. Most companies will have an acceptable threshold for this type of activity. When it is done on daily basis, it is ethically inappropriate as it is an abuse of system resources and a nuisance to other personnel.

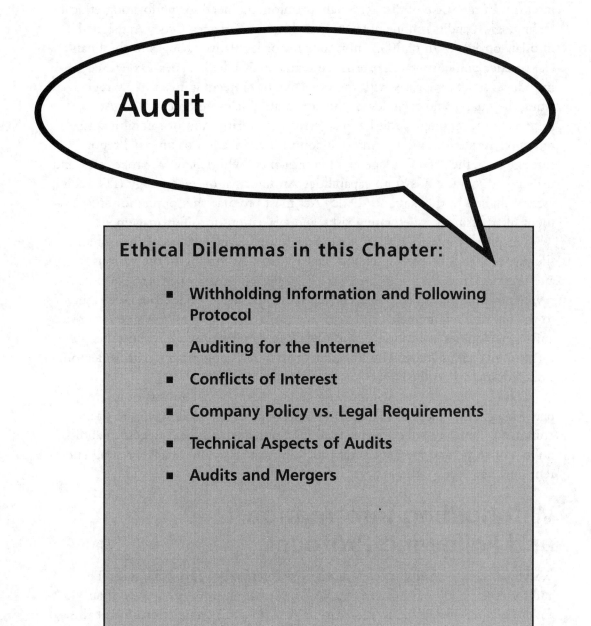

Chapter 2

Audit

Ethical Dilemmas in this Chapter:

- **Withholding Information and Following Protocol**

- **Auditing for the Internet**

- **Conflicts of Interest**

- **Company Policy vs. Legal Requirements**

- **Technical Aspects of Audits**

- **Audits and Mergers**

Introduction

Audits are crucial for determining system integrity and business practice integrity. In the wake of disasters such as Enron, the need for performing ethical technological audits is imperative. Acts such as the Sarbanes-Oxley Act signed into law on July 30th of 2002, introduce major legislative changes to the financial practice and corporate governance regulations. The Sarbanes-Oxley Act introduces strict new rules with the objective of protecting investors by regulating the quality and accuracy of the corporate disclosure process. This Act impacts the technology audit because it requires verification of careful record retention, implementation of internal controls, verification of financial reports through data, the use of independent consultants, "whistleblower" procedures, and real-time disclosure of system capabilities. An information technology (IT) audit rightly aligned to the Sarbanes-Oxley Act must produce the sources for an assessment, all assessment issues, rating risks, and evaluations for IT management.

The purpose of an IT audit is to carry out periodic reviews of the systems, the controls, and the corresponding security risks. According to the various auditing standards, the audit function allows professionals to perform periodic reviews of the security risks and corresponding controls to incorporate changes to the business requirements and priorities. An audit also considers system threats and vulnerabilities in relation to the latest known viruses, worms, and other forms of malicious attack. The IT audit verifies that appropriate controls demonstrate consistency in the effectiveness against attack.

This chapter addresses withholding audit information, conflicts of interest, performing incomplete or partial audits and their validity, following the chain of command, company policy versus legal requirements, technical aspects of audits, politics of audits and mergers, audit problems that arise, and finally, keeping current on audit issues and practices.

Withholding Information and Following Protocol

Withholding information occurs in many different ways during an audit. The auditor may rightly or wrongly withhold information from the results of an audit. They may reveal audit information prior to audit completion so that the company being audited can fix the problems and thus no report is issued on those problems. They may also withhold information from senior management.

Independent Audit Failures – Do You Report or Keep Things Quiet?

You are an independent contingency auditor hired by a brokerage company. You quickly discover that they do not have a backup machine for their primary mainframe computer. This mainframe stores and processes all of the financial data for the business. They ask you not to report about this problem in your audit because they are in the process of buying a backup system and it will take only six months to purchase and implement the redundant system. Do you bite your tongue and give them the necessary time to ascertain compliance, or do you report on this failure of contingency in the auditing documentation reports?

Conservative You cannot leave something as significant as no backup for the production systems and production financial data off your audit report. Even if they have a plan in place to create a backup data source, it will probably take much longer to implement that plan than expected. Worst of all it could just be talk. Never omit system-critical information from an audit based on plans or promises to fix the glaring problem.

Liberal In this one instance you may decide to omit the major failing of the company's contingency plan for their production systems, but do not lie on the audit documentation. Explain the circumstance and review them in a positive manner, but duly note that they do not have a backup production machine for their financial data. However, if for some reason you decide you can trust them and they will implement the new system within six months, take your time on the complete audit and do not submit the audit report until their backup system is online and functioning according to contingency plans. You may choose to do this because if you report this type of system vulnerability, in most cases, the business will perish from the negative press of failing to maintain compliance with contingency standards.

SUMMARY

When you come across a glaring problem during an audit, it is a bad idea to try to cover it up for the company you are auditing. Avoid this practice at all cost. It will have serious ramifications on your reputation as an auditor and may result in worse circumstances for the company. If you decide to risk your reputation to help the business out, be certain you do so within all of the legal boundaries and make sure they can follow through with their promises of contingency compliance.

Divulging Problems for Immediate Fix – To Tell or Not to Tell

You are auditing a system, working closely with an IT team with whom you have developed a friendship. You discover a problem and are tempted to communicate that problem to the IT team so they can fix it immediately. You would rather not cite them for the problem if they can apply a quick fix. Do you think this is appropriate since they will address the problem immediately?

Conservative You need to stay within your professional boundaries even if you develop friendships with clients. If the rules are to perform the audit and report on it, avoid trying to help the audited company. This will negatively affect your reputation. You must separate business from friendship. Performing your job is not personal.

Liberal   If you can help a business out while performing an audit and stay within the legal boundaries, do so. This is an excellent business ethic. Providing negative audit feedback while you are in the process of performing the audit will be greatly appreciated and allow the company to address the problems immediately. If you find a serious problem that the business is not aware of (for example, their database backups were failing), refusing to tell them may be unethical because that problem could damage the business. Consider what you communicate to the company in terms of how it will benefit them but not interrupt the integrity of the audit.

SUMMARY

Whether you decide to help the company by providing audit information early so that they can fix the system prior to completion of the audit or whether you decide to stick to the original plan, just make certain you are within the law and within your own ethical boundaries. The right answer to this question lies in the agreements you set up in advance of performing the audit and the seriousness of the problems you discover during the audit. The right ethics may fall in the conservative or liberal perspective depending on all of the facts.

Following the Chain of Command – What do You do with Contradicting Orders?

The Chief Information Officer (CIO) of an insurance company hires you to perform an audit on their network information systems infrastructure. He provides detailed procedures for you to perform this internal audit. Once you begin the audit, the President of the company gives you contradictory instructions. The President asks you to address the business processes from the point of view of data flow rather than the technical infrastructure procedures the CIO requires of you. Will you follow the instructions of the CIO or the President of the company?

Conservative Follow the instructions of the CIO. He is the more technical of the two and the one that hired you. Communicate what you plan to do with the CIO and explain that you are receiving contradictory instructions from the President. Your ethical loyalty lies with the person who hired you to do the job. He is also the one who knows the technology requirements of the business due to his role as CIO. However, by no means be rude to the President.

Liberal You should write an e-mail to both the CIO and the President of the company and ask them to work out the differences in their audit requirements. If you follow the guidelines of the CIO, the President of the company can accuse you of not doing the job correctly, and if you follow the President's request, the CIO will accuse you of failing to do the job for which you were hired. This may be the plan they have had all along. That way if a serious problem with their system arises during the audit, they can say the audit was invalid and request a second one. This will give them additional time to fix the system. You will be the only one looking bad in the end. Beware of shady strategy when you are dealing with conflicting interests of heavy hitters within an organization.

SUMMARY

In most cases, it is best not to get too paranoid. Even though politics are always at play in business, try not to read too deeply into scenarios. Opt for open communication between the CIO and President. If you cannot get that, try to get them to give you the specifications in writing.

Auditing for the Internet

When performing audits for the Internet, the audit process defines what actions are necessary to ensure the adherence of Internet privacy policy and security controls. This process is divided into two sections: one for a general-level audit and another for an aggressive audit. The aggressive audit procedures will try to determine if the controls put in place will protect the privacy of users against a directed attack.

In this section, we discuss how to ethically perform an audit for online Internet privacy policy and online controls. We also discuss whether the auditor has a duty to warn others of serious system security problems.

Auditing Online - Policy or Privacy?

You are auditing an online policy for an Internet Service Provider (ISP) company. This allows you to have access to all of the logging information of the system. The online policy covers how this particular company treats personal information they collect and receive, including information related to the past use of products and services online. Is it within your job function to check these logs, which might in turn expose you to the personal information of users of the ISP?

Conservative Stay on the conservative side and avoid reviewing the details of log files with personal computer online use information. Perform your audit and interview the system administrator about these log files if necessary. Invading other's privacy is against good ethics regardless of how justified you are in doing so. Therefore, unless there is a specific need for you to review this sensitive information, do not do so.

Liberal When performing an audit for an ISP, it is within your job description as a systems auditor to review the log files. Do not get fascinated by what you see and start reviewing specifics out of curiosity. Just do your job in a professional manner. Communicate with the system administrator so that they are aware of the fact that you will be reviewing the log files, which contain private information about their users. Make sure you obtain the system administrator's approval prior to reviewing the log files.

SUMMARY

In most cases, avoid reviewing the details of personal user data for an ISP. If you must, access personal Internet use log files carefully. Determine if it is a function you must perform in order to fulfill the requirements of the ISP system audit. Make sure you have proper legal authority to perform this service. Also verify that you have permission from the system administrator.

Auditing Online Controls for Security – Do You Remain Impartial?

You are performing an audit for the data processing systems of an online e-commerce company that is very popular in the industry. You discover that they do not use any type of encryption when gathering and processing credit card information online. You know that this is a huge security risk and will write it up accordingly in your audit report. Based on this knowledge, is it appropriate if you personally do not purchase from them anymore?

Conservative Stay on the safe side and do not change your buying habits because you have inside information. In most cases, when performing an audit you are to remain impartial to the information you find. If you discontinue purchasing from this company, some may consider this evidence against you for breaking neutrality.

Liberal No one in their right mind expects to continue buying from a company if they know their online credit card information is not safe with that business. You would be going against your own personal ethics if you continued putting yourself at risk. The company certainly cannot expect you to remain impartial when it comes to your own credit card information being at risk.

SUMMARY

It makes sense that you would not want to risk your personal credit card data to an insecure system. However, the information you gather during an audit is private and you are expected to remain neutral in the face of what you see. Changing your behavior based on information gathered from an audit is your own personal decision.

Auditing Duty to Warn – Should You or Shouldn't You?

Regarding the previous issue of credit card information being at risk, is it appropriate for you to warn your friends and family of the danger in buying from this company? Are you ethically responsible to warn other users of this security weakness? Would warning others be in breach of your ethical responsibility to the company for which you are performing the audit?

Conservative Avoid warning others of system security issues when performing an audit. This may be difficult to do since you want to protect your friends and family from danger, but you are under agreement to keep the information confidential. Breaking that agreement is unethical.

Liberal It is unethical to break a confidentiality agreement, however, you do have the right to warn your friends and family of the dangers of this e-commerce company. It would be unethical not to. Imagine if one of your family members ended up being a victim of credit card fraud because of this security weakness. However, avoid making a blanket public statement to all of the users of the e-commerce site. This will make your breach obvious and force the company to punish you for neglecting your contract with them.

SUMMARY

Deciding between warning your friends of a system that is in danger of violation and staying within confidentiality agreements is very tricky. There are rules of conduct on both sides. The side of the conservative possesses the ethics of confidentiality. The side of the liberal provides the duty to warn. If you feel you need to warn your friends or the public of a serious problem, consult with a lawyer to make sure you are not jeopardizing yourself legally. The same is true if you feel you need to remain silent due to confidentiality obligations.

Conflicts of Interest

When performing auditing duties, it is important to maintain both the actual and perceived neutrality of the audit. Auditors must maintain their independence from sales and personal interests in order to administer their audit responsibilities in an impartial manner with integrity.

When auditors consider undertaking management decisions such as purchasing for the company which they are performing the audit for, they must consider the impact that such involvement might have, or appear to have, on their ability to discharge their professional duties impartially. If a company permits auditors to participate in management activities, the hiring company must be aware that these activities may lead to professional conflicts of interest on the part of the auditor.

This section discusses conflicts of interest the auditor may face, and how far they may take them. We first discuss crossing the audit lines too far by pushing products on a company you are auditing. Next, we learn about referral fees, gratuities, gifts, and relating to management. This section concludes with the topic of divulging audit information to the public or competitors.

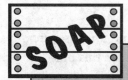

Life as an Auditor

Life as an auditor is filled with many ethical and social situations that arise from your work. How you act in each situation will govern your ability and successfulness in the said role.

As an auditor you are to perform an unbiased review of a service or product, and give an honest, independent report on the situation. Auditors are called on to help protect investors, employees, and the com-

Continued

pany itself from possible risk, and mitigation of any risk should an unseen problem occur.

However, it is far too easy to become entwined with a company, or employee within a company when performing an audit. Friendships, business relationships and hidden agendas all add social and ethical "strings" that may influence the facts.

Because information you gain as an auditor may impact the financial outlook, or place a roadblock on an important date for a company, it is not unheard of for an auditor to also be lent on emotionally or ethically. I have often heard of clients asking for information to be withheld from a final report or delayed in the release while a solution is implemented, fearing that the truth will harm the business.

It is, however, the auditor's job to simply find the truth, reporting on a given situation honestly. Any auditor that accepts a bribe or allows a client to influence the final report is causing more harm to the company than good, no matter how well their intentions may have been.

Enron is a prime example and should be a turning point for all business processes. No matter what the intentions can be, an audit has to be accurate and has to be published as widely as possible and not be influenced by any other factor.

Auditors must remain the inhuman, emotionless workers of the world with no strings attached who simply find the truth.

Because we all know, it is out there.

Paul Craig, CEO, Pimp Industries

Crossing the Audit Lines
Too Far – Should You Offer Solutions?

You are auditing an Executive Information System (EIS) to determine if it is secure from outside attack. The company expects you to perform the audit for this purpose exclusively; hiring was for no other reason. However, the system administrator from what you can tell thus far, may accept any ideas you have to improve security. You have a friend who owns a software business, which develops tools for EIS information security. He asks you to plug his tools whenever you are on an auditing job. Must auditors ensure that the advice or services they provide do not include management responsibilities such as purchase recommendations, which normally remain with the management of the audited entity?

Conservative An auditor should not use any information gained during an audit for personal gain or in any manner that would be contrary to the law or detrimental to the legitimate and ethical objectives of the organization. When a company permits you as the auditor to provide advice or services other than to an audited entity, take appropriate precautions limiting any conflict of interest that may result, and refuse to take part in management responsibilities.

Liberal There is nothing wrong with plugging your friend's product to the company, which needs such a tool, especially if it is a good one. You can help your client and friend out at the same time. This is wonderful ethics. However, if the tool will not fulfill your client's particular need for their EIS security, it would be unethical to push it on the client.

SUMMARY

Some auditors simply perform audits and avoid any type of system recommendations. Others use the opportunity to offer additional consulting services and recommend products. There are strengths and weaknesses in both scenarios. Straightforward auditing is strictly informational, providing audit results and specifics, whereas the auditor that recommends solutions goes above and beyond the call of duty.

Disclosing Referral Fees – Must You Tell?

You opt to go ahead and plug the EIS security product mentioned in the previous issue to the company where you are performing an audit. Are you required to disclose the fact that you will receive a referral fee from the vendor for advocating their product to your client?

Conservative If you decide to recommend a product to a company you are performing an audit for, disclose all of the information; be straightforward and honest. They will appreciate your honesty and in most cases will not begrudge you the referral fee.

Liberal There is no need to tell the company you are auditing that you will receive a referral fee for recommending the EIS security product. That is between you and your friend, the vendor of the product. There is nothing unethical about getting a referral fee.

SUMMARY

Disclosing referral fees to your client is completely up to you and your personal ethics. These choices dictate the type of relationship you will have with the client. Do you keep everything on the table, upfront and divulged, or will you reveal only what you must? That is up to you to decide.

Receiving Gifts as an Auditor – Should You Decline?

You are performing an external Securities and Exchange Commission (SEC) audit for a brokerage company, reviewing the financial algorithms and system architecture diagrams of the trading system. Is it important to protect your independence and avoid possible conflicts of interest by refusing gifts or gratuities from the company that you are auditing? Will this influence be perceived as influencing your independence, integrity, and audit results?

Conservative External auditors must not participate in any financial gift activity or informal relationship that may impair or judge to presume impairment of their unbiased assessment and ultimate judgment of the system audited. This participation includes those activities or relationships that may be in conflict with the interests of the company under audit. Most especially, this includes accepting gifts or gratuities from the company or another organization that is a competitor of the company you are auditing.

Liberal The answer to this ethical dilemma depends on the nature of the gifts and/or gratuities. If you are working at a company during the holiday season and they give you a personal gift, there is nothing wrong with that as long as it does not influence your audit. However, financial gifts and gratuities are a little trickier since you work for an external audit company and they are the ones paying you. Avoid accepting money from the company you are auditing to keep your conscience and performance clear.

SUMMARY

In most cases, if you are performing an external SEC audit on critical brokerage trading systems, politely decline gifts and gratuities from the

company you are auditing. There are some small cases in which it may
be ethically correct to accept a holiday gift of little financial value.
Nevertheless, even that is a risk to your integrity as the external auditor.

Relationships with
Management – Will it Affect the Results?

You really hit it off with the manager of the technical department where you are
performing an external audit. He invites you to go out for drinks with the team
after work. You believe that auditors must avoid all relationships with managers
and staff of the audited entity and other parties associated with them, to ensure
integrity of your work and a perception of independence from the organization.
In this case, you do not feel he will influence you in any direction by compromising or threatening your auditing ability to act independently. Do you agree
with this ethically?

Conservative   You must decline the invitation for drinks from the
department manager. Unfortunately, you cannot, in good conscience, go out
to drinks with the manager of a company of which you are performing an
external audit. If you would like to develop a friendship with him, do so
after the audit is complete.

Liberal   There is nothing wrong with going out for a few drinks with the
department manager where you are performing an audit. As long as you are
off the clock and do not let the relationship with him sway your audit in
any way, there is no ethical compromise made.

SUMMARY

Some auditors will lean on the conservative side and avoid all social
interaction where they are performing an external audit. Others may be
socially active and have no problem with that behavior ethically. The
most important aspect for both considerations is that the auditor does
not let any actions or relationships with employees of the company
affect the audit results.

Using Audit Information – When is it Okay?

A company hires you as a consultant for one year to perform an internal audit of a famous online trading company. You just finished the internal audit on this well-known company and would like to write an article for an information security magazine based on the audit results. Do you feel that auditors may use information received in the performance of their duties for advancing their own careers?

Conservative   Internal auditors, even if they are independent consultants, must respect the inherent value and proper ownership of information they gather and receive during the audit process. They should never disclose that information without appropriate consent from the audited company unless there is a legal or professional obligation to do so.

Liberal   If you are not under legal obligation to the online trading company, you can use that information in whatever way you see fit. You may feel it is perfectly ethical to write an article about your findings, which will bring you notoriety in the auditing industry. However, you may not be able to find another auditing job after revealing all of this information, because some businesses may find you lacking integrity by divulging such information.

SUMMARY

With or without a confidentiality agreement, internal system auditors expect to maintain some level of confidentiality with their clients. Breaking this confidentiality with the client will reflect negatively on you as well as them. However, the information you gain on a job is yours to use within the legal constraints and you may write up your findings by keeping the company name out of the article.

Divulging Audit Information to the Competition – What About Your Reputation?

Is it ever acceptable to divulge information about a company you have audited when it would provide a significant advantage to their competition, presuming you can do this within the constraints of the law and any non-disclosure agreement you may or may not have signed? What if you received significant payment from the competitor company for this sensitive information?

Conservative Selling information from an audit to a competitor company is simply wrong and reflects poor ethical standards. In many cases, it is also an illegal activity. If somehow you get around the legal issues, you are in deep water ethically. Avoid this dangerous business game at all costs. Another name for this type of activity is "espionage," which is a form of malicious attack.

Liberal Very few people would say that espionage is ethically correct behavior. Even most liberals agree to stay out of the area of selling audit details to competitors of the company where you are performing an audit. If your morals dictate that you can do this without breaking any laws, then do so at the risk of your reputation.

SUMMARY

Selling IT secrets from the audit of one company to another is a direct abuse of power on the part of the auditor. There is never a circumstance where this type of behavior is ethically prudent. A few ethical circumstances may exist in the military when dealing with warfare and terrorism.

Company Policy vs. Legal Requirements

One of the most difficult things to face when conducting an audit is factoring the requirements of company policy versus various legal requirements. What makes this aspect difficult is that there are federal legal requirements, state legal requirements, and industry legal requirements, which all need to balance against the corporate policy.

In this section, we delve into aligning an audit to the Health Insurance Portability and Accountability Act of 1996 (HIPAA) laws and other ethical issues when performing an audit. We discuss the details of when it is necessary and whether it is ethical to turn audit results over to a government agency such as the Internal Revenue Service (IRS) if they require them for legal reasons. Finally, we discus the requirements of the Sarbanes-Oxley Act when performing an abbreviated system audit.

Policy and Law in the Medical Profession – Should You Report Them?

You are performing an internal systems audit for a doctor's medical practice on the business policy throughout the system. This particular IT audit is a success in terms of the business' corporate policy, which was the purpose of your employment with them. However, the audit is an utter failure in terms of medical legal requirements such as HIPAA. Do you report both or just stick to what you were required to audit which was adherence to the business policy throughout the system not, HIPAA laws and regulations? How do you handle this circumstance?

Conservative You must make them aware of the company's failure to comply with HIPAA. It is possible that they are not aware of the requirements of HIPAA and by divulging this information to them you will prevent serious problems in the future. You may also choose to report them to the appropriate legal authorities concerning their HIPAA non-compliance in order to protect your reputation. If you complete the audit without doing so, your reputation as an auditor may come into question later because of their lack of HIPAA compliance. Stick to the book when you discover serious legal compliance issues when performing an audit, even if the legal compliance to laws and regulations was not part of your hiring expectations for the internal systems audit.

Liberal It is imperative that you explain to the company you are performing the internal audit for that they do not comply with some very critical industry legal regulations that protect patient information. Provide them with the requirements of the HIPAA mandate and explain your findings to them. They will greatly appreciate this information. You do not need to go to the authorities and report them. If they want to stay in business, they will address the non-compliance immediately, as long as you have explained the seriousness of the issue at hand adequately. Even if they do not address their HIPAA non-compliance, you have done everything required of you.

SUMMARY

When performing an internal audit you may come across serious legal requirements that are not in alignment within the company you are auditing. The more knowledgeable you are about all of the security and IT regulations the more of an asset you are as an auditor. In this issue, you performed an audit for a company as an internal auditor reviewing business processes in the information systems. However, you discovered a greater problem. In most cases, it is not necessary for you to report them to authorities as soon as you find the problem. Give them time to address it and the knowledge they need to do so. This is not covering it up, but rather allowing them a little space to handle it internally.

@#&!?!

Auditing Should Be More than Regurgitating Information Gained from the Client in Interviews

When performing an audit, there should be more to it than just interviewing people. Once you receive standards documentation from the client, run tools to check for compliance. Checklists alone are not enough to verify compliance. Also, architecture should be reviewed with PRACTICAL suggestions for remediation based on the knowledge of the clients networks and business that you gain in the interview process.

Derek Milroy, GSEC, CISSP, MCSE, CCNA
Consultant

Turning Over Audit Results to the Government – What are the Legal Requirements?

The IRS has requested that you provide copies of detailed audit documents relating to a prior client's information systems, in order to determine their assets for a tax lien and possible acquisition by the government for tax evasion. It appears they were delinquent on their federal taxes for several years in a row. You are not able to locate the client to obtain formal permission to release the documents over to the IRS. Should you turn the information over to the IRS or try to hold out until you speak with the client directly?

Conservative   Standard ethical and legal code for auditors dictates that they should not knowingly be a party to any illegal activity, or engage in acts that are discreditable to the profession of auditing or to the organization they are auditing. You were not aware of the illegal activity of this company when you were performing the audit services for them. However, since you are now aware of the legal issues surrounding this company, turn the information over to the IRS immediately.

Liberal Do not indiscriminately hand over all of the audit information about your client. Wait until you can get in contact with your previous client. You do not have the right to just divulge all of the information about them. It may be a mistake or someone posing as the IRS who is actually a hacker. Wait until you receive proper authority from the old client before you release all of the details of their audit. This is not something that should be done hastily, even at the request of what appears to be the IRS.

SUMMARY

When dealing with government agencies such as the IRS you must do your homework. Once the request is posed to you seek out credible advice as to what you are required by law to do. Do not just blindly do what the IRS says out of fear or avoid them on principal. In most cases, you will have to turn the information over, but make sure you are doing it within the constraints of your agreement with the client and the law.

Reducing Lengthy Audits for Completion – Is this Audit Valid?

When you perform audits, you follow the standard 7799 procedures, which are incredibly exhaustive. In addition to the 7799 procedures, you follow a set of procedures that address the Sarbanes-Oxley Act requirements for audits. You need to do an audit in one week for a new company; therefore, you must cut down the audit to only the essentials. You decide on a partial audit because you can complete an abbreviated form of the 7799 audit requirements within the allocated timeframe even though you cannot do the full audit as required. You will also implement all of the procedures for the Sarbanes-Oxley Act. You have decided in the past that you can do this abbreviated audit on occasion to ascertain a sense of where to begin or to save time when necessary. Do you find reducing lengthy audits for any reason to be ethical? Would you consider this audit valid and effective if you did not implement the Sarbanes-Oxley Act procedures during the process of auditing?

Conservative You should never cut away any of the meat of an audit because it makes the audit invalid. There is no such thing as an abbreviated audit. Just communicate with the company and explain that there is not ample time provided for proper auditing procedures. Never shorten an audit for any reason. A technical audit by definition is a thorough analysis of all parts of an information system, its controls, and its security risks. This includes the most important aspect of maintaining compliance with legal issues such as the Sarbanes-Oxley Act. Failing to address any part of the audit results in a risk to system security and incomplete audit results.

Liberal In some rare circumstances you may be required to produce quick assessments or audits regarding the IT of a particular company. Avoid this type of audit as much as possible. Nevertheless, if a company needs an assessment by a certain deadline there is no reason to turn away the work. Make sure you cover all of the major areas and legalities, especially the procedures for the Sarbanes-Oxley Act. Specify in your audit results that it was not comprehensive and requires a follow-up, more thorough audit.

SUMMARY

In most cases, reduced material in an audit means reduced quality and inaccurate results. It is up to you as the auditor to decide if it is worth the money to take a job that you know you cannot perform to the best of your ability due to the time constraints. Never perform an audit that does not check the basic legal requirement of a system such as failing to verify compliance with the Sarbanes-Oxley Act.

Technical Aspects of Audits

Performing effective technical audits on networks or information security systems often requires employee interviews, existing policy reviews, and physical inspections. The physical inspection is an in-depth technical analysis of the information system. In order to perform the assessment, the security assessors must know and understand existing vulnerabilities for multiple systems and have the tools to test for the presence of these vulnerabilities.

In this section, we cover the ethical issues that arise when performing port scanning and penetration tests for a system audit.

Port Scanning for Audits – Should You Ask Permission?

You are performing an internal network audit. You decide to utilize port scanning technology to determine network security and vulnerability. Since you are performing port scanning to diagnose network problems and to detect vulnerabilities on the network, is this legitimate activity if you do not inform the company that you will use this means of detection for the audit?

Conservative Port scanning is a highly invasive activity and should not be done on an audit unless absolutely necessary. If you deem it necessary, you should obtain proper approval from the company that you are performing the audit for, because the information taken from a scan can often leave the target system violated and therefore vulnerable. This type of activity, even if it occurs for benign reasons, is misconduct and generally unethical.

Liberal Port scanning is part of an assessment and necessary in many different types of network auditing scenarios. You received the authority required to do whatever is necessary to perform the audit when you accepted the position. There is no way to generate an effective network audit without using port scanning. Go ahead and do it; you do not require special permission.

SUMMARY

In auditing, some of the normal rules of conduct do not apply. Depending on the circumstance, the auditor may be required to perform activities that would normally be considered taboo. If you are required to perform port scanning you should communicate what you are going to do to the system administrators and management team. Depending on the circumstances of the assignment, you may deem it unnecessary to apply for formal approval from the system administrator and network personnel.

Audit Penetration Tests that Go Wrong – Should You Have?

To adequately perform a network audit, you go above and beyond the requirements of your job and attempt to hack into the network without consulting the company first. You do this to determine how easy it is for an intruder to break into the system and plan to write this information in the audit reports. However, once you penetrate the network something goes terribly wrong and the entire system crashes. Are you at fault or was this just part of your job?

Conservative You went too far in this particular network audit. An audit is meant to review the system not penetrate it or simulate a malicious attack. Deciding to perform a penetration test, especially without proper consent, was your mistake and you need to remediate the circumstances and assume responsibility for your error. You are ethically at fault.

Liberal The company that brought you in to perform the audit left the methods you utilize for the network audit up to you. The penetration test you performed failed miserably. Better you point out the network's weaknesses now than someone with malicious intent doing so later. Have the network administrator and technical team work on the system failure until they find the problem. This is not your fault, and you are not ethically accountable for the results of your action in this case.

SUMMARY

It is important when you perform an audit that you are in close communication with the system administrator if you decide to test network integrity. In most cases, penetration testing is not part of an audit. Try not to be too creative when auditing network infrastructures.

Audits and Mergers

Businesses tend to perform IT audits prior to large corporate mergers to gauge that both parties comply with the law, and determine how much money it will require to amply secure and integrate the two IT systems. Merger audits ascertain the work requirements of connecting two independent computers systems so that they may communicate with one another once the business merges.

This section focuses on the ethical dilemmas auditor's face when performing an audit for companies that are merging. It addresses handling multiple client audits and provides information on mergers.

Handling Multiple Client Audits – Should You Provide Details?

You are an auditor representing two clients who are in the process of a merger. Both of your clients pressure you for information about the other's systems as the audit proceeds. When you accepted the position of auditor, the agreement indicated that you would provide all of the auditing data at the end of the audit and divulge the results first to each company. Since they are merging, it seems harmless to provide that information. Do you communicate anything to them?

Conservative   Since the merger and the audits are not complete yet, it is not prudent to provide the details of the audit as you perform it. Providing negative information about either business to the other may interfere with the merger process. Since your agreement requires you to wait until the audit is complete and not provide the information directly to the merging company, you must adhere to that agreement without exception.

Liberal   If the IT team asks simple questions about the merging company's systems so that they may better prepare for the merger, it is not a big deal to reveal some information verbally. Just do not indicate any audit failures on the part of either company. However, if you can provide information that will save both businesses time and money then do so.

SUMMARY

In most cases, it is always best to stick to agreements firmly. However, on the job you may find this hard to do when there is pressure from both sides because of the massive workload coming up with the pending merger. Consider carefully the consequences of revealing data to either company. There are some instances where you may deem it necessary to provide limited information about the audit for business expedience purposes.

Providing Information for an Acquisition – Should you Suppress Audit Problems?

You are performing an audit on a small company that will soon be acquired by a much larger business. The large business hired you to perform a thorough audit of the smaller company. You find some serious system problems at the smaller company and write them all up. Just before you present the findings to the large business, the management and many of the employees from the smaller company ask you to suppress the information because they will all lose their jobs if this merger does not go through. Do you suppress this information on your report?

Conservative   An auditor is required to disclose all material facts known to them. If they fail to disclose such information, it will distort the reporting of the activities under review and thus reflect negatively on the auditor's credibility. The purpose of this particular audit is to reveal system, business process, and security weaknesses. Suppressing audit issues is never ethically appropriate.

Liberal   You may choose to suppress audit problems if the smaller company can fix them in time for the merger. This is not a wise choice for an auditor to make, but out of compassion for all of the people involved, you may find that personally you do not want to see the company go under. If they cannot supply the fix in time then you must report all of the audit data.

SUMMARY

Suppressing audit data is not a good idea. Avoid this type of activity as much as possible. In some rare instances, because of your personal ethics, you may choose to do so if you possess the assurance that the problems will be resolved quickly and efficiently and benefit the greater good.

Chapter Summary

This chapter discusses the ethical considerations of the information systems auditor. We reviewed issues you may face when performing audits and withholding information or failing to follow correct protocol. Failure to follow protocol includes accepting requests from the companies you are auditing to hold negative reviews back from the audit report.

After learning how to rightly report audit data we dove into the sensitive area of auditing for the Internet. Internet auditing includes when to apply the principles of the auditor's duty to warn in instances where public credit card data is at risk, and how to rightly review customer use log files with integrity.

We thoroughly covered the subject of handling conflicts of interest such as accepting gifts and gratuities and recommending products. Each of these issues places the auditor in a compromising position if not handled carefully.

In the legal section, on company policy versus legal requirements you learned how to balance the requirements of a specific policy audit while also including legal necessities such as HIPAA rules and the Sarbanes-Oxley Act. You learned that in some cases you need to educate the audited company on legal issues that they do not address within their systems.

Following legal issues, we touched on the technical aspects of audits, drilling down to technical procedures such as port scanning and including penetration tests when auditing and their corresponding results.

In the section on audits and mergers, you learned to draw boundaries where necessary and remain flexible at the same time when performing audits for multiple companies in the process of a merger. This section also included handling acquisition audits and the issues that arise when addressing sensitive confidentiality matters.

At this point, you possess the ethical knowledge of what is within reason and what is going too far when performing a system audit. The bottom line for most of the issues was stick to your original agreement and stay in communication with all parties involved in the audit.

Frequently Asked Questions

The following Frequently Asked Questions, answered by the authors of this book, are designed to get you thinking about the ethical circumstances you may face when performing audits. Unless legal issues are involved, then answers in the FAQ may not be right for your organization.

Q: Is it ever appropriate to withhold negative information on an internal or external systems audit documentation report?

A: The entire purpose of an audit is to reveal system weaknesses; therefore, withholding this type of information defeats the purpose of the audit. It is never appropriate to fail to report on all known system problems or failures to comply with policy or the law. In some instances, you may decide it is ethically the right choice to stall the report process thereby giving a company more time to comply as long as you remain within the constraints of the law.

Q: When you perform an audit for an ISP, do you have the right to review the system use logs and view private customer information such as the details on Web sites users accessed?

A: If you must review log files for an audit and that information is in writing, then it is acceptable to review the log files. The moment you are bound up in the personal information within them, you are breaking ethical boundaries.

Q: Is it acceptable ethically for auditors to recommend external vendor product solutions while they are performing an audit?

A: There is nothing wrong with making product recommendations when you are an auditor. Some companies may really appreciate the input. Others may find it offensive. Use tact and do not let other products influence the quality of the audit or the audit results. If you only recommend quality products, you remain within ethical boundaries. However, if you recommend a tool a company does not need simply because you will receive a referral fee, then you are breaking the code of ethics.

Q: Is there any circumstance where you should divulge the details of a private internal audit to a government agency?

A: When required by law to hand over audit results of a company to the government, you must do so.

Q: Is port scanning an ethically acceptable practice when performing system audits?

A: If you perform port scanning in relationship with the IT team and systems administrators then it is a perfectly acceptable means for performing network audits. If done out of relationship with the business you are auditing it may not be ethical and may cause problems with the system you are auditing.

Q: When you perform an audit for two companies that are merging, are you required to release all of the information for both companies equally?

A: Releasing audit information is completely dependent upon the hiring terms and laws in place in regard to the audit. Stick to your initial agreements with the companies and you will not violate ethical protocol.

Chapter 3

Vulnerability Disclosure

Ethical Dilemmas in this Chapter:

- **Vulnerability Nondisclosure**
- **Full Disclosure**
- **Public Disclosure**
- **Ethical Duty to Warn**
- **Limited Disclosure**
- **Black and White Hackers**
- **Patch Development**
- **Responsible Disclosure Plans**

Introduction

The discovery of system vulnerabilities within software and operating systems is inevitable within the information technology (IT) industry. Regardless of the time spent testing during product development, flaws are nearly always present during the initial rollout process. Based on this common problem, one would think a system for discovering and fixing these technology flaws already exists. However, the current industry process for disclosing vulnerabilities ranges from doing nothing at all to damaging business processes by leaking vulnerability data to the black hat community.

This general lack of structure in communicating and fixing product flaws invokes a fiery debate within the information security community, which has been going on for almost ten years. Yet to date there is no formal, acceptable, and enforceable standard of practice for vulnerability disclosure. The various sides in this debate express valid concerns both for and against the different means of disclosure such as full disclosure versus limited disclosure. This vigorous debate resulted in a new term consideration called "responsible disclosure," which is discussed at the end of this chapter.

This chapter discusses the various points of view and corresponding ethical issues of vulnerability disclosure. The chapter begins with a consideration of the popular notion of nondisclosure, addressing whether you can in fact control information and if it is ever appropriate to avoid the disclosure process altogether.

Following nondisclosure, we discuss the process of full disclosure and the ethical consequences of performing a full disclosure, including how they affect the IT community and the black hat community.

We then delve into sections on public disclosure and the ethical duty to warn. Following public disclosure is limited disclosure. Limited disclosure is a modification of full disclosure whereby a company reveals enough information about a system flaw that their clients gain awareness of the problem, but not enough data for black hats to abuse the limited disclosure. After we talk about the various forms of disclosing flaws in information security products, we discuss how hackers abuse these flaws. We then consider the ethics of patches and how they address IT product flaws.

Finally, we conclude with the new paradigm consideration of responsible disclosure, and whether there is a way the IT community can perform useful and responsible disclosures without alerting the black hat community to system vulnerabilities.

Vulnerability Nondisclosure

A nondisclosure policy within a company means that whomever signs the nondisclosure agreement agrees to keep the vulnerability information within that organization tightly contained so that no one outside of the organization, especially the general public, ever learns of the existence of product vulnerabilities.

Some vendors and security institutions try to promote a policy of nondisclosure. They feel the need to control vulnerability information and only trusted individuals receive information about product or system flaws. In this way, businesses believe they can protect vulnerable systems until a fix is available.

Road to Hell Pavement Company, Inc.

The seemingly timeless debate regarding vulnerability disclosure was once something I loved to follow as an outsider. I had strong opinions, but no real relevance to them, as I had neither discovered one nor felt it likely that I would. All of that changed a couple of years ago, in the midst of some work for a large organization that must remain unnamed due to an nondisclosure agreement that is still in effect. I headed up a small team whose task was to find any and all issues with a virtual private network (VPN) product that was about to be implemented. Unfortunately, not only did we find problems, we found *many* problems, and did not even finish examining all the things we wished to check before time (and funding) for the project ran out. The vendor addressed the first three issues which were found (all of which within two days, before we even got into reverse engineering, I should add), which is the good news. The bad news is that it is the overwhelming consensus of the team that more problems are lurking in the software, both at the server and the client end. At one point, one of those fears was confirmed; a friend of mine complained to me one day, about a year later, about how someone could just copy the software VPN client from one machine to another, and all the information (save the password) needed to log into the VPN remotely would follow with that one directory; this is abhorrently bad security for such an application, and it was sheer torture keeping my mouth shut as I listened.

Unfortunately, the client has not given permission to disclose; they never will, in all likelihood. For whatever reason, the client follows the vendor's lead on the matter, and thus is opposed to any disclosure. This

Continued

is unfortunate in the greatest extreme, as I have watched many large and critical organizations implement the software over the past two years, undoubtedly unaware of what may occur if a black hat were to discover the weaknesses that still hide within. Just asking nicely about disclosing, well after the known vulnerabilities were fixed, has brought the threat of a lawsuit from the client; there is little doubt what would occur should one of us decide to disclose spontaneously. But it is no small thing to remain silent as to the problems that can affect others, either.

Rob Shein
EDS – Washington, D.C.

Can You Really Control Information? – Adopting Nondisclosure Policies

In a vendor product company, the major flaw when thinking of nondisclosure is the belief that someone can control the information. There is no way to assure that the selected individuals can be trusted not to use privileged vulnerability information for their own gain. Furthermore, some of the individuals employed by vendors and security firms have questionable histories. Can you really trust reformed individuals with past careers as black hats or grey hats to act responsibly with privileged vulnerability information?

Conservative Adopting a policy of nondisclosure has several advantages. A nondisclosure empowers management and IT personnel with control over information within the organization. In addition, in the case of disclosures, it gives them control over vulnerability information, which will keep the wrong information out of the hands of black hats and other malicious people or organizations. Failing to disclose system vulnerabilities keeps the company reputation intact. The real advantage of nondisclosure is to the vendor alone. If a vendor can keep the vulnerability a secret while it is fixed, they can avoid any negative press that may be generated.

Liberal A policy of vulnerability nondisclosure has more disadvantages than advantages. There is no way to assure that the black hat community or other malicious attackers does not already possess the vulnerability information or that they will not discover it on their own before a public disclosure is made. There are four primary reasons why a policy of vulnerability nondisclosure is a really bad idea.

First, if vulnerability information is leaked or simultaneously discovered, the black hat community has an opportunity to actively exploit the vulnerability without public knowledge. Systems will be left exposed during the time it takes the software vendor to patch the product.

Second, since the vulnerability is not disclosed publicly, administrators do not have the opportunity to protect vulnerable systems. If a vendor fails to disclose serious system vulnerabilities, their clients will determine they are unethical and even dishonest.

Third, because there is no negative press for the software vendor, they are not motivated to repair the flaw in a timely manner.

Fourth, it is very difficult to clearly define the trusted selection of individuals with access to sensitive vulnerability information. Because of these reasons, a policy of nondisclosure is obviously less than desirable.

SUMMARY

Vulnerability nondisclosure in most cases is a bad idea for all of the reasons mentioned in the liberal point of view. Failing to disclose system flaws tends to cause more harm than good. However, from the point of view of the vendor, nondisclosure may be useful in some circumstances when you can quickly remediate a flaw thus not incurring any negative publicity for the vendor.

The Black Hat Community – Vulnerability Issues and Organizations

The black hat community practices a policy of nondisclosure. When a black hat discovers vulnerabilities, they retain the information or judiciously distribute it only within a black hat group. These black hats then use the vulnerability to penetrate unprotected systems for whatever covert purpose they desire. Eventually the vulnerability information leaks out into a public forum. However, before this time expires, systems and their administrators have no defense against exploitation. Do organizations like black hats have the right to conceal vulnerability issues for malicious purposes?

Conservative   The black hat community is unethical by its very nature. They are just adding additional intolerable behavior by failing to disclose system weaknesses when they discover them.

Liberal   Everyone has the right to information. Putting aside malicious attacks derived from nondisclosure of information, the black hat community may or may not disclose information weaknesses they discover. It is perfectly ethical to gather information and remain silent about the data. The ethics fall into the utilization of the information collected.

SUMMARY

Ethics and the black hat community is an interesting subject. Regarding nondisclosure, some may argue they have the right to collect and withhold information, while others argue that because of what these individuals do with the information they collect their intent indicates that they do not have the ethical right to collect information or fail to disclose system weaknesses.

Full Disclosure

Full disclosure means many different things depending on the person you speak with and the vulnerabilities at play. What does full disclosure mean to you? In textbook terms, the definition of full disclosure is the process of broadly disseminating as much information as possible regarding product or system vulnerabilities so that potential victim's possess the same information as the potential attackers. A revelation of this type of disclosure ensures that product developers and clients with foreknowledge of product weaknesses possess the necessary time to implement defensive action against system vulnerabilities.

There are four primary ways potential victims ensure their systems withstand the vulnerability after a full disclosure. The first is to activate system protection by developing and implementing Intrusion Detection System (IDS) signatures. IDS signatures provide secure detection of the exploit in question. A second means of protection is implementing a temporary fix or workaround such as shutting down a vulnerable service or blocking traffic at the firewall. The third means of detection by systems administrators who utilize exploited code, is to scan the network for vulnerable systems or to test the possible vulnerability of systems not yet patched. Finally, on the vendor side, programmers of the product in question can review the structure of the flaw and attempt to avoid similar situations in future development.

Those who support full disclosure argue several advantages to this process. This section addresses full disclosure from the ethical points of view of the conservative and the liberal.

Ethically Handling Security Vulnerabilities – Who do You Notify?

You are a network engineer consultant performing diagnostics on a job. You discover a severe vulnerability in a firewall purchased from a vendor solution. In response to this vulnerability, you install a new, more secure firewall solution from another vendor. What do you do with the vulnerability information you have about the other product?

Conservative Call your coworkers and warn them of the problem. Immediately notify the Computer Emergency Response Team (CERT) of the vulnerability so that they can notify the vendor and publish the facts after the vendor has fixed the problem and disclosed the product weakness themselves. Avoid directly publishing the vulnerability to protect the vendor's reputation and your own, since your business uses the vendor solution and was vulnerable.

Liberal Warn everyone you know. Perform a full disclosure, since CERT is slow in issuing proper warnings and many businesses may experience a dangerous hack in the meantime. Find a well-known researcher who is willing to publish the vulnerability. Full disclosure is the right answer because it motivates the vendor to provide a timely patch or workaround to a new vulnerability. If the vendor fails to provide a timely fix and full vulnerability disclosure is public, the resulting negative media will cause damage to the vendor's reputation and revenue. Further, in order to avoid future negative media, you will force the vendor to produce better software to avoid this type of media a second time.

SUMMARY

There are two points of view when making the decision to perform a full disclosure. The first is to follow a chain of command starting with notifying your organization and your clients, then bringing the weakness to a qualified organization that handles the disclosure process from there, usually in a limited disclosure manner (discussed later in this chapter). The second point of view immediately discloses all vulnerability information since they feel that organizations like CERT are too slow in reporting vulnerabilities and clients need to know the full details as soon as possible to better arm themselves against attack. Whichever means you adopt, consider the repercussions of both before acting.

The Game of Disclosure

Vulnerability disclosure is a high stakes game, with much fame going to the person or team that discovers a vulnerability, and much egg on the face of the company with the vulnerability. It can be very frustrating to be an established, legitimate vulnerability discovery team that duly notifies a company when a vulnerability is found, and then waits for the company to respond and patch the vulnerability. Many researchers have been "scooped" by other, less scrupulous individuals who will release a vulnerability without notifying the affected company, long after the first researcher has discovered and usually well documented the same vulnerability. Confidentiality and secrecy are often keys to the discovery-patch-announcement cycle that vulnerability disclosure follows today.

Jens Haeusser
Manager, Information Security Office
University of British Columbia

Performing a Full Disclosure – How Much do Others Know Already?

You are about to perform a full disclosure including the script code and all other details on a security weakness within the Internet browser system your business utilizes. You argue that you must fully disclose all of the information because you assume organizations like Black Hat already possess the information and you want the vendors and clients to have this information in order to catch any damage caused by malicious attacks. Are you correct in this assumption?

Conservative While it is true that the talented black hat community may likely have prior knowledge of an exploit, the hordes of script kiddies do not. Fully disclosing a vulnerability including exploited code, arms the script kiddies with weapons. Following the full disclosure, the script kiddies will possess the automated exploit and may launch attacks upon anyone in the public who utilizes the browser in question. Even if the script kiddies are oblivious of any technical knowledge, they probably have what they need to launch an attack from the disclosure. In addition, if the capable black hats do not posses prior knowledge of a new vulnerability, full disclosure drops this information in their laps and makes it significantly easier for them to develop exploited code and automated tools.

Liberal Full disclosure advocates assume that the black hat hacker community is already aware of product vulnerabilities by the very nature of the black hat organization. By fully disclosing vulnerability information, administrators of vulnerable systems obtain the data needed to take counteraction and provide protective measures. Full disclosure is imperative so that administrators and programmers fully understand the vulnerabilities in order to prevent and defend against them. Through full disclosure systems, administrators and programmers obtain access to the full technical details of the vulnerability and consequently can take appropriate defensive action.

SUMMARY

Although the concept of full disclosure does not preclude vendor notification, most conservatives point to the lack of a grace period during which the vendor can address the flaw as a major disadvantage. In full disclosure, the vendor receives notification simultaneous to the time of disclosure vulnerability information to all others. Because of this, systems are vulnerable during the amount of time it takes the vendor to address the vulnerability and the client to put defense measures in place. However, from the liberal point of view, waiting to post full disclosure is allowing a time bomb to go off in your organization. Failing to perform a full disclosure deprives systems administrators from the adequate time required for effective defensive measures internally.

Public Disclosure

The vulnerability life cycle publicity stage begins after thorough testing of patch development efforts. During this stage, the originator, coordinator, and vendor cooperatively develop the content of the public disclosure in a manner agreeable to all parties. The public disclosure process is similar to full disclosure with one exception; the public disclosure will not include any exploited code. However, full disclosure of technical details is included with a tested patch, potential workarounds, and possibly an IDS signature. The idea here is to give administrators and programmers enough information to defend against the vulnerability, but make it difficult for the script kiddies to launch an attack exploiting the known vulnerability. The timing of a properly conducted public disclosure must coincide with patch availability. However, if there is a known leak of the vulnerability or it is already being actively exploited the public disclosure will preempt patch availability.

ISS Handling Vulnerabilities – Should You Pay?

During the latter half of 2002, Internet Security Systems (ISS) received considerable criticism over the handling of several vulnerabilities. ISS discovered flaws in Internet Software Consortium BIND software, Apache Web server software, and Sun Microsystems Solaris X Windows font service. In all cases, ISS notified the vendor and worked with them to coordinate a public disclosure with patch availability. Irrespective of who is at fault in the handling of each incident, these procedures were not well received by the general public. In the case of the ISC Bind vulnerability, patches were not distributed quickly enough. The vendor patches for the Solaris Font problem were flawed and had to be recalled. Finally, the Apache patch was not distributed until after public disclosure, even though black hats had been exploiting the vulnerability for over four months.

Because of these events, ISS was motivated to release a public policy describing each step it would take when disclosing a newly discovered vulnerability. The ISS disclosure policy contains several of the key responsible disclosure concepts with one notable exception: ISS declares that it will disclose the vulnerability to paying subscribers of its service one day after notifying the vendor. Further, they may incorporate testing for the new vulnerability within their security products. It is interesting to note that one of the key goals of responsible disclosure is to keep knowledge of vulnerabilities within the smallest circle of people until a patch can be developed and made public. What is to prevent a black hat from subscribing to the ISS subscription service and receiving a notice of the vulnerability one day after the vendor is notified? Is this type of selective disclosure ethical?

Conservative ISS will not be disclosing technical details about the vulnerability, but the black hat will know what type of vulnerability exists and in which part of a vendor's product. That knowledge may assist the black hat in developing an exploit and using it on vulnerable systems before a vendor patch is available. In addition, it is not ethically appropriate to make money off exploitation information. This places ISS in a compromising position because they do not make money unless there are exploits.

Liberal Making money from passing along exploited information is an honorable trade. If it is important for an organization to obtain this information, they will be willing to pay for it. It does take significant time and energy to accurately research potential vulnerabilities and address them intelligently. Black hat organizations may end up with access to this data; however, there is nothing unethical about the information.

SUMMARY

Some may consider it unethical to charge money for product vulnerability information and argue that this type of service provides data to the black hat community at a fee while not all of the IT community will have access to the vulnerability data. Others argue that there is nothing wrong with making a profit from the disclosure process, whether the black hat community retrieves information in this manner or not.

Vulnerability Disclosure by Security Research Companies – Should They Tell?

With greater frequency, security research companies receive criticism for disclosing vulnerabilities for the sole purpose of generating favorable press coverage. The media coverage a security company receives may mean substantial revenue in the form of new or larger customer contracts. Because of this, the public is starting to question the true motivation behind some of the vulnerability research and disclosure organizations. In some cases, the disclosures of vulnerabilities by security firms are the result of intense stress testing of products. The likelihood of these vulnerabilities coming to life outside of a falsely manufactured lab environment is small, if not impossible. Should disclosure of vulnerabilities discovered in a lab under unusual circumstances such as intensive stress testing be made available to the public?

Conservative Publicizing vulnerability discoveries only helps hackers and is not ethical behavior. If you apply the right type of pressure to nearly any vendor product, you will find weaknesses. Real threats are the purpose of full disclosures, not "what if" scenarios. This is also an environment where security companies can pick on certain vendors by stress testing only their products. The scientific results are not conclusive enough to support publicizing stress tests unless it is done by an impartial body of experts who have nothing to gain from publishing such results.

Liberal Disclosing all data about systems the public uses is an effective tool against malicious attack. Based on that data the clients determine if the system weakness will ever occur in their production environment. Publicizing system vulnerabilities under a stress test environment is an asset to the IT community.

SUMMARY

Depending on the type of stress test, inaccuracy of advertising system vulnerabilities may occur and unnecessarily tarnish the reputation of a particular product or vendor solution, thus making this type of information disclosure inaccurate. However, the more information a system administrator has at their disposal the better they can protect the information systems in their charge.

Ethical Duty to Warn

A person or business has a "duty to warn" if utilization of their product may cause harm to the user. A business' first obligation is to redesign the product or apply necessary patches to eliminate the danger. If for some reason that cannot happen, the person or business must provide other means to protect the user from the danger associated with their product. If the problem still exists, they must sufficiently warn the user about it. If a bug or vulnerability is open and obvious, then there exists an ethical duty to warn.

This means that products and vendor solutions must apply some consideration of consumer expectations and perform appropriate risk tests. Since the manufacturer is the expert on the product, failing to warn of vulnerability by an employee is unethical behavior.

This section discusses two different scenarios of duty to warn. The first one advocates the more conservative approach recommending warning of product weaknesses, and the second issue addresses a case when it may not be appropriate to warn the public of system weaknesses.

Writers Exposing System Weaknesses – Should You Disclose All Information?

You are writing a white paper for a new operating system. It is common to mention strengths and weaknesses in a white paper, but only to a certain degree. The operating system you are writing about has a serious security weakness. Is it your duty to insist on revealing this important information in the white paper or through some other means of communication?

Conservative Overall system integrity is critical when selling a new product, especially an operating system. Insist that some sort of warning go into the white paper and corresponding system documentation. Without this, the company will be putting themselves at risk for any system damages incurred because of the operating system. Explain the importance of this to senior management. They will appreciate that you brought this matter to their attention.

First, similar to other forms of discloser mentioned, you should always notify the vendor before any public disclosure is made. Do not expose the information outside of the vendor. Conduct this contact in such a way as to confirm that the vendor has received the notification. If you feel you cannot communicate directly to the vendor about system vulnerabilities, use a third-party coordinator who will assist in facilitating the communications discoverer and the vendor.

Liberal It is certainly not your place as a writer to require inclusion of certain system vulnerability information in the white paper you will receive payment to produce. This is especially true if the information has the potential to be detrimental to the sales of the product. Mind your own business and do the job they hired you to do. Leave the facts and the problems up to management.

SUMMARY

Determining whether it is your duty as a writer to warn your readers of system problems is a choice you must make. Are you ethically entitled to the duty to warn? The benefit of warning your readers is they will know you are thorough in your research and trustworthy, which in turn improves your reputation as a writer. The down side of providing such warnings is that some companies may not choose to hire you because they simply want someone to write, not tell them what to do and force them to reveal every down point of their product.

Instilling Public Fear with Full Disclosures – Err on the Side of Caution?

You work for an air traffic control tower and you discover a system vulnerability in one of the software tools you use to track planes. This is really big because it potentially endangers many lives. Is it ethically acceptable to publicly disclose this information on national television? You know this type of disclosure may instill fear and panic in the public.

Conservative This particular type of disclosure is best handled in a more private manner between the initial discoverer of the vulnerability and the vendor. During the time after initial contact and until public disclosure, all communication lines between the vendor, discoverer, and originator should be kept open and confidential. Any miscommunication during the entire disclosure process could lead to premature disclosure and potential public panic. It is important that the vendor attempt to reproduce the vulnerability in order to verify its existence. The originator should provide the vendor and coordinator with all the necessary information and aid reproduction in any way. This will determine if there is in fact an error. Disclosing air traffic software vulnerability data without absolutely confirming the system weakness is completely unethical. This type of vulnerability must be handled in this manner without public disclosure.

Liberal The public has the right to know if the air traffic control system for airplanes and an airport is inoperable or defective. This is a case where public disclosure may save lives and the information must be published immediately upon discovery.

SUMMARY

Publishing information immediately upon discovery is not always a good idea. It is best to contact the vendor and perform the necessary tests to validate that there is in fact a valid vulnerability. Once you discover there is an accurate vulnerability it is your ethical choice to determine whether you feel you have the ethical duty to warn the general public of the air traffic control problem or handle the matter in a more confidential manner.

Limited Disclosure

Limited disclosure is similar to nondisclosure because the sharing of vulnerability information occurs within a small group of people. The unique difference is that nondisclosure occurs within the organization and limited disclosure may include individuals outside of the organization at the organization's discrepancy. During the initial phases of limited disclosure, access to the full details of the vulnerability is granted to a small group of individuals. This group consists potentially of three different parties, the discloser, the vendor, and possibly a third-party coordinator. Unlike full disclosure, the limited disclosure process does not provide the full technical details of the vulnerability at the time of final disclosure. Release of those details occurs only when the vendor fixes the system weaknesses. The reason for this limit on technical data is advocates of limited disclosure claim that users, programmers, and administrators do not require detailed technical information in order to patch or defend systems. In addition, fans of limited disclosure assert that the disclosure of full technical information only assists the black hat community.

There are several problems with the concept of limited disclosure. As with nondisclosure, we face the dilemma of whom to trust with the initial vulnerability information. It will be very difficult to enforce ethical behavior among those that may stand to gain from the disclosure or exploitation of an unknown vulnerability.

Without mandatory public disclosure, there is nothing to motivate the vendor to develop a timely fix. Since the vendor can delay the final disclosure until they fix the flaw, delaying final public disclosure ultimately delays the fix indefinitely.

Finally, since the amount of technical information in the initial disclosure is greatly limited, customers may not be able to take early defensive actions.

IDS Signatures and Defensive Measures – Should You Provide Details?

You are a systems administrator and hear a rumor that there is a problem with one of your administration tools. The vendor has disclosed nothing to you thus far. Without detailed technical information, IDS signatures cannot be created to counter this problem. You know that your detection systems will not be effective because the development of tools to detect vulnerable systems and test vendor patches will be impossible to develop since the information about the vulnerability is not revealed. With all of these facts in play, do you as a system administrator feel that a company has the ethical right to refuse to provide disclosure on the technical details of their product's weaknesses?

> **Conservative** From the systems administrator point of view it is unethical to delay or avoid disclosing product vulnerabilities. The discovery of a vulnerability already actively exploiting systems is a no-brainer. The weakness must go through a full disclosure so that they system administrators may create IDS signatures to counter the problem and update the corresponding defensive technology required. In these situations, systems exposure and exploitation are disastrous during the period of time while the vendor delays disclosure until they are ready to release a patch. Even if publishing of a final disclosure occurs before the vendor releases a patch, administrators still lack the sufficient information required to deploy the necessary countermeasures. Finally, without a complete understanding of the structure of the flaw, the programming team for the vendor product will continue to make similar mistakes when coding future products. All of these reasons are solid argument for the necessity of full disclosures.

> **Liberal** Even though failing to disclose information may be harmful to clients, vendors are not ethically required to perform a full disclosure. Limited disclosure is not unethical. A limited disclosure protects vendors' and clients' sensitive information from falling into the wrong hands.

SUMMARY

This issue is a principal versus practical discussion. From the point of view of system administrators, in most cases full disclosures are necessary for them to adequately perform their services for all of the reasons mentioned. However, some people may still not feel that vendors are ethically required to produce full disclosures on product vulnerabilities, and that those disclosures feed the black hat community and script kiddies.

Black and White Hat Hackers

The people who oppose full vulnerability disclosure do so because they feel that publishing system vulnerabilities provides an opening for "black hat hackers" to perform malicious attacks on vendor products. Revealing the details of system weaknesses fuels hackers with the knowledge they need to abuse those weaknesses. In addition, "white hat hackers" whose responsibility is to find vulnerabilities, have their own set of moral issues to address when reverse engineering products for the protection purposes of discovering vulnerabilities.

This section discusses the means by which hackers abuse the full disclosure process. It also discusses the ethical repercussions of such abuse, both to the hackers and those who provide full disclosures. Next, we delve into white hat hackers and whether reverse engineering products is ethical from the point of view of system protection.

Hackers Make Use of Vulnerability Disclosures – Is Full Disclosure Necessary?

You work for an information security company and uncover evidence that a black hat is making use of significant operating system vulnerabilities. You know that the way to avoid this type of exploitation is if businesses do not provide full disclosures. From an information security point of view, can you argue that full disclosures fuel hackers and are thus unethical?

Conservative The most important matter for information security professionals is system integrity. The prevention of exposing system weaknesses to malicious attacks is the first priority. Anything that can potentially generate an attack requires confidentiality and protection. Although full disclosures in some cases, may speed up the process of protecting vulnerability, they are a liability within themselves to the information security officer. Publishing attack code is simply unethical and provides new ideas for future attacks. It provides a library of resources to malicious coders.

Liberal Public disclosures are necessary for customers to defend their resources. Even if malicious attackers were not aware of the security weaknesses and malicious code ideas already, they would soon be aware of them on their own so it does not provide fuel for the work. It is nearly impossible to provide effective security for a system when the information security officer receives obscure information regarding system vulnerabilities.

SUMMARY

This debate on full disclosure is heated and there is no right answer. Both points of view have strengths and weaknesses. However, because of vendor resistance to fixing security vulnerabilities, the more likely road most information security professionals will take is that of full disclosure. Full disclosure forces vendors to provide patches for known security weaknesses. If vendors were quicker on their toes when responding to weaknesses in their products, full disclosure would not be a necessity and the argument would look very different.

The Government on Hackers – Should You Reverse Code?

The cyberspace security department of the U.S. government urges white hat hackers to discover security vulnerabilities in vendor software. However, the government wants this data about product flaws to go only to the vendors and the government. This is in direct contrast to what some IT professionals feel they require when keeping their system integrity intact. The government allows security professionals to discover vulnerabilities, but communicates that reverse engineering code done by anyone other than a computer security professional is for immoral purposes. This means that unless you are an information security expert you cannot look too deeply into vendor products to find vulnerabilities, thus hindering your ability to apply necessary protection for the systems under your responsibility. Is it immoral to reverse engineer code if your intention is to protect the system you administer or work with?

Conservative Reverse engineering code must remain in the realm of information security professions and not in the hands of system administrators or programmers. It is unethical to reverse engineer code from a vendor even if your intention is to find vulnerabilities and protect your own system from such a product weakness.

Liberal Systems administrators and developers need to keep in mind the integrity of the products and environments under their realm of responsibility and the sensitive data within those environments. There is nothing wrong with ensuring the protection of customer credit card information if you have reason to believe that the software product you use to process credit card transactions is not secure. The most ethical choice in such a circumstance is to reverse engineer the vendor tool, find the weakness, report it to the vendor, and apply protective measures on your system to prevent abuse of this vulnerability. Failing to do so would be unethical.

SUMMARY

This issue is very tricky to sort through because of its complexity. On the one hand, government agencies state that reverse engineering product code is immoral for some technology professions to perform; on the other hand, failing adequate protection of customer information is without a doubt unethical.

Patch Development

During the process of detecting and fixing product vulnerabilities, the correction stage begins with patch development. Patch development is a necessary step when addressing product vulnerabilities. The range of time it takes to see a resulting patch from vulnerability discovery varies greatly depending on the vendor and the complexity of the product or system weakness. In some cases, patch development may take a great deal of time if the flaw is inherent to the structure of the product. The vendor may also have to address other similar tools, which have the same problem within their product line. This is especially the case when vendors develop products utilizing a central code library.

Following is an excellent example of the complexity of patch development in relation to the disclosure process. We discuss an ethical issue with Simple

Network Management Protocol (SNMP) vulnerabilities. This section also addresses the pitfalls of patch releases including patches that combine system fixes, and quick patches that crash the system they are supposed to fix.

Taking the Market Advantage – Should You Communicate?

You found vulnerability within a product you developed utilizing SNMP. This problem consequently exists in other products utilizing SNMP. Notification of additional vendors and release of the details of such vulnerability is necessary for properly testing their products for this weakness. However, if you do not notify the other vendors and fix the problem within your software, you can publicize the error and gain a market advantage. Is it ethical to fail to disclose information about an SNMP weakness if it will give you a market advantage?

Conservative The involvement of multiple vendors can lead to confusion and miscommunication especially on an issue that affects competitors. Since the right thing to do is to communicate the SNMP vulnerability, every effort must be made to keep all actions coordinated. If a single vendor releases vulnerability information prematurely, the customers of the remaining vendors will be left exposed.

The companies must work together to test all patches and ensure they are affective for the various products utilizing SNMP. Differences in environments and system configuration may cause a patch to have negative side effects. Once the patches are successful all of the products utilizing SNMP will be safe.

Liberal Knowledge of a problem in a resource shared by competing vendors provides a business edge. Use that to your advantage. Finding a problem with a shared resource and addressing it within your product is your prerogative. You are not ethically required to share this information for any logical reason. You can be certain your competition would not make that communication to you. Seize this opportunity to leave the competition in the dust.

SUMMARY

The obvious ethical choice for the larger picture is to communicate serious vulnerabilities in the SNMP code to all who use it in their products. However, most people do not base their personal ethics on the greater good for mankind; they base them on smaller matters and personal relationships. Some feel it is not their ethical responsibility to communicate an SNMP weakness to their competitors. They many even consider this type of communication a violation of corporate loyalty.

Combining System Fixes with Security Patches – Adding More Risk?

One problem with full disclosures is the race to create a patch that fixes the security issue. When addressing disclosed vulnerabilities, some companies often combine system fixes with security patches. You as the system administrator find this process complicates the vulnerability fix because it may affect other areas of your system. Additional system fixes added to patches cause new problems to arise, which cannot be easily isolated. Is it ethical to respond to a full disclosure by combining system fixes with vulnerability patches? In addition, sometimes the patch is developed so quickly that is contains errors and crashes the system it was designed to fix. Is it ethical to respond to a full disclosure by issuing quick patches, where proper patch testing did not occur because of a full disclosure?

Conservative System patches for disclosed vulnerabilities should be independent of any additional system fixes or upgrades. Security vulnerabilities require effective solutions done in the most secure manner attainable. Complicating vulnerability with additional system fixes is an unethical way to handle security patches. This is especially true in the case of creating a vulnerability patch too quickly without proper testing of the patch on the operating system. There is always the danger of increasing the damage rather then addressing the problem. Full disclosure is not an excuse for quick patches that cause system problems to arise.

Liberal One of the results of full disclosure is quick fixes that may be ineffective or damaging to the system they are trying to address. This is just part of the reality of the full disclosure process. It presses the vendor to make an immediate response even if they are not technically prepared to do so. There is nothing wrong with combining vulnerability patches with additional minor system patches as long as they do not cause a problem.

SUMMARY

Regarding the issue of combining fixes with vulnerability patches, some may consider this adding additional risk to the initial problem. Others may feel that providing additional fixes does not cause a problem and may not feel this is an ethical issue. In addition, when a patch is not aptly tested, problems do arise. This may be a negative consequence of the full disclosure process.

Responsible Disclosure Plans

The purpose of "responsible disclosure" is to allow customers of a vendor product ample time to protect their systems from exploitation and attack. Responsible disclosure refers to the amount of time required for black hats to generate an attack after acquiring knowledge of system vulnerabilities. A malicious attack may occur at any time; however, responsible disclosure addresses the period of time it takes the vendor to provide a patch once they know of the vulnerability. The primary goal of responsible disclosure is to minimize that period of time to reduce the occurrence of attack. In theory, if a vendor properly follows the responsible disclosure patch procedure, the patch release will occur prior to black hat knowledge of the vulnerability. This will allow responsible customers to protect their systems from exploitation. It is important to note that if the black hat community begins an attack prior to public disclosure then the timeline for public disclosure requires immediate escalation. This will allow customers to take precautions on the systems administration end to protect against possible exploitation.

The first part of this section addresses ethical issues of responsible disclosure from the point of view of the U.S. government. In December 2002, Dennis Fisher with the help of the SANS Institute requested input on The Fisher Plan. According to the SANS News Bites e-mail list, The Fisher Plan arose in the days following October 2, 2002, when Richard Clarke told two hundred people attending the SANS/FBI Top Twenty Vulnerabilities briefing in Washington,

"Look for vulnerabilities. If you find one, tell the vendors, and if they are not responsive, tell the government." Dennis rightfully pointed out that the government is a large organization and connecting with the right person would be nearly impossible.

The second part of this section addresses issues in association with the proposed responsible disclosure forum. The responsible disclosure forum is a means by which different parties can debate and mediate their vulnerability disclosure points of view. The responsible disclosure forum is an attempt to reach a compromise between all sides in the disclosure debate. Individuals and businesses either participate in the disclosure forum, or are considered members of the black hat community. Although this is a unique statement when you consider other responsible disclosure proposals, it is an important component. There needs to be a deterrent to irresponsible disclosure. Without civil or criminal laws to punish irresponsible disclosure, public black listing may be an effective option.

The Fisher Plan, Government Disclosure – Is it Necessary?

The Fisher Plan proposes a government reporting center that holds responsibility for vulnerability reproduction, vendor coordination, determining a deadline for repair based on the severity of the vulnerability, exerting pressure upon vendors to fix vulnerabilities within the set timeline, coordinating a public disclosure, and possibly issuing financial compensation to the discoverer. The group proposed in the Fisher Plan will face many challenges. Do you feel it is necessary and ethical to regulate the disclosure process?

> **Conservative** The Fisher Plan is a welcome and necessary process for vulnerability disclosure. Without some type of regulation, black hats will always hold the advantage. What better organization to conduct this type of reporting center than the government, which possesses centralized channels of communication and ample funding for security activities. It is unethical to fail to have a process such as the Fisher Plan already set in place.

> **Liberal** Discovery of systems vulnerabilities is inevitable. The good people will discover some and the bad people will discover the others. It is in the best interest of those companies and individuals that do not want to be associated with the black hat community to follow a responsible disclosure policy. All parties interested in improving the state of information security are going to have to come together and compromise to build a team of

industry experts so that the disclosure process does not fall over to the government. It is best in the hands of the private sector business and other intermediaries.

SUMMARY

Regardless of whether you favor a government process or private process for handling vulnerability disclosure, there is no doubt that the IT community must discover a way to rightly address disclosure issues. Vendors must receive notification and clients must receive the vulnerability information for proper protection of their information systems. In the end, all of this needs to occur in an expedient secure manner.

The Responsible Disclosure Forum – Should One Be Created?

At the center of the responsible disclosure forum is a single "core group." This core group must be larger and more diverse than the individual groups currently in existence for the disclosure process. With a responsible disclosure forum, disclosures of all new vulnerabilities go to this group. Therefore, this group wields a lot of power over businesses. Their responsibilities include following preset procedures that earn the trust of the IT community. The core group will act as a coordinator and will be responsible for reproduction, coordinating communication, and severity assessment. It is important that forces other than their own internal needs motivate a vendor. Maintaining the integrity of a "trusted" group will pose a significant challenge both practically and ethically. Do you feel the IT industry is ready for a trusted core disclosure forum, and that individuals within that group who represent different business areas will act in the best interest of all parties?

Conservative In a perfect world, having a trusted group is optimal and what the IT community should work toward. In reality, this group requires a layer of accountability to protect all parties. A second group can hold the trusted group accountable and receive early warnings with enough information to prepare defenses and detect exploits. However, an additional group adds risk and considerable effort must be applied to not publish detailed technical information, scripts, or tools that would aid untalented script kiddies in launching attacks.

Liberal A trusted group is a viable solution to the standardization of the vulnerability disclosure process. Any process, even if it has weaknesses, is better than no process at all. Granted, not all individuals can be trusted to keep the greater good in mind; however, the IT industry is ready and desperately needs 'a trusted core disclosure forum.

SUMMARY

The conservative point of view adds weakness to the overall idea by having a second group to add accountability to the trusted group, which will require more work because this team will need to assure that vulnerability information is not prematurely disclosed. In addition, protection mechanisms need to be put in place to prevent black hats from infiltration of the second group. Any enlargement of the circle of trust before adequate patch development and testing will increase the risk of information leakage but is necessary in terms of accountability. The liberal point of view that there must be something in place, even if it is not perfect, is definitely an agreement that cannot be denied.

Chapter Summary

In this chapter we discussed the ethical considerations of vulnerability disclosure. The first topic of conversation was whether nondisclosure is advisable under any circumstances. We determined that if disclosing system vulnerabilities will result in conditions of public safety, it may not be a wise to opt for nondisclosure. In most other circumstances, some form of disclosure is required.

You learned that full disclosures are the revealing of all vulnerability details including the technical details and scripts prior to patches, which fix the vulnerabilities.

Another aspect of disclosure we discussed was the process of disclosing information in a public manner. You learned that public disclosure is similar to full disclosure with one exception; the public disclosure will not include any exploited code.

Next, we delved into the dilemma of the ethical duty to warn. We discussed whether clients have the right to know of weaknesses in vendor solutions and whether writers are ethically required to communicate such vulnerabilities.

In contrast to full disclosure, the discussion on limited disclosure highlighted how a limited disclosure protects from malicious attacks but may have inherent weaknesses. These weaknesses occur because limited disclosure may not apply the necessary pressure for vendors to develop patches readily enough.

Black and white hat hacking was considered in relation to the vulnerability disclosure process. You learned why those who oppose full vulnerability disclosure do so because they feel that publishing system vulnerabilities provides an opening for black hat hackers to perform malicious attacks on vendor products. In contrast to the black hat attackers, white hat hackers assist in finding vulnerabilities for protection purposes.

You also learned that patch development is critical to the disclosure process. The range of time it takes to develop a patch from when the vulnerability was discovered varies greatly depending on the vendor and the complexity of the product or system weakness. This development process affects which type of vulnerability disclosure will most effectively address the problem.

This chapter concludes with the consideration of responsible disclosure plans. Responsible disclosure plans do not exist yet; therefore, this section was based on studies in the area of creating trusted groups or government mechanisms to handle the disclosure process in a standardized manner.

Frequently Asked Questions

The following Frequently Asked Questions, answered by the authors of this book, are designed to get you thinking about the ethical circumstances you may face when performing vulnerability disclosures. Unless legal issues are involved, then answers in the FAQ may not be the right answer for your organization. Some answers may be more ethical than others, but the true response is up to you.

Q: Are there any types of vulnerabilities that are inappropriate ethically to disclose.

A: Vulnerabilities that potentially endanger the public, should be handled carefully and by the appropriate authorities. It is unethical to adopt a policy of nondisclosure for these types of vulnerabilities.

Q: What types of defensive action can be taken against system vulnerabilities once a full disclosure has been made?

A: There are four types of defensive action that may occur after a full disclosure has been made: 1. Developing and implementing an (IDS signature to allow detection of the exploit; 2. Implementing a temporary workaround such as shutting down a vulnerable service or blocking traffic at a firewall; 3. The system administrator may use exploited code to scan the network for vulnerable systems or to test the possible vulnerability of systems that have been patched; and 4. Programmers of the product can review the structure of the flaw and attempt to avoid similar situations in future development.

Q: Is it ethically appropriate to disclose vulnerabilities for the purpose of publicity or to make a competitor look bad?

A: Exposing product vulnerabilities specifically for the purpose of publicity is ethically inappropriate because it puts vendors and clients at risk, especially in the case of credit card information. If you choose to expose competitor vulnerabilities to the public, try to protect their clients from unnecessary personal damage.

Q: What is the difference between limited disclosure and full disclosure?

A: During the initial phases of limited disclosure, access to the full details of the vulnerability is granted to a small group of individuals. This group consists potentially of three different parties: the discloser, the vendor, and possibly a third-party coordinator. Unlike full disclosure, the limited disclosure process does not provide the full technical details of the vulnerability at the time of final disclosure. Release of those details occurs only when the vendor fixes the system weaknesses.

Q: What is the process of reverse engineering code within vulnerability disclosure?

A: Reverse engineering code is the process of taking an executable and deriving source code from that executable. In the vulnerability disclosure process, this is done to detect and verify code vulnerabilities.

Q: Why are quick patches, which are not thoroughly tested, a hindrance to the vulnerability disclosure process.

A: Quickly developed patches that do not go through a thorough testing process, may wreak more havoc on a system than malicious attacks. When a patch is not properly tested, it may contain bugs or additional security weaknesses.

Chapter 4

Digital Postmaster

Ethical Dilemmas in this Chapter:

- **Viewing E-mail**

- **Can You Take E-mail Back?**

- **Spam, Spam, and More Spam**

- **Cyber Stalking, Threats, and Harassment**

Introduction

What is the role of the postmaster in a digital organization? What are the constraints that influence a postmaster's professional duties that can give rise to ethical dilemmas? There are regulations that keep the postmaster busy such as archiving and the storage of e-mail server logs. In addition to the regular e-mail delivery duties, postmasters are often responsible for administering antivirus and anti-spam software as well. Administering content filters in an attempt to halt the incessant barrage of offensive and disk space-clogging spam is no easy task. Balancing all of these competing interests can result in tricky situations for the postmaster, complicating an already challenging job with plenty of ethical pitfalls.

This chapter discusses the ethical issues that the postmaster may encounter on any given day while performing their various duties. It begins with the ethical considerations of viewing e-mail content and also headers and traffic patterns. It then explores the conflicts that arise when postmasters receive requests to "take mail back" in contravention of policy or even legal mandates. Next, it considers the skyrocketing amount of spam that inundates our networks, and how the pressure to stem the flow creates ethical dilemmas for the postmaster that administers the spam filters. The chapter concludes with the disturbing problem of cyber stalking and harassment via e-mail.

Before we delve into the actual scenarios, consider the nature of e-mail as a communications medium. E-mail is both a delivery mechanism for attachments and a storage mechanism for the archiving of action items, messages, and files. It is a calendar, an action list, a FedEx courier, and a filing cabinet.

Most consider e-mail to be ephemeral, informal and private, yet it is actually a very permanent record that is useful for opposing counsel and regulatory agency investigators. Some of the most notorious corporate scandal investigations of late involved e-mail as a key piece of evidence, not to mention humiliation.

Now that we have raised the stakes of ethical decisions regarding e-mail, we will explore some scenarios from the postmaster's perspective.

Viewing E-mail

Some businesses have strict policies regarding viewing other people's e-mail. In many cases, e-mail is a business record; to view an e-mail message concerning a management action is the same as pulling someone's employment records out of the file cabinet in Human Resources. However, the anonymity of the Internet allows us to think that no one is looking, which can quickly lead to compromised ethics. No one suffers greater temptation in this area than the people with system privileges, the postmaster, and the system administrators, because they have the computer authority to view any e-mail file. This section addresses the ethics of viewing e-mail, traffic analysis, and mailing lists that do not belong to you.

Handling Bounced E-mails – To Look or Not

Before there were mass mailing worms, when you saw an e-mail bounce, there was usually a good reason. As the postmaster, you know that e-mail can be notoriously unreliable; one incorrect character in an e-mail address will cause it to bounce. And if an e-mail bounces, it means it failed to reach the intended recipient. What are some of the competing interests regarding the postmaster's role in handling bounced e-mails? On the one hand, they can help get the e-mail to its intended target, and on the other hand, the second they focus on a particular message they start to learn a lot about its content and may see things that they should not see. Even the subject line often contains sensitive information.

Conservative   There are no "competing interests" in this case, as there should be a policy of not reading the content of the e-mail, or even the subject line. "Look away" should be the golden rule unless there is a legitimate investigation involving specific e-mail addresses. Even then, the postmaster should not be reading e-mails, but giving copies of the e-mail to the investigators.

Liberal   You can peek here and there; an extra pair of eyes is always good to have when there is so much abuse and misuse of e-mail. Besides, you have a good excuse to look at the mail; it bounced and you need to find its rightful owner.

SUMMARY

The postmaster's main job is to get the e-mail from the legitimate sender to the legitimate receiver. The only time the postmaster should read e-mail content is when there is an investigation authorized by law enforcement or the internal security department. Company policy should be explicitly clear and enforced in this regard. E-mail users have a responsibility as well; if you are sending sensitive information by e-mail it should be encrypted by PGP or S/Mime.

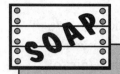

The Heartbroken Postmaster

An e-mail postmaster not only has the responsibilities of maintaining the security and availability of the e-mail system, but he or she also has access to a great amount of confidential and private information. The Electronic Communications Privacy Act of 1986 requires that system owners keep confidential, under penalty of law, the mail messages of users on that system. Postmasters are not to explore users' Inbox's unless directed to do so in support of an investigation process. One such postmaster was faced with an ethical decision during a time of personal crisis in her life. She and her husband worked for the same organization, and she suspected that he was having an affair. She decided to check the contents of his e-mail, which in turn revealed the affair. Once she confronted her husband, he filed a complaint about what she had done. Although her supervisor was sympathetic about her situation and what drove her to make that decision, he still had to terminate her employment. In the end, the unethical postmaster was heartbroken and unemployed.

Angela Orebaugh, Security Consultant

Traffic Analysis – Looking at Who Gets What

You know that reading the content of e-mails is perhaps the highest level of intrusiveness on confidential communications, but what about reading e-mail logs that show details of who's sending e-mail to whom and when. Traffic analysis does not involve content, so it is okay, right? In addition, traffic analysis is a method that intelligence agencies use to glean information about enemy activities, even when they cannot decipher their encrypted communications. Who communicates with whom, when, and how often, can be almost as important as what is said. Is it appropriate to look for patterns in e-mail and try to determine what they mean in terms of personal relationships and other aspects of people's lives?

> **Conservative**   Since traffic analysis can reveal so much about a user's private communications, this is an unethical way to circumvent any existing policies that prevent you from reading the content. The subject, to and from addresses, and the frequency of the communications all add up to a serious breach of privacy.

Liberal If the header information is the only part of the e-mail you can see, what is the problem? The policy says, "Do not read the e-mails," so you do not read them. You are just looking out for abuse and someone trying to hijack the server for spamming others.

SUMMARY

Traffic analysis reveals surprisingly detailed information that is very private. Keep this practice limited to authorized investigations and legitimate troubleshooting in order to preserve your users' expectation of privacy, as defined by company policy.

The Role of the Postmaster

The position of postmaster in an organization is a vital, if often overlooked position. While it is generally possible for employers and IT staff to read all e-mail messages in a company, it takes a special effort and an active attempt to do so. The postmaster, on the other hand, can potentially see any e-mail that is sent to or from a company WITHOUT trying, since they receive bounced and misconfigured e-mail messages. Most postmasters have stories to tell about the confidential, private, and often embarrassing e-mails that find their way into the postmaster mailbox. It is therefore critical, when choosing a postmaster for your organization, that the employee be trustworthy, loyal, and close-lipped, and preferably with a selective memory.

Jens Haeusser
Manager, Information Security Office
University of British Columbia

Mailing Lists – What about Reading *Public* Content?

Many users subscribe to public mailing lists. The content of these lists are logged and available on the Web. Is it legitimate to peruse these e-mails, since they are available to the public anyway? What if you were reading a public mailing list and saw a posting from someone in your organization that mentioned very sensitive or classified information?

Conservative   Treat this as regular e-mail; there is sensitivity to the mere fact that the user subscribes to the list. The lists' content may be public, but what if a user wants to lurk and read, but not participate in, the logged traffic? Treat the membership itself as confidential information.

Liberal   This is in the public domain. It is like a magazine subscription— no big deal. If they did not want it to be read by others, why would they join a public group and use it as they do? Report the individual.

SUMMARY

The rule of secrets is that if you tell no one, it is a secret, if you tell one other person, it possibly remains a secret, if you tell five people, you have told the world. While some consider mailing lists "public," not all mailing lists receive full posting on the Internet. There is sensitive information in this type of traffic, which varies from personal interests and hobbies to identifying with political agendas or seeking support for a medical condition. The question is whether the employee is demonstrating good judgment, and if they are posting sensitive information to a mailing list. The answer is "probably not."

Stumbling Upon E-mail – What Happens When You Look?

As the postmaster, you occasionally receive an e-mail that is not for you personally. Is reading mail that you "stumble upon" ever okay? What are the circumstances where you should act upon information gleaned from unintentionally reading someone's e-mail?

Conservative   You should never read e-mail that you "stumble upon," because it violates the privacy of the users. An image of child pornography in the e-mail is the strongest exception to this rule. This content is illegal according to federal law and you must report it to law enforcement immediately, as spelled out in the policy and procedures manual.

Liberal It is legitimate, especially if I can use it as an excuse to look into the e-mail habits of certain people that I do not like or trust.

SUMMARY

Make sure you are not "stumbling into" too many e-mails from a particular person or targeted group; this is unethical and discriminatory. If in the course of performing legitimate postmaster work, such as content filtering or validation of a backup tape, you happen to find something illegal or abusive, you should escalate the matter. This could include legal, security, and/or law enforcement, based on company policy. This is especially true when it involves child pornography, which is contraband by federal law. With regards to combating spam, remember that it is not always necessary to read the content of an e-mail to figure out whether it is spam or not, so minimize the intrusiveness of the vetting process by reading only the e-mail header info first.

Viewing Customer Content – If You Cannot See it, How Can You Help?

The following chat is an actual exchange between a user of a Web mail service and its technical support department. The user wrote to tech support, asking them to resolve a problem with the Web mail. It was making him log out and log back in each time he downloaded an attachment to the computer via the Web mail interface. If we look at the exchange from the customer's perspective, there is obvious surprise by the customer at the technical support department's actions in attempting to resolve the problem. What are other alternatives to handling this ethical circumstance, if anything?

```
Customer:
Every time i download an attachment, I have to logout and login in order
to access my other e-mails.  The webmail locks up due to the attachments…
I thought you might want to know, please let me know what the problem is.
It's not my computer; it's every computer I use to work with this webmail.
```

```
Webmail:
Hello,
For attachments, I need to know which e-mails.  I looked through a few e-
mails and can only see image files.  How are you downloading the e-mails,
i.e. what links are you using?


Customer:
Hello,
1.  I did not give you authority to look at my e-mails. Do not look at my
e-mails.
2.  Unfortunately this is the case with image as well as Word, PowerPoint
etc.
It is something with this service as it is consistent with different
computers and different types of attachments.  I am not using links. This
should not be a specific case to my inbox... Are you not hearing of this
from others?
Can you setup another account and see if this is the case with that one?
VERY frustrating.


Webmail:
Hello,
I have no way of knowing your problem without investigating.  If you do
not provide enough details, I have no idea what I need to look at. If this
is how you see it, then all I can say is: NO DETAILS, NO ASSISTANCE.  I
receive no errors when going through your account.
```

Conservative The technical support department should get permission from the customer to do this. Note in this example that technical support downloaded "a few attachments," which could mean 5 or 100. The customer might feel this is a breach of privacy and thus a violation of trust. SHOUTING AT THE CUSTOMER, as happened here, is also not good Internet etiquette coming from the support department, especially when a customer feels violated.

Liberal The customer wants help so technical support tried to replicate the problem in order to solve it. That is how things work. Technical support was just doing their job, and did not do anything unrelated to the technical issue at hand. Users should know that there is no privacy on the Internet.

Besides, technical support is monitored for closing tickets in the shortest amount of time. Such is life in the technical support department.

SUMMARY

Common courtesy would dictate that technical support make it explicitly known that it would have to download attachments from the customer's e-mail, and then let the customer decide what to do. Minimizing the number of attachments viewed is the best solution; if the customer knows up front, there will be no surprises and no breach of trust or privacy. Always keep in mind the *expectations* of privacy that users have by default, and be sympathetic when telling them that you have been looking through their e-mails. They might not appreciate your efforts to "help" them if they get the "shock and awe" effect of someone looking at the contents of their e-mail and attachments without explicit permission.

Disk Space Hogs – Follow Company Policy

You are the postmaster at a large company and the CEO was running out of disk space on his share of the e-mail server. The company policy is to file a request to the postmaster to increase the disk quota, and then bill the excess storage space to the departmental budget of the person making the request. You thought it was odd that the CEO needed more space, as the allocation was very generous, so you read the entire e-mail file on the server in order to determine the real cause of the problem. You concluded that the CEO was wasting space by abusing the e-mail system for personal use, and that the CEO should stop hogging storage by accepting all those jokes and tasteless graphics. He then sent the CEO an e-mail to that effect, refusing to upgrade the storage. Was this a mistake ethically?

Conservative   The policy is already in place, so follow it. Disk space is cheap and not worth even one minute of a CEO's time. Upgrade the disk space and leave the content undiscovered. Reading the CEO's mail is not only unethical; it exposes you to sensitive information far above the "need to know." Strategic company decisions and other such discussions, not to mention the CEO's personal communications with family and friends, take precedence to curiosity about what is taking up all that disk space.

Liberal This brave soul took the CEO to task for misusing e-mail and hogging valuable disk space. "Speaking truth to power" has to occur once in a while so that the higher-ups know they have to obey the policies they create for the rest of the company. The job entails managing the disk space, a limited resource, so that e-mail storage is available to everyone. If the higher-ups get away with it, everyone else will clog up the servers with useless e-mails.

SUMMARY

There is no good reason to read the CEO's mail or anyone else's if there is already established policy to routinely upgrade disk space, especially if they are paying for the burden on the storage resource. This one should not be a tough call.

Can You Take E-Mail Back?

Certain sectors have strict regulatory burdens regarding document retention. Policies in the workplace should reflect legal requirements in terms of retention and destruction of e-mail records. Unfortunately, some of the regulations and policies may conflict resulting in ambiguity as to what is really required, so we do our best to follow the policy that legal and IT management gives us. As one of the lawyers we spoke to when preparing this chapter said: "It's becoming increasingly difficult to really know what's illegal these days." Some situations are tricky whereas some are more clear cut. Choose wisely.

Sins of Omission – Is it Legal?

An emerging market segment in the information security and legal compliance industries deals with "information lifecycle management." These products encode each e-mail and document with some sort of tag or protective wrapping that enables the owner to have control over the use of the document. This includes "rights" such as forwarding, printing, or modifying the tagged message document. These products can help e-mail administrators keep control over the spiraling amount of e-mail on their servers and storage networks. One such product even has a feature that sets expiration dates on e-mails in order to have them automatically "shred" themselves just past the pre-designated mandatory retention period set by regulations and internal policy.

Some of these commercial products also have a feature that allows you to stop the automatic destruction process from the central console, in order to comply with legal discovery requests such as in a lawsuit or investigation.

You manage one of these futuristic consoles and get a legal discovery request for an electronic copy of all e-mails from the Vice President of Operations' e-mail account that has just been served with a subpoena. You get a panicked visit from the Vice President of Finance strongly urging you to stall the recall order for just a few hours, when the e-mails will have expired. He explained that he had been going through his e-mail logs and figured out that an incriminating e-mail will conveniently disappear very soon, all you have to do is *"allow it to happen"* and not act upon the letter from the Vice President of Operations until it is too late. Is it ethical for you to follow the instructions of the Vice President of Finance?

Conservative Be polite yet firm and stop the destruction process from occurring immediately. Asking the Vice President to put that request in writing will let him know you are serious about keeping your job and avoiding your own legal problems. Take notes of what you did and when, as well as who asked you to take unethical and illegal actions.

Liberal You are just adhering to the existing schedule. Backups should not be done during business hours, so all you are doing is letting the e-mail management system do what it is supposed to do: Destroy old e-mails. Take a long coffee break and let it slide. You might get a raise for being a "team player."

SUMMARY

Allowing the destruction of discoverable evidence is not only unethical, it is illegal. The court may haul you in to testify as to the document destruction procedures that normally occur and all the actions you took that day, including when you knew about the subpoena and who you talked to about it. While this is a sin of omission, it is also unethical to rationalize not complying with legal orders. E-mail and other electronic records now constitute the majority of discovery requests.

Morale over Safety – What if You Had to Choose?

You work as the network administrator for a small government contractor. The company deals with some controversial aspects of the government and has been receiving its fair share of threats via e-mail, snail mail, and phone. The Director of Physical Security tells you to update the contact list for physical security issues; as the bomb threat investigator, he is used to being replaced with another officer. Later that evening you find a couple of minutes between backups, and send out a routine e-mail to the 50 employees in the company, notifying them of the change in the contact list.

Ten minutes later you receive an e-mail back from the CEO, chastising you for sending out the e-mail, as it is "his job" to address these issues. He asks you to recall the e-mails if it is possible. Note that there is no factual error in the e-mail, so you suspect that he just does not want to talk about this subject. It could be a political issue and not a safety issue driving the recall request. Do you follow the request and recall the e-mails?

Conservative   You do not recall the e-mails, especially since their purpose was for safety reasons. Also, the CEO's desire to recall them makes you very uncomfortable. Ethically, you feel that the recall will withhold important information that can save time in a crisis. You think the CEO just wants to avoid the subject altogether, and that by keeping safety issues off the minds of the employees he can help keep morale up.

Liberal   This is the boss here, and what he wants he gets. Recall the e-mails, and set an appointment with the Director of Physical Security to discuss communications regarding safety issues. That way you can get him to address this situation promptly, as he has more pull with the CEO.

SUMMARY

Make sure you understand why the Director is asking for the recall, as your assumption about his motives may be incorrect. If it seems like the Director is just trying to bury the whole safety issue, you have a larger problem. In this specific case, recalling e-mails may not be a regulatory compliance issue, as the contractor does not fall under the same rigid document retention laws as those that govern the financial sector, for example. Still, your sense of right and wrong has to guide you in terms of what may be lost in conveying important incident response information to the users in your organization. Sometimes you have to take a stand.

Spam, Spam, and More Spam

This section discusses the ethical issues of spam, a topic we did not wish to include in the book, but to many people it is the most important ethical issue of all. Obviously spamming is unethical and using mass mailing worms to send spam is unethical. However, that does not justify some of the community responses to spam. The following sections discuss the use of spam filters, spam killers, and blacklisting.

Tuning the Spam Filter – False Positives

You constantly receive requests to solve the spam problem at work. As with any security tool, the spam filters you work with are not perfect. On one hand, people have lost important e-mails when the spam filter generated false positives, and on the other hand, people who are still receiving spam are yelling at you because they want you to be more aggressive in filtering. What do you do in this circumstance?

Conservative Spam is annoying and even offensive, but the postmaster's first responsibility is to get legitimate mail through. Tune the spam filter so that it lets in a little more spam while ensuring that all the real mail gets to the people that need it. Have an awareness session about the issue and explain to the users that you made a decision to err on the side of caution concerning their important communications.

Liberal The people hate spam. You are getting a lot more complaints about spam than about what e-mail users are missing and do not know about. What they do not know cannot hurt them.

SUMMARY

Spam has gotten so bad in the last couple of years that it is becoming more than just an annoyance. There is ongoing research to find the best combinations of methods to weed out the spam from the legitimate e-mail traffic.

"Research-grade" Spam Killers and Blacklists – Do They Work?

You are still trying to solve the spam problem at work, which keeps getting worse despite your best efforts. You do a Web search for spam solutions and come up with a seemingly perfect solution that makes sense to you. It is the latest and greatest and it jives with what you think is the perfect spam solution, a nifty new way to blacklist spammers. However, it is an experimental effort at the research phase and still has many kinks in the compilation and maintenance of the black-lists. This could be the perfect solution, but it could also block e-mails from legit-imate sources. Is it ethical for you to implement this new solution knowing that you may block e-mails from legitimate sources?

Conservative "Research-grade" spam killers are just that, research. Specifically, blacklisting of spammers can be utilized maliciously to shut down legitimate e-mail traffic from innocent sites. Since there is no verifi-cation mechanism to the "reporting" function in blacklisting, the result is abuse of the blacklist. The cure may be worse than the disease.

Liberal Spam has to go, and this is the tool to do it with. You trust your superior technical skills and though this tool is not officially commercial - grade and ready for production use, you can tweak it just right. There are no perfect tools.

SUMMARY

Spam will get worse before it gets better, but experimental software and the mail server do not mix. Users see e-mail as one of the most critical business applications and depend on it to convey legal, financial, and security-related messages and alerts. Not only is this research grade "fix" bad change management, it is ethically incorrect to use software that has not been proven in the production environment.

Cyber Stalking, Threats, and Harassment

Cyber stalking, threats, harassment, and other abusive behaviors occur through e-mail on a daily basis. There is something about e-mail that can make otherwise timid and shy people very aggressive and threatening. This is especially true if there is a perception of anonymity on the part of the abusive party.

Online Stalking – No Big Deal?

Someone is stalking one of your users. She keeps getting suggestive and progressively creepier e-mails from a person that is obviously using a pseudonym. She says she is scared that this person is going to come to the office and hurt her, though the content of the e-mails she showed you do not explicitly say that. Since the e-mails do not yet rise to the level of a criminal threat of death or bodily harm, the police probably will not take the case. The woman is obviously under duress by these e-mails and is asking for your help. What do you do?

Conservative Yes, it is only e-mail but there is a real person sending those e-mails and certainly there is a real person being victimized in your organization. Refer this to the security group and retain a log of printed e-mails with full headers for later use. Most likely, security will have you quarantine all the e-mail from the stalker as well as anything outgoing to the stalker's e-mail address. Look into the cyber stalking laws in your state.

Liberal This is the Internet and cowards will do what they do from far away. The police department cannot do anything yet since it is not a direct threat, so let this little annoyance run its course. There is no real threat here, so just block the offending e-mail address and the stalker will eventually go away.

SUMMARY

Cyber stalking is a serious matter despite the fact that it is online and not facilitated by phone or snail mail. Cyber stalking often transitions into physical stalking and can escalate into a violent workplace incident. Even though it is "just e-mail" right now, it can have a devastating effect on the victim in terms of mental health and productivity. Treat these cases with the same care as you would serious harassing and stalking behavior originating offline. Also note that in some states, inaction on this kind of victimization may become a legal problem if the victim (the user in this case) sues on the grounds of "hostile work environment" if the company does nothing, since the company has been notified.

Chapter Summary

Being a postmaster can strain even the most ethical person's judgment. There are always technicalities and end runs around the letter of policy in your organization. The postmaster controls the vital communications infrastructure that thousands of users rely on to transmit and receive critical information. Users abuse e-mail in ways that waste time, bandwidth, and disk space, not to mention sending harassing and offensive content. This abuse can make the most ethical postmaster want to take action, but as we saw in the section on viewing e-mail, this desire must be tempered by privacy considerations. Ethical use of the power that comes with the postmaster's privileges dictate that there must be a basic respect for the confidentiality of the e-mail content, and even traffic patterns, that come to light when looking into legitimate e-mail problems.

The example of the traffic analysis in the beginning of the chapter illustrated this ethical principle: It may not be explicitly forbidden, but it still violates the spirit of the policy that protects user privacy. Users are typically shocked to learn of the kind of monitoring that goes on in their organization.

From an ethics standpoint there is a duty to inform users of the kind of monitoring they are subjected to. It is good business and good ethics to manage their expectations of privacy to reflect company policy and legal requirements, such as the growing number of regulations affecting the retention of e-mails as a business record.

These regulations may create ethical dilemmas, which we explored in the section on "taking e-mail back." This may seem harmless enough to some, but deleting e-mails may be a serious breach of company policy, and possibly against regulations and laws regarding obstruction of justice.

Hopefully, each organization has its own written policies that govern the legitimate use of e-mail. Policies should govern the handling of issues arising from abuse by both users and administrators, in a fair and consistent manner. We saw in several of the scenarios how a postmaster can go on fishing expeditions in order to find "the goods" on certain people, whether via viewing e-mail headers, content, or "stumbling upon" e-mails from a particular person. This is abusive and unethical.

Selectively applying policy is discriminatory and unethical, as well as a great way to lose in court against employees. Though many policies in the U.S. explicitly take away the users' expectation of privacy, this may not work in places such as the European Union, where privacy is considered a human right.

In such an environment, violating a user's privacy may only be done when there is "concrete suspicion of misuse" or some other thresholds that are higher than in corporate America. This gets tricky when setting global policies for remote offices in different states and countries. Be aware of the local legal and regulatory issues emerging in your specific jurisdiction and adjust policy and awareness training accordingly.

In the section on spam filtering, we discussed the tremendous pressures on postmasters to block this malicious traffic from getting to the users' inboxes. That pressure can cause an otherwise terrific postmaster to take shortcuts in evaluating filtering schemes, creating the possibility of excessive false positives that deny legitimate e-mails to users. We also discussed the unintended consequences that follow the use of "research grade" filters that rely on unreliable blacklists, creating denial-of-service conditions for innocent third parties.

The cyber stalking discussion gave us a chance to think about the impact that stalking via e-mail can have on users in an organization. Just because e-mail is the medium for this malicious behavior does not mean that there are not devastating consequences for the victim. Treating cyber stalking victims with compassion and respect is the ethical duty of the postmaster, who should treat cyber stalking as a serious problem, referring it to the security department for further investigation and handling.

While there have been leaps and bounds in IT in the past few years, the role of the postmaster may be different today than it was in the early days of e-mail. E-mail use now constitutes the majority of the communications in most modern organizations. The sheer volume grows daily by multiple gigabytes in some companies, and the legal community now prizes these e-mail records as a treasure trove of potentially incriminating evidence.

Keep in mind the trust that users and management have invested in you to safeguard the confidentiality of the e-mail messages in your charge.

Frequently Asked Questions

The following Frequently Asked Questions, answered by the authors of this book, will get you thinking about the ethical dilemmas you encounter during your role as a postmaster. Remember, unless legal issues are involved, we are not holding you to a particular right answer to any of the material in this chapter. Some answers may be more ethically sound than others, but the correct responses as applied to the particular situation are up to you and your flexibility in the ethical realm.

Q. Is viewing the content of e-mail ever all right?

A. Typically, the company policy will state that there is no expectation of privacy concerning e-mail that resides on the company network. This does not necessarily mean that the postmaster has free reign in reading the content of any e-mail. Ethically speaking there should be a legitimate reason for viewing content, such as an investigation into a breach of company policy or abuse of e-mail resources. If the postmaster selectively reads e-mails and targets specific people for extra "attention," they may be setting themselves and the company up for a discrimination complaint.

Q. Should you ever "take mail back?"

A. Since e-mail is a record and in some cases mandated to be retained for certain periods by federal law, the decision to take mail back involves careful choices between legal and regulatory mandates that, unfortunately, often conflict with each other as well as company policy. This is a difficult topic and causes many reputable companies their reputation. In some cases, it can even lead to criminal charges of obstruction of justice if there is an attempt to conceal or destroy evidence contained in the e-mails.

Q. What are some of the ethical dilemmas that the postmaster faces due to the deluge of spam?

A. Spam seems to be getting worse, with some estimates claiming that spam now constitutes a majority of e-mails on the Internet. The pressure on the postmaster to keep this annoying and offensive traffic out of the users' inboxes is tremendous. This pressure can cause a postmaster to take drastic measures and shortcuts in evaluating filtering tools. Tuning the spam filter must take into account the fact that every filter has false positives and that legitimate e-mails may be lost in the desire to keep Spam out.

Blacklists are one way to filter spam, yet they are notoriously unreliable in that anyone can "report" a site as a spammer, causing a denial of service on a potentially legitimate site. This has already happened to several international security-related organizations. The use of research grade filters on production networks is unethical and irresponsible, as they rely on these free-for-all blacklists and can harm innocent third parties.

Q. Is cyber stalking and e-mail harassment that serious?

A. Cyber stalking and e-mail harassment can be extremely serious. Remember that there is a real-life person sending those e-mails and that the one receiving them in your organization is certainly a victim. Cyber stalking can take tremendous tolls on victims, just as stalking over the phone line or snail mail would. Stalking is particularly insidious since it often stops just short of overt threats so that the victim may not be able to get help from law enforcement in states where cyber stalking laws are weak. Perhaps the most worrisome aspect of cyber stalking is that it often transitions into physical stalking, which sometimes results in violence against the victim. This is a serious issue and should be brought to the attention of the security department and if appropriate, law enforcement.

Chapter 5

E-mail Scams

Ethical Dilemmas in this Chapter:

- **Monetary Gain**

- **Identity Theft and Scams for Personal Information**

- **E-mail Chain Letter**

Introduction

E-mail scams are rampant on the Internet and most people do not know what to do when they receive them in their e-mail box. Unfortunately, many have fallen victim to them. Individuals who are scam savvy just delete and forget about them. However, some scams can fool even the most competent and aware individual. The following is a sample of such a scam that is sure to catch unsuspecting people off guard. In this example, the scammers pass themselves off as the Federal Deposit Insurance Corporation (FDIC) and use real federal government agent names.

```
-------- Original Message --------
Subject:  Important News About Your Bank Account
Date:    Mon, 26 Jan 2004 15:25:18 -0400 (EST)
From:    FDIC <Rajinderpal_Arsavir@aol.com>
To:      <XYZ@aol.com>
To whom it may concern:


In cooperation with the Department Of Homeland Security and federal, state,
and local governments, your account has been denied insurance from the
Federal Deposit Insurance Corporation due to suspected violations of the
Patriot Act. While we have only a limited amount of evidence gathered on
your account at this time, it is enough to suspect that currency violations
may have occurred in your account. Due to this activity, we have withdrawn
Federal Deposit Insurance from your account until we can verify that your
account has not been used in a violation of the Patriot Act. As a result,
Department of Homeland Security Director Tom Ridge has advised the FDIC to
suspend all deposit insurance on your account until such time as we can
verify your identity and your account information. Please verify through
our IDVerify below. This information will be checked against a federal
government database for identity verification. When we have verified your
identity, you will be notified of said verification and all suspensions of
insurance on your account will be lifted.


http://www.fdic.gov/idverify/cgi-bin/index.htm


Failure to use IDVerify below will cause all insurance for your account to
be terminated and all records of your account history will be sent to the
Federal Bureau of Investigation in Washington D.C. for analysis and
verification. Failure to provide proper identity may also result in a visit
```

from local, state, or federal government or Homeland Security Officials.
Thank you for your time and consideration in this matter.

Donald E. Powell
Chairman Emeritus FDIC

John D. Hawke, Jr.
Comptroller of the Currency

Michael E. Bartell
Chief Information Officer

It is imperative for e-mail and Internet users to understand exactly how thieves steal sensitive financial information through e-mail scams. Scam artists are ingenious at creating e-mails that sound legitimate and that also have a psychological affect on the recipient. The psychological affect is a big part of the scam, throwing the recipient off guard enough to respond to the scam.

The dangerous e-mail scams will request credit card information, bank account numbers, and social security numbers. **NEVER** provide this information to anyone unless you initiate the conversation. **NEVER** disclose this information through e-mail.

The issues in this chapter represent a small sampling of the various e-mail scams circulating today.

Monetary Gain

In one sense, if an individual loses money on a scam for monetary gain, they deserve it. The reason we say that is that greed is the number one reason people fall for these types of scams. This is nothing new; flim flam artists have been a part of human culture throughout recorded history. In a culture that believes in the concept of an "honorable thief," a good defrauding might actually be applauded. The only thing technology has changed is the number of "marks" that can be targeted per hour. However, fraud is certainly not ethical, and even if greed was the motivator, when a senior citizen loses everything they have, it is beyond sad. Each of us should invest the time to talk to our parents, uncles, and aunts about these types of fraud.

Help Me Move Money from My Country – Governments Must Set the Tone

There is a very common e-mail scam floating around that requests that you help a representative from a foreign government move money from one account into another. This scam is shrouded in humanitarian principles and is very effective. According to the Electronic Privacy Information Center (EPIC), it nets over 100 million dollars in scam money. The most recent version of this money transfer scam tries to pull at your heartstrings by including letters from a woman who is dying, or soldiers who need help. This e-mail commonly comes from Nigeria; however, the sender may be from any country. Since this e-mail often originates outside of the U.S. where the computer laws are more lenient, do you feel the perpetrators must be held equally accountable ethically?

Conservative Regardless of the laws, attempting to steal money from unsuspecting individuals is unethical behavior.

Liberal This case is slightly different than U.S.-generated scams. They are certainly inappropriate, but the individuals cannot be held personally accountable because their government does not hold them accountable. The government of a country must set the ethical standards for their people.

SUMMARY

Regardless of the origin of an e-mail, financial scams targeting individuals for money are morally wrong. Trying to obtain money from others under false pretenses is morally unacceptable.

@#&!?!

Is Return Fire Ethical?

Recently, one of the major Internet Service Providers (ISPs) began a program of scanning back against anyone who sends e-mail to one of their customers. In this case, they are attempting to prevent the receipt of mail from open proxy servers in order to reduce the amount of spam. As I understand it, their policy is such that if you do not wish to be back scanned, do not send e-mail to them.

On the surface, this sounds admirable and ethical, however, there is a flaw in their logic. This would be similar to the concept of a retail store reserving the right to inspect any packages that are brought into the establishment; if you don't want to be inspected don't enter their business. This works well for retail establishments, however, it appears that the practice may actually cross the line when it comes to back scanning and attempting to exploit proxy servers. In this particular case, the ISP needs to send some specific queries toward the origin of the e-mail, and attempt to send mail to determine if it is an open proxy. In other words, they must use the computing resources of the sender, something that is indistinguishable from a malicious and illegal attempt to use a proxy, while scanning ports may be annoying or rude, actually attempting to construct a message and sending it from someone else's server is illegal.

To understand the reason why this is over the line, let's examine the retail analogy a little further. In this case, it is no longer simply inspection of what is brought on to the property of the retailer; instead it is more like the retailer sending someone over to the house of the customer to test the security of their customer. Further, there is the assumption that the computer sending the e-mail is within the rights of the consumer to consent to a search based on usage; very often the sending mail server is owned by a third party and the assumption of consent to inspection through usage cannot be construed.

In this case, the hacking by a legitimate ISP for admirable reasons is still unethical and the methods used are just as illegal for them as they are for the hacker.

Bryce Alexander
Network Engineer
The Vanguard Group

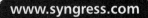
www.syngress.com

"Free Credit Report" E-mails – Can You Tell the Difference

Lately, there is a set of e-mail scams running rampant on the Internet that offer free credit reports. Of course, they need your social security number to do this. They are often intermingled with legitimate business marketing ploys offering free credit reports. The legitimate businesses use the free reports to draw customers into their credit monitoring and repair services. In the case of the counterpart scams, the scam artist is trying to obtain your social security number to commit identity theft. Do these types of scams, which compete with real businesses, damage the legitimate credit reporting businesses? If so, is it ethical to deter people from legitimate business by using the same means to scam people?

Conservative False scams should not affect legitimate business; if you are interested in obtaining your credit report you can get one for free from the credit agency. Therefore, the advertising is not very effective to begin with. In addition, if you fall for the marketing ploy of the legitimate credit business, you need to perform some research and check with the Better Business Bureau to determine if the company is valid. This requires a little more work on the part of the consumer.

Liberal From the point of view of the legitimate consumer credit report business, fraudulent offers severely damage their reputation as well. Individuals will tend to discard all communications regarding free credit reports. Scams targeting legitimate businesses have an added ethical mark against them because they not only impact the victim but the business as well.

SUMMARY

We have already determined that scams are unethical. This issue addresses whether they are unethical towards businesses that market their services in the same manner. Some people may feel they are not adding any additional ethical concerns by targeting legitimate businesses because the consumer can easily determine a false advertisement from a real one.

eBay and PayPal Scams – You Should be More Aware

Samples of large-scale financial scams affecting a lot of customers are the eBay and PayPal scams. The user receives an e-mail stating that their account will be shut off it they do not send their credit card number, social security number, and other account information immediately to the sender of the e-mail. The sender's e-mail name may have the words PayPal or eBay in it. This e-mail often scares people into action because they do not want to lose their account privileges. Therefore, they reply to the e-mail and send their personal information. However, eBay or PayPal did not request this information; it was from a scam artist. The customer has just exposed himself to credit card fraud. This type of scam is both unethical and illegal. However, do you, as the customer have a responsibility not to fall for such an obvious scam?

Conservative You are not at fault; you just need to be careful with your personal information. Even if there is an eBay or PayPal logo on the e-mail, you must verify everything directly with eBay and PayPal. Call the number on the Web site where you have the account. Again, never send personal information via e-mail to anyone.

Liberal You are somewhat at fault regarding this issue. Anyone who sends their personal information via e-mail to someone representing an electronic funds transfer company, must take some blame for the ignorance of their actions.

SUMMARY

There is no doubt that the customers need to be more aware of scams. One way to do this is to subscribe to information security services that periodically send warnings of new e-mail scams.

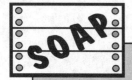

E-mail Philosophy

Some 200 centuries prior to the birth of Arpanet (and the Internet), a system named "cursus publicus" (or public message) was born. Cursus publicus was the name given to the postal system conceived by the Romans to deliver mail at a speed of up to 170 miles in as little as 24 hours. A system was devised to ensure that each and every correspondence traveling over cursus publicus were inspected to prevent abuses of the system for private use and self-gain. In 1680, William Dockwra of London, England came up with a system he named the "penny post." Correspondence was marked with a stamp in order to provide the receiver with an indication of the letters' date and place of origin. Years after its conception, Dockwra's service was closed never to return, as it was deemed that the service was creating a monopoly.

Years later, approximately two centuries before the conception of the Internet and at the height of the Industrial revolution in England, saw the birth of the kinetic postal system as we know it today. Since then, as the postal systems boomed, we have seen the birth of such things as airmail, commemoratory stamps, mail order magazines, and the inevitable arrival of the unsolicited mail-shot. I remember reading an article in an English financial newspaper that estimated that almost half of the mail sent through the oldest, conventional postal system in the world consists of advertising and other miscellaneous mass-mailings—amongst other things, promising recipients "guaranteed immediate wealth," "work from home," and "get your diploma in just two weeks." Sound familiar?

As much as it seemed to work at the time, in this day and age, a kinetic mail system as draconian as that which the Romans conceived in 62 BC is clearly not a practicable option; however, it was only the other day that I read of the plans of a large software vendor, suggesting that charging for the transport of e-mail was the only way to stop Spam and other unsolicited mailings. As it stands, due to the sheer volume of advertising that passes through the kinetic mail system, it is estimated that most western postal services would simply collapse due to their financial dependency on well-paying mass-mailing businesses, if mass mailings and advertising through the kinetic mail system were to stop. Is this really the situation we want to create in the cyber world? And if we do, will it really prevent electronic advertising campaigns and e-mail scams in the future?

Continued

The problem of mass electronic mailings and electronic scams cannot be solved through education or by legislation. The little impact of the "Can-SPAM act," the hundreds of malicious e-mail attachments that people insist on opening, and the failure to stop mass advertising by the kinetic postal services, has proven to me that the answer is no, at least for the time being. We cannot defy the laws of physics and prevent all postal advertising in the kinetic world, but there is still time for us to take heed of the past and present and change the way things are done in the cyber world; the technology ball is in our park for now.

Think before you click!

Tom Parker
NetSec Inc. "Managed Security – Business Relevance"

Chain Letters

Chain letters seem to be the same whether done in paper or e-mail. Since they have been done in e-mail, they are an Information Technology (IT) issue and so we consider them in the following.

E-mail Chain Letters – Do They Harm Anyone?

Most people have received chain letters at some point in their lives. E-mail chain letters are the next generation of this scam. A very popular chain letter scam that many people fall for is one stating that Bill Gates is testing an e-mail software tracking system and is requesting the help of the public. The scam states that Microsoft will pay you a certain number of dollars for each person that you forward the e-mail to. The engineering genius behind these scams intends to slow down the Internet and work similar to a computer virus. Since there is no financial loss, is this type of scam ethical?

Conservative Any e-mail that requests you to forward it to a large list of your friends or family is a scam. Regardless of whether there is a personal financial loss, e-mail chain letters are still unethical. Another name for this type of scam is the pyramid scam. Pyramid scams affect the performance of the Internet and can also shut down e-mail servers.

Liberal Since for the most part these scams do not perform any harm to the individual, one can determine that they are ethical. Pyramid scams for the most part are not intent on stealing money or identity. Nor are they dangerous in the same manner as identity theft scams or credit card scams.

SUMMARY

Regardless of the dangers involved, whether they are minor irritations or serious threats of identity theft, e-mail scams are unethical and have a negative impact on the Internet and the individuals and businesses using the Internet.

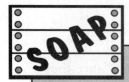

Does the End Justify the Means?

I think we can all agree that the process of attempting to reduce the amount of spam we receive on a daily basis is an ethical activity. Where many people part ways, however, is in the ethics of how they implement that process. In my mind there are two options: implement a process that places the cost burden of the implementation on my own organization, or implement a process that places the cost burden on all other organizations, including the ones that never generate spam. Let me give you an example that describes the difference in greater detail.

Back in December of 2003 I made a post to the North American Network Operators' Group (NANOG) mailing list. Shortly after making the post, my organization's alerting system lit up like a Christmas tree. Someone had just made 16 attempts to relay mail through our mail server. These were not your average relay attempts, but some pretty intricate patterns that are known to work with many low-end mail systems, anti-virus SMTP relays, as well as Microsoft Exchange. Obviously my first thought was that some spammer was trolling the list, saw my post, and was now probing to see if I could be used as a spam relay.

I had just started investigating the incident when our alerting system went off again. This time it was 24 IDS alerts from the same source IP address. Sixteen of the alerts were due to the relay attempt described here, while the remainder warned of attempts to access various well-known proxy ports. Finally, our alerting system warned that our firewall

Continued

had detected a port scan from the same source IP address. One hundred and four additional ports had been probed looking for services such as Telnet, FTP, Network Data Management Protocol, Microsoft RPC services, X-Windows, Oracle, RADIUS, and a host of well-known back door Trojans. Obviously we were pretty convinced at this point that the source IP address had evil intent, and proceeded to start investigating the source of the attack.

For the sake of brevity, I'll skip the details of our investigation work. Suffice to say that the source IP address in question was 209.208.0.15, and it is controlled by njabl.org. If you access their Web site, you will learn that this activity is considered a "feature," and that it is done in an effort to reduce spam. By subscribing to their service, you are permitted to check any IP address that attempts to send you e-mail to see if it is a known spam relay. If the IP address is not listed in their database, njabl.org will perform the probes and use that information to determine if the source IP is a potential spammer. So, someone on the NANOG mailing list had subscribed to this service and our network was being probed because I had posted to that list.

Let's skip the discussion of whether block lists are actually effective since it is so easy for spammers to simply move on to a new IP address. Instead, let's focus on the ethical issues of this type of spam control. Some organization had subscribed to this service in order to help reduce their cost of fighting spam. My organization experienced a financial loss, however, as our security analysts now needed to investigate the incident to first see if it was successful, and then to decide how to best mitigate future episodes. You might be thinking, "just block the source IP address and be done with it." The problem here is that many block lists will actually add you to their blacklist if you attempt to block their probe attempts. The thought process is, "if you are trying to hide from us then you must be up to something." So a proper analysis needs to be done in order to chart the best course of action. Obviously, this ties up resources even longer, resulting in either further financial loss.

I posted information about the probes to the NANOG mailing list just as a heads up to people, since they might see the same thing (see "Extreme spam testing" in the 12/03 section of the archive). My reasoning was that I wanted to spare other organizations from having to do the same investigation work. The responses I received back were pretty interesting. While some people agreed that the activity was not very ethical, many spoke up and felt quite justified in the activity. Their thought process was that spam has become so bad that anything that can be done to help reduce it was acceptable activity. In other words, it was okay to act

Continued

like a black hat because the intention was good, the ends justifies the means. One poster even went so far as to say the real problem was that I scrutinized my logs and had an IDS.

Viewing the njabl.org Web site, I get the feeling that they realize they are pushing the ethical boundaries. To quote from their customer requirement section:

"Ideally, all contributing mail server's SMTP banners should also include something along the lines of: "By connecting to this server, you agree to be open relay tested."

This is pretty laughable. To start, transmitting e-mail is not an interactive service. By the time your mail server is talking to their client's mail system, you have no way of opting out of the connection. In fact, this is pretty similar to the old spammer trick of claiming you opted into their spam list even though they never gave you a way to opt out. Laws were created to regulate this kind of unethical activity.

Also, the system is broken. Even if I had some way of opting out of the connection, it was not my mail server that connected to their client's system. My mail server created a connection to the NANOG mailing list server, while it was the NANOG server that connected to their client's mail server. The appropriate system to check would have been the NANOG mail server, not mine.

So what is the ethical approach to spam control? Many people use tools such as SpamAssassin or Bayesian filters to control the amount of spam they receive. While these tools are not perfect, my experience has been they are far more accurate than block lists. They also have the additional benefit of not generating any outbound suspicious traffic, which can cause a financial loss to everyone else.

Chris Brenton
SANS Instructor and Private Consultant

Identity Theft and Scams for Personal Information

The most inscrutable chapter of the Christian Bible is Revelation. There is a discussion in that book about the "mark of the beast." Apparently, it is a sign on the hand or forehead that uniquely identifies an individual. In the past, every time I have heard this I have shaken my head and thought this is impossible for two reasons, technology and privacy; who would sign up for that? Technology is not an issue anymore. I will never forget having a chip inserted into my dog, Yogi, so that he could move to Hawaii with us. They put it in with a hypodermic needle and scanned him with a wand to make sure the chip worked. But what of the privacy concerns of being a scannable human being? What would drive anyone to wear a visible mark on their forehead or hand? If you do not believe that this is possible, consider the growth in identify theft. This is the mother of all cyber tsunamis—more and more people are getting hurt and hurt badly. The only realistic solution is to make your identity part and parcel of who you are. In this section, we consider a number of the growing identify theft scams that are creating enough pain that I believe governments and people may consider ill-advised remedies in the not so distant future. If it is an opt-in program, I recommend you opt out and stick with the "check your credit report twice a year" approach to identity defense.

"Find Out Everything on Anyone" Scams – the End Justify the Means?

Another common e-mail scam requests money to provide you with a CD-ROM or access to a database program where you can research personal information about anyone you like. This information is obtained through public records, pretexting, or stolen personal information. Is it ethically appropriate to purchase these services if you are trying to find an old high school friend for benign reasons?

> **Conservative** Even if your motives are pure, you should not purchase information gathered illegally under any circumstances. This action promotes more illegal activity. You should contact your local district attorney's office or department of consumer affairs and report this scam.

> **Liberal** You are not ethically at fault for obtaining information that will help you find your long lost friend, since your motives are positive. The government has access to this data; you should too.

Summary

Accessing information that went through an illegal or questionable data collection process appears to be a black and white ethical issue, but this is not necessarily the case. Private investigation firms sometimes use this information when looking for a lost child or loved one. Although the end does not justify the means, some would beg to differ.

Con Artists and E-mail Questionnaires – Presume it is a Scam

You receive an e-mail from an old friend from high school; at least they appear to be an old friend of yours. In the e-mail, your friend asks you a series of questions including your favorite things to do or collect, your birthday, current address, phone number, spouse's name, and so forth. You answer the questions and look forward to reacquainting yourself with your old friend. Have you done something wrong? Were these questions unethical to ask?

Conservative Do not answer these questions. Do not provide false information instead of the correct answers. This is a con. The reason why the con artist asks you about your favorite things is because they are trying to guess your passwords. This is not an old friend even if the e-mail indicates their name. They are trying to get information from you to steal your identity or hack into your bank account.

Liberal A normal response to receiving an e-mail from an old friend is to start communicating. There is no way you could have known a con artist sent you the e-mail.

SUMMARY

Since e-mail is not face-to-face, it is very difficult to determine whom you are really speaking with. This is also true in chat rooms where you may meet people who later want to know more about you. If you receive any e-mail out of the ordinary, presume that it is a scam, even if it is from a long lost friend.

@#&!?!

E-mail Ethics: Think Before You Click

The foundation of all ethical behavior is the willingness to understand how your actions will be perceived and to adjust those actions accordingly. For the most part, this system works pretty well. Unfortunately, there are times when well-meaning people commit what I like to call "the

Continued

wrong execution of the right idea." Two great examples of this are the "Reply-all storm" and the "Excessive Signature."

The "Reply-all storm" starts off innocently enough when someone addresses an e-mail to too many people. This typically happens when someone sends out an announcement meant for a local group ("Sandy's service anniversary celebration will be today in room 52") but accidentally addresses the mail to a much wider audience ("all 32,000 US employees"), most of whom don't even know Sandy, much less care where her party is. This is bad enough, but hey, accidents happen. The problems really start when some well-meaning person tries to point out the mistake, but hits "Reply all" and sends back a message to all 32,000 U.S. employees saying something like, "You sent this to the wrong group." This goes on for several rounds until someone gets wise to what's happening and "Replies all" with a message (usually in all caps) saying "STOP ANSWERING WITH REPLY-ALL!" This goes on for several more rounds, chewing up everyone's in-box space, time, and network bandwidth until everyone gets tired of the game or the administrator steps in and kills all the messages.

Who's the wrong party here? he originator of the message for over-addressing the note in the first place. But IMHO, those who insisted on using Reply All to advance the sorry state of affairs, are the more egregious offenders. They had the power to limit the annoyance of the exchange by addressing their replies only to the originating sender. Instead, they chose to broadcast their repeated messages to the whole world. The moral of this story: think before you click. Think about who really needs to see your message. If it's a large group then use Reply All. But if it's only one or two people, please address your message to only those chosen few. We all have overloaded inboxes and anything we can collectively do to reduce that load is the helpful and ethical thing to do.

Another pet peeve of mine is the abuse many people commit with their e-mail signatures. The first type is the person who insists on using 1 MB graphic bitmaps or animated GIFs in their signature. PLEASE STOP! Those of us who regularly download e-mail on slow hotel dial-up connections really do not appreciate the extra few minutes needed to download your cute animated company logo. Another annoyance is the long legal disclaimers that seem to be popping up all over the place. Some are as much as eight to ten lines long. Tagging that on the end of a one- or two-word e-mail unnecessarily expands the amount of bandwidth needed to transmit. Again, think before you click. Do you really need a legal disclaimer on a message that says just "Thanks" or even the aforementioned meeting announcement?

> Think before you click. Think about what your message says, who you're saying it to, and how you're saying it. It's the socially responsible and ethical thing to do.
>
> *Stephen Fried, Lucent Technologies*
> *Director, Security Architecture*

Account Verification or "phisher" Scams – Should These Domain Names be Issued?

Individuals purchase domain names that are very similar to the domain names of credit card companies, electronic funds transfer sites, and other financial transactions sites. Scammers purchase these domain names exclusively for fraud and identity theft. For example, someone may purchase the site called XYZ-CREDITCARDS.com when there is a legitimate credit card site called XYZCREDITCARDS.com. Once the con artist owns the domain, they will issue millions of e-mails to unsuspecting people asking the customers of XYZCREDITCARDS.com to verify their credit card account information. They must update this data on the fake site. The information they collect includes social security numbers, bank account numbers, home addresses, telephone numbers, everything. Is it ethical to issue domain names to people that are similar to the domain names of valid financial online businesses?

Conservative It is unethical to issue domain names to people if they are too similar to the domain names of existing reputable financial institutions. This is a recipe for disaster. The only reason why someone would want to have a domain name similar to the name of a real company is because they want to commit e-mail scams and fraud posing as a representative of that business.

Liberal It is not ethical to control the issuing of domain names because scam artists abuse this freedom. If one business has a similar name to another, they should not have to go through layers of bureaucracy to obtain the domain name. Even worse, they should not be refused a domain name because someone else uses it.

SUMMARY

This issue considers how to protect innocent victims from a scam yet not impinge on the rights of valid businesses. There is no right answer.

@#&!?!

Spam vs. Spam

A techno-savvy friend with a deep-seated hatred of spam recently began receiving unsolicited e-mail from some company whose schtick was free goods in exchange for referring other names to them so they could spam even more. This friend, "Matt," went to the company's Web site and gathered some information, then scoured the Web and managed to find the online resume of one of the company's employees. This resume happened to include the employee's phone number, address, and personal Web site url. Matt took that information and posted it on a public Web discussion board, along with a scathing indictment of the company's practices, and suggested that other spam-haters "give him a call."

Even though he posted this message anonymously, the bulletin board software records and displays the IP addresses of all anonymous posters.

The next thing Matt knew, his employer's "abuse" e-mail address received a cease-and-desist order from the targeted employee's lawyers, and Matt's computer was taken offline by a sysadmin. The lawyers insisted that the message be removed from the bulletin board, and Matt contacted the board operator who said it would be deleted in a week, but not immediately. Furthermore, the guy's phone number has most likely already been redistributed via e-mail forwards (which Matt's message encouraged) and indexed by search engines, so even if the original message gets removed, the calls will probably continue for awhile.

Meanwhile, on the advice of his employer's legal counsel, Matt has written a detailed apology to the company and to the "victim," which he plans to post on the same discussion board as the original message. But it remains to be seen whether Matt's own employer takes any further action against him.

Continued

www.syngress.com

Oddly, the legal reason given for the cease-and-desist was not the publication of the personal information (which was already publicly available), or the encouragement to harass, but rather "defamation."

This was based on the minor fact that Matt's message described the employee as the "owner" of the spamming company, when he had really been only a manager and had recently quit.

John Fielding
Software Engineer

Chapter Summary

As you can see from the Soapboxes, people have strong opinions about Spam and scams! We each have an ethical and professional responsibility to maintain a thorough knowledge of e-mail scams so that we may better defend ourselves, our organizations, and families from fraud and identity theft. This chapter only covers a sampling of the thousands of scams blanketing Internet e-mail today. Successful scam artists make millions of dollars with these scams. They also face the potential of jail. Finally, if there is a rule of thumb, it would be to never provide personal or account information through e-mail or in response to e-mail.

Frequently Asked Questions

The following Frequently Asked Questions, answered by the authors of this book, are designed to get you thinking about the ethical considerations of e-mail scams and how you can protect yourself from identity theft and fraud. Unless legal issues are involved, then answers in the FAQ may not be the right answer for your organization.

Q: How can you protect yourself from e-mail scams?

A: Never send personal information such as social security numbers, credit card numbers, or bank account information through e-mail for any reason.

Q: How do you tell the difference between real businesses such as agencies that will supply a free credit report and fake businesses out to steal your identity?

A: Contact the Better Business Bureau to determine if a business is valid prior to accepting any offer through an e-mail advertising campaign.

Q: If you receive an e-mail that requests that you update your personal information for your credit card company into their Web site, which is a valid domain name that is the same as you credit card company, should you do it.

A: NO! Scam artists are known to purchase domain names similar to those of real businesses. This is known as a "phisher" scam. Never input your personal information into a Web site in response to an e-mail request.

Chapter 6

Information Security Officers

Ethical Dilemmas in this Chapter:

- Hacking
- Penetration Tests
- Viruses and Worms
- Encryption
- Handling Network Security Information
- Ensuring Information Security on the Personnel Level

Introduction

The role of the Information Security Officer (ISO) includes the responsibility of effectively securing their organization's data systems and information resources. They hold the balance between security and getting the job done. Proficient ISOs can network well and bridge the gap through their communications skills between managers and systems administrators. ISOs understand the threats and risks to the corporation and corporate technology. They identify best practices and utilize them to protect information resources. The ISO must effectively communicate these best practices to everyone in the organization. Finally, a strong ISO utilizes their knowledge to create a diversified protection strategy.

This chapter discusses the ethical issues facing the ISO, including handling issues such as hacking, penetration testing, viruses and worms, encryption, network security, and personnel security.

Hacking

Computer hacking is a form of malicious attack whereby a person known as a "hacker" breaks into a computer system that they are not authorized to use. This includes attempts to bypass the security mechanisms of an information system or network for the purpose of obtaining damaging information.

This section deals with the ethical dilemmas an ISO faces when it comes to combating hackers. We will touch upon whether there is ever an appropriate circumstance to hack into a system for the purpose of business warfare or education. We will also discuss different types of hacking scenarios and the corresponding ethical choices that must be made by the ISO in relation to each one. These issues include operating systems (OS) attacks, cracking passwords, and spoofing.

Hacking for Business Warfare – Is it Just a Part of Business?

Your boss comments that he thinks your competitor's Web page has guessable Uniform Resource Locators (URLs) and shows you a couple of examples. He then asks you to see if you can get more information from their Web site. He mentions that all companies do this to their competitors and it is normal in the industry. Will you hack for your boss to get the competitive edge on other businesses or out of a desire to keep your job?

Conservative   Hacking into competitor's Web sites is completely inappropriate behavior. These actions border on illegal activity. Tell your boss that you cannot hack into a competitor's Web site for any reason.

Liberal   Business is war and utilizing technology to succeed in business is common practice. If you stay within the law of information technology (IT) you are not doing anything wrong. You can be certain that your competitors are doing the same to your company.

SUMMARY

When senior management makes requests that border on illegal activity, do not immediately comply. Always consider the repercussions of any action you perform and where you stand ethically on the matter. Do not needlessly put yourself or the company in danger or surrender your personal ethics out of pressure to keep your job.

Giving in to Distributed Denial of Service "Hacktortionists" – Do You Pay?

A hacker contacted the Chief Executive Officer (CEO) of your company and demanded a payment of thirty-five thousand dollars or he will incur damage to the system. If your company does not pay, the hacker will launch a Distributed Denial of Service (DDoS) attack. This attack will cost your company far more than the thirty-five thousand requested from the "Hacktortionist" if it is successful. The CEO of your company asks you, the ISO, what you recommend and how to respond. What do you say to him?

Conservative   Your job as ISO is to ensure the security of the system. A DDoS attack will take down the system and cost many times the amount the hacker requested. There may also be irrevocable damage done in the process. Even though this behavior is unethical, advise the CEO to pay the hacker and contact the appropriate authorities to track them down.

Liberal   Do not pay off the hacker. Endless copycats will prey on your company! Since you are forewarned, secure the systems and bring in extra help for recovery as well as to track and identify the hacker. Report the threat immediately to the proper authorities.

SUMMARY

Corporations give in to "Hacktortionists" for two primary reasons. Number one, the cost of recovering from a DDoS attack is greater than the pay-off amount. Number two, the reputation of the business faces ruin in the media if the results of such a destructive attack are released to the general public. This is especially true if the company possesses personal data such as credit card numbers or medial information.

Hacking for Education – Is it Just About Learning?

For some hackers, hacking is an educational process. It is about learning operating systems and system weaknesses, not making a name from themselves or performing destructive activities like other egomaniac hackers who want to hear their alias name on the daily news. Is this type of hacking more acceptable than hackers who want to be famous?

Conservative No form of hacking is acceptable. Breaking into someone's house just to test your locksmith skills and see how quiet you can be, even if you do not remove or look at anything in the house, is still breaking and entering. The same is true with hacking. The motive does not justify the activity.

Liberal Hacking for education is basically inappropriate under most circumstances. However, if you have no negative intent this is ethically more forgivable then someone with malicious intent. Even if you report the vulnerabilities you find to the company you hack into, it is still not right ethically.

SUMMARY

There is not an ethically correct reason to hack into someone else's computer system. The only organizations that may allow their employees to hack other systems is government or military agencies for the purpose of national security. In this type of scenario, your actions may be honorable. In any other case, stay away from hacking unless you are performing authorized penetration tests for your own company.

OS Attacks – Go After the Bad Guy?

Hackers and worm writers frequently make operating system attacks on Microsoft systems because many hackers do not like the ethics of Microsoft. Is it appropriate to attack a company because they have a bad reputation in the industry or their peers or customers view them as unethical?

Conservative Hacking of any type is ethically wrong regardless of your feelings toward the business you attack. You would be stooping to the level of the company you are trying to punish.

Liberal Business is war and sometimes the only way to balance out the scales with an unethical company is to play the game too. However, you do need to consider the other people it affects besides just the company. Hacking also affects all of the users of their software and the businesses of those users may be negatively impacted.

SUMMARY

The footprint of Microsoft software is so large that it is not clear a significant number of attackers are actually targeting them. Although hacking another company's computer system is unethical, there is often a round of applause when an attack on an unethical business occurs. You must decide what sits right with you.

Cracking Screen Saver Passwords – Should You or Shouldn't You?

You need to install a patch on a user's computer and they are out to lunch. They have a screen saver password, which you could easily crack. Do you do it?

Conservative Avoid cracking a user's screen saver password and simply wait for them to return from lunch. This sets a poor example for the users. Even though you know what you are doing as the ISO, others without as much knowledge and access as you may see what you do as an example and try to do the same.

Liberal Cracking a user's screen saver password is not a big deal. Just get into the machine and do your job. This happens quite often. Every time you perform updates after hours, you must do this anyway. Other employees must understand that this is part of your job.

Summary

The ISO must set an example for the rest of the company. In most cases, it would be wise to set the right ethical example of not cracking others passwords. However, when you have to get the job done, you must do it at times.

Spoofing – Does it Serve a Purpose?

Internet Protocol (IP) spoofing often occurs on secure systems by super hackers who are not out to do any malicious damage. They are just trying to outdo renowned security gurus. Is this type of spoofing acceptable since they do not damage the system and they do show you your systems' weaknesses so that you can fix them?

Conservative   Spoofing in any of its forms is unacceptable behavior, even if you do not have malicious intent. It is not your place to point out the security weaknesses in another person's system, especially for the thrill of getting one up on a security guru.

Liberal   There is something good about spoofing renowned security gurus. This type of play between sharp technologists helps identify security weaknesses. As long as no damage incurs, this prevents future damage from a malicious source.

Summary

Technologists like to outsmart each other. It is a game to them. Sometimes these games can help serve security for each other's organizations, and other times it just eats up valuable resources and energy. At its worst, this behavior accidentally causes destruction.

Penetration Tests

Penetrating testing is the process of ethically authorized hacking and probing a corporation's information systems and networks to determine potential security weaknesses or vulnerabilities that a malicious attacker might exploit. The penetration testing method involves an investigation of all security features of the system in question. The penetration tester then attempts to breech security and penetrate the system and network. The tester simulates a hacker by using the same attack scenarios, methods, and tools of a real malicious attack. After the test, the penetration tester submits a report on the system vulnerabilities and suggests procedures for implementation to make the system more secure.

The following sections deal with the ethical dilemmas an ISO must address when performing penetration tests. Ethical issues when testing for security vulnerability and hacking to determine system weakness are detailed below.

Testing Security Vulnerability – Should You Help the ISO?

An information technology employee wants to test the company's computer security vulnerability level. In the process, she discovers a major flaw in the computer security. Not wanting to get in trouble for "hacking" the company's computer system, she writes malicious code that will help her fellow coworkers including the ISO discover the vulnerability themselves. Is this type of behavior ethical?

Conservative Performing a system vulnerability test without the consent of the ISO is completely inappropriate. Writing malicious code to point out the weaknesses discovered is just plain crazy. She not only went out of bounds on this one but also attacked the company to avoid communicating what she found. The employee knows what she did is ethically wrong and exemplifies this by the way she chose to shroud herself after the fact.

Liberal Although performing a penetration test without prior consent of the ISO is against policy, in this case it was informative and showed initiative. She should have stopped at that point and presented her findings to the ISO. She was wrong in writing malicious code to point the problem out to her coworkers.

SUMMARY

Trying to help the ISO by finding weakness can cause more damage than they prevent. It is better to avoid "helping" the ISO, since they are the experts, not you. If you do find a security weaknesses, immediately bring it up to them. Never launch malicious code at your own company for any reason, even if your intentions are good.

Don't Be Afraid to Attack Your Own Network (or Products)

As a security professional, you should encourage the security analysis of hardware and software technologies that you use on your network or in your organization. Of course, it must be clearly defined that such activities should only take place on test and development systems and products, *not* live network components.

Set up test networks and product configurations in your laboratory and allow employees to look for security vulnerabilities. Reward them for their success. It will strengthen the security of the organization and at the same time foster creativity, education, open-mindedness, and competitive spirit.

Incorporating third-party security audits of your network configuration or product development lifecycle can also help to discover previously overlooked vulnerabilities. Having a fresh set of eyes can go a long way.

It's frustrating, but typical, to watch corporations introduce new technologies onto their live network without testing them. They don't understand exactly what threats they are protecting against and why.

Do not be afraid to explore. Try to break your product, software, or network—there's no harm in that. Fix the problems and try again. Be proactive. Don't wait for a malicious attacker to find the problems for you.

Joe Grand
President & CEO
Grand Idea Studio, Inc.

Appropriate Hacking to Determine Weaknesses – Know What You are Doing

You have just completed a training course on hacking. Exercising the course material you have just learned, you begin penetrating your company's computer security to see if there are any existing vulnerabilities. Is this appropriate action to take as the ISO?

Conservative Even if your intention is to check the integrity of the systems, which lie under your realm of protection, hacking may bring about damage to operations. Since you just took the course, you may not have the expertise yet to perform a vulnerability test without causing unnecessary damage to the systems you are supposed to protect. If you would like to perform this type of penetration test, hire a consultant that is experienced and proficient in this type of exercise.

Liberal Part of your job as the ISO is to determine and assess the vulnerability of the systems you protect. Start with a simple penetration test that you know you can recover from, then build slowly from there until you have performed a full blown penetration test.

SUMMARY

Assessing the security of the systems you are responsible for as the ISO is a challenging job. Be certain you know exactly what you are doing when you hack into the system. If you are a novice, take it slow or leave the job to an experienced professional that can perform penetration tests without putting the system at risk. If you feel the knowledge you have is sufficient, perform basic tests on your system. Start with running these tests in the test or development environment, not in production.

Failure of Penetration Testing Software – Who's at Fault?

The software product you purchased to perform a penetration test on your information system appeared to be effective until an attack took your company's network down. The product did not find the weaknesses that the attacker utilized. Is this the fault of the vendor or should you have utilized human resources as well for the penetration testing?

Conservative You really should have performed two types of penetration tests to ensure the integrity of the system. Best practices recommend performing human penetration tests with a professional tester, as well as utilizing software that specializes in penetration testing.

Liberal Get a refund on the penetration testing software tool. It obviously did not do its job. Now you need to start all over again and purchase a new tool or bring in a specialized security professional to perform the penetration tests.

SUMMARY

Trust in any single tool is a recipe for disaster. Not all vulnerability assessment software tools meet the mark; some are better than others, none are close to perfect. Make sure you thoroughly research a tool prior to purchase. Do not place the security of the information systems you are responsible for in the hands of marketing hype. Take your time and shop around, ask questions, call references, and really know what you are buying so that you have the piece of mind that it is an effective solution to the information security needs of your business. When it comes to protecting corporate resources, it is always good to double up and use a tool and human resources, especially in the case of penetration testing.

Viruses and Worms

Viruses and worms are forms of malicious code designed to disable or destroy information systems. There are many types of viruses and worms. In addition, programmers launch new ones on a daily basis. Some, such as Code Red, are devastating, while others are just a nuisance. Spam is also a form of malicious code, which has grown significantly due to its marketing potential.

This section discusses ethical issues such as the development of viruses, virus tolerance levels, due diligence, system crashes, attacking attackers, and bypassing alerts.

Virus Development for Profit – Is it Appropriate?

Worm and virus writers make a profit from their malicious code through spam. Some experts say there is a connection between the people who write malicious code and the spammers. Is it ethically appropriate to make money writing malicious code for the distribution of spam?

Conservative Developing spam or similar viruses for profit is completely wrong. In most cases, it is also illegal and should not be tolerated under any circumstances.

Liberal Writing viruses for marketing purposes such as spam tarnishes the reputation of the programmer; however, it is not ethically wrong. There are laws that ban or regulate unwanted e-mail, but nothing as of yet, which denies it in every sense. If spam programmers are within the bounds of the law, their behavior is not commendable but acceptable.

SUMMARY

Writing code that throws spam into e-mail boxes is not an honorable job, but it is not completely unethical either, unless it causes damage to the recipient's system. After all, we have lived with cold calling and door-to-door salespeople and we will probably all live with spam to some extent. Laws also vary from country to country, and therefore, spam may be an acceptable part of business in some countries, and no one has the right to stop that.

Bounty Hunters for Virus Writers – A Deterrent?

Some companies offer cash bounties for information leading to the conviction of a virus writer that targets vulnerabilities in their products. Since these virus writers incur expensive damage to the companies and clients, is it ethically appropriate to put a bounty on their heads?

Conservative It is better for the vendor to focus their financial resources on better securing their products then to spend the money on the offensive. This is a waste of financial and human resources. If they put that money into making the software more secure there would not be any successful attacks.

Liberal   This is a step in the right direction to thwart off malicious attacks. If a company can afford the bounties, they have every right to go after the culprits who are out for their destruction.

SUMMARY

The ethical result of bounty hunters will determine if the human and financial resources are worth it. It may just be a waste of time and energy; then again, it may be a powerful deterrent in the war against malicious attacks.

Acceptable Virus Tolerance Level – Is there One?

You are an ISO responsible for the senior systems administrator who seems to be having trouble keeping computer viruses out of the system. There tends to be a new attack every day. What is the acceptable tolerance level for a systems administrator if viruses frequently infect the system for which they are responsible? Do you expect there to be a certain level of tolerance for frequent virus attacks or should you fire the administrator after the first one?

Conservative   One attack is acceptable; however, daily attacks are way beyond the acceptable range of tolerance. You should fire the systems administrator and replace them with someone who can better assess the needs of the system and reduce the number of security incidents. One detected attack per month that is not damaging to the system is an acceptable range. Any attack that significantly damages the system or allows compromising of the data warrants bringing in someone new who can actually do the job.

Liberal   You should research the nature of the attacks both in-house and on security Web sites such as SANS.ORG to determine if this is affecting everyone in the industry or if just your company has a weakness. Recommend to the administrator that they consider different security options when administrating the system.

SUMMARY

The acceptable tolerance level that an ISO needs to set for an adminis-trator is dependent on the factors involved. If attacks on the system occur daily and all other corporations are having the same problem because of a new virus, it may not be the fault of the administrator. However, if your company is the only one affected by these attacks, you need to reassess overall security and the qualifications of the adminis-trator responsible for virus prevention.

Viruses and Due Diligence – Does it Work?

In the previous example, would it make a difference to you if they had done due diligence or not to prevent the attacks?

Conservative If the administrator performed due diligence and the attacks still occurred due to a weakness in his virus protection strategy, it would be even worse, because that would prove that he really does not know what he is doing and should be let go immediately.

Liberal Since the administrator did all he could do and you have verified that fact, you may just have to accept that sometimes virus attacks happen and you just need to stay on your toes at all times performing restoration measures.

SUMMARY

Due diligence can work in the favor of the administrator or against him. If he did due diligence and your company was the only one under such heavy virus attacks means that his best is not good enough. However, if everyone in the industry is facing these attacks and he did due diligence, your company may not suffer as greatly as other companies and the administrator deserves a pat on the back. The correct ethical response is relative to the full details of the circumstance.

System Crashes – Should You Reformat the Hard Drive?

A virus takes out the computer of an executive at your office and they tell you that you can do whatever you want to get it running again. The destruction is obvious and there is nothing that will fix the problem at this point. You cannot perform a backup, so you opt to reformat the hard drive. When the executive returns, they blame it on you and say you had no right to wipe out their machine and consequently try to get you fired. Are you at fault?

Conservative When performing a reformat of a hard drive for an executive or anyone for that matter wait until they are present so you can explain what happened and not end up the scapegoat. Since there was a complete crash on the executive's system, there is nothing that can remedy the situation. However, you are at fault for reformatting the hard drive prior to communicating properly with the executive. Even though the crash was not your fault, you left yourself open to be the one to take the heat.

Liberal You are certainly not the one at fault. The executive is going to take you down for his own mistake. He has the power to do this. On the other hand, maybe he does not understand what happened technically. Either way you will be the one to blame even though you did nothing wrong.

SUMMARY

Determining fault is very tricky when it comes to technology. Very few people understand the complexities of technology and how malicious attacks affect computers. If you try to explain this circumstance to a non-technical user, they may not be able to grasp what happened and since they cannot understand it, they just presume you messed up somehow. You made a mistake by formatting the hard drive without really covering your bases; it left you open to take the fall. The executive made many mistakes: obtaining the virus and then blaming you. If you still have your job, set up formal procedures where you obtain a signature on a sign off sheet when you must reformat someone's hard drive. In the future, this will relieve you of the painful consequences.

Attacking Attackers – Go on the Offense?

You discover and identify someone who is hacking into your system. Is it appropriate to teach them a lesson and hack them back, or send them a destructive virus?

Conservative It is never appropriate to use malicious means to retaliate against someone for attacking your system. This will just result in a never-ending cycle of attacks. Contact them on the phone or in person and try to handle the circumstance in a mature manner, which will not result in a future attack on the system under your responsibility. Document all of your findings carefully in case you need to prosecute the attackers.

Liberal Sometimes the only way hackers get it is on their own terms. Give him a good whack with a destructive virus and try to destroy his system. Therefore, he will no longer be able to attack yours.

SUMMARY

ISO's need to use many different tactics when addressing security breaches. In most cases, going on the offense is not a good idea because you could end up in legal trouble. However, there may be instances where you find it is your only option.

Bypassing Alerts – Never a Good Idea

The software you use to review the integrity and security of the system provides too many alerts, so you quickly review them every day and determine that they are false. It turns out that one of them was true and a virus attacks your system. Are you at fault for not checking more carefully, or is the software company at fault for making it too hard to tell a fake alert from a real one?

Conservative You are at fault in this circumstance. Even though the alerts are tedious, just glancing over them is a total waste since you are not paying close attention and presume they are redundant. Some alerts will be false alarms or warnings but others are important. It was your job as the ISO to review these alerts and determine which ones you needed to respond to and which you did not. You were wrong in basically ignoring them and the virus attack ethically falls in your court.

Liberal   You are not at fault, but the software company is definitely at fault. Creating a product that is difficult and tedious to use does not help in securing a system. Alerts should be focused, not general, and help the ISO perform their job, not hinder it.

SUMMARY

In the above ethical dilemma, both the vendor and the ISO are at fault. The vendor is at fault because their tool is determinately tedious and generalized, and the ISO because they were lazy.

Encryption

Encryption is the procedure of encoding or scrambling plaintext data to make it difficult for someone else to see the original data sent with the exception of the intended receiver. An encryption algorithm complexity utilized determines the level of protection provided by encryption. Encryption protects e-mail, secure on-line transactions, File Transfer Protocol (FTP) sites, and much more.

This section delves into encryption ethical matters including backup keys, virtual private network (VPN) encryption, sending unencrypted documents, industrial espionage, law enforcement and encryption, and selling encryption tools globally.

Backup Keys – Are they Necessary?

The CFO of the publishing company you work for quit abruptly and went over to the competition. The CFO securely encrypted all of his data and you, unfortunately, do not have any backup keys. We know that what the CFO did was bordering on unethical behavior, but did you as the ISO do something unethical by failing to have backup keys?

Conservative   Backup keys are critical to the survival of the business and you have failed in your role as the ISO. The company and you should own a secure backup set of all encryption keys for this very type of circumstance. You cannot retrieve his data without the keys. A bad situation just got worse.

Liberal You are not responsible for the CFO quitting the company in a terrible manner and running to the competition, probably with his encryption keys and a copy of the encrypted data. Most small companies like the one you work for do not have backup keys for encrypted data. It is not your fault.

SUMMARY

Staying abreast of the most recent requirements in information security is a tiring job but necessary to protect your company. Always keep current on the most recent tools such as key backup and recovery systems that will protect your company.

VPN Encryption – Utilize for Personal Gain?

You have made a few bad investments and need to earn some extra cash fast. Finding a high dollar market in day trading, you develop a way to share these stock tips utilizing your company's encrypted VPNs. Is it ethically appropriate to utilize corporate encryption for personal means?

Conservative You should never use any type of company resource for personal means, especially encryption from the corporate VPN. You should know better if you are an ISO.

Liberal It is not a big deal to utilize encryption of the VPN to do a few personal stock trades. It is probably against the rules but you did nothing ethically wrong.

SUMMARY

For the most part, avoid using corporate resources, especially information security resources, for personal means. In some cases, you or others may determine it is unethical. In most cases, it is simply not smart.

Sending Unencrypted Documents – Should it Ever Occur?

You are aware that it is against company policy to send confidential documents that have not been encrypted over the company network. However, you are under deadline and need to send some files to your assistant who is working from home. This is probably not too big a deal, right?

Conservative You should never for any reason send unencrypted confidential data over the company network. You are at fault here. You are certainly not maintaining a secure code of ethics as an example for the corporation.

Liberal This type of behavior may occur with non-technical users but there really is not an excuse for the ISO to send unencrypted files.

SUMMARY

You may witness employees making the mistake in this issue but it is not one that the Information Security Professional should ever make.

Victim of Industrial Espionage – Who's Responsible?

A competitor has intercepted some e-mail between the CEO of your company and another partner, which contained highly confidential information. The CEO failed to encrypt the data even though there is encryption software installed on his machine. Is this your fault?

Conservative If the CEO did not encrypt his highly confidential e-mail, you must have not done your job in terms of security awareness and the blame falls on you. The role of the ISO is to secure the data and systems of the corporation. This includes educating the employees and the executives on what they must do to ensure privacy and security.

Liberal Since the CEO had the encryption software at his disposal, it is not your fault that he failed to use it. This failure on the part of the CEO resulted in a competitor now having access to very sensitive information.

SUMMARY

Ethically speaking you should have properly prepared the CEO and all of the employees in the company for this type of scenario. The CEO was wrong and you were too in failing to properly educate him on the security requirements of information technology.

Is Industrial Espionage Ethical? – Common Behavior

In the previous example, was the company who intercepted the e-mail behaving ethically?

Conservative No. Intercepting e-mail and stealing sensitive corporate secrets is not ethical and poor business practice. It is not necessary to take from others to get ahead.

Liberal All is fair in love and war. The competitor knew your company better than you knew yourselves and preyed on a security weakness. You must anticipate these types of actions in the corporate world and appropriately prepare for them.

SUMMARY

Industrial espionage is the practice of stealing data and ideas from another corporation, which is quite common. All businesses need to guard their computers, sensitive documents, personnel, and offices from this type of behavior.

Law Enforcement and Viewing Irrelevant Data – Do You have a Contingency Plan?

One of the employees at your company was caught red-handed accessing illegal Web sites on the corporate machine. The local law enforcement agency came in and accessed all of the information on his computer and the network, even everything that was encrypted. Was this type of behavior appropriate? Should you have protected the data in some way from irrelevant review?

Conservative The law enforcement agency had every right to review all of the data on the accused machine as well as the corporate network, since the accused performed these activities at work. Let them do their job and hope that only the accused is punished and not the company as well.

Liberal There are many tools on the market that will help the police decrypt and find all of the relevant illegal material they are looking for without exposing all of the sensitive corporate information. You should purchase one of these tools to add a layer of protection to the data when or if it is necessary for a police investigation. These tools will allow the police to search for information relative to their investigation.

SUMMARY

You should always attempt to secure the network to the best of your ability. This includes contingency plans for the security of the encrypted information even in a case such as mentioned above.

Selling Encryption Tools Globally – Did You Do the Research?

You have created an excellent encryption product that is about to go on the market. Your company is an international business. At a trade show in Europe you sold a few copies of the tool to overseas companies. The U.S. government and the military also acquired your product. Have you done something ethically wrong?

Conservative The example above is an ethical and legal problem. According to the rules of national security, the distribution of algorithms and information must remain within the U.S. In the past, other companies have been prosecuted in federal court for these same acts. You have made a huge mistake. Tell the U.S. government that you sold copies of this algorithm internationally.

Liberal You should have done your homework prior to selling the tool. Since you did not know the law and reason for strict rules for encryption tools, you are not ethically at fault but you may be held accountable legally for your ignorance.

SUMMARY

Whenever you develop tools for information security be certain to do research on the legalities of those tools. Since the laws are still catching up to the rapid advancement of IT, new ones are passed daily that affect your business. Run all new information security developments through legal council prior to placing them on the market for the general public, especially before you go global with a tool

Handling Network Security Information

Network security information is the reporting of security information and weakness such as malfunctions and intrusions that affect the security of the network.

Ethical issues concerning the reporting of software failures that cause a breach in security and stealth sniffers monitoring corporate networks are discussed in this section. In both cases, awareness is key. The ISO has the demanding responsibility to ensure that all employees are aware of the corporate security policy and that all systems are closely monitored by them and remain secure.

Software Malfunctions – Should You Report Them?

An employee of your company fails to report a software malfunction, which caused data to be exposed to the Internet. Was their failure to report the incident unethical?

Conservative Failing to report a breach in security is just as bad as creating one yourself. If the ISO is not made aware of system problems, they cannot adequately protect system resources and information.

Liberal The employee may not have known any better and failed to report the problem because they did not understand the risk it posed to overall information security. They did not do anything unethical.

SUMMARY

ISO's should provide adequate security awareness so that an issue such as this one does not arise. If the employee was previously made aware of the security implications and still failed to report the incident, they are in breach of their ethical responsibility to the corporation.

Stealth Sniffer – Improve Security

You have discovered a stealth sniffer monitoring your network. Does anyone have the right to do this?

Conservative   No one has the right to monitor your network. This is unethical behavior and should be addressed as such, whether the person is an employee of the company or a competitor involved in industrial espionage.

Liberal   If your network is not secure, you are welcoming an attack and spies. Address the issues that enabled this person to run a stealth sniffer and monitor the system.

SUMMARY

The ISO must assume responsibility for all security breaches. They must also further improve the system to prevent them. Running a sniffer may be unethical on the part of the person doing it; however, you as the ISO fall into the realm of unethical behavior if you do nothing to remediate the situation.

Ensuring Information Security on the Personnel Level

ISO's also hold responsibility on the personnel level. Issues such as lying to clients about the integrity of information security fall under the realm of the ISO.

Other ethical dilemmas discussed in this section include sex in the workplace caught on security tape, handling evidence, and security reprimands.

Lying to Clients Regarding Corporate Security – Is This Ever a Good Idea?

Your boss asks you to tell the clients that your company's security is completely tight, that it is impossible to breach the system. You, as the ISO, know this is not the case. The system is only as secure as it can be, but no system is invulnerable to attack. However, most of the competitor company's marketing propaganda says that they have unbreakable security. Can you honorably make this statement to the clients for your boss?

Conservative As the ISO, you must keep the highest level of integrity. Do not communicate anything that is not true. If your boss or the marketing team is communicating inaccuracies about system security, correct them on their error. Promising completely secure system protection is an impossibility and outright lie.

Liberal You can make a statement to the client that indicates that the infrastructure is secure to the best of your ability. Word it in a way that makes them feel confident in the security of the system without making a blanket statement guaranteeing absolute security, which is not possible.

SUMMARY

Marketing hype often exaggerates the environment of information systems. An ISO needs to be strong in their influence on the communications distributed by marketing and other departments. The ISO must ensure that nothing is communicated that will come back to haunt the company because it is grossly inaccurate.

@#&!?!

Doing the Right Thing Under the Pressure of Sales

Some time ago I headed security efforts for a company that provided Web-based financial services as an Application Service Provider (ASP). My responsibilities included interacting with potential clients and explaining the safeguards we had in place to ensure confidentiality and availability of our service. My first sales engagement was a meeting with one of the company's earliest prospective customers. One of the client's concerns

Continued

was our lack of a disaster recovery facility that would forestall service interruption if the primary site became inaccessible. Our sales associate reassured the representatives, "The secondary data center will be operational by the end of the month." They looked at me for confirmation.

I hesitated for a moment, knowing that my colleague was exaggerating our preparedness. By correcting him, I might jeopardize this critical deal. On the other hand, with a simple nod I would be supporting a commitment we probably could not keep. I wanted to say "yes," realizing how important the disaster recovery site was to closing this deal, and how much we needed this client. Our company considered this engagement a cornerstone in our development, a way of demonstrating to other prospects the market's acceptance of our product. There was a good chance of closing the deal at that meeting if I could commit to having the site ready in time. The secondary data center was being built, but we were unlikely to finish it by the end of the month. I would be misleading the client by promising to have the site ready so quickly.

"We are in the process of setting up the secondary data center," I explained. "I will check the estimated completion date, but there is a chance the site will not be ready by the end of the month." Although we did not close the sale that afternoon, the client did sign up for our service once the disaster recovery site was completed in the following month. When the sales pressure is on, it may be tough to do the right thing. Sometimes it is tough to determine what the right thing is.

Mark Markevitch
Independent Consultant

Sex in the Work Place – How to Handle It?

A contractor and employee are caught on a security camera having sex in a dark hallway during their night shift. You are the ISO on duty watching the security screens. You are responsible to take action to stop the incident but fascinated, you allowed this event to play out in full. Are you at fault?

Conservative Yes, you are at fault, and unethically so. You should have disrupted the incident immediately.

Liberal One can hardly expect you to go up to your two coworkers in a precarious situation such as this ethical scene. You were tactful in waiting until it was over to address the incident. However, you lacked tack in apparently watching on the security camera.

SUMMARY

An ISO needs to be ready to deal with personnel security incidents as well as computer-related ones. It is always better to do everything by the book. However, some incidents may be too embarrassing to address according to policy. Choose what feels ethically correct to you when these incidents occur.

Handling Evidence on Personnel – A Difficult Situation

When you confront the couple about the incident on tape, embarrassed they beg you to destroy the evidence. Should you erase the tape?

Conservative No. Erasing the tape will put your job in jeopardy. In addition, what if something happened during that time period and now you have no record of it. Do not destroy this tape and risk losing valuable security records. Maybe it was all a scam to divert your attention.

Liberal If you know the couple well and their reputation at the company and are certain they are not a security threat, do them the favor of erasing the tape to save embarrassment on their part and having to explain on your part why you did not interrupt them.

SUMMARY

Erasing security tapes is not a good idea under any circumstances. This is a difficult situation that the couple put themselves in, not you. Being forced into this type of circumstance will test your resolve in protecting the corporate assets according to policy with integrity.

Security Reprimands, Contractors vs. Personnel – Treat Equally?

Upon reporting the incident of sex in the workplace on film discussed in the past few issues, should the contractor and employee be reprimanded differently because of their work status, or in the same manner?

Conservative   Treat both the contractor and employee equally in this circumstance, because they were both responsible for the same act. Senior management should meet with them to determine whether to terminate employment for both parties. You may consider firing them or allowing them to stay on the job in a probationary manner. Their additional request to destroy the surveillance tapes is a significant mark against them, which requires careful consideration because destruction of evidence is a serious breach of security, and weighs heavily towards the side of letting both employees go.

Liberal   Since the contractor and the employees hold different employment status with the company, consider them each differently according to the agreements made by each of them in their hiring. In this case, release the contractor from their contract with your company and put the employee on probation.

SUMMARY

Contractors do not tend to remain at a company for a long period of time due to the nature of their work. You may want to allow the contractor to finish their contract and not renew it. A corporation does not have as much of a commitment to a contractor. To avoid future problems with this couple, the contractor may end up sacrificed.

Chapter Summary

In this chapter, we discussed the ethical considerations in the technology role of ISO's. We defined an ISO as a person who effectively secures their organization's information, technology, and resources. We detailed ethical matters such as hacking, viruses, worms, encryption, handling network security information, and ensuring information security with personnel.

We reviewed the ethics of hacking, which included whether there is ever a circumstance when hacking is ethically correct. Following on the tail of hacking you learned the tolerance level for virus attacks on the system expected of the ISO. You now know where to draw the line indicating appropriate level of ethical responsibility.

You learned how to handle encryption and the rules of encryption in a reasonable manner to ensure security of corporate data. Next, we delved into network security information and the protection of it.

Finally, we discussed personnel and the potential dilemmas you may face as an ISO with the shocking things that can occur in the workplace.

At this point, you should be knowledgeable of the ethical responsibility of the ISO.

Frequently Asked Questions

The following Frequently Asked Questions, answered by the authors of this book, are designed to get you thinking about the ethical circumstances you may face when pursuing a career as an ISO. Unless legal issues are involved, then answers in the FAQ may not be the right answer for your organization Some answers may be more ethical than others, but the true response are up to you.

Q: Is it ever appropriate ethically to hack into a computer system that is not your own?

A: In most cases you should avoid hacking into computer systems as it puts you, the ISO, at risk personally. Even if senior management asks you to hack into a competitor's system, refrain from the activity. Hacking for educational purposes is also not a good idea. The only circumstance where hacking may be appropriate is if you work for the government or military and hacking into enemy systems is part of your job to protect innocent lives.

Q: Is it ever appropriate to perform unauthorized penetration tests on a system that lies in your realm of responsibility?

A: Again, in most cases, the answer is no. Performing *unauthorized* penetration tests may put the system at risk. However, performing penetration tests in the testing environment may be acceptable in your role as ISO but not acceptable on the part of a programmer or other technical personnel at the company.

Q: Are you, the ISO, at fault if the system you are supposed to protect is frequently attacked by computer viruses?

A: The bottom line is yes, you are responsible to protect the system from frequent virus attacks. There may be circumstances where there is nothing you and the industry as a whole can do to protect a particular type of malicious attack that catches everyone off guard. Nevertheless, you must be able to significantly protect the system from most forms of attack if you have the appropriate resources and skills to do so.

Q: Is it ever appropriate to send confidential material via e-mail that is not encrypted.

A: Sending unencrypted confidential e-mail is never appropriate. It is forgivable if the sender was not aware of the security policy against such behavior. However, the ISO is then at fault ethically for not properly communicating the security needs of the corporation.

Q: If an employee fails to report that they have witnessed a software problem on the network that exposes sensitive information, are they being unethical or is the ISO simply at fault?

A: Both the ISO and the employee are at fault. The employee is unethical because they are not reporting problems to the ISO, which could be damaging to the system. The ISO is at fault for not closely monitoring the network and detecting this type of security problem.

Q: How should you handle requests to lie to competitors about the security of the system, which is your responsibility as the ISO?

A: Never lie about the security of the system you administer as the ISO. You can highlight the strong points but never say your system is impenetrable for the purposes of marketing.

Chapter 7

Programmers and Systems Analysts

Ethical Dilemmas in this Chapter:

- Coding Practices

- Code Maintenance

- Code Review

- Code Design and Testing

- Programmers and Viruses

- Programmer Security Responsibility

173

Introduction

This chapter covers the ethical issues that programmers and analysts may encounter. We discuss the ethical dilemmas resulting from coding practices, reviewing code, malicious attacks, secure programming, software deployment, code design, and program testing.

We start by defining the roles of programmers and analysts. Programmers and analysts are the information technologists who develop computer applications utilizing various programming languages and macros.

In this chapter, we refer to programmers and system analysts in various ways depending on the role they are playing, including application and software developers. It is important to know that they all perform the same information technology (IT) role with slight variations. For example, a software developer is a programmer that focuses on the creation of a software product that can then be packaged and sold. A systems analyst in some cases is someone who writes code for the operating system such as UNIX shell scripting.

Programmers work off of design specifications. Specifications are detailed instructions written by business analysts or system users, which define the requirements for a given application slotted for development. The programmer takes these requirements and converts them to a program design.

There are four primary phases of software/application development: design, plan, prototype, and implement. If any of these steps are skipped, a problem may develop. This chapter touches on and provides scenarios of ethical matters for each phase of the software life cycle development process. We also discuss common programmer ethical dilemmas.

Coding Practices

This section discusses ethical quandaries regarding bad code, weak code, the correct use of system memory, utilizing system resources, redoing code due to business rule changes, staying current with coding best practices, and pseudo code. This will give you a thorough understanding of the ethical issues programmer's face in their general coding practices.

The primary ethical concerns of programmers result from either lack of proper communication between business users and developers, insufficient knowledge in their proclaimed area of programming expertise, simple boredom or laziness, and most common of all, a lack of time allocated for proper project completion.

Bad Code – Whose Problem is It?

Bad code is code that is written in a manner that does not fulfill the business or technical requirements defined by any given project. Writing bad code can mean several things. Sometimes it is just a matter of not taking fully into account the complexity of the specifications. At other times, developers are simply working off of patterns that they have used successfully in the past that may not necessarily apply to the current project. Bad code can also result from rushed deadlines and production pressures. Finally, and worst of all, bad code can come from developers who do not have the technical expertise to get the job done, but somehow managed to bluff their way through the technical interview. The choice of how to handle them falls into the hands of the programmer. The following scenario addresses reworking bad code that was written by a coworker and friend:

You are performing software development with a computer graphics group. The team is motivated to produce an award-winning product for the next release. However, one member of the team, "Allen," produces dubious code and seems incapable of doing better. The project schedule is in serious jeopardy. One of your fellow programmers, "Rick," suggests that you and he just rewrite the code written by the weak team member Allen, so it works properly. He says that no one need ever know that the two of you rewrote Allen's code to make it work properly. Is this type of cover up performance ethical?

Conservative Rewriting programs for someone else on your team is inappropriate and slows production down, wasting your time and the company's time. You should sit down with management and explain that this one person is significantly affecting the goals of the department and company. You should never do someone else's work for them, no matter how well meaning your intentions.

Liberal Your desire to help the team and your friend is well intended and may work as a one-time fix in this case. There is nothing wrong with helping a friend out. You need to watch each other's backs. You may need help sometime in the future and he will owe you one.

In addition, you may also want to consider talking to Allen and encouraging him to brush up on his programming skills so that he is up to speed. For Allen's benefit, you should also tell him that you are making changes to his code. This will ensure that he can respond appropriately if there are any questions directed to him in the future or any program maintenance work that comes back to him. It will also help him learn how he should have written the code.

SUMMARY

It is a tricky business to help someone do their work without notifying management. Expectations are set around a person's performance; in this situation you will create a false sense of Allen's ability. If you really want to fix the code, you should seek permission from the project leader to do so.

Working on a team brings to light many ethical issues. When you cover up for someone else's failings, it can put the team and project at risk. However, there also needs to be a human element in business.

No one is perfect and any expectation of that is unrealistic. Most people find it better to work in an environment where they feel supported rather than in a cutthroat environment where everyone plays the blame game. How far you take that support is up to you. In addition, how often you point the finger is up to you as well.

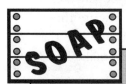

Microsoft Windows NT

Does it infuriate you when a PC user calls and says that their machine is running slow? The first thoughts that come to mind would be a memory issue or a network card problem, if hooked to a network, or disk space problem. But after investigation, you find that the real problem is Windows NT's baseline OS doesn't include defrag software. The end user has to buy something like Disk Keeper to rid the hard drive of severe fragmentation. Also, even with Disk Keeper you have to run the software repeatedly and it still doesn't fully rid the hard drive of fragmentation. Yes, Windows NT was far better from a security standpoint than Windows 95/98, but get real; even these baseline operating systems included some form of defrag software. It would be like using all your money to buy what you thought was reliable transportation but it couldn't even get you out of your driveway.

Jeff Payne
GIAC Certified
IA Analyst Inc.

Weak Code – Is it Ever Okay?

Weak code falls into the category of laziness, carelessness, or results from over-working a developer. In the following circumstance, weak coding practices are due to being overworked, which commonly occurs in application development environments that have unrealistic deadlines generated by the business users or management. In the following two scenarios, consider how you would respond to weak code.

You are tired from working a week of consecutive ten-hour days to get your project done and decide to cut corners wherever you can, which results in writing lazy code that will just get by. The code you end up writing will work fine and does not have any security weaknesses, but you know you could write it much better and utilize computing resources better. Is it okay to write weak code when you do not have the time to do the job better because you are being grossly overworked?

Conservative Your company pays you good money to create the optimum solution, not the minimum optimum solution, for your develop-ment efforts. Cutting corners never pays off and you will probably have to come back and rewrite your weak code anyway. Dig deep and do the job correctly, even if you are tired. You will be glad you did. Nothing feels better then knowing you did a job to the best of your ability.

Liberal When push comes to shove, it does not make any difference what kind of code you write as long as it gets the job done effectively, within budget, and on time; that is the bottom line for management. That is what you are being paid for, not to create a code masterpiece. There is no need to spend three hours working on code that you could write in one just to make it fully optimized. If you always did that, you would never get any projects done on time.

Summary

In all areas of business, we are faced with the dilemma of doing the job versus doing the job to the best of our ability. Doing the job right tends to pay off in the end, but not always if you miss your deadline. Finding an ethical balance that you can live with between giving it your all and pulling projects in under deadline will give you peace of mind in the work place.

Correct Use of Memory – Fixed Versus Dynamic

Memory allocation is an important matter for lower level programmers such as C, Java, and UNIX developers. Properly using system memory can be an ethical issue because wasting memory costs the IT department money and can interfere with other developers' work. Consider the following scenario:

You are developing a program for an accounting firm, which draws data from an accounts database table. The size of the data you extract may vary depending on the records for any given month. Is it unethical or just poor coding practice to waste memory by declaring the maximum possible size rather than dynamic allocation?

Conservative If you are wasting memory, you are wasting system resources, which results in wasting the company's money. Any act of wasting money is unethical. How would you feel if it was your money and someone was not handling it with utmost care and respect? You would not want someone else to waste your hard-earned cash.

Liberal In this case, maybe you did not choose the most optimum programming solution, but this is really no big deal compared to today's hardware system resources. We are talking about worrying about a fraction of a cent here. If every programmer had to worry about these matters, no work would ever be done.

Summary

Programmers are hired for their expertise in developing software. The allocation and use of memory is entrusted to them. If they remain within a certain range of acceptability, this should not become an issue in most cases. Everyone takes shortcuts from time to time. Many of these short-cuts are generated because the developers are under aggressive and sometimes impossible deadlines. Other times, these shortcuts are bad habits that they have developed over time. In either case, it is worth-while to consider both extremes and find out what you feel comfortable with as an application developer. Maybe you have never considered how you waste money through your coding practices. It is worth some thought.

Ethical Use of System Resources – Are You Using or Abusing the Privilege?

You are a computer genius working at a securities company and can write code that will bump up the speed of the host computer while it is performing complex trading calculations. Is it ethically appropriate to alter the speed of a computer, which will be running your application?

Conservative You need to be very careful when altering the system resources of a machine that will run your software. It is not recommended to reallocate the fundamental core speed of host machines. This practice is unacceptable due to the risk imposed on the host machine. Think about the fact that if there is the slightest problem or security weakness in the software that you have developed, you can impose serious damage to the host computer. Let the client upgrade their hardware on their own. Do not interfere with this type of dynamic memory boost, even for the client's benefit.

Liberal If you know how to write code that speeds up the processing power of the host machine, you should review it with your technical project leader and, if they approve, go for it. This will give your product a significant edge on all of your competitors. The clients will most certainly appreciate the additional speed and processing power. Just be sure you thoroughly perform error handling and penetration testing on the product before it is released to the general population.

SUMMARY

Altering system resources on a host machine is not against the law or necessarily immoral, but it could result in problems, depending on the structural integrity of the software manipulating the client resources. You will see the negative results of this ethical dilemma if your software has a bug that permanently alters a host machine or makes is susceptible to a malicious attack.

Redoing Code Due to Management Changes – Should You do It?

Often on IT projects, the technical team is required to get started prior to when the management team has actually completed the full project planning. Sometimes management will notify the programmers that the coding standards or even the planned software project itself has changed to implement new business rules. This type of business requirement change results in reworking code and sometimes tossing out weeks or months of development work. The following issue addresses this problem.

You are halfway through a large program that will be used by the order fulfillment department of a fiber-optics company. Your IT manager implements new standards for everyone to follow. Do you go back and rework everything you did? Do you start the standards from the point you are at? Do you say forget it and use them on the next project?

Conservative If management has provided you with standards, it is your responsibility to utilize them to the best of your ability. Go back and try to update the code you have already written to meet the current standards. If you cannot update it, you must rewrite it. This is part of the job. Roll with the punches. Be sure you speak to your manager so that they know that reworking and rewriting your earlier work will set the project back in terms of the aggressive deadline.

Liberal Just because management did not perform their job correctly is no reason for you to suffer the consequences. After all, if the project is not completed on time because of this change, you will be the one to eat it, not management. Just implement the standards from the point you are at in development and do not worry about the work you have already done. You will never get the project done on time if you back track at this point.

In addition, if implementing the new standards throws the project off too much because you cannot use existing libraries, do not implement the standards at all. It is not your fault they were tossed into the mix at this late phase of the development effort.

SUMMARY

One constant in application development is that things are always changing. Operating systems are upgraded that require reworking old code, business rules change, and IT projects are often dumped or redesigned in mid-development. Learning to adapt to change is essential for programmers and analysts.

Staying Current with Coding Practices – What if It's Not in Your Schedule?

Most of your development team has remained current with recent coding languages, practices, standards, and changes in the development industry. You do not have time for the extra education required to stay current. Do you feel it is ethically correct to remain in the dark when it comes to the current coding standards and practices?

Conservative Part of a programmer's job is to stay current with the most recent developments in IT. This includes educating yourself on the most up-to-date compilers, programming techniques, secure coding practices, and standards. It is a given in the development industry that you will grant yourself a continuing education in your job role and potentially expand beyond your area of expertise. Therefore, it is not acceptable if you fail to keep yourself informed of the best and current means to perform your job as an application developer.

Liberal If your company does not pay you to take educational seminars and provide you with up-to-date resources, it is not your responsibility to do so on your own. Granted, you want to keep your skills fresh and marketable, but there is only so much time in the day to realistically do this. Educational seminars can be costly if you have to foot the bill yourself.

Spending all of your time working or in school will consume your life. That is not a fair or a happy way to live.

SUMMARY

Keeping up to date on recent software tools and development practices requires a significant amount of time on the part of the programmer. Some programmers do this automatically because they are excited about new technology in their area of expertise. Others may simply not have the time because they carry a large workload at the office. A third category of programmers may simply not want to update their skills and coast for as long as they can. Find out what type of programmer you are and if you feel good about it.

Commenting Code – When is It Okay Not to Do It?

The practice of commenting code is important for the other developers who will later maintain, fix, update, or rewrite the code you create. Commenting practices vary from developer to developer. Some programmers hate commenting, and therefore never do it. Others want to make themselves indispensable and do not comment because they want the work returned to them. Others comment consistently. Consider the following scenario:

You are a top coder at your company and you never comment your code because it takes too much time. This is primarily to keep up with what you are required to produce. Is it unethical to fail to comment code due to a lack of time?

Conservative Most programming standards dictate that developers must provide code comments. This is sensible because it allows for easier updating of the program and helps others understand what the initial developer was doing. Programmers should make commenting code a standard duty. If they do not, they are intentionally making it harder for those that will maintain their code. Saying that it takes too much time is not an excuse. In the long run, it will waste time for the business.

Liberal The bulk of programmers do not comment their code. In most cases, if there is a problem with code a developer has written, they will fix it themselves. When faced with the choice to finish a project on time or comment the code and run over schedule, the wise choice is to get the job done quickly.

SUMMARY

Aggressive deadlines in development result in an array of ethical dilemmas. The above example is one such circumstance. It is always best to weigh the advantages against the disadvantages when making a determination such as commenting code.

Omitting Code Comments for Job Security – Should You Play the Game?

You are a top coder at your company, and you never comment your code because you want to ensure job security by making it difficult for others to understand. Is it unethical to avoid commenting your code for the purposes of job security?

Conservative Failing to comment code to ensure job security is definitely not ethical. It is also a form of sabotage. Making things hard for the company and team due to your own insecurity is just wrong. Any practice that reduces the quality of your work to gain job security is unethical.

Liberal Office politics are tricky and sometimes you do not have a choice but to play the game. If you do not play the game, you usually lose. The ethical people are not always the ones on top. Unfortunately, it is usually the reverse. People who know how to play the game are the individuals calling the shots. Therefore, if you write excellent code, it is smart in some cases to ensure your job security by making it a little harder for others to decipher your work. Additionally, in this way no one else can take credit for your work because they would be required to speak to you in order to understand it.

Summary

Job security is a very interesting ethical matter. Most people build a little job security into their jobs. Some people in IT are terribly bad at playing politics so they use their technical knowledge as a non-political strategy to stay in the game.

Pseudo Code – Is It Worth Your Time?

Pseudo code is the step-by-step description representing future code that will be written in its place. Pseudo code is not often practiced outside of the computer school environment. Take into account the following scenario:

You never pseudo code even though it is company policy. A non-technical manager using methodology books wrote the company coding policy and most of the technical people think the corporate policy makes no practical sense. You think pseudo coding is a complete waste of time, and therefore, you are saving your company time and money by not pseudo coding. In this case, is it appropriate to go against company policy?

Conservative   In most cases, you should follow the standards set by the company. Standards are written by experts and are tried and true. In a few cases, it is useful to address unnecessary standards with your manager. You should sit down with your manager and explain the pros and cons of pseudo code. Tell them that you can save the company time and money by not adhering to this standard. Explain why it is unimportant technically and that it will not affect the quality of your work.

Liberal   There is no need to make a big deal out of a standard such as pseudo code, which no one in the industry does anymore. Do not pseudo code. There are plenty of standards that are not followed, because the development team thinks the standards document is a joke. Most programmers have honestly not even reviewed the standards because they did not want to waste their time. At least you know what they are.

This is a case of realism versus textbook (at best). In theory, all kinds of standards and practices are important, but in real life, development efforts with real deadlines and most standards and methodologies do not apply. This is especially true if the standards were written by non-technical personnel.

SUMMARY

Often, developers are faced with long drawn out methodologies and standards that, if followed, would prevent all projects from ever being completed. Given enough time to elaborate standards and methodologies is beneficial to software development, but with the deadlines imposed on programmers they are forced to find the best possible solution somewhere in the middle. Senior management does not always understand this.

Code Maintenance

Maintaining code poses different ethical situations than the original generation of code. Programmers who maintain code have the job of going through existing code and making minor adjustments due to changes in the production environment, database, business rules, or overall system architecture. The next two issues involve modifying the original code of a program.

Modifying the Original Secure Design of a Program – Is this Ever Appropriate?

You are a maintenance programmer working on a program that has a security model with bounds checking. You add a new function that does not perform bounds checking. Is it ethical for a maintenance coder to modify the original secure design of a program in this manner?

Conservative When performing maintenance work you must stick with the existing design and security model of a given program. It is never appropriate to add functionality that does not adhere to the original secure design of the system. You are wasting your and the company's time.

Liberal It is not always necessary to following existing secure design concepts of a program when you are simply adding functionality. The overall secure structure of the program should be enough to maintain its own integrity, even if you do not add bounds checking to your new function.

SUMMARY

Adhering to a program's secure structure when you are doing maintenance work is primarily dependent on the type of maintenance work you
are doing. If the new function overrides or alters the functionality of the
program altogether and you do not implement bounds checking, you
may be ethically wrong. However, if the additional function you are
adding has no effect on the overall security of the program, there may
not be a need to address it.

Affecting the Overall Quality of a Program – What is Acceptable?

Is it ethical for a maintenance coder to write a less quality add-on function than
the code written for the original program?

Conservative Continuation of quality is a requirement for maintenance
programming. Any additional code added to a program should have the
same level of quality.

Liberal The reality is that compensation for maintenance programmers is
far less than for the original developers, because they are often not as skilled.
Trying to match the quality of an existing program may not be realistic for
a maintenance programmer.

SUMMARY

Quality is important in the maintenance of existing applications; however, the resources on hand must be taken into account and an acceptable quality assurance level must be set. Not all programmers are
phenomenal, and to set a standard for all work to match may be unrealistic. However, system security should never be the aspect of maintenance code that is comprised for any reason.

Code Review

Thus far in this chapter we have discussed standards and methodologies from the point of view of the programmer. Now let's take a look at it from the point of view of the reviewer role.

The code review process occurs in three different ways: by a third party, by coworkers, or by automated software. The process of reviewing code provides a check and balance for development efforts. A simple code review checks the basic vulnerabilities of the program. The more complex security conscious code reviews are referred to as penetration tests. These tests probe and attempt to penetrate the security of the program and system in which it is running.

This section discusses lazy reviews, following standards, and automated code review.

Lazy Reviews – Do You Do It?

Your team takes turns reviewing each other's code on a monthly basis. You know everyone writes decent code. Is it acceptable not to perform the review of your team's work if you do not have the time?

Conservative Absolutely not! A code review checks for more than just good coding practices, it verifies the integrity and security of the system. No one writes perfect code. It is important for every developer to have a second set of eyes to review their work.

Liberal If your coworker has just created routine code that they could write blindfolded, taking the extra time to review it when you already know it is fine is a waste of time and energy. This is especially true when you have so many other projects to focus on.

SUMMARY

Getting lazy reviewing code or just feeling it is not necessary could save time or cause real damage. The complexity and priority of the project that requires review plays a role in the necessity of a thorough review. When the code to review is repetitive, maybe it is a waste of time to check every line. But then again maybe not, that is for you to decide under the unique circumstances of your job as programmer and code reviewer.

Following Standards – How Strict Should You Be?

When reviewing code, you discover that one of the programmers did not follow the coding standards but otherwise their work is good. Do you make them rewrite it or let it slide knowing it may cause someone else more work in the future?

Conservative   Your job as the code reviewer is to make sure applications meet coding and security best practices. If the programmer knowingly failed to implement company standards, they should expect to be required to rewrite it after the code review. If you let one programmer get away with it, they all will try and you will end up with quite a mess on your hands.

Liberal   If the code is good and secure, there is no need to waste time and money making the programmer rewrite it on principle. Instead, tell them in a friendly way that you let it slide since it was such excellent code, but they should review the programming standards set up by the department for future use. There is no need to make a big deal of it, but have them try to make the adjustment for the next project they work on.

SUMMARY

When deciding to enforce standards on programmers after a code review, consider if the time and energy required will justify the changes in the code. If so, require the programmers to go back and redo their work to the department standards. If not, you may be slowing down the entire project and creating a lot of enemies. Remember, the goal of software development is to create the best possible program in a time efficient manner. The only absolute requirements are that the program performs operations according to specification and that it does not pose a security risk to the system.

Automated Code Review – Do You Trust the Software or Yourself?

Automated code review includes the use of software applications to review programs. There are many tools on the market that perform this function. The following example discusses the ethical circumstance of relying exclusively on automated code review. For instance, you use an automated code review tool to review your own Visual Basic code. When you run the software on the code you just built, it detects structural problems that will take you weeks to correct. You are an expert in Visual Basic programming and personally do not trust automated code reviews so you do not update your code accordingly. Did you do something wrong?

Conservative The purpose of an automated code review tool is to more quickly find mistakes you would not otherwise find through a personal or peer review. Research the recommended changes and implement them. It is never appropriate to ignore the recommendations of any type of code review.

Liberal You have determined that automated code reviews can be generic and trust your expertise in Visual Basic programming. Why waste the time and energy in implementing a structural change that is not necessary. The automated tool may only be programmed to find one type of structure and therefore be incorrect itself.

SUMMARY

Implementing an automated code review and following up on that review with changes to your code has strengths and weaknesses. If you know that the structural changes the tool is recommending are irrelevant you may decide to skip them. However, on the other hand, if you do not know as much as you think you do and fail to implement changes in your code based on the review, you may have a lot of extra work to do in the future as well as set the project off of its deadline.

Code Design and Testing

The code design and testing phases of application development occur at opposite ends of the life cycle development process. However, they are discussed jointly in this section because they are codependent. Some IT departments perform testing instead of code design and then rework the program at the testing phase. This type of coding is known as "ad hoc development." Other IT departments perform ample code design and thus have minimum reworking to do at the testing phase.

The subjects discussed in this section are skipping the design phase, ad hoc development, and skimping on the test phase.

Skipping the Design Phase – A Bad Idea?

The design phase of programming is the structural program development. This is where you lay out the process flow and overall feasibility.

You decide to skip a thorough design phase for your system because you hate designing and love coding. Once you get to the testing phase, there are major structural problems but the code is great. Do you go back and restructure it or just write workaround code to make it usable?

> **Conservative** You should have done the job correctly from the start of your development efforts. Now that you have determined that skipping the code design phase really does not work, you should go back and perform a code design and rewrite your code so that it works correctly with a strong architecture behind it.

> **Liberal** It is too late in the game now to go back and rework the design of the application. Write the appropriate workarounds that will make your application function correctly. Based on this experience, you may want to consider taking the time in your next development effort to work the kinks out at the time of code design.

SUMMARY

Skipping phases of the software life cycle development process always comes at a price. Unfortunately, the above issue is quite common in software development. It tends to occur with the most talented computer programmers who feel that they are beyond design.

Ad Hoc Development – Is a Structured Plan Better?

Most organizations do not have time to fully implement a structured development plan that utilizes best practices. Therefore, the unofficial standard at some companies in regard to application development is ad hoc coding and then deployment.

Your company is one such organization that develops on an ad hoc basis. You know that this method of application development does not fulfill even the most basic application system requirements. What do you do in this circumstance?

> **Conservative** You should take the initiative to propose a full life cycle development process to your manager and IT team. Writing code under the current circumstances of your job will only generate future problems. You will be thanked for your foresight.

> **Liberal** Unfortunately, many development efforts occur in an ad hoc manner. If you are working in an environment like this, you may choose to go with the flow or set up a process for yourself to use that is more structured. Proposing an entirely different means for development efforts may set you at odds with the entire team and probably will not be implemented anyway.

SUMMARY

When you work for a company that performs ad hoc application development, you have the personal ethical choice to implement a more structured means for your own development process. You also have the choice to take it to the next level and share your process with the rest of the team and/or management.

Skimping on the Testing Phase – Is Automated Testing Enough?

The primary purpose for testing an application prior to its entry into production is to verify security. Skimping on the testing phase can result in exaggerated problems for the future of the application. Most departments do not spend enough time testing applications prior to placing them in production.

Sometimes this happens because the developer is used to their code and confident in what they have written. Thus, they feel it is not necessary to test it. Other times they just check for obvious errors and pass the application to the deployment team. For these reasons, it is always optimum to have a different person perform testing on a given application.

You have just completed an application that is a month overdue. You use an automated testing tool to verify that it does not have any major bugs or security weaknesses. Is automated testing enough or are you ethically required to perform full testing?

Conservative   Automated testing does not necessarily cover all of the bases of human testing. It may cover different areas that human testing misses. To properly complement automated testing, you should now perform a peer test of the application. Have a coworker test the system for you.

Liberal   Once you have completed automated testing, you have done your job according to the company standards. It is not your responsibility to enforce additional testing if that is not the company policy. It is not even realistic to perform that testing given that the application was supposed to be deployed one month ago.

Summary

Going above and beyond the call of duty to ensure that your application is as good as required is a personal decision. In most IT departments, you will find a range of personnel from those who do the minimum just to get by to those who are so thorough they slow the entire process down. Finding the right balance of thoroughness and expediency is important to a successful development process.

Programmers and Viruses

The intentional and unintentional introduction of viruses into development and production environments requires significant ethical consideration. Viruses are sometimes propagated through a development environment due to carelessness. Programmers populate them in the production environment, when an application either intentionally or unintentionally introduces them.

The following issues, including the correct use of company resources, propagating viruses on the corporate network, downloading shareware, and malicious attacks, ethically illustrate this concern.

Using Company Resources for Continuing Education – What About the Risk?

The most common place to find computer viruses is a university technical lab. The following issue addresses the ethical concerns of contracting a virus on your corporate laptop by using company resources in a university lab. For instance:

You are a junior programmer at a start up company. You are attending night school to finish your education in computer science. You use your company laptop to perform homework assignments at the university lab, which puts the laptop at risk. Is it appropriate to put company resources at risk in such away?

Conservative Even if you are pressed to use company resources for your continuing education, it is not appropriate. Company resources are for company use only. Any use of the corporate laptop outside of company use is not acceptable.

Liberal Since you are using your company's laptop to further your education in computer science, which will in turn benefit your company, this type of use is acceptable. It would be different if you were using it for other means.

SUMMARY

Using your corporate laptop outside of work is a sensitive matter. Many businesses allow their developers to take their laptops home, especially when the workload is large and they will be doing additional coding outside of the office. The acceptable range of personal use for corporate laptops varies from business to business.

Contracting a Virus and Propagating It to the Network – Should You Confess?

This next issue follows up on the previous issue of the use of corporate resources. The only difference is that in this case you have contracted a virus from the university computer lab:

In addition to using company resources for your continuing education, you unknowingly contract a computer virus. This occurred while you were working in the computer lab at the university, which you know is prone to computer viruses and worms. The virus proceeds to infect the entire network at work. Do you tell your boss how you got it?

Conservative Taking your work computer to a computer lab at a university when you know you are placing it at risk is just plain dumb and ethically inappropriate. University computer labs are known for having every virus imaginable and you were not ignorant to that fact. You made a huge mistake.

Tell your boss what you have done and any details you can remember that may help them combat the virus, which has now attacked the corporate network. Pray that you do not cause too much damage.

Liberal Wait and see what happens. Maybe it is a simple problem and will be handled quickly. If the computer virus seems to be complex, talk to your teammates who are trying to fix it and explain what happened with your machine. Maybe that will give them the knowledge they need to clean up the virus without getting your boss into it.

Finally, reconsider whether you should go back to the university computer lab in the future. It might not be worth your job.

SUMMARY

Admitting to propagating a virus on your corporate network can be scary business. This is especially true if you have used company resources potentially inappropriately. It is always best to tell someone if you know how the virus was propagated, because it will help them fix the program more quickly.

Downloading Shareware – Is There a Standard Policy?

A lot of programmers use shareware to obtain code that they would otherwise have to spend a significant amount of time developing.

A programmer downloads shareware code from a non-trusted source to save time developing the same code. They fail to share this action with the Information Security Manager. Is this inappropriate behavior on the part of the programmer?

Conservative This is highly inappropriate behavior and can affect the integrity of the entire system. All shareware code downloads should be discussed with the Information Security Manager prior to any download. Your company may also have a standard policy to not use shareware. This action was done in ignorance.

Liberal If you have to run everything by the Information Security Manager, you will never get any work done. There must be some trust for you as a programmer, that you are knowledgeable about what you are downloading. Programmers use endless shareware libraries. This is standard practice in application development.

SUMMARY

Downloading shareware opens an entire box of ethical issues. In the one addressed above, the programmer and the Information Security Manager should set up a shareware standard in advance. If the Information Security Manager is too stringent, the programmer will have difficulty getting the job at hand done. This will consequently result in an uncooperative relationship between the programmer and the Information Security Manager.

Coding Attacks – Are They Ever Justified?

A malicious attack is designed to disable, obtain information from, or damage a computer system. In terms of coding, the goal of an attack is to destroy or derive information from a system. Most attacks result in an effect on the business, which can have a negative impact on the image of the company or availability of services rendered. There two types of coding attacks that occur at different phases of the application life cycle: architectural/design level attacks and implementation attacks.

The more difficult of the two to resolve are architectural and design. The next level of attack is the implementation level. Implementation level attacks occur at the coding stage. The code level vulnerabilities are the simplest type to repair. What would you do in this next scenario?

You have a grievance with the company you are working for that has treated you unfairly. Knowing that architectural level attacks are hard to find, you build one into the system you are coding. Are you justified in this type of behavior?

Conservative   It is never appropriate to perform any type of malicious attack regardless of how unfairly you have been treated. In most cases, this type of behavior moves you out of the ethical arena into the illegal.

Liberal   Business is war. If you have been severely mistreated and have no other recourse to take, you may consider this type of behavior. However, with malicious attacks you must understand that you are venturing out of the ethical behavior dilemma and into the illegal.

SUMMARY

Generating a malicious attack against a company you work for is dangerous and not a very smart idea in general. Putting ethics aside, placing yourself in greater risk by toying with the idea of a malicious attack results in much worse consequences then just unfair treatment at the office.

Programmer Security Responsibility

Determining the development security responsibility of a programmer is no small matter. Information security touches many areas of application development including application program interface (API) calls, Common Gateway Interface (CGI) flaws, temporary fixes, disabling system warnings in macro development, and using back doors. The following examples address each of these issues.

The Power of the Programmer

A programmer or a systems analyst effectively has more power than any other user of computer systems. Programmers, through code, can change the behavior of an operating system, modify the way other programs work, or even change the way system hardware is configured or functions. Overall, that is a very large responsibility to have.

So how do most programmers relieve the stress of responsibly wielding this power or the stress of short deadlines and impossible project goals? Easter eggs! An Easter egg is a little 'surprise' that a programmer has hidden within an application. It's usually a fairly small amount of code the displays the programmer's name in a unique way or causes the program to act slightly differently than originally intended.

Are Easter eggs ethical? After all, they consume system resources, take additional coding work, and are generally not bug tested as well as 'official' code. Look at it like this... Considering the power a programmer wields and the things a programmer could do to a system, adding a couple of Easter eggs is pretty harmless. I would much rather see the name of the programmer displayed in twelve different fonts than have my CD-ROM suddenly stop playing any CDs except for Pink Floyd music CDs.

Jeremy Faircloth
Systems Engineer and Author

API Calls and Security – Finding the Right Balance

You are writing code that calls functions from the Windows API. You just assume that the API is secure. Is it your responsibility to check this fact out and build additional security into your error-handling routines if the Windows API does not meet your company's information security standards?

Conservative When developing code it is best not to assume anything. Therefore, in the above circumstance, perform the necessary research to ensure that the calls you are making to the Windows API will be secure on both fronts by determining whether the API itself is completely secure.

Liberal It is not your responsibility to check every Windows API function to determine if it has the appropriate security and prevents risk. This would result in an excessive amount of time spent on research that may not be accurate anyway.

SUMMARY

When you are utilizing external interfaces and tools, you are posed with potential security risks. If you take the time to check every external function or library you may never get your code written. Finding a proper balance between getting your work done and ensuring security is up to each software developer.

CGI Flaws – Who is Responsible?

A CGI is a predefined standard used for interfacing World Wide Web (WWW) information and database servers with external software applications. CGI programs are common in Internet development work. You are writing CGI code for a Web application in the perl programming language. You were not aware of a corporate policy that involves checking input buffer lengths that can create a security vulnerability. Consequently, the corporate Web server is attacked. You wrote excellent code but did not properly check the input buffer lengths. Is the attack your fault?

Conservative It is your responsibility as a programmer to familiarize yourself with corporate standards, security practices, and policy. Therefore, you are to blame for the security breach of the corporate Web server.

Liberal Many corporations do not fully communicate corporate policy and standards. This communication is the responsibility of the project manager or team leader. If there was a failure to communicate specific policy on the part of the project manager, you are not liable for the security breaches incurred because of it.

SUMMARY

Determining responsibility due to a failure to follow corporate policy is a common problem. In most cases, the programmer will take the heat simply because they are lower than management on the totem pole. Failing to implement security standards is a bit more serious because of the implications to the business and system integrity. There are some areas where programmers need to be more proactive; this may be one of them.

Temporary Fixes – A Common Practice

A temporary fix is usually a workaround that makes a computer program function correctly but is not the optimum solution for the problem. The next issue addresses the weaknesses and responsibility for implementing and updating a temporary fix.

You are past your deadline and have a couple of fixes that must be implemented in order for your code to run properly. Time is very tight so you apply a temporary fix with the intention of creating a more secure fix when you have more time to spend on it. Is it ever appropriate to implement an insecure temporary fix when the pressure is on for project completion?

Conservative It is never appropriate to implement a fix on a computer program, even if it is temporary. A temporary fix can result in a breach of system security. In the above circumstance, you should simply tell your manager that the appropriate fix will take more time and consequently you will not meet your deadline. If your manager tells you to apply the quick fix explain to them that it will not work.

Liberal In a perfect world, it is always better to take the time to create a secure program fix. The reality of computer programming paints a vastly different picture then the ideal world. Sometimes there are aggressive deadlines that must be met, and it is common practice to implement patches after a software release.

SUMMARY

This issue weighs the business realities against the technological demands and the results of those high-pressured demands. The reality concerning temporary fixes is that they are common practice. These fixes are systematically followed up with software updates and patches. Some of the most well known software companies in the world such as Microsoft make this common practice in the case of operating system patches that address security weakness.

Disabling Warnings in Macros – Not a Big Deal?

You are an Excel programmer and are annoyed with the system window pop-up every time you open your Excel code, which says that macro viruses are possible and asks are you sure you want to open this application. You decide to disable the warning. Is it ethical to disable system warnings for your own expedience and convenience?

Conservative It is always better to stay on the safe side and not disable any system pop-up windows. They are there for a purpose and even if it slows you down a bit, do not alter or remove them for your own convenience.

Liberal As an Excel macro programmer, you have expertise in this area and clearly know what you are doing. Disabling a pop-up window that is simply annoying is not a big deal.

SUMMARY

Programmers adjust their systems on a regular basis to make their jobs easier. Since they have more knowledge than the average user of the operating systems they are conducting development efforts in, they may know how to streamline simple system warnings to make their jobs easier and more efficient. It is important to remember that sometimes a little knowledge can be a very dangerous thing. If you decide to circumvent system pop-ups or other system procedures, be certain you know exactly what you are doing.

Using Back Doors – A Catch 22?

Back doors are created by application developers to provide a way into the system in case something goes wrong with the primary application. For example, if the application locks up you will need a way to get in and free the system resources. Without a back door, you cannot do this.

Knowing that it is a security risk to use back doors in your application development, do you do it anyway because you know you will need to get into the system via other means if a problem occurs? Is the creation of a back door appropriate in this case?

Conservative Never put the system you are developing in at risk by using back doors. It is as simple as that. If something does go wrong in your application, it will be difficult for you to get in but not worth the security risk you would otherwise impose on the system.

Liberal This issue is a catch 22 scenario. The security policy rightly states that you should not use back doors when developing applications and this makes complete sense. Back doors are a huge security risk. Nevertheless, if there is a problem with the system, you will be required to quickly get into it by some means to prevent major consequences, which requires you to create a back door. As the programmer, you have to have a back door so you create one knowing the risk.

SUMMARY

Back doors to applications are a significant security risk, but not being able to get into an application is a serious development issue when a problem arises. Speaking to your system administrator may give you new ideas for handling this catch 22 situation. They may have alternate means for handling this problem besides the use of a back door.

Cracking Passwords – Should You or Shouldn't You?

Cracking passwords occurs for malicious reasons as well as innocent ones. The next issue discusses one such potentially innocent reason to crack the system administrator's password if you are a programmer.

You need to install your software onto the test box and the system administrator with the password is out sick. You can guess or crack the password of the test box and therefore install your software. Is it ethical to do this?

Conservative You should wait until the system administrator returns to work. You have not been given blanket access to the test box and therefore you should certainly not try to crack the administrator's passwords. If something goes wrong on that server, you will be the one held responsible.

Liberal Since you are under a tight deadline and can guess the system administrator's password, go ahead and get started on your work.

SUMMARY

If you cannot wait another day because you are under such a tight deadline, reference the employee address book and call the system administrator at home for the password and permission to use the testing box. In most cases, they will not give you the password on the phone but may be able to provide you with the appropriate privileges remotely so that you can use the test machine under your own user identification.

Software Deployment – What is the Best Way?

Deploying software is the final step in the development process not including ongoing maintenance. Within the area of deployment, the developer faces additional ethical concerns. One such concern is departmentalized deployment.

Departmentalized deployment is a means to deploy a recently developed software application that isolates different departments, rolling out the software one department at a time. This allows the development team to see how the new software affects each department and their corresponding systems. This process simplifies and provides easier isolation of problems and fixes.

You know it is more secure to deploy software in a departmentalized manner; however, you do not have the time so you roll it out all at once. Are you wrong in doing this?

Conservative Deployment of software is a very important step in user acceptance. If it is deployed in a rushed manner, it could potentially cause an inconvenience for the users. They will not want to use the new system in the future. This will stain the image of the new application. It is better to take the time and deploy the new application in a departmentally structured manner.

Liberal Again, we are faced with the reality of the software development process against the ideal circumstances of development. Sometimes you do not have the time because the system you built is needed immediately so you must deploy and hope there are not any major problems. In addition, global deployment can be somewhat protected by testing in a simulated test environment that mirrors the development environment.

SUMMARY

The results of deploying applications all at once can pose a problem with regard to user acceptance for that application. However, if all goes well, it is a non-issue. Only the developers and the testing team can make this call.

Chapter Summary

In this chapter we discussed the ethical considerations of programmers and analysts. We defined programmers and analysts as the information technologists who develop computer applications utilizing various programming languages. You learned that there are many different titles a programmer can have, which identify whether they develop package software solutions, operating system functional programs, or other forms of application development.

In the conservative and liberal ethical responses, we reviewed bad and weak coding practices. We included the ethics of code reviews comparing automated reviews with peer and third-party reviews. You learned about the relationship between programmers and malicious attacks such as viruses and stealing. You learned how to ethically handle these circumstances. In addition, we considered the ethical responsibility of keeping information systems secure when writing code and the expected responsibility of the developer. Finally, we discussed the ethics of application deployment, structured design, and testing.

This chapter thoroughly highlighted the ethical pitfalls of computer programming, making you aware of what risks you could consider taking to speed up production and what risks are simply not worth the results.

Frequently Asked Questions

The following Frequently Asked Questions, answered by the authors of this book, are designed to get you thinking about the ethical circumstances you may face when performing computer programming or systems analysis. Unless legal issues are involved, then answers in the FAQ may not be the right answer for your organization. Some answers may be more ethical than others, but the true response is up to you.

Q: What is bad code and what are the ethical ramifications of writing bad code?

A: Bad code is code written that does not fully take into account the technical specifications provided and falls short of the application requirements. In some cases, people who are not qualified for the work at hand write bad code. Ethically speaking, if a corporation hires you to do a job, you should have the appropriate capability to perform that function in a time-efficient manner. If you take a job that you are not qualified for, you can tarnish your reputation as a programmer and influence the productivity of your department.

Q: Describe the code review process including potential ethical pitfalls within these processes.

A: The code review process is the phase in the software development life cycle where checking of code occurs for security weakness and overall usability. Ethical issues occur in the code review process when this step of the application life cycle development is skipped or glazed over.

Q: What are the ethical responsibilities of computer programmers when it comes to the generation of viruses due to their negligence?

A: Computer programmers have the unspoken responsibility to prevent virus and worm infection on company resources. When programmers do not handle their equipment in a diligent manner, they put the business at risk of contamination. This carelessness can cause serious damage and impedes the development process altogether.

Q: Do programmers carry the weight of security or is this just the role of the Information Security Officer?

A: All personnel within a corporation should be security conscious. This is especially true of computer programmers. When developers implement insecure code or back doors, they put the company at risk. It is up to the programmers to calculate if the risk is necessary given the application requirements.

Q: In application deployment is there an ethical requirement of the developer to perform deployment in a certain manner?

A: The answer to this question is heavily dependent upon the expected project deadlines and physical deployment environment. In some cases, global deployment is necessary and can be somewhat protected by testing in a simulated test environment that mirrors the development environment. In other circumstances, avoiding departmental deployment out of laziness can be disastrous.

Q: As a developer, are you required to follow a code design process, or is it acceptable to handle coding errors in the testing phase of application development?

A: Again, this question depends on the environment of the IT department and their expectations. The code design process does circumvent future reworking of the code at the testing phase. However, your technical lead may not require or desire you to perform a code design phase within the development life cycle.

Chapter 8

Database Administration

Ethical Dilemmas in this Chapter:

- Database Development and Ethical Pitfalls
- Handling Data, Program, and Hardware Backups
- Data Models and Database Architecture
- Obtaining Knowledge from the Data
- Ascertaining Data Requests from Users
- Massaging and Cleaning Data
- Data Forecasting and Trend Analysis

Introduction

The database administrator (DBA) is a key player in information technology (IT). Most businesses cannot operate without an operational database and someone to administer it. The DBA is responsible for all of the data within a corporation. Data is stored in a database, which may come in various formats such as flat file, relational, object oriented, multidimensional, and many other proprietary formats. Data is formatted and managed within these databases for easy input and access. Many business applications are built around the database to perform day-to-day business processes.

Database administration within IT falls under three primary roles as listed:

1. The Operations DBA performs the day-to-day database maintenance, backups, and operations of a corporation's production databases.

2. The Development DBA or Architectural DBA performs database development efforts including architecture, planning, modeling, cataloging, and designing new or existing database systems.

3. The Data Administrator performs data processing at a senior level, which includes managing a company's data and metadata. (Metadata is data that describes other data.)

In this chapter on database administration, we discuss the ethical dilemmas DBAs find themselves in with the incredible access to information they possess.

We review ethical issues for the three aspects of database administration: operations, development, and senior database processing . The topics covered in this chapter include the personal ethics involved in database development by DBAs, ethical considerations for database administration qualification, data and program back up issues, handling third-party or vendor database solutions, data modeling dilemmas, how to ethically use knowledge gained from previous employment without breaking non-disclosure agreements, how to rightly handle knowledge obtained from the database, how to rightly distribute data from the database to business users, determining effective use of data types in database development efforts, working with the data in an ethical manner, massaging data accurately, and the ethical pitfalls of data reporting, forecasting, and trend analysis.

Database Development Ethical Pitfalls

What is behind Google, the IRS audit system, your airline flight reservations, or your credit rating? A database of course, or more likely many databases. The wise manager fears the database development process because, of all software projects, this is the easiest one to lose control of and face incredible cost overruns. Attention to detail, spot-checking, and making sure you have the right team are all critical, but perhaps the key member is the DBA. As mentioned in the introduction, a DBA is an IT trusted employee who administers the corporate database(s). The issues in this section on DBA discuss development database administration ethical dilemmas when faced with data discrepancies and the misuse of the DBA password by developers.

Data Discrepancies in Database Development – What if Your Boss Wants you to Keep Quiet?

Discrepancies in data can occur for many reasons and range from incorrect data input to data conversion problems. The worst type of data discrepancy is one in which an employee is stealing from the company. In this type of circumstance, financial data shows balance discrepancies. The following is an example of this worst-case scenario.

You are consulting for a company, building an executive information system (EIS). When you delve into their legacy data that you ported to a data warehouse, you discover a major financial discrepancy in their accounting records. You report this to their Chief Financial Officer (CFO) who looks at the data and keeps you at the office until late in the evening executing queries. During this time, he is obviously very upset. He tells you to keep everything completely confidential to him only and not tell anyone in the company or outside of it. What would you do in this circumstance?

> **Conservative** It is never a good idea to keep a major discrepancy a secret. If you have a good relationship with the IT manager, you should get them in the loop on what is happening. Just explain to the CFO that you need to have your manager aware of what is going on since you report to him.
>
> **Liberal** When something heated happens like this issue, it is best to take the approach of wait and see. If you jump the gun and notify authorities or someone else in the company, you may find yourself in the midst of a very

bad scene. Wait a few days, see what happens, then determine if you are legally required to communicate anything about this event.

SUMMARY

It is quite an ethical dilemma to be caught in the middle of a major financial discrepancy at a company. Finding a serious problem like this requires serious consideration; you do not want to end up in legal trouble yourself for hiding information. In most cases, the CFO in this example will have to tell someone else rather quickly even if they are the ones at fault, because the new system will make the discrepancy obvious. However, if the CFO asks you to change the data to hide the discrepancy, you must draw the line and notify your IT manager or the company Chief Executive Officer (CEO).

DBA Password Use and Misuse – Should You Implement Changes?

Using the DBA password for purposes that have nothing to do with database administration is a common problem for DBAs working in database development efforts. The following issue addresses this ethical scenario of allowing access to the DBA password for development work.

You begin working for a new company and discover that they use the DBA password when writing embedded Structured Query Language (SQL) code. You know this puts the entire database and data at risk. Do you refuse to allow the practice of using the DBA password?

Conservative You should not allow developers to use the DBA password in their applications when executing embedded SQL code. Immediately change the DBA password and issue a memorandum to the developers that the DBA password will no longer work in their code. They may get mad and have to rewrite some code but that is better than a breach in database security.

Liberal The reality is that developers often need database administrative privileges. There is no sense in making all of the developers hate you by changing the DBA password and requiring them to rewrite endless past code. What is done is done. Encourage the developers to use other logins and passwords whenever possible within their code. If you rock the boat on your first day, you can guarantee you will be out the door in no time.

SUMMARY

Implementing changes as a new DBA to a company can be tricky. The development team is used to working a certain way and will resent you for requiring them to do a lot of work. Whether you choose to be con-servative and change the password or you choose to be liberal and leave it, you may also want to consider implementing a development logon and password for future work. T his development logon and password allows the developers to perform some administrative privileges but does not provide the global access of the DBA password.

DBA Qualifications – When are You Qualified?

Qualifications for DBA's are vast. It is not always easy to determine if someone is qualified for the role unless you have an experienced DBA on staff that can per-form a technical evaluation of potential new hires. When putting yourself for-ward as a DBA there are many ethical questions you should ask yourself. First and foremost is, are you truly qualified? The following issues illustrate such as problem.

You have been a database programmer for several years and have been studying database administration. You apply for a job as a DBA and in your resume describe your previous database development work as database adminis-tration to get you in the door. You feel you can handle the DBA job but do not have the applicable work experience that would otherwise make you qualified. Is it ethical to put yourself forward as a DBA without the formal education and job experience?

Conservative It is never appropriate to put yourself forward as a DBA if you do not have certification in database administration. Enroll in night courses to learn the necessary skills required to be an effective DBA. A DBA is not a job that can be learned as you go. You are trusted with a company's information; any mistake on your part could result in disastrous conse-quences for the company that employed you.

Liberal   If you know that you possess the skills of a DBA but not the formal training or experience, there is nothing wrong with honestly communicating that and accepting a job as a DBA. Many people in the IT industry are self-taught and sometimes they are the best ones for the job.

SUMMARY

Self-taught IT professionals are commonplace in the industry. Self-taught professionals often end up in DBA positions. This is due to the demand for DBAs compared to the supply of them. However, there is a significant difference between the self-taught professionals who are skilled and those who are deluding themselves. If you are self-taught and want to apply for a DBA job, take a skills assessment test to determine if you have what it realistically requires when ethically putting yourself forward for the role of a DBA.

Handling Data, Program, and Hardware Backups

We have discussed the development of a database, but the operational issues are just as important and fraught with danger. Technology refreshment and maintenance programming are two classic danger points. We discuss the selection of a second rate solution because of kick backs and the importance of accuracy in managing data types. Backing up databases for system redundancy is a key role of the DBA. Backups are done to ensure that the data is lost not in the case of an overall system failure. A system failure is a database corruption, network failure, power outage, virus problem, or other such scenario.

The following issues discuss the ethical ramifications of failing to perform a data backup, how to address damaged data backup disks, and selling old backup drives that still contain company data. These are all very tricky issues, none of which possesses a simple ethical answer.

Failing to Perform Required Data Backup – What if You Miss One?

You fail to perform a database backup on Friday as mandated by the technical manager. Do you wait until the next scheduled backup or do you go ahead and do it the following Monday when you remember?

Conservative You should immediately perform the database backup on Monday. Performing a backup during operation hours will slow down the production system, but it is more important to have the data backup. You have made a huge error by forgetting the backup and should immediately account for it.

Liberal The reality is that some companies do not even perform weekly backups. If you do the backup right away, the production system will slow down. Your error will become grossly obvious to everyone in the company and business as usual will be affected. Wait until the end of the day on Monday and stay late to perform the database backup. In some cases, you may decide to skip it altogether and just wait for Friday to do the backup.

SUMMARY

Database backups are an important part of the business contingency plan and should be done like clockwork. If for some reason you are unable to perform one due to system changes, are out sick on the scheduled day of backup, or forget altogether, it is wise to do it on the next available evening. This will ensure that if there is an overall system failure there will be current backup data and data structures for the implementation of contingency efforts.

Handling Damaged Backup Disks – What if You're to Blame?

You are in the process of reconfiguring your boss' computer and drinking a cup of coffee. You have off loaded all of his sensitive data onto backup disks and have reformatted his hard drive. When you go to set down the coffee, it spills onto backup disks containing all of your boss' data. What should you do?

Conservative   Clean the disks and see if the data has been damaged. If it has, go immediately to your boss and explain what happened. Maybe he has another backup at home or on the network drive.

Liberal   You should have backed the data up on the network rather than on backup disks. Finish your work, copy what you can onto his newly formatted drive, and pray he does not know what is missing. Odds are he will not notice the difference.

SUMMARY

Redundancy is very important when performing any type of system backup, be it an entire database or the information on a laptop. It is always advisable to keep are hard copy of all data on an external hard drive, as well as a copy on the network or on disks. Triple redundancy will save a lot of problems and possible lost jobs.

Selling Old Backup Drives – What if Your Company Cannot Use them Anymore?

The company you work for has a lot of old data backup drives and you discover a business that is willing to buy them from you. The format of these old drives is such that very few people have the ancient technology to read them. You do not have the technology at the company anymore to read them yourself and delete the old data. Should you just sell them?

Conservative   Making a personal profit from company hardware in your possession is completely unethical. Selling old data backup drives under these circumstances is completely inappropriate. You should have the old data backup drives professionally destroyed. The company will be at risk if you sell the old data backup drives. Do not sell them.

Liberal   Often one of the perks of a job is handling old hardware. Some companies do not care what happens to the old hardware and leave it up to the people in charge. If you have that kind of leeway, there is nothing wrong in using that hardware in an intelligent manner to make a profit for yourself. Just make sure that you do not put the company at risk. In addition, since the technology is so old, there is only a slim chance that someone could actually see the data on the disks. The business you plan to sell them to will have to delete all of the data anyway to fully utilize them.

SUMMARY

Making personal money from retired hardware or software is a tricky issue. Often there is not any corporate policy to dictate what to do in these circumstances. Consider security risk above all else first. Then make the determination of what you should do if faced with this type of circumstance.

In most cases, the only secure means of handling this situation is to destroy the old backup drives. If, however, you decide to sell them, you may want to add a clause that you supervise the deletion of old data on those drives. It may be worth it if you can obtain a significant amount of money from the sale of the drives.

Regarding this same issue, would it make a difference if you were handing the money over to your department to purchase new technology?

Administrating Data Types and Allocating Memory – Are You Looking at the Big Picture?

As a development DBA, you must set up new databases for the company. Part of the process of developing a database is defining data structures and types for the data. There are many ways to define data structures and types, from the highly optimized use of memory allocation to the rather sloppy but flexible memory use. In addition, though it is a lot of work, an ethical developer will ensure that the data types are sufficiently well defined to allow for consistency checking to prevent "dirty data." The following is an example of taking the sloppy yet flexible way when allocating memory for data types.

You are building a new database that will have data from multiple sources that may be different lengths and require a range of memory allocated to it. You have set all character data types up at the maximum length level so that you do not have to go back and change anything later if the fields need to be larger. This means that you are wasting a lot of server space that will require the company to buy new servers more often. However, you are keeping the database flexible for the different types of data that will populate it, thus, saving yourself time in the long run. Is this an appropriate choice within the development demands of your job as a DBA?

> **Conservative** You should always perform your job function in an economical manner, keeping in mind the details of the technical requirements while simultaneously taking into account the big picture of the business and the financial results of your development work. Wasting memory will result in an inefficient system. Go back and do the job right.

> **Liberal** Oftentimes when developing a database, the exact technical requirements are not clear or specified up front, and therefore, you need to build a lot of flexibility into the database. Allocating additional memory for data types is common practice. You have done nothing wrong. If anything, you have done the right thing by keeping the database as flexible as possible.

SUMMARY

Most people have a hard time looking at the big picture and the minute technical details at the same time. If you are someone who can that is wonderful, but it is not realistic to expect it of the majority of IT personnel. The DBA on a development effort has the responsibility to build correct database functionality first and assess financial result of those efforts second. This is assuming they are not considering anything astronomical in price with little value return for the company.

Purchasing Third-Party Database Solutions – A Risky Business?

The role of purchasing and configuring third-party or vendor database solutions often falls in the hands of the DBA. Common third-party solutions include financial database solutions, contact management systems, and electronic data feeds such as those used for stock data in the brokerage industry. The following is an example of some of the difficult ethical issues you may face when interacting with vendors.

You are given the task of finding a new contact management system for your company that will integrate well with the database you have already built. One of the vendors offers you a referral cash bonus if you select their product, which is not the optimum solution to the company's database needs. There are certainly better options out there that would integrate more smoothly with your current database and overall systems environment. Do you take the money and accept a contact management system that is not optimal?

Conservative When in the market for an external vendor application, your job as a DBA is to always find the optimum solution for the technological and business needs. Under no circumstances should you select a tool that does not fit those needs, even if it provides you with a "referral fee" or other bonus, which is merely a bribe.

Liberal There really is not a huge difference between the vendor applications; some are simply better than others. In reality, you are the one that is going to have to do the configuration work so it really does not matter which you select as long as the end result is the same. A bonus is really nice when you are seriously underpaid considering how many hours you have to put in as a DBA. You work weekends and nights, and are on call in case there is the slightest problem. You owe yourself this bonus.

SUMMARY

Accepting money as a referral fee or commission for purchasing a product is tricky business. If you decide to do this, you should really consider what type of people you would now be in a partnership with. Are their ethics a little shaky? You may have problems down the road with this type of vendor.

Data Models and Database Architecture

Data modeling is the process of creating an architecture diagram that represents the entities and their corresponding relationship within a corporate database. Data models start at the logical level outlining business units and end up at the detailed physical database level, which includes memory allocation, file allocation, and data types.

In this section, we have included two ethical issues you may face when performing database architecture functions and creating data models. Consider each issue carefully. Determine how you would handle the same circumstances. The first scenario describes re-using data models you have built at a previous job, and the second outlines ethical dilemmas in the creation of database specifications.

Keeper of the Gate

If you were responsible for a water reservoir then one of your primary concerns would be protecting the purity of the water. If you owned a restaurant, one of your primary concerns would be the cleanliness of the facility and the purity and freshness of the ingredients. For a DBA, or anyone concerned with data entry, it is imperative that you do everything you can to prevent data corruption. After all, once motor oil is in a reservoir, it is all but impossible to get it out; you almost have to empty the reservoir and scrape the mud from the bottom and refill. Cleansing data isn't quite as hard, but it is as expensive. It requires specialists to write hundreds of scripts to test for this and that condition. However, if software checks are added to test every one of those conditions during the development phase then you do not need to bring in a high-priced specialist to cleanse your data. And if you do have to bring in the high-priced specialist and you do not add those checks to the system, you will be right back where you started within a year. The operations folks have responsibility too; suppose you were trying to enter the amount of a payment and you were told to enter round numbers, $99 instead of $99.99 because it is faster. How long would the database remain accurate? A minute? One of the times of greatest danger for a database is during a maintenance update. All too often, the maintenance coder removes critical checks and balances, either to get the job done faster or because they do not understand the total system. The DBA must be the keeper of the gate; the database is only valuable to the organization if its data has integrity. Your responsibility includes investigating every possible source of database contamination.

Stephen Northcutt

Re-using Data Models from Previous Jobs – Is this Okay?

You have saved all of the old data models you created on previous jobs. You are now working for a competitor of one of your previous jobs and they ask you to create a data model for their database, which is similar to one that you created for their competitor. Assuming that you believe you are not in breach of a non-disclosure agreement or non-compete agreement, do you go ahead and build an identical data model?

Conservative In most cases concerning this issue, you probably signed a non-disclosure agreement for the previous job and therefore you are not at liberty to disclose the data models from that job. Nor are you at liberty to model a competitor's database after one from a previous job, if you signed a non-disclosure agreement. Simply tell your new employer that you are under legal obligation to your former employer and cannot create an identical database or show them any of the database documentation from your previous employer. They will understand and respect you for your integrity.

Liberal The experience you gained from your previous employer is yours to keep and not owned by them. It would probably be inappropriate or illegal to show your new employer the data models or other database documentation from your job. However, the skills and knowledge you gleaned from your last job is yours, and if you build a similar database and reference the models privately you are not doing anything wrong.

SUMMARY

If an employer requires that you sign a non-disclosure agreement or agreement of non-compete, read it carefully before you sign. Have legal representation review it so that you are aware of what you are giving over in regard to your own intellectual property and that of the hiring company.

Creation of Database Specifications – What if They're Not Building it Right?

You have been hired by a startup company to build an object-oriented database. Once you have been hired you discover that the database is a relational database, not object-oriented. The manager of the database team is not technical and has been talking up a storm to prospective clients and the rest of the company about the advanced object database his team is building. Do you burst his bubble or just play along?

Conservative You need to explain the technicalities to your boss and provide information on the difference between an object-oriented database and a relational database. Do not let him further humiliate himself. He is providing inaccurate information and will thus jeopardize the business altogether. It is your job as a technologist to clear this inaccuracy immediately. You cannot expect a business manager to understand the difference between an object-oriented database and a relational database.

Liberal It is not for you to correct your boss. Anyway, these days there is a lot of ambiguity between relational, object, flat file, multi-dimensional, and other types of databases. Sometimes one aspect of the database will be flat file, another relational, and yet another object- based. The odds are that the clients really do not know the difference themselves.

SUMMARY

Often the details of technology can mystify non-technical management. They may throw around the latest hot ideas in IT and say that they are implementing them. Try to keep your management team informed of the technical developments and be proactive in explaining what you are building for them and what you are not building. This may save them some embarrassment and prevent the company from misrepresenting itself technologically.

Obtaining Knowledge from the Data

DBAs are privy to an incredible amount of client, coworker, and business information. Therefore, database administration is a trusted role within the organization. This means that the DBA is trusted with information that is of a confidential nature and should be handled with discretion and sensitivity. It is important for the DBA to handle this power at their finger tips in an ethical manner.

Developing Selective Blindness

Remember when you were a kid and your mother asked you to go get something out of the kitchen, you came back to tell her that you couldn't find it and it was right in front of your face? (Okay, some of us have been guilty of that as recently as last week, but I digress.) To be a good DBA, you need to develop a similar "blind spot" when dealing with your company's data. Yes, it's true that you have access to pretty much anything you'd want to see. And it's also true that in the course of designing or troubleshooting a database, you'll probably need to examine live data, be it financial, payroll, or human resources-related. In these cases, you should be able to look at the contents of a query or report without really *seeing* what's on it. This means that any inadvertent discoveries you make, like "Nancy makes more than me" or "Maria took 37 sick days last year" is something that you're ethically bound to keep to yourself. Your coworkers wouldn't take any more kindly to you invading their privacy than you would if they invaded *yours*.

Laura E. Hunter
Network Engineer & Technical Trainer

Knowledge Regarding Coworkers Pay from the Data – Should You Say Something?

You are checking out the data integrity after a database upgrade and perform some SQL queries on the sales data table to make sure everything is as it should be. You accidentally discover that some of the sales people are getting higher commissions than others. The percentages seem to be random, not based on experience or sales performance. You are close friends with some of the members of the sales team. Do you say something to your friends or just keep quiet?

Conservative   Disclosing information about salaries is not up to you and is in breach of your responsibility of protecting the data as DBA. You are in a trusted role as a DBA and should not disclose information to the employees within the company for any reason whatsoever. This type of behavior is completely unacceptable.

Liberal   Since the company you are employed by is doing something a little shady with their employees, you do not owe them anything. Friends are friends, and they should know that they are being seriously jilted. Tell your friends but ask them not to spill the beans so that you can provide them with future information. While you are at it, you should check the salaries of other IT personnel to make sure you are being paid what you deserve.

SUMMARY

The role of the DBA provides many challenges. The DBA has access to detailed client records, credit card information, employee payroll data, and much more. In some cases, there are legal and government requirements for how this data should be handled in regard to privacy. In other cases, there are no legal requirements or company policies and it is up to the DBA to determine what their own personal ethics are in relation to the information they have at their fingertips.

Knowledge Regarding Private Company Information – Should You Look?

You are the DBA at a backup data center. Your company provides back up and redundant data services for several different businesses. Your job is simply to back up the data and make sure the data replication technology is working appropriately. Is it acceptable for you to check out all of the information in the databases of all of your clients?

Conservative   Privacy is a very important matter with clients. They are entrusting you with their sensitive data and are not expecting you to snoop through it. Be professional and do not inspect or review the data entrusted to you.

Liberal   Part of the job of an administrator in a backup location is to verify data integrity, which will require you to review the data from time to time. There is nothing wrong with reviewing the data. If, however, you divulge information about the data, that is another story.

SUMMARY

As the administrator of back up and replication services, reviewing data entrusted to you should be done when necessary as part of your job function. Reviewing data for nosey purposes should not be done; however, there are no rules against it in most cases.

Knowledge of Private Personal Information – Security vs. Invasion of Privacy?

The Internet Service Provider (ISP) you are a DBA for collects detailed data about users' online activities. It keeps track of the Web sites users go to. Is it appropriate for you as the DBA to review this data and see who is accessing pornographic sites or have other unusual sites that could be embarrassing to the ISP user?

Conservative   You are entrusted with sensitive information about ISP users and should never abuse that trust. Reviewing usage is not appropriate.

Liberal   As a DBA for an ISP company, you should review the usage of its users. It is your responsibility from a security point of view. If the users are accessing illegal sites, your company could be at risk. This is a security function of your job.

SUMMARY

Reviewing sensitive information about ISP clients is a touchy issue. By reviewing what sites they visit, you may obtain information that someone is trying to learn how to build a bomb or other terrorist activity, which could target your company and hurt other people. However, customer information must have some level of privacy. Check the customer agreement the clients have with your company to determine what you can legally do with client information to balance out your role of security versus invasion of personal privacy.

Ascertaining Data Requests from Users

As a DBA, you receive requests for data sets from developers and business users alike. These data sets are formatted into reports, graphs, bar charts, and tables for many business purposes. It is your responsibility to provide them with the accurate and properly formatted requested data. This data is then used to make important business decisions such as purchasing inventory, determining profit and loss, and assessing corporate stock values.

Handling Unusual Requests for Data – Is there a Clear Policy?

A business user requests data about a department that she does not work in. You presume she is checking up on a coworker she does not and like trying to get them fired by pulling up dirt on them. She would get this dirt from the data set provided by you. Do you provide the information or deny the request?

Conservative Part of your role as DBA is to protect the data and see that the proper procedures are followed in regard to data access. You should not provide data to someone if that data is outside of their range of responsibility, without approval from the person owning the data.

Liberal Your presumptions may be wrong and if you get too paranoid you will be a hindrance to business rather then a support. It is your responsibility to provide the information requested by business users, not question their data access unless it is against the company policy. In this circumstance provide the data and stay out of company politics. Maybe her coworker is performing poorly and this information is necessary for the business to function properly.

SUMMARY

Companies should have clear policies regarding data access. Most do not. If you work for one that does not have clear policy in regard to data access, it is a judgment call on your part to provide data to the business users. Use your common sense and always keep in mind the rules of information security even if your company does not address them.

Assessing Management Requests for Data – What is the Procedure?

The manager of new business development for your company has requested historical information about existing business clients in the database. The manager of existing clients has told you not to provide data about his department to anyone. The manager of new business requires this information for projections to determine his goals and new business objectives. What do you do?

Conservative This scenario is different from the previous issue because the new business manager has a right to the data to properly perform their job function. However, it is always intelligent to play it safe and formally request permission of the manager of both of these departments (new business and existing business) to provide the data to the new business manager. Follow the proper chain of command and you will be in line with business procedures.

Liberal The existing business manager has no right to limit data access to the new business manager. The odds are that he is trying to give the new business manager a hard time out of job competition or maybe he is hiding something. Provide the necessary data to the new business manager but do not make a big deal of out it.

SUMMARY

When you have control of a corporation's data as a DBA, you inevitably end up in the middle of a lot of company politics. Try to stay as responsible and neutral as possible, but do not give in to company politics to the point where it hinders your job responsibility. If your company does not have clearly defined policy regarding data access, set up a policy and propose it to the IT and business managers. Therefore, questionable access can go through the correct procedure.

Providing Sensitive Data via E-mail

The manager of sales has requested that you send a report out via e-mail to all employees and contractors working for the company, which contains current sales data and sales forecasts. You consider this information to be sensitive. Some of the contractors at your company who would receive the e-mail also work for competitor companies; therefore, competitive data would go out to the competition, which is not a good idea. Do you send the report?

Conservative Refuse to send out sensitive data to a global companywide e-mail list. Not only would competitors directly get the information, but e-mail format is also easy to simply forward on and the sensitive company data could end up on the Internet somewhere.

Liberal Talk to the sales manager regarding your concerns if this data goes out to a corporate wide mass e-mailing. Explain to them the dangers and request that they send a modified form of the data to a specific group of employees. They may then see the risk for themselves and decide to simply report on the data at the next company meeting.

SUMMARY

Sending sensitive data out on e-mail is always dangerous. This is especially true for a company wide mass e-mailing. It is your responsibility as the DBA to think through these scenarios and find a solution that does not hinder the business, but refrains from exposing company information to competitors.

Massaging and Cleaning Data

Data massaging is the process of cleaning existing data either within the database, within an application that utilizes the database, or when data is used for reporting purposes. The complexity of data massaging can range from simply removing white space or nulls after the data to changing it altogether. The following two issues discuss changing the data for marketing purposes and exaggerating sales data.

Changing the Data for Marketing Purposes – Is it Legal?

You are pulling this quarter's data together for the corporate financial report that will go out to the investors. Your boss asks you to remove some of the low figures because they take down the whole report. Do you do it?

Conservative Changing financial data can get you into a mess of trouble. Refuse to remove the low figures and explain that you do not want to put yourself at legal risk.

Liberal In this issue, if your boss wants to remove a whole section of data from the report that is his prerogative. Just make sure that it does not make the report inaccurate. It is up to him to limit the results on the report. Be careful not to venture into the area of altering or deleting data.

SUMMARY

Unfortunately, this type of request happens all of the time when issuing financial or marketing data. Not reporting on sections of data when it is not required is less of an issue than actually altering data. This problem ventures into the area of legal issues and should be handled with utmost care and responsibility. Keep in mind the law and your own personal ethics when making the decision to format financial or marketing data.

Exaggerating Sales Data for Your Boss – Are You Painting a False Picture?

Your boss is up for a promotion and asks you to make him look good when you generate the financial reports from the database, which will be reviewed by senior management. He asks you to exaggerate the sales for his department by including some potential sales he has going on. (He claims he will definitely close these sales within one week.) Do you feel this is ethical?

Conservative Including potential sales into a report on sales is not acceptable. Encourage him to try to close the deals before the reporting cycle begins. You cannot create a false report for senior management. It will ultimately fall back on you and put your job in jeopardy.

Liberal If you know the record of accomplishment of this sales person and he can make the sales happen, you might as well include them in the report. You are taking a chance, but it is not one that could put your job or the company in a difficult situation. This is just status reporting.

SUMMARY

DBAs receive requests when they have to generate status reports from sales data. Salespeople can be very persuasive in such circumstances. First, make sure that you will not be painting a false picture of the data before considering altering a report based on projections or improved status.

Data Forecasting and Trend Analysis

Data forecasting is the process of using historical data to predict the future. In most cases, this type of technology is utilized for purchasing inventory, stock predictions, sales predictions, and overall business assessments. The following two issues, fudging numbers in data forecasting and inaccurate trend analysis graphs, discuss ethical dilemmas that arise when using forecasting tools.

Data Forecasting Tools that Fudge Results – Should you End the Relationship with the Vendor?

You work on a team of DBAs and discover that the data-forecasting tool your company uses was fudging numbers to be more accurate. Senior management is dependant on this tool for inventory purchases and marketing. There does not seem to be a problem with the business because of the data-forecasting tool. Should you keep quiet and leave the subject alone or speak to senior management about the inaccuracy of the tool?

Conservative You should immediately report any inaccuracies within the data-forecasting tool to senior management and suggest that they do not use it until you work out the bugs with the company that sold the tool to your business. Even if there are no problems with the business, using an inaccurate tool is completely unacceptable.

Liberal Contact the company you bought the tool from and explain the errors you have found in the forecasting tool. Explain how you feel it is fudging numbers for greater accuracy. Do not bring the problem to the business users yet since it is not causing a disturbance to the business. You may be wrong in your determination of the inaccuracy of the tool.

SUMMARY

When dealing with vendor software, you may come across problems and find you have to baby-sit some third-party database solutions. Keep tabs on all vendor tools that fall under your domain and stay in close relationship with the vendor. Making determinations to end a vendor relationship based on problems with their software should be carefully considered.

Pulling Inaccurate Trend Analysis Graphs – What Will be the Result?

You discover that the graphs in your bosses trend analysis reports that he is about to present to the board of directors are wrong. The data is correct but the graphics are wrong. He cannot reschedule the meeting. Do you tell him and ask him to pull the graphs?

Conservative You should never put your boss in a position where they present inaccurate information to the board of directors. Ask him to pull that report and explain that the data is correct but the graphs are wrong.

Liberal If the data is correct, tell your boss to go ahead with the presentation and explain to him that the pictures are a little off but the actual data is correct. The odds are that no one will even notice.

SUMMARY

When you must make determinations on whether to pull reports at the last minute due to inaccuracies in data, keep in mind the results of both scenarios: what kind of effect will there be if your boss walks into a room with no report versus your boss walking in with an inaccurate report that he can explain.

Chapter Summary

In this chapter, we discussed the ethical considerations of DBAs including having the appropriate qualifications to be a DBA. We defined the three primary roles of the DBA as the information technologists who 1) perform database operations and administration, 2) develop and design new databases, and 3) are administrators of data process and metadata.

You learned that there are many different ethical dilemmas a DBA may face while performing their job function.

In the conservative and liberal ethical responses, we reviewed the pitfalls of data backup and utilization of third-party database solutions. We discussed how to ethically utilize data model knowledge from previous jobs without breaking a non-disclosure agreement or holding back on your current job. You learned how to handle the knowledge you gain from the incredible access you have as a DBA. We discussed how that knowledge could be used and abused, administered and withheld appropriately.

You learned how to ethically handle these circumstances in a responsible manner.

This chapter thoroughly highlighted the ethical pitfalls of database administration, making you aware of what risks to consider when generating reports on data and working with management on financial data reports.

Frequently Asked Questions

The following Frequently Asked Questions, answered by the authors of this book, are designed to get you thinking about the ethical circumstances you may face when performing database administration functions. Unless legal issues are involved, then answers in the FAQ may not be the right answer for your organization.

Q: What is a DBA?

A: A DBA is a member of the IT team who is responsible for one of the following areas of database administration:

1. The Operations DBA performs the day-to-day database maintenance, backups, and operations of a corporations production databases.

2. The Development DBA or Architectural DBA performs database development efforts including architecture, planning, modeling, cataloging, and design of new or existing database systems.

3. The Data Administrator performs data processing at a senior level, which includes managing a company's data and metadata. (Metadata is data that describes other data.)

Q: What kind of ethical dilemmas can a DBA get into when using knowledge they have obtained from a previous job?

A: A DBA can be in breach of non-disclosure agreements or non-compete agreements.

Q: In what ways can a DBA abuse knowledge they gain from data?

A: A DBA can abuse the data under their responsibility by snooping on people for non-security purposes. Another way DBA's abuse their power is to provide information unfairly to different managers or employees.

Q: What are the types of data reports that may be requested of the DBA from the business users?

A: The types of reports that may be requested of a DBA include marketing, sales, financial summary, or any type of compilation of data from the database for employees or senior corporate management.

Q: Is it ever appropriate to change the data in a database for any of the following reasons:

- To clear nulls or white space

- To add data from potential sales for reporting purposes

- To remove a block of data from a marketing report

- To change existing financial data for a board of director's report upon request of a senior officer

A: In some cases, it is part of the DBA's job to clean up dirty data, which includes removing white space or nulls, properly formatting addresses when doing a database conversion, or other such cleanup efforts. It is never appropriate, regardless of who mandates it, to change existing data or delete important financial data.

- To clear nulls or white space – Yes

- To add data from potential sales for reporting purposes – Maybe

- To remove a block of data from a marketing report – No

- To change existing financial data for a board of director's report upon request of a senior officer – No

Chapter 9

Information Service Providers (ISP)

Ethical Dilemmas in this Chapter:

- Internet Service Provider Customer Services

- Computer Viruses, Worms, and Trojan Horses

- Internet Service Providers' Security Practices

- Cable Modem Hacking

- Intellectual Property

- Internet Service Provider Information Sharing

- Domain Hijacking and Name Confusion

Introduction

Everyone accesses the Internet through an Internet Service Provider (ISP), which is a company that has the necessary host computers and telecommunication lines to connect computers to the Web. Big companies serve as full-service ISPs, providing firewalls, filter spamming, e-mail services, and connection to the Internet. They are also in a position to spy on and filter information. As you read this chapter, you should consider your company to be the ISP in many of the issues.

ISPs originally did not want to police customers' e-mails or be responsible for the content on Web sites that they host. Just as the phone company is not liable for a death threat that is carried across its wires, ISPs saw themselves as a neutral service focused on providing bandwidth and uninterrupted service; not concerning itself with what people did with the service. But, unlike the phone company, ISPs store data on computers and have terabytes of data flowing through their wires. Government policy such as the Patriot Act have forced ISPs to start scrutinizing and setting policies based on this new reality.

Most people do not think about their ISP very much; indeed they may not even realize that they have one if they are using a portal such as America Online (AOL), which provides ISP capability and more, all bundled into one service. Other major ISPs have caused their users significant grief in recent years. In late 2003, Comcast raised their connection rates for cable modem users by over 20 percent, simply notifying their customers with a statement in their bill. Qwest suddenly got out of the ISP business in 2002, converting their customers, ready or not, to MSN. MSN support was in no way ready for the many service issues that arose, and people had trouble accessing their accounts.

Despite these episodes, ISPs provide a valuable service and for the most part do it in a conscientious way. This chapter discusses the kinds of optional services ISPs can provide their customers, how they deal with viruses, worms, and hackers, and how they handle protecting intellectual property. This leads into whom they share information with and how. It closes with a discussion of domain name stealing and rights.

Internet Service Provider Customer Services

ISPs can extend their core services in several ways that are normally to your benefit. However, sometimes, you may not want the enhancements they are sending your way.

ISP Ethical Responsibilities

Many ISP's consider themselves to be just a "pipe" for their customers and have no responsibility to provide security for that customer. This pipe can be broken by security issues, and many of these security issues can be addressed by the ISP before the customer is ever affected. For example, detecting, controlling, and preventing denial of service attacks on ISP customers would be a great value-added service. Is it an ethics question to provide these services? I would say it is an ethics question to not provide customers with at least options for these kinds of services. Obviously, the price for the service is not free, but there are many organizations that would pay a "little bit" extra for the added protection.

Security comes in many forms to include the standard BIG 3: Confidentiality, Availability, and Integrity (CIA) and I would add in here Communications. ISP's can help themselves and their customers by focusing on security issues they can control.

- **Confidentiality** This is a tough nut to crack for ISP's. They can do things to protect their internal architecture and assure protections are in place to minimize their systems from being used to intercept and exploiting information passing across the ISP's backbone. This includes preventing and detecting sniffers and protecting the backbone from being hacked.

- **Availability** ISP's can take measures to assure their backbones and connections are secured to help prevent denial of service and other availability issues for the clients. By the ISP recognizing denial of service attack or other attacks on availability, they can keep themselves operational and their customers operational. ISP's cannot force a client to implement security on their end, but they can help to prevent some security issues from reaching the client.

- **Integrity** Similar to Confidentiality, ISP's can take steps to protect their internal infrastructure so the ISP is not a source of problems. They can also offer customers solutions to improve integrity on the customer networks.

- **Communications** ISP's need to communicate with their customers, the security features they do and do not have in place.

Continued

ISP's also should offer value added security recommendations and solutions (whether at a cost or not) so customer's have options. From a communications standpoint, ISP's shouldn't attempt to hide security issues, but address them proactively and when necessary react with drive and conviction to resolve the security issues. ISP's can also be a source for getting the word out on security issues and solutions.

I have seen a trend of ISP's moving toward providing security features, options, and solutions for their clients. I believe this trend is due to some consideration of ethical responsibility and that there is money to be made in providing security solutions to customers.

The moral of this story: ISP's, take the high road, be a provider of recommendations and solutions that will help your customers. It will help build a long-term, trust relationship with your customers.

Greg Miles, Ph.D., CISSP, CISM
Security Horizon

Updates of ISP Software – Should You Download What You Need?

Your company's ISP is offering an updated version of the latest e-mail software, promoting new corporate monitoring capabilities that sound like spyware to you. Not wanting it to be used on you, you download an older but compatible version of the software, without going through your system administrator. Will this ensure they will not use the software to spy on you?

Conservative No. There is no way to ensure that you are not being spied on. You should be vigilant in looking for clues. What are you so afraid of if you are not doing anything wrong and have nothing to hide?

Liberal If you are concerned about it, you should ask your system administrator if they are using the monitoring capability and discuss the implementation of the corporate monitoring policy with them. It is the most direct way to know what is going on.

SUMMARY

E-mail spyware tracks all incoming and outgoing messages, and often also records chats, instant messages, and keystrokes. Through spyware, an employer can discover most transgressions from its employees. Whoever installs the software normally has control over it, and it is invisible to others. If your system administrator re-installs the software later, they will have the ability to spy on you. The latest anti-spy software can quickly determine if your system has spyware on it. It detects and purges spyware, and removes traces of what spyware looks for.

Pop-up Advertising- Should ISP's be Responsible for Blocking Them?

Should ISPs be responsible for filtering-out uninvited "pop-up" ads? To get rid of them you have to click on them to close the window. ISPs can eliminate these little nuisances so you never see them.

Conservative Your ISP is paid to be your brother's keeper partially for situations like this. These kinds of ads are particularly annoying because not only did you not request them, but they require action on your part to make them go away. When you click on the pop-up window to close it, you may mistakenly hit the advertisement itself, which immediately sends you to the advertiser's Web site in a new full-screen browser window.

Liberal Advertising is protected by the First Amendment of the U.S. Constitution. ISPs should not put themselves between you and the companies sending you the information, unsolicited or not.

SUMMARY

Pop-up ads can appear anytime you are connected to the Internet. After their initial debut, pop-up ads became more prevalent until filters arrived to screen them out. AOL had users up in arms about pop-up ads until Version 8, which included a pop-up killer. Pop-ups invoked special ire from AOL customers who were traveling and paying connection fees to dial in from the road, only to have to deal with unsolicited advertising. Pop-up ads are a prime example of an extra service ISPs can provide— putting a filter in place to keep them from getting through to the ISP's customers. ISPs can make this an optional service; AOL created a simple pull-down option for it on their home page. (The AOL filter even filters pop-up ads generated from the AOL Web site.)

Pop-up spammers exploit a feature of the Microsoft Windows operating system known as Messenger Service. Windows Messenger Service is designed to provide users on a company's computer network with messages from the network administrator. For example, an administrator might send a message to all users that the company's network will be shutting down in five minutes, or a printer might send a "job complete" message using the service. If your home computer is connected only to the Internet, you likely do not have any practical uses for Windows Messenger Service. It is a good idea to turn Messenger Service off if you do not use it, because other problems could enter the network through it. Microsoft has since recognized this weakness, and now ships new systems with Messenger Service turned off.

ISP - Updating Your Operating System?

In addition to the pop-up killer they offered, AOL wanted its customers to know the value of turning off Messenger Service. It developed a tool that AOL users could run to turn off the feature entirely, but few bothered and complaints about pop-up messages kept growing. In the fall of 2003, AOL began turning the feature off for its customers who have administrative privileges, by automatically going into their systems and turning Messenger to "Off." AOL did this procedure without telling them.[1] Was this appropriate?

Conservative   It is a very dangerous precedent for an ISP to go into your computer and turn processes and settings on and off. In this case they were making changes to software that comes from another company, Microsoft, which is especially egregious.

Liberal   AOL only did what Microsoft now does on new computers; a strongly recommended practice. If they were to inform their customers they might only confuse them, or at the least distract them with unwanted technological information. Advanced users can always turn the service back on.

SUMMARY

In endeavoring to make matters simple for their users, AOL takes a strong paternal approach to taking care of its customers' computers. Their target audience would not know how or why to disable Messenger Service, and would likely be too intimidated to attempt it. While AOL's intent may seem charitable, the driving factor was to reduce the number of support calls it kept receiving about the unwanted ads. Whatever their motives, they were performing a free service for their customers; an AOL user might respond to a pop-up ad that contained a virus and spread it further. Normally, a customer would find it troubling for an ISP to update their operating system, even for a good reason, without telling them first. However, in the case of AOL, this kind of protection fits entirely within the model of complete service, making the Internet connection a simple matter. This philosophy forms an unwritten customer relationship.

You Cannot be Stephen Northcutt; You Use AOL

I notice my co-authors are bit rough on AOL from time to time in this chapter, so I wanted to issue the counterpoint. I have used AOL for seven years. The parental controls were great when my son Hunter was growing up. AOL has been available in every hotel business center, kiosk, or Internet café in every country I have visited. The interface is fast and I like the feeling of community. If they would only support a text- and folder-based filing system and encrypted communications, I would recommend them without reservation. I try to only use my Stephen@sans.org e-mail address for company business, but from time to time on travel, especially internationally, for one reason or another I cannot get my VPN tunnels established and have to resort to AOL for business. I can't tell you how many times I have gotten a reply back saying, "You can't be Stephen Northcutt, you use AOL!" I am not certain a snobby attitude about which ISP you use is an ethical issue, but it does strain the bounds of politeness.

Stephen Northcutt

ISPs Blocking E-mail – Do You Have a Choice?

AOL recently installed filters to prevent customers from visiting Web sites that are operated by spammers who use these Web sites to harvest e-mail addresses. They also filter their incoming e-mail, sending unknown messages to a junk mail filter. One day in April 2003, AOL reported blocking 2.4 billion spam messages in a 24-hour period. When you block 2.4 billion e-mails, chances are you will lose some valid messages. It has been stated that AOL did not sufficiently explain the ramifications to their customers, who were suddenly missing regular e-mail from entities such as church and school groups. Were the ISPs wrong to implement the filters this way, since most ISPs and mail programs allow the user to maintain a personal blocking list?

Conservative   Anything to get rid of spam is welcome. We e-mail citizens may experience some hiccups along the way as we get our systems operational, but that is to be expected in this complex technology.

Liberal   Your e-mail is becoming more sacred as the means of communication you rely on. The U.S. Post Office would not suddenly decide which newsletters and leaflets should go into your mailbox and throw the rest away, and neither should your e-mail provider.

SUMMARY

While e-mail is growing in importance in our lives, it has not yet taken the status of the U.S. mail. No one is ever surprised to learn of a mysterious e-mail disappearance or non-transmittal. ISPs with a vested interest in their customers using e-mail as their primary communication means, should be careful not to cause major disruptions such as this one. Matters like these also occur when someone changes their e-mail address; there is a loss of contact until the system is corrected. The ISPs were right to take bold action to add spam e-mail filters; however, they should have communicated better to their users how to avoid these problems.

Program Backup from Your ISP – Should They Ask First?

Is it appropriate for an ISP to make data backups if their clients do not request it?

Conservative   No, and for several reasons. Businesses in general should not volunteer services that are not requested, as they can get in over their heads. All services should be documented so that the customer knows what and what not to expect. An ISP should not extend beyond the contracted services, since customers who are sensitive to security and privacy would not want an unauthorized copy of their data floating around.

Liberal This would an easy service for an ISP to provide at low cost so, yes, they should do it. Many people do not perform backups regularly. The ones who do are usually those who suffered a system crash nightmare. For those few customers who have privacy concerns, if there is an emergency some day and they need yesterday's data, they will be extremely grateful that their ISP can come to the rescue.

SUMMARY

This issue typifies the kind of dilemma ISPs face. They have great control and access to their customers' computers and data, which they can use in helpful ways. Customers may be happy that you made a back up of their data, or if they have secrecy/privacy issues, they may be really upset. If the Internal Revenue Service (IRS) comes with a warrant for all of a customer's data, for example, they may not expect that you will be able to furnish it going back one year. Maintaining backups is a good service for an ISP to provide, but they should inform the customer that they are doing so.

Computer Viruses, Worms, and Trojan Horses

It is a complex, ever-changing world out there with various nefarious elements such as viruses out to thwart productivity. ISPs see it both in attacks on themselves and passing through their gates to us. The ISP is our first line of protection and defense against the outside online world.

A worm is a form of virus that self-replicates and resides in active memory. It does not alter files nor is it passed through them; worms can infect other computers without assistance. They do not enter a system through e-mail attachments or an infected floppy disk, but rather through a computer's ports. For example, an intruder can sneak into an open port that is listening to a chat service. Worms duplicate themselves and are usually invisible to the user, who detects them only when their uncontrolled replication consumes system resources, slowing or halting other tasks. One particular form of worm uses a bot or Web robot (or bot) to go to another unsuspecting computer and perform a preprogrammed task. Most bots on the Web are good agents that are sent by search engines to look for Web site content to respond to a search inquiry. But some, such as the following, are up to no good.

Trojan Horse

A Trojan Horse, akin to the one in Homer's story of Troy, is a malicious program that pretends to be a benign application. Trojan Horses are not viruses since they do not replicate, but their programs can be just as destructive. For example, a Trojan Horse may arrive in an e-mail message posing as an update to your antivirus software. Invoking the update would post a normal-looking installation window on your screen while taking other actions not apparent to you, such as deleting files or changing your system settings.

Distributed Denial of Service

Hackers have been known to go after a company's Web site because of a grudge or perceived wrongness in the company's attitude. Take the well-documented case of a series of assaults by a 13-year-old on Gibson Research Corporation (grc.com), all because Steve Gibson reportedly referred to hackers as "script kiddies" in a newsgroup discussion. The kid was insulted and assailed the grc.com server, hosted at their ISP Verio, until the Web server shut down, giving GRC's customers a denial of service. This kind of attack is called a Distributed Denial of Service (DDoS).[2]

To enact a DDoS, the hacker first sends a worm to enter some unsuspecting person's machine through an open port, making the computer the DDoS "master." From this master system the intruder finds and invades other people's computers through the Internet. When computers send files on the Internet, they are broken into packets during the transmission. To launch the attack, the hacker, using a single command, instructs the controlled machines to send streams of packets to the ISP target server. The flood of incoming data forces the Web site's server machine to shut down, thus denying service to its legitimate users. DDoS attacks are difficult to trace because the hacker orchestrates the entire attack using other people's computers. Enough time has usually passed from the invasion to the attack to foil any investigative attempts to trace the worm's origins.

Loss of Revenue Due to ISP Failure – What Does the Service Agreement Say?

You have a small business selling custom fishing lures over the Internet at www.catchyourbass.com, hosted by Topstar. Your Web site goes down for several days during June, your best-selling month, because of DDoS attacks on another Topstar customer's Web site that is hosted on the same server as yours. Topstar puts temporary filters in place to protect the server, and seemingly gets the situation under control. Shortly after the filters are removed, the attacks begin again. Topstar finally moves your Web site to a different server and is investigating the matter, but in the meantime you have lost revenue. Should Topstar be held responsible?

> **Conservative** It is always difficult to claim potential lost revenue unless you have at least a five-year steady sales history. Even if you do, the attacks were not Topstar's fault, and as long as they are making every effort to respond to the situation, they should not be held accountable.
>
> **Liberal** Several days outage is quite long, almost an eternity in this age. You should be able to claim damages from the downtime.

SUMMARY

Read your service agreement to determine Topstar's liability. The agreement should spell out exactly how much outage is permitted and for what reasons. Many ISPs, such as Earthlink, have clauses in their service agreement excluding any liability whatsoever resulting from Denial of Service (DOS) attacks. Others, such as Verio, disallow any responsibility for circumstances beyond their control, including those caused by hackers.

Loss of Service Due to the ISP Coming Under Attack – Should You be Reimbursed?

You have contracted a certain amount of bandwidth from an ISP for an upcoming Webcast. During the Webcast, the ISP receives a major DDoS attack and the streaming Webcast fails. When you mention this to the ISP, they tell you that it is not their fault that they came under attack. Can you hold the ISP accountable and get your money back?

www.syngress.com

Conservative In this situation, you have a clear expenditure for which to seek reimbursement. However, the ISP is also an innocent victim. The hacker is the one who owes you money. You should ask the ISP to help find the culprit.

Liberal The ISP agreed to provide you with a service and did not deliver. It seems you should at least get your money back, and even some compensation for the financial impact to your business from not being able to conduct the Webcast.

SUMMARY

Again, most ISP policies specifically exempt them from any losses due to hacking. However, for goodwill they may pay you back for the cost of the Webcast in a case like this where you clearly have money out of pocket. They may have some insurance policy in effect that would pay for your expenses. But unless your Service Level Agreement states otherwise, you may have to face the reality that you bought so much bandwidth, only to have it used by a hacker.

ISPs' Security Practices

To maintain security, one needs to consider implementing policies and good practice just as much as security-related products. ISPs play a key role in computer security, as their operations rely on making systems accessible over the Internet. ISPs expose various services on different hardware to all sorts of users; users to whom they set connections, grant access, and authenticate and enforce usage rights.

It is not our intention to delve into all of the ins and outs of an ISP's business and security policy, as it is beyond our scope. There is a useful list of such policies on the Microsoft Web site, with specific suggestions as to how ISPs can best serve their Windows customers.[3] Underlying these policies is the fundamental question of how much the ISP should act as your protector without you knowing it. The following issue provides a good example.

Should an ISP Block Microsoft Ports?

A small number of ports commonly used for Microsoft file sharing and related services, are some of the most common ports for worms to enter. Should your ISP block traffic to them to further protect service to your network?

Conservative   Yes; an ISP is inherently in a stronger position to keep current on the best security practices. If these are good ports to cut off, the ISP should feel empowered to block them and not consult with their users about each and every one.

Liberal   Your ISP should not take away any of your freedom without telling you. Maybe you are an advanced user who can make some use of these ports, and blocking them would stifle innovation. Besides, if you cut off these ports, couldn't the hackers just find other ones to use?

SUMMARY

It is impossible to ensure protection against all vulnerability, but there are some significant steps ISPs can take to greatly improve security, and this is one of them. A large percentage of malicious traffic such as worms, uses certain ports, specifically ports 135 through 139 and 445. Blocking these ports will isolate any infected machines and slow the spread of malignant, autonomous code such as the bots used in a DDoS attack. In fact, Microsoft advocates denying all traffic on these ports as a best practice.[4] Microsoft file sharing is used in internal networks, such as when you have two or three PCs networked together in a home office and you want to pass files from one to the other.

Johannes Ullrich of the Sans Institute says these ports should indeed get closed off, and further points out that, "Blocked ports should not give end users a false sense of security. Like a seatbelt in a car, blocking ports should not encourage unsafe computing, just as a seatbelt should not encourage poor driving; instead, blocking ports should be viewed as a preventative measure."[5]

Cable Modem Hacking

Typically, ISPs offer cable modem service at 1.0 to 1.5 Megabits/second (Mbps) when passing data to a computer, and 128 to 256 kilobits/second (kbps) when sending files from a computer to the Internet (known as downstream and upstream speeds, respectively). That might sound like a raceway to a dial-up user, but for some broadband users, it apparently is not enough. Computer hackers have been known to perform hacks that "uncap" their cable modems, a process that breaks the boundaries of bandwidth limit and produces incredible speeds for the hacker—up to 10 Mbps. If you had a 1 Megabyte file you could transfer it in one second. Uncapping modems is popular with individuals that download and trade movie clips; it is also against the law because it violates the service agreement with the hacker's ISP. It is also socially unethical because it takes speed away from their neighbors who have the same ISP. Consider how a hacker's ISP handled the situation in the following legendary Internet story.

Banned From Using Broadband for Life – Too Severe a Punishment?

In April 2002, a 19-year-old computer hacker from Colorado uncapped his cable modem connection because he craved faster speeds to download software from chat rooms. It only took AT&T, his ISP, six hours to uncover the youth's antics and cut off his service. The company was not amused and banned him from using their high-speed service for life. Since the service was in his father's name, he was also directly affected, and could no longer telecommute because the entire household reverted to a dial-up connection. AT&T reportedly handles such matters on a case-by-case basis; perhaps there were aggravating circumstances.[6] From what we know, would you say they were too harsh on the young man?

> **Conservative** No. The hacker was not only stealing from AT&T but also from their other customers. He performed an illegal act and is lucky to have not been prosecuted.

> **Liberal** It seems rash to impose a life sentence on anyone, especially someone under 21 years old, for a first-time offense. After six months of slow dial-up speed, he was undoubtedly reformed and deserved to have his family's service restored. In return, perhaps he would be willing to do a service for AT&T, such as write about his experience to warn others not to do what he did.

SUMMARY

ISPs put capacity limits in their subscriber's modems to keep users from taking more than their fair share of available bandwidth. If a user uncaps their modem and starts hogging bandwidth during peak hours, other ISP customers will experience reduced performance. The culprit here would likely be harming others beyond the impact to AT&T. As to the results of this case, it turns out the severity of the consequences have mitigated through time. In 2002, subscribers typically only had one ISP available—their phone service provider. With new technology developments, customers can buy high-speed Internet service from a variety of ISPs, using a DSL or cable modem connection.

Originally, uncapping required a sophisticated hacker to accomplish, making it a rather obscure phenomenon. In 2002, a hacker called DerEngel posted his creation called OneStep to a Web site, targeted to certain types of modems and making the uncapping process more accessible to non-programmers. When some Ohio residents used the software in the summer of that year, their ISP, Buckeye Cable, soon learned of their actions. Because of the number of free riders, Buckeye claimed enough damages to meet the $250,000 limit for federal investigation. They called in the FBI who raided 17 homes, served warrants, and confiscated equipment (and some pirated movies). Seven of the perpetrators were charged with fifth-degree felonies (punishable by up to one year in prison) and had their lives turned upside down.[7] Some of these culprits do not fit the normal hacker profile; they are writers and small businessmen who wanted to be able to use the Internet faster and found an online tool to do so, without realizing how much trouble they could get into. Most ISPs simply disconnect service when they uncover people tampering with their modems.

Modem manufacturers and ISPs keep improving technology to attempt to outwit the hackers, and thus remove the temptation in the first place.

Intellectual Property

The Digital Millennium Copyright Act (DMCA) of 1998 significantly modified copyright law in the U.S., with the intent of protecting U.S. companies from copyright infringement over the Internet. It adds new teeth to copyright compliance and, in tandem, limits the copyright liability of ISPs and other online services. The DMAC gives ISPs legal protection against being sued due to any of their subscribers infringing on someone's copyright, if the ISPs adhere to certain requirements. In order to sail into the "safe harbor" set out in the DMAC, the ISP must designate a person as its agent for receiving copyright complaints. If a grievance is received, the law lays out the steps that the ISP must follow to retain its legal protection.

Today, ISPs typically post all relevant information in the Policy section of their Web sites to ensure compliance. But the DMCA has been used in ways beyond the typical case of a corporation's copyrighted material, such as software, being pirated and sold as legitimate. Consider the example of the Church of Scientology, which has a longstanding battle with the site www.xenu.net, which is run by a Norwegian man that is critical of the church. Under the DMCA, the church has attempted to bar the site from U.S. audiences, saying www.xenu.net infringes on its copyright. Because www.xenu.net is hosted in Norway, its ISP does not need to heed the DMCA. There are similar issues here in the U.S.

Misuse of DMCA to Hide Flaws – Should the Material be Removed?

Concerned citizens and groups have raised many concerns about electronic voting machines in wake of the 2000 election. Diebold, Inc., a manufacturer of such machines, has been sending out many cease-and-desist letters to ISPs, after internal documents indicating flaws in their systems were published on the Internet. The company has cited copyright violations under the DMCA and has demanded that the documents be taken off the Internet. As an ISP, would you require one of your Web sites to remove the material?

Conservative Yes, because the DMAC clearly states how ISPs must proceed to protect themselves from lawsuit. Telling your Web sites to quit posting information about Diebold without the company's written consent will clear you of responsibility. The Web is full of misinformation and you can do your part to reduce it.

Liberal No. The law is being misused and it is appropriate to challenge it in court. Right or wrong, people have the right to question the manufacturer's capabilities and to post their questions, findings, and beliefs on the Internet. It is a basic freedom of speech. If an ISP believes their subscriber sites are not acting maliciously, it should not be quick to ask them to remove controversial material under the name of copyright infringement, regardless of concerns about the law.

SUMMARY

This is a book about ethics, not law, but sometimes it is hard to tell where one stops and the other starts. Certainly, for the ISP to ignore the DMCA request puts them at risk. From an ethics perspective, the DMCA is being used in ways probably not envisioned by its creators. For new laws to be fully defined, each case must go to court to clearly define their applicability. The DMCA effectively makes the ISP's agent a judge as to decide whether a Web site is out of order when the ISP receives a complaint. The ISP, not having any political or religious convictions, can take the safe road and ask a Web site to remove any offending material that generates a takedown letter. But this business-first approach does not serve the spirit of free press, and may impact the ISPs reputation in the **liberal** press.

DMCA and Universities as ISPs – Are They Still Independent?

As a network provider, a university serves as an ISP with DMCA rights and responsibilities. Imagine you are a network administrator at your state's university, charged with complying with these rules. You come across a student Web site protesting Nike's overseas practices, full of disparaging information and questionable facts, using the Nike logo as part of the graphics. What should you do?

Conservative As an administrator, you are in a unique role to help clear up some of the nonsense on the Internet. Corporations are lambasted for policies that are poorly understood by their critics. Nike is not likely to look kindly upon the site if it finds out about it. You should contact the student and ask them to pull the offending information from the site before someone else does.

Liberal This may fall under "fair use as parody." The student has a right to his opinion, however inflammatory, and the site may serve a useful role to provoke debate on the issue of globalization of trade. In any event, you should leave it intact unless and until ordered otherwise.

SUMMARY

A university serves many constituents, including students doing class-related work, professors doing research, and the broader community with non-profit entities. Again, although the DMCA was created to protect the ISP role, the effect has been to tighten up the university's policies in this area. For example, the University of Texas' Web site explains at some length how it is in an ISP role for its many academics and constituents, and what it must do to comply with the DMCA to avoid copyright infringement.[8]

The academic area is one where many sites are cited and many companies are referred as part of student projects, course work, and professors' research. It is a side consequence of the DMCA that the university network, in its ISP role, needs to review and publish its copyright policy. Universities should be clear about not yielding their rights as independent voices on the Internet.

ISP Information Sharing

Due to the nature of how they work, ISPs have access to considerable information about their customers, including the Web sites they frequent, the e-mails they send, and credit card and other financial records. In the normal course of events, this information is not collected for any individual customer, but resides momentarily on the ISP server as part of their activity.

The ISP's role in sharing information changed greatly when the government passed the Patriot Act in October 2001, and follow-up legislation. The act names ISPs and libraries as institutions that, when subpoenaed, must provide the U.S. government with all of the information they have about their customers. This brought the ISPs into the forefront as keepers, or in this case, potential sharers of information about its customers. The Federal Bureau of Investigation (FBI) can and does install its sleuth program, Carnivore, onto ISP servers to track information about suspected people.

Consequently, ISPs have less resistance than they used to have about disclosing what they once considered proprietary customer information. They have now begun to share customer information in other instances such as the following:

ISPs and Privacy Rights – Is it Confidential?

An ISP promotes that it will not share customer and employee information, but you learn that they have in fact shared that information with partner companies. Users begin to receive e-mail solicitations corresponding to their Internet browsing. How much of an issue is this?

Conservative The government should have all of the resources within its power to investigate suspicious people. It is completely inappropriate for an ISP to use the same information in a commercial sense.

Liberal ISPs should resist sharing their customer information with any external entity.

SUMMARY

ISPs may inappropriately sell or share information with marketers who would love to have a list of e-mail addresses tied to certain browsing behavior. The problem is that such acts are difficult to catch and to prove. Most ISPs treat customer information as confidential and behave ethically in regards to it.

Music Downloading and ISPs – Should They Share the Information?

The subject of customer privacy also comes into play in the ever-hot topic of music downloading. The DMCA allows copyright holders to subpoena ISPs for the names of people they believe are using their copyrighted material without permission. Under the legislation, the Recording Association has asked certain ISP's for the identities of their customers who download music files. A court clerk without a judge's action can issue these subpoenas. Should the ISPs comply with the request?

Conservative The recording industry has had tremendous difficulty trying to catch cyber music thieves. The ISPs should comply with the request and give them the lists.

Liberal The act gives too much power to corporations, in this case the recording industry. If the ISP releases the customer identities, the subpoenas are likely to snare unsuspecting grandparents whose grandchildren have used their personal computers, and innocent university students whose room-mates have shared their computers.

SUMMARY

The DMCA has significantly redefined when an ISP should release cus-tomer information, and the law is still forming in litigation. Several ISPs, including Pacific Bell Internet Services and Verizon, were sufficiently dis-turbed by the new lowering of the bar of customer privacy protection to fight the subpoenas in court, asking that they be declared invalid.

As one ISP spokesperson explained their perspective, "We really believe that anyone who can take the time to fill out a form letter, can get it stamped by the court clerk and get the name of an Internet user…The potential for abuse is very great."

@#&!?!

Do Not Shoot the Messenger!

The MPAA/RIAA's action against Napster for illegal music downloads is an example of the pursuing the right thing for the wrong reason. No one dis-putes that downloading music or movies in violation of their copyright restrictions is illegal. However, the actions against Napster were an example of shooting the messenger instead of the message writer. ISPs are like the phone company and Postal Service and its equivalents. They manage the infrastructure of the network. They shouldn't manage the content of the traffic on the net.

Universities are basically ISPs and shouldn't interfere or monitor the content of network traffic unless there is a compelling reason to do so. It would be extremely difficult to determine if certain traffic was illegal. For example, we discovered traffic on port 12345 and immediately assumed it was a NetBus attack. It was a vendor application that happened to use port 12345 to communicate between its clients and server.

P2P software is not illegal. The content of the messages transmitted is what could be illegal. The only way an ISP can detect transmissions of copyrighted material is to examine all of the packets in the traffic flow. There are other ways to detect this misuse and these methods do not vio-late the privacy of the sender and receiver of the messages.

Continued

> We do not prohibit the use of P2P programs. There are legitimate reasons for using the software. We DO prohibit the transmission of illegal copyrighted materials.
>
> *Randy Marchany*
> *SANS Instructor*

Handling Network Security Information – Should You Ever Release It?

You are the head of a mid-sized ISP, and one of your customer's calls to say her computer was hacked. She has a pretty good idea who did it, and is savvy about how to prove it. She wants all of the information corresponding to a certain IP address to nail the culprit. Should you provide her with the information?

Conservative In no way should you give anyone information from another's computer unless it is to the U.S. government. You do not know what the woman's true motives are; maybe she has a lawsuit brewing against a former business partner, the alleged "hacker."

Liberal The ISP should do everything it can to help its customer. Preferably, you will not need to give her information about another customer, but if that will help solve the crime, you should do so.

SUMMARY

If she was hacked, you as the ISP should be in the forefront of uncovering everything about the event as it happened over your systems. An ISP should not release customer information to others, unless under court order.

Domain Hijacking and Name Confusion

Domain hijacking is the process of stealing a domain name from another entity. It is not common nor easily done, unless you happen to be a hacker. Sometimes an unknown site legitimately has a name that is associated with another, more famous, entity.

To Protect Your Business – Hijack a Domain Name?

You are the head of Brest Golf Carts, a highly reputable business started by your father, Jerry Brest. You do an increasing amount of reselling online for golf cart parts and accessories at www.brestgolfcart.com. Someone has a porn site up at www.brest.com and your customers regularly go there in error. You hate these instances, realizing that people could associate your father's good name with pornography. A friend of yours is talking about something called "domain hijacking" and you feel desperate enough to consider asking him to attempt it. Is this the best alternative you have?

Conservative Domain hijacking involves illegal hacking. There is no way you should pursue it. Even the act of going to a site to learn more about it could get you into trouble. Inform your customers of your Web site name and publicize it well, or change the company name.

Liberal One can sympathize with your problem. Maybe you could find a form of hijacking that would not be too illegal; perhaps you would not have to do any stealing yourself. However, there are legal means that you can pursue and probably should. You need a good intellectual property lawyer.

SUMMARY

Hijacking is illegal and unethical. The rules that control Internet names must be strictly maintained or there would be havoc. Internet names cannot be determined based on personal requests.

If you had a trademark on the name "Brest," you would have the rights to the Web site name due to Clinton-era legislation called the "Anti-cybersquatting Consumer Protection Act." This Act gives clear protection and allows for damages in cases where a domain name holder is acting in bad faith or is out to hijack a trademarked name, especially if the holder is making money on the name. For example, back in 2000, Yahoo successfully argued that names such as ayhoo.com, eeeyahoo.com, and yafoo.com, are too easily confused with yahoo.com.[9] The trademarked companies usually win even in instances where someone else has previously taken the domain name.

Short of having a trademark, you have to wait for the domain name registration to expire and hope to jump on it. Lapses in the registration process occur, for example, when the holder changes e-mail addresses without notifying the domain name service company, during the renewal interim of one to two years.

WhiteHouse.com Example – Should You Even Get Involved?

The Whitehouse.com site, which features a mix of pornography, political satire, and live chat, began in June 1997 as a free speech site. Within three months, they decided to switch to an adult format and became highly successful partly because of their high-profile name. Most popular Internet sites use the suffix .com in their domain names and Whitehouse.com is often the beneficiary when Web surfers search for the White House home page (www.whitehouse.gov).[10] If you were the site's ISP, would you continue their service knowing they are capitalizing on the White House name?

Conservative Misuse of a name, especially a venerated name such as this one, is entirely unethical and despicable. Under-age children can easily stumble across the Web site. It is the kind of mistreatment that brings out rage in the American public. Your business reputation as an ISP is at stake. You should ask whitehouse.com to change format or move elsewhere.

Liberal Since whitehouse.com has the name legally, you do not need to get involved with your customer's business. Since the site is successful, they will undoubtedly keep their account up-to-date. If you do not host them, someone else will.

SUMMARY

The U.S. government has not taken out a trademark for the name "White House" and so the site owner, New Jersey entrepreneur Dan Parisi, is within his legal rights to use the name. On the other hand, Parisi also had the site www.madonna.com, which the singer Madonna successfully took over in a court battle, because she has a trademark on her name.

ISPs have a moral dilemma when their Web site customers act in ways the ISP does not condone. The ISP is in a unique position to give the tricky Web site some direct consequence of its behavior. Sure they can legally do business this way, but you do not have to make it easy for them. If you were to reject the site you could publicize the incident in the computer industry magazines, invoking other ISPs to follow your lead.

Chapter Summary

The ethics of ISPs involve some weighty matters of privacy and evolving law. Hopefully the issues we have shared here have given you some insight as to what these matters entail and how they may affect you. Over the next few years we expect to see ISPs take the responsibility of being the "poor man's firewall" more seriously. Taking $9.99 to $39.00 a month from a customer and doing nothing when that customer comes under attack may be ethical, but it leaves room for a more proactive business model. Leadership is the key. If you know of any ISPs that are doing good work protecting their customers, or that have really effective security awareness programs, drop me a note at Stephen@sans.org and we will try to get their stories out there.

Frequently Asked Questions

The following Frequently Asked Questions, answered by the authors of this book, are designed to get you thinking about the ethical circumstances you may face vis-à-vis your ISP. Unless legal issues are involved, then answers in the FAQ may not be the right answer for your organization.

Q: Who are some of the best ISPs? How can I choose one for service?

A: Industry periodicals provide ratings of ISPs, but they are often just about who is the biggest. Ask your neighbors and friends who they use and how happy they are with the service. It is quite a competitive industry, so you can try one and if you are not happy switch to another.

Q: How do I go about switching ISPs? Isn't it complicated to get hooked up to the Internet through a new ISP?

A: The ISP will take care of everything for you. You should expect some down-time, but no more than a day.

Q: What are the ramifications of changing from one ISP to another?

A: It usually means that you have to change your e-mail address; some customers stay with an ISP just to preserve their e-mail address. People change e-mail addresses all the time; it is probably the one time that it is appropriate to send an e-mail to everyone on your list.

Q: Do some ISPs have stricter policies than others about guarding your privacy? How can you know which one to choose?

A: Again, there are industry articles on the subject, but it is probably best to find out who provides service in your area and talk to them and read their policies.

Q: Does an ISP need to tell you when they have given your information to someone else?

A: If they have sold their subscriber list, they probably will not volunteer the information, but they should tell you when formally asked. In the past, when the U.S. government asked for information, ISPs would notify you. The law is changing in this regard with the follow-up legislation to the Patriot Act. This is a matter of hot debate in Congress and with civil liberty groups.

References

[1] Jesdanun, Anick. "AOL quietly changes Windows settings to combat pop-up spam." Security Focus. October 23 2003. url: www.security-focus.com/news/7278 (January 19, 2004).

[2] Gibson, Steve. "The Strange Tale of Denial of Service Attacks Against GRC.COM." October 6, 2003.

url: www.grc.com/dos/grcdos.htm (January 17, 2004).

[3] Kimber, Lee and the Coho Internet team. "ISP Security Practices List." (January 15, 2003).
url: www.microsoft.com/serviceproviders/columns/isp_security.asp (January 18, 2004).

[4] www.microsoft.com/serviceproviders/columns/isp_security.asp

[5] Ullrich, Johannes. "Internet Service Providers: The Little Man's Firewall?" 2003. SANS Institute Reading Room. url: www.sans.org/rr/special/isp_blocking.pdf (January 17, 2004).

[6] Poulsen, Kevin. "Cable Modem Hacking Goes Mainstream." SecurityFocus. May 8, 2002.

url: online.securityfocus.com/news/394 (January 16, 2004).

[7] Bode, Karl. "Nailed to the Wall. Ohio uncappers face legal nightmare." Broadband Reports.com. November 21,2002. url: www.broadbandreports.com/shownews/23727 (January 16, 2004).

[8] www.utsystem.edu/ogc/intellectualproperty/dmcaisp.htm

[9] Flynn, Laurie J. "Whose name is it anyway? Arbitration panels favoring trademark holders in disputes over Web names." New York Times. September 4, 2000. Page C.3.

[10] Cooper, Charles. "Whitehouse.com cries foul on America Online." ZDNet News. September 17, 1998.

url: http://zdnet.com.com/2100-11_2-511995.html (January 19, 2004).

Chapter 10

Brother's Keeper

Ethical Dilemmas in this Chapter:

- Coworkers' Inappropriate Habits
- Job Performance of Others
- Concerning Others' Compensation
- Business Ethics of Others

Introduction

"Am I my brother's keeper?" is one of the oldest and most famous questions of all time. We can surmise an appropriate reply as "No, you do not need to know where he is at all times, but you should be aware of how he is doing to ensure no harm comes to him." We naturally apply this logic to our lives and all those around us; certainly no one should ever cause another person harm.

With this philosophy in mind, this chapter explores the issues you may face in the workplace as you observe the actions of your coworkers. When is it right to intervene over concern of what someone else is doing? We cover some of the typical issues of this nature, and also some different cases you may not have ever considered.

Coworkers' Inappropriate Habits

In a work environment you have a chance to see people in all kinds of circumstances. Others around you may not be as careful as they should be with company rules, policies, and procedures. They waste other people's time and risk company security without thinking about it. Should you ignore it? They may do things at work that are not necessarily right, but are they wrong? Even if they are wrong, are you the right person to do something about it? We want to be treated like professionals, but we are not always willing to act like professionals. Information Technology (IT) jobs are being outsourced at an unprecedented rate. Perhaps we should take a close look at ourselves and ask if our collective behavior is part of the reason.

Sleeping During Meetings – What if You Catch Someone?

At a team meeting your manager, Sheila, is giving a rather lengthy update about the company's safety policy. You realize Dan, one of your teammates across the table, has fallen asleep and a long line of drool has formed from his mouth down to the table. Sheila cannot easily see Dan from where she is sitting. Should you attempt to wake him up?

> **Conservative** No, you should not interfere. You may make things worse by bringing attention to him. Even if you could wake him without notice, it is not your job to get involved.

Liberal Yes, if you can do so discretely and it is a one-time occurrence; you could save him some embarrassment. If Dan is known for sleeping at meetings it would be better not to intervene at any given time, but let him know when you are alone with him that his sleeping at meetings is noticeable.

SUMMARY

This is a judgment call for you to make, depending on how well you know Dan. His napping is harming no one but himself. It is not your place to correct his behavior unless you are good friends and regularly look out for each other. Maybe Sheila will realize that her content is not rousing if she sees him dozing. Better to let the situation unfold without getting involved.

Internet Hoaxes – Your Coworkers Gullibility

A technical writer in your group repeatedly sends the team e-mail warnings of issues she has seen on the Internet, virus threats, and so on. Most if not all of them turn out to be hoaxes. Recently, she passed on an alert that the signal from your cell phone could cause a spark and fire if used while you are pumping gasoline. You respond to the e-mail to let her know she sounded a false alarm, but she took no notice and now she is at it again, this time with a dire warning about Acquired Immune Deficiency Syndrome (AIDS) being spread through the use of public toilets. What should you do?

Conservative Go to the woman's manager and to let them know the impact the writer is having on your work. The manager should put a stop to this time waster.

Liberal Take some time with the writer to explain about Internet hoaxes and show her how to get educated about what is real before sending out such futile warnings.

SUMMARY

Delete the writer's e-mails without opening them, if they are not work related. You did what you could to try to stop her. She undoubtedly believes what she is sharing is valuable to some in the group, and whatever you say will fall on deaf ears. Her own behavior will catch up with her, as others will get tired of the continual stream of junk information. You do not need to try to solve this problem.

Blast from the Past – When Material is Not Properly Deleted

One day while working on a coworker's computer you discover the source code from a small software outfit that your company evaluated last year. As part of the process, your coworker should have removed the source code as mutually agreed by the companies. What should you do?

Conservative Report your discovery to management and let them decide what to do. They know the terms of the original agreement and the likelihood of the errant code causing problems.

Liberal Tell your coworker of your discovery and ask them to immediately delete the source code. As long as they do so quietly and quickly, probably not much went wrong from it having been on their computer all this time.

SUMMARY

Companies take the security of their source code quite seriously; your coworker has shown little respect for it. The fact the source code has been left so long means it is now in all the system backups and deleting it from their computer is not sufficient to purge it. Though no harm will likely come from your coworker's neglect, you cannot decide this for sure by yourself. You need to report the incident to management and inform your coworker that you are doing so, so he will not be blindsided by what happens.

Disclosing Information – What if Your Coworker Shares too Much?

In a meeting with representatives from an outside partner, one of your coworkers divulges what your company plans to include in its next software release without having them sign a Non-Disclosure Agreement (NDA). You learn about the occurrence after the fact when he is telling you about the meeting in casual conversation, even bragging a little about how well it went. When you voice concern about what he revealed, he says he believes the partner people will not do anything wrong with the information, and it would be embarrassing to chase them down now with an NDA. What should you do?

Conservative You need to immediately let management know what has happened. They will want to contact the partner directly to put an NDA in place. There is usually little downside to an NDA, although the partner may balk at signing one after the fact. Your manager is the best one to handle the ramifications of your coworker's neglect.

Liberal Your coworker needs to learn how to properly use NDAs. Help him draw one up for this meeting, retroactively, and send it to the partner yourself if he will not. Work with him to make sure he is prepared for such meetings in the future.

SUMMARY

You need management to help you do everything possible to rectify the situation. Otherwise, the partner would feel they could share it with others in the industry. People like to have product secrets to share, especially if they are someone else's. It makes them valuable to industry pundits and makes them feel more powerful. Your coworker is not ready to conduct meetings with people from outside companies. By blowing the whistle on this one, you will raise his attention that he needs to be more professional in business meetings.

Lowered Awareness – When Your Coworkers are Potentially Lax about Security

You work in a secure building. One of your coworkers, Paul, has been known to lend his keys out to his carpool mate, Sarah, from an office building across the way who sometimes borrows Paul's car during lunch. She then uses the keys to enter the building and return them to Paul's desk. What should you do?

Conservative Report what has been happening to management. It is clear that Paul does not understand the importance of and process of keeping the building secure.

Liberal Suggest to Paul that he should make another arrangement for lending his car to Sarah so that he is not giving her his key to the building. If the loose activity stops now, no real harm will be done and no one will need to be the wiser.

SUMMARY

Keeping a building secure is the responsibility of all who work there. Therefore, you are responsible for reporting what you see. If you wish to inform Paul first so he will not be blindsided by your actions, fine. It takes the eyes and ears of all to note a security gap like this one. A security breach often starts with something innocent that gets exploited by those who know to watch for it. You cannot estimate the possible losses caused by Paul's activities, and need to sound an alarm. While telling Paul to stop giving out his key may work for now, it does not address the need for him to change his way of thinking about a secure building.

Questionable Internet Viewing – What do You do About Offensive Material?

While walking by a coworker's cubicle, you see that he is looking at sexually explicit photos on the Internet. He takes no notice of you as he browses from site to site. What should you do? You know this is inappropriate behavior, you know that it could lead to a reprimand or termination, and most importantly you know that many people would be offended by this should they see it. If such behavior is unchecked, it could represent a pervasive atmosphere of sexual harassment leading to a lawsuit that could seriously damage your employer and endanger your job. What should you do?

Conservative You should quietly leave and report the incident to your manager. Pornography, including soft porn, has no business in the workplace. If it happens again, you should report the incident to an even higher level of management.

Liberal Make your presence known, thereby letting your coworker know how easily his behavior is observed by others. He should then stop on his own without you needing to take further action.

SUMMARY

This issue is much more serious than someone napping in a meeting. But while looking at pornographic sites is against most companies' policies, your coworker is not doing any actual harm to anyone. Let him be and form your own judgment as to his character. Presumably the system administrator's will discover his actions soon enough. If you were the one to turn him in it would ruin your ability to constructively work together in the future. If you signal to him that you are watching, he is likely to continue his behavior, but in a more circumspect manner, and resent you for your knowledge. The system administrator's are charged to police this kind of inappropriate surfing and are quite good at knowing how to handle it.

@#&!?!

The All Night Audit

I was working on a long security audit of our offices in one of the largest cities in America. The equally long report was mostly completed, and I was bleary-eyed at 5:45am after an all-nighter, reading the last of the 15-45MB event logs that I insist on pulling off of servers being audited. I was racing to finish the report to turn it in by the time my boss sat at his desk that morning. At 5:48 a.m., I sat bolt upright, wide awake. It wasn't the sunrise or the caffeine kicking in...it was the log entries!

Buried in that Windows Server System Log with document and image print entries to the printer, I saw:

```
SYS  3/15/2001   0:51:53 Print  10   Information  None  IMAGING
Document 112 http://www.smutfantasies.com/join.html owned by IMAGE
was printed on HP LaserJet 4 via port LPT1:. Size in bytes: 404822;
pages printed: 0


SYS  3/15/2001   0:53:34 Print  10   Information  None  IMAGING
Document 113 http://www.freshmenteens.com/pt=pmb2148/tour2.htm owned
```

Continued

```
by IMAGE was printed on HP LaserJet 4 via port LPT1:. Size in bytes:
537786; pages printed: 0

SYS  4/2/2001  18:57:43  Print  10  Information  None  IMAGING
Document 130 http://www.girlswithguys.com/videos/ owned by IMAGE was
printed on HP LaserJet 4 via port LPT1:. Size in bytes: 531265;
pages printed: 0

     SYS  4/2/2001  19:01:31  Print  10  Information  None
IMAGING  Document 137 http://www.livenudesex.net/mastergate/ owned
by IMAGE was printed on HP LaserJet 4 via port LPT1:. Size in bytes:
277656; pages printed: 0
```

...And many more, and much worse.

The pattern showed use after work, into the night, and even coming in on weekends. This was the manager for the contractors' group in the office, and a friend of the local president.

Was it wrong since it wasn't detracting from working hours? After all, they did work hard and the output was good.

Would looking at such sites (some show no pages printed) alone be an offense or violation of the contract?

Whose computer was it anyway?

Oh, and this was printed via the print queue on

1) a domain controller that the contractors had 2) full access rights to, ...and 3) from a generic account that all in the group used.

The logs actually showed 1? years of this activity, becoming bolder over time. No administrator had ever reviewed the contractor's server logs, even though it was a full domain controller.

With key ties to the local management, the manager had become confident that not only was he not going to be caught, but he could continue indefinitely without being reported by his underlings, or face retribution from local management if found out. He was wrong on all counts. When the National Audit Office and Security Management Team I worked for reported it to regional management's attention, he lost his job and embarrassed the local management.

Computer and company property use and abuse must be defined and guidelines promulgated in company policies and employee handbooks. Ethics training clearly lets the entire staff know what is expected, and what is forbidden. Fair and consistent enforcement is also needed.

Ima Nauditor
Fortune 1000 company

Job Performance of Others

It is unavoidable that you will be affected by other people's job performances at work. They surround you, they infringe on you, their poor performance can reflect on your performance. Although these specific situations might not apply to you, at some point you will have a coworker that is not doing their job the way you think they should. How you handle these issues shows the kind of character you have.

Skipping Standard Operation Procedure – When Your Coworker Does It

You are a member of a group of software testers for an application-specific database management product. One of your fellow testers, "Amy," routinely skips through portions of the test believing that the test plan is a waste of time. She says she knows what the tricky parts of the program are and can more constructively go right to them.

> **Conservative** You should let the test leader know of Amy's habits, because she is endangering the results of the entire test suite. You will likely make your future work life with Amy uncomfortable, but if you do not inform the lead tester, your own sense of completeness and pride in your work will be tarnished.

> **Liberal** Since Amy seems unwilling to change her practice, it is doubtful you will get anywhere in talking to her further. If you report her, you will alienate her. Continue to do your work according to the test plan, and respond honestly to any questions about how the tests were run.

SUMMARY

You must inform the others of Amy's way of working, since what she is doing directly affects the work you are doing. You are part of the team responsible for product testing. Tell your manager. You can inform Amy ahead of time that you feel compelled to take the matter to management, but do not expect her to change her ways. Even if she were to change, you still need to inform the test lead because the testing that has gone on so far is affected. If the lead tester wants to let it go, that is their decision. If Amy is right that there is a problem with the test plan, the plan should be changed for all.

Reporting Errors – What About When it's Only Your First Day?

You were just hired at a new job and discover that the code of one of the programmers is wrong and producing the wrong results in the production system. Do you report this to your team leader, or just mind your own business?

> **Conservative** Whenever you see someone doing work wrong you should report it. Following this philosophy makes it easier for you to proceed and not take into account personalities or make excuses for whatever shortcomings you find in their work.

> **Liberal** Being new on the job, the last thing you want is to become labeled as a stoolie for management. Your first priority should be to be a team player. Talk to the programmer in question and offer to help fix their code. Hopefully you can resolve the problem without needing to report it to others.

SUMMARY

Since this error has gone to the production system, you need to report it to the team leader to resolve it as quickly as possible. Harm is being done to your company's reputation and business, and you have an opportunity to do your part to correct matters. Your fellow employees will see the merits of your actions if they have the right interests at heart.

Warnings Unheard – When you Raise an Issue that is Ignored

You work as a software auditor for a defense firm that is under contract to meet a Department of Defense (DOD) standard. You review the software specification documents for the latest missile guidance program, find numerous deficiencies, and write a report about them. When you deliver it to the Program Manager, he acknowledges receiving the report and then throws it in the shredder bin. Unnerved, you return to your desk and read the DOD standard and learn that his only obligation is to receive the report, not do anything with it. You have put considerable time into preparing this report and believe that following its recommendations would significantly improve the software's quality. Should you confront the Program Manager and request he read the report, take the issue to management, or do nothing?

Conservative You should do nothing. You have fulfilled your responsibility and cannot invoke another to do so.

Liberal It probably will not do any good, but confront the Program Manager. You can take the issue to management to at least have the satisfaction of having said something, but do not expect much to happen.

SUMMARY

When companies and individuals work in a contract arrangement there is a common tendency to work to "contractual minimalism." This means doing the absolute minimum the contract specifies, not a shred more, and is especially pervasive in those under government contract. Instead of considering what the intent of the contract is and trying to fulfill it, people look at the letter of specification. You may justifiably think less of such people, but they are within their rights to act this way, even in cases of outrageous behavior such as this one. You have learned something of this individual's ethics to remember for the future, but other than that, you should do nothing.

Concerning Others' Compensation

No matter how much we like our jobs and work for professional fulfillment, the base of the whole experience is what we are paid for doing it. Nothing gets people more upset than the idea of being unfairly paid in relation to their coworkers. In general, for large organizations the best approach is to establish pay and performance bands and treat everyone equally. However, sometimes for one reason or another, two employees of fairly equal rank and ability may be compensated at different levels. Perhaps one employee was hired away from another job and a certain salary level was needed to bring them on board. Or possibly, an employee may have been hired during heady economic times such as the dot.com bubble. Whatever the reason, this can certainly lead to a number of fascinating ethical situations.

Salary Discrepancy– Why is Someone Else Being Paid More?

While dropping off a memo on a coworker's desk, you notice his briefcase open and a recent pay stub sitting in it. Although he is five years your junior and does comparable work, you see he is making $500 more per month than you are. You wonder if you make less because you are a woman or because maybe he has been more demanding of a higher salary. What should you do?

Conservative   You should do nothing other than try harder to improve your own performance. You should not have looked at your coworker's salary in the first place. You do not know how management views your relative contribution. Maybe they think his work is more valued for a reason you do not know. Forget what you have seen.

Liberal   You could raise the question of your pay with your manager, saying you are concerned about being paid fairly without explicitly saying what you have learned. You could also pursue this with Human Resources and find out what the typical pay structures are for men and women in your company, and what, if any, work has been done to make sure they are equal.

SUMMARY

This is the classic ethical issue that happens in work groups. All is going along fine on the team until someone finds out how much the others are making. Once this happens, it is hard to go back to the way things were. In this situation you cannot let it be known that you have learned of your coworker's pay, as you had no business snooping in his cubicle. It is okay to ask what Human Resources knows about male versus female pay, although pursuing this may leave you frustrated. If men and women are being paid fairly at your company, this matter is not about your gender. If not, it is a huge commitment to try to change things—one that you cannot do alone. In this situation you would be hampered in your fight by your inability to say that you know your coworker makes more money than you do.

Your best bet is to drop the matter and figure that in the next few raises things will even out. If indeed he is being paid more than you for comparable work, you will come to be valued more and given more opportunities, while he will come under increasing pressure to perform. Good work speaks for itself.

Payment for Duty – What if They're Not Doing Their Job?

One of your coworkers, "Marshall," tells you he is having trouble with motivation at work and is not performing up to par. While previously he had been a strong contributor and you believe he is highly paid, he says he now finds the work boring and is having trouble focusing. Your team makes a joint effort on the project, and it is not apparent how much any one individual is contributing. Marshall confides in you, "Really, I have not been producing much at all. They ought to fire me." What should you do?

Conservative Alert management that all team members are not pulling their weight, and leave it to them to sort out who is doing what.

Liberal Suggest to Marshall that he look for work elsewhere that would engage him. It is often hard for a non-motivated person to engage in a job-search, but that is likely the best solution for him.

SUMMARY

When something is shared in confidence you should respect that fact and not tell anyone else about it. In your conversations with Marshall, you could pressure him to take some kind of action to move out of his rut for the benefit of all. Otherwise, before long, management is bound to notice his lack of performance. Forget wondering about how much he is being paid for what he is doing. In this day and age, his laggard performance will catch up with him very soon.

Business Ethics of Others

This section considers cases where an employee is clearly violating your company's Standards of Business Conduct. There is no doubt that what is happening is unethical by any standard. The simple, or perhaps not so simple question is, what is your personal responsibility? How and when do you intercede in such situations? This is a tough problem; despite some whistleblower protections, many people that have stood up for what is right have paid a high cost.

www.syngress.com

Personal and Professional Business– When it isn't Separated

You work as a financial analyst for a line of inkjet printers in a major computer company. The Senior Vice President of Marketing, Stephan North, has heavily promoted the acquisition of GIAC Printers, a small inkjet printer company. As you look at the company's business, buying GIAC Printers makes no sense to you as it adds no value to what you already provide. In your evaluation process you discover that the Chief Executive Officer of GIAC Printers is an old college friend of Stephan's. In company meetings, a few mid-level managers challenge the strategic value of acquiring GIAC Printers. Stephan defends the idea strongly without revealing that he has what you believe to be a personal stake. What should you do?

Conservative Share the information with your manager so that they can decide how to confront Stephan. The organization risks financial harm from Stephan's actions; you should make all efforts to prevent this from occurring.

Liberal Show Stephan the information you have about his relationship to GIAC Printers and make him realize that it should be made known to the organization. This way he can save face and will think better of you than if you went around his back to reveal what you know.

SUMMARY

In many companies, finance is responsible for the moral compass of the organization. You need to take a strong stance and make sure the information you have reaches the Financial Controller, if not the General Manager. Your company stands to lose a lot of money if it proceeds with a dubious acquisition or merger.

@#&!?!

Openly Wireless

Wireless networks certainly create interesting ethical situations. A client of mine is a network cabling guy who was really proud that he could get into the wireless network of an attorney in town. Do I call up the attorney and inform them of their "openness"?

What about my neighbors? Do I say hello to new neighbors by saying "Hi, you don't know me, but you really need to do something about your WEP"?

Susan Bradley

Overheard Conversations – What Should You Report?

You work in an office with cubicles and while it is possible to hear what is happening on the other side, people generally tune out each other's conversations. For the last six months you have been across the wall from a coworker named Sam whom you do not know very well. Sam speaks in hushed tones during phone calls, which has naturally aroused your curiosity. You start to deliberately eavesdrop on his conversations and within a day or two it is obvious that he is running a side business selling real estate in Hawaii from work, using the company's phone. Do you say anything?

Conservative Yes, absolutely. Go to your manager with what you know. This is a form of abuse of the company that should be stopped before it goes on too long and others become aware of it.

Liberal Let Sam know you have heard what he is doing so he will stop making the phone calls at the office. If it stops soon it will not cause much damage.

SUMMARY

Running a side business from work is a serious breach of most company's Code of Business Conduct. It is in your best interest and the company's to make Sam's actions known to whoever is necessary to stop it. Telling your manager should suffice.

Whose Job is it Anyway?

This chapter deals with the issue of being 'Brother's Keeper'. There are many situations where you may find that you have to make decisions on the proper ethical path to take. One possibility that is always available is the 'do nothing' approach. While this in itself may be considered unethical at times; it's not always a good idea to step into a situation where you're not otherwise involved.

When you aren't involved in a conversation or situation that some of your coworkers are having that may be unethical, a very tempting solution is to eavesdrop or involve yourself just enough to get the information necessary to report the situation to someone else. However, if you do participate in that fashion and then don't report the behavior for any reason, you are just as liable as the original participants. Sometimes the best approach is to just leave well enough alone and let someone else deal with it.

Jeremy Faircloth
Systems Engineer and Author

Deliberate Misconduct – Should You Blow the Whistle?

Marcia was given responsibility for the physical security of company gear, including some high-end camera equipment. As her coworker, you realize she abused this privilege for personal use by taking the equipment home when not authorized. Not wanting to get her in trouble, you do not report the incident. However, a month later you begin to see a pattern of personal use of more types of equipment. Do you now report the series of mistreatment?

Conservative Yes, it is past time for you to blow the whistle on Marcia's behavior. She has apparently started to think of the equipment as her own, negating her position of responsibility.

Liberal Tell Marcia what you have observed and let her know that if she does not stop you will report her to management

SUMMARY

This is a case of more than misuse of company resources; Marcia is also abusing her position of responsibility. If others become aware of her actions, they might start to think of such positions as lax. If Marcia wants to use the equipment for personal use she needs to get authorization. Since she has been making a habit of misuse, it is unlikely she will stop after a simple conversation with you. By bringing in management, you will let her know the seriousness of the situation.

Disgruntled Employees – What if You Think There is a Reason to Worry?

You work with a coworker who routinely complains and makes idle threats. Recently passed over for a long-awaited promotion, the disgruntled employee threatens to sabotage the encrypted company files and databases. You were the only one to hear his threat. What should you do?

Conservative Immediately take this issue to your manager. A saboteur could cause a lot of damage to the companies' records and business. If your manager is unavailable or unresponsive, take the matter higher.

Liberal Talk to your coworker to see if you can get him to calm down about the situation. Make him realize that sabotage will hurt all of you, and he would likely be caught. If he still seems bent on destructive action, let your manager know your concerns.

SUMMARY

This is a clear situation where harm will come if your fellow employee takes action. You cannot risk taking time to contemplate the matter or try to act as a counselor yourself. You need to immediately inform upper management of what you have heard, through your manager or directly.

Chapter Summary

With the variety of quandaries our coworkers throw our way, it is difficult to come up with one guiding principle of how you should respond. Start by asking what harm is being done by the action, either to yourself, a fellow employee, or to the company. The greater the danger of harm, the higher in management you should report to. Also ask yourself if you are in as good a position as any other to report the problem. In some cases, there are people charged with this kind of oversight and it is better to let them do their job. You do not want to stir the waters with a coworker if it is not necessary. You are usually on safe moral ground if you take a hard and unpopular stance and inform management of what is happening.

Frequently Asked Questions

The following Frequently Asked Questions, answered by the authors of this book, are designed to get you thinking about the ethical circumstances you may face in relation to your Internet Service Provider (ISP). Unless legal issues are involved, then answers in the FAQ may not be the right answer for your organization.

Q: If you observe a coworker or manager doing something against your organization's policy and report it, you are protected by whistleblower legislation, true?

A: It depends. There are regulations. For safety there is The Occupational Safety & Health Act of 1970, in the federal government there are a number of regulations, and California state employees are protected by California Labor Code Section 1102.5. However, if it is merely a violation of your organization's policy instead of a violation of a law or statute, there may be no protections at all.

Q: Isn't it every employee's duty to report Internet porn in the workplace since this is degrading to women and can lead to additional problems?

A: Internet pornography is a massive problem; the majority of porn surfing happens during work hours. Reporting porn, while potentially somewhat valuable, is clearly a losing game. The better approach would be to make it very hard to access. Most commercial firewalls have a subscription service and there are tools like Websense and Surf Control. One thing is certain, though, it is the ethically challenged senior manager that knowingly allows porn surfing to become an employee perk.

Q: If I do turn in a coworker, what are the chances of this leading to violent reprisals?

A: Statistically very low. Less than 10 percent of employees are concerned about violence in the workplace. However, studies of the so called "angry white man syndrome" show that if you are worried, you may well have good reason to be. In workplace killings, workers often were able to guess the name of the killer and often stated there were indications and warnings that employee might snap.

Q: If a coworker is angry at the organization all the time and mentions being passed over for promotion, should this be reported?

A: Employees that feel they have been robbed of something they were entitled to have been known to act in a very unethical manner. Feelings of entitlement are one of the common personality traits of most individuals convicted of espionage in the United States. However, realistically, most Human Resources departments would not take action simply because an employee is angry. Unless you have specific behaviors to support the observation that the employee is angry, the odds are very low anyone would listen to you.

Chapter 11

End-user and Employee Computer Security

Ethical Dilemmas in this Chapter:

- Work/Life Boundaries
- Distractions within the Computing Environment
- Viruses
- Physical Security
- Money Matters
- Helping Your Fellow Employees
- Dealing with Management
- Roles within the Company
- Procurement
- Offensive Issues

Introduction

This chapter explores some typical issues that may occur while you are using your computer at work or at home. It is based on real life stories and situations that you are either already familiar with or will be at some point on your journey as an end user.

Company policy is an overriding factor in determining how you should act at work. Some policies are vague or silent in areas such as whether or not you can serve on the board of directors of another company. Additionally, a particular group may also have unwritten policies that go beyond the company policies. Then there are company rules that are difficult to adhere to so they are often ignored, such as policies against receiving gifts from anyone outside the company. If you do business in Asian countries such as Taiwan, Japan, and Singapore, you would cause offense if you refused a gift from a business relation who gives presents as signs of appreciation. Some companies allow their employees to accept such gifts, but it must be returned if it is of value. You must determine what is valuable—a decorative fan would probably be okay to keep, but not a miniature CD player.

This chapter opens with a discussion of the work/life balance and the resulting quandaries. It proceeds into matters that appear in the computing environment, touches briefly on pay and other money-related issues, and then goes into the endless ethical quandaries that arise in dealing with one's manager. We explore typical issues for several specific end-user roles. Though they may not all pertain to your job, they give insight into the kinds of ethical issues your fellow workers encounter. We close with an example of an "offensive issue," something that you normally would not consider doing. The feeling of being wronged sometimes drives people to behavior they would normally regard as distinctly unethical. Hopefully, you will not find yourself doing the same.

The individuals of each company are where "the rubber meets the road" on ethical issues. Unlike areas where policy guides one through, in the episodes portrayed here the individuals had to face the situation unprepared, with only their good sense to guide them. Over time, people form their own strong sense of ethics in the workplace, allowing them to chart a clear course through any potentially scandalous circumstance they may encounter.

Work/Life Boundaries

Working people must know where to draw the line between work and home life. The answer varies by individual and by company culture. High tech companies broke ground when they allowed people the freedom to work on their own schedule and dress in a very casual manner. Internet start-ups took culture to a new level, with employees with pierced tongues listening to rap music as they design Web sites. Many of today's companies realize that they get much more productivity from their employees when they work from blurred work/life boundaries. Some people who work all hours of the day and night consider the office a second home. A few years back on the road leading to one of the Microsoft campuses in the Seattle area, there was a sign reading, "Work from home. Good pay, flexible hours, call 800-xxx-xxxx." Then a few telephone poles later a sign read "Live at work. Next right."

Telecommuters have work/life balance questions inherent in everything they do. For the most part, people who work in these flexible environments end up giving much more to the company than they receive. As one developer put it, "The company has no qualms about taking over my personal life," so he feels entitled to use some company resources in return. The following issues give you an idea as to what is normally acceptable.

Work E-mail Address – What if it is Your Personal One as Well?

You use your business e-mail address only; you do not have a separate one for personal use, which is within company policy. Personal mail comes in, including letters from your sister, recipes, and basketball notices. Is this okay?

> **Conservative** Even though it is acceptable to receive personal e-mail according to company policy, you should be cautious about exposing your privacy and the privacy of the people who write to you.

> **Liberal** If you feel trusting toward your employer and have nothing to hide in your e-mail, this should work out fine. Many people do it. Having one e-mail address makes it simpler for you and your contacts to maintain.

SUMMARY

This is a prime indicator of how intermingled you are with your company. People with one e-mail address have fluid work/life boundaries in many regards. They check their e-mail at home and respond to messages coming in from overseas after hours. At work they jot a quick message to a friend confirming they can come for dinner this weekend. This works fine if you and your contacts do not mind the fact that a silent reader could be monitoring everything you write.

Company Resources – Using Them for Personal Use

You work at a software company in the media business and have available to you all that technology has to offer. You are responsible for a class project for your daughter's school's auction. The class decided to build a doghouse that is larger than life, and indeed, on the Saturday morning of the auction you learn it will not fit into the banquet hall holding the event. You rush to work and put together a multimedia presentation about the doghouse, including a 3′ × 6′ mounted color poster, blown up from a scanned photograph the teacher took of the kids making it, with verbiage describing the whole process. The crowd loved the result. As a matter of fact, your poster was a bigger hit than the doghouse itself. Were your actions acceptable?

Conservative No. You have gone overboard using company resources for personal use. You have used expensive inks and papers plus energy, without even knowing the costs.

Liberal Since you are doing this project on your own time and for a one-time event, it should be okay as long as it is not against company policy. Plus, by doing projects like this you are keeping yourself current on how to use the latest tools in real-life situations

SUMMARY

Whether this is permissible depends on the company. While there are hidden costs to using company resources, there are also hidden benefits. You were able to promote your company resources in a way most advertisers would love, making sure everyone attending the event knew of your company's contribution.

Company Materials – What if Others Use Them for Personal Business?

While searching for your document on the remote printer, you look at other employee's output and come across a letter not pertaining to company business. Should you take this issue to your manager or ignore it?

Conservative You could talk to your manager to make sure that there is nothing improper happening. They can make the decision whether or not to intervene.

Liberal You should not mention the letter to anyone else. It is not your problem and you do not know the background or justification for what you saw. You should have identified your printed sheets without reading the contents of others.

SUMMARY

Having a shared network printer is an unfortunate necessity. Most companies cannot afford to provide everyone with their own high-performance printer, but for confidentiality reasons that is exactly what is needed. People print many legitimate documents not suited for the eyes of others. In this situation there could be a valid reason for the letter in question. If something shady is going on, it will come out in other ways. The best ethical practice is to keep your eyes open for what you are looking for at the printer, and keep your curiosity under control.

Distractions within the Computing Environment

Computers present a thousand ways to distract us from the important things we are supposed to be doing. The most focused employees manage to stay on task, while others are easily persuaded to spend time "searching" the Web.

Use of the Company Internet Access – What are Your Boundaries?

America Online (AOL) is your company's Internet Service Provider (ISP). When you log on, you are greeted with a link to the latest Sports Illustrated pictorial highlighting the annual swimsuit issue. Is it okay to click on this link?

Conservative   No. The content is non-work related. Besides, you would be showing poor taste and it may offend your female coworkers.

Liberal   Since your company has chosen AOL and has not blocked its ads, you are within reasonable bounds to peruse them as long as you are not taking more than several minutes to do so. It could provide a pleasant quick break from work without leaving your desk.

SUMMARY

Following this link seems like a dubious idea, one where the possibility of the downside outweighs the benefits. How far you would be out of line depends greatly on your corporate culture, but even in a lax environment some would find this objectionable. If you are interested in viewing the site, better to write down the link and visit it from home.

Pop-up Ads – What Happens when They are Out of Control?

You are researching a work issue on the Internet and cannot resist responding to a splash screen advertisement for a new diet with a photo of a woman in a bikini. You get into a slippery slope problem where they have related links and pop-up advertisements about dieting, recipes, and the latest slimming fashions. Some of it is rather interesting, but you are feeling a bit overwhelmed and out of control and the pop-ups keep coming and even if you close one another starts up. What should you do?

Conservative   You need to log off of the computer and run Spybot Search and Destroy to clean up after your surfing binge.

Liberal Ignore the pop-up windows and go back to what you are supposed to be doing. They will die off eventually.

SUMMARY

When you are being hit by unsolicited advertising you are likely receiving cookies, spyware, and so on. Logging off of the computer will at least stop the invasion. Harmless though it may be, you may want to report it to your system administrator. If you start browsing predatory Web sites, at a minimum you must take steps to clean your computer.

@#&!?!

SANS is Causing Pop-ups?

As a SANS employee, I am expected to keep my computer protected with all security updates and features and my antivirus and personal firewall up to date as well. You can imagine my surprise when I went to a secure SANS Web site and it spawned a popup! I killed my browser, in case the problem was resident javascript code or some such, restarted it, tried another SANS secure site and another, totally unrelated popup came up. This was right in the crest of a mass mailing virus and I receive a lot of attachments so I started my AV and found nothing. Some Web site that I had visited had managed to install spyware on my system. I had always been wanting to try the google toolbar, which has pop up prevention, so I took that moment to install it. So far, fingers crossed, no pop-ups. If you find pop-ups distracting, or if they lead you into dangerous workplace behavior, maybe you should try the google, or another pop up protecting, toolbar!

Stephen Northcutt

Spam Messages – What if You Respond Using the Company's Computer?

In your e-mail inbox there is a spam message directing you to a tantalizing hot new Web site. It is after normal business hours but you are logged onto the company's computer. Is it okay to check out this Web site?

> **Conservative** No. You have no business looking at sex-related sites at the office, even after work. You will create a track record of every site you visit, and more of them are likely to start popping up in windows without your control.

> **Liberal** This might be okay if you know how to cover your tracks, and if there is not a strict company policy against viewing sexual photographs. You might find, however, that the images quickly get cruder than you bargained for. Most of what is out there is hard pornography.

SUMMARY

You should delete the message without opening it. If you do not, you are likely to get caught later with sexual content on your computer. Most companies have a specific policy against this very thing, and even if yours does not now, it likely will in the future. Do your x-rated browsing elsewhere.

News Items – Is it Okay to Read the News at Work?

Today a prominent political figure passed away and your ISP features a late-breaking article. Is it okay to read about the latest news on company time?

> **Conservative** You should stick to work-related business while at work. Following to this rule keeps things clean and simple. Reading the news may seem okay, but it is a short step over to see how your favorite baseball team is doing in today's game, which is clearly unacceptable.

Liberal As a salaried employee, you should be free to keep up with the news as long as it is not for too much time each day. In the past, people would scan the newspaper over coffee when they arrived at the office. Knowing what is happening helps you socialize with your workgroup.

SUMMARY

How you handle this question depends on your company culture, but for many it is acceptable to do some monitoring of the news at the office. People with flexible work/life boundaries consider it entirely normal to go out onto the Internet while at work. It fits into their life. Contemporary companies are concerned about your overall productivity, not how you are spending any given moment. Items in the news may be relevant to your work. In most offices you need to resist going into the more recreational aspect of the news, and stick with the headlines, business, and science articles. Any such reading is best done early or late in the day and for less than 15 minutes.

Job Search and the Company Internet – Is Looking Okay?

You want to find a new job and spend hours searching the company's on-line job postings to find something else within the company. Is this appropriate to do while you are on company time?

Conservative Such searching should be done on your own time, but you can use the on-line job postings.

Liberal Yes, part of healthy employment is making sure you are in the right position. How can you tell that if you do not periodically keep abreast of what is available? This searching can take hours and it makes sense to do it on company time, since they will benefit if you move to a more productive position.

SUMMARY

How valid it is to job-hunt at work depends on how long you tend to stay in one position. In other words, how often do you search job postings and how legitimate is your desire to make a change? If the change is indeed good for all, and you have been in your current position for at least a year, it is reasonable to spend company time searching to see if you can find a better way to contribute.

Looking Outside the Company

You are searching for a better job throughout the industry and want to use the company's fax machine and Internet in your search. Is this is appropriate?

Conservative No. This needs to be done on your own time with outside resources.

Liberal It is difficult while working to have the time during the day to pursue another job. It is a small cost to the company for you to use the fax and Internet. Just do not make your actions too visible to others who may want to follow suit.

SUMMARY

There is a major ethical difference between the previous issue where you are looking within the company, and this one where you are searching externally. It is not likely in the company's interest to have you leave or they would be helping you to do so. Therefore, you cannot expect to use their time or resources.

Configuration Control – Should You Use the Company's Laptop for Personal Reasons?

Your company has provided you with a state-of-the art laptop computer that you are free to take home in the evenings for business and personal use. A system administrator set up your computer to company standards for going on the internal network. You are accustomed to managing your own computer and like things configured to your tastes. Even though the company standard software is Microsoft Office, you prefer installing and using the WordPerfect Suite. Should you do so with this laptop?

Conservative No. System administrators cannot afford to take the time to diagnose and maintain non-conforming computers. If your computer starts having difficulties, they are likely to save your files (or get them from the latest backup), wipe your disk clean, and start over with the standard configuration. If you choose to do your own support, you will likely miss automatic software updates and nightly backups. More importantly, the administrators would consider you a renegade. They would have no sympathy for you if a virus infected your computer or if some other major problem arose.

Liberal Installing software is hardly a crime. If you are competent enough to manage the computer, you should feel free to do so. You will likely incur the dislike of the system administrators, since part of their job description is to serve you in this manner. However, if you stay out of their way, there should be no harm done.

SUMMARY

Everything depends on whether your company considers the laptop to be a personal computer or a business computer. In this case, they have standards and deviating from these standards is not appropriate. Installing software may not be unethical in itself, but it can have unexpected results which can take time to fix and hamper productivity. While you may get away with doing your own configuration at a small start-up company, for most environments this will not fly and sooner or later you will need to conform.

Access Control – Should You Use Passwords that Are Not Meant for You?

You work in marketing for a small software company. In the hallway during the lunch hour, you overhear one system administrator tell another the new root password, "sunshine," for the computers in your area. You periodically work into the night after the administrators have gone home. During your trade-show days you developed general experience in setting up and troubleshooting computers. Sometimes the system hangs up after hours and it would be useful for you to have the password to reboot it. Should you advise system administration that the root password has potentially been exposed, or quietly have it available in case you need it?

Conservative You cannot employ the password without permission. Using the password may cause repercussions you are not even aware of. Someone may become aware that the login occurred, which would instigate a troublesome investigation. You should tell the two administrators you overheard them, so that they will be more discreet in the future. They will undoubtedly change the password immediately.

Liberal There is no need to report your knowledge of the password as long as no one else heard it. What the administrators do not know cannot hurt them. You are not even sure if you will ever use the password. You are liable to get the two administrators in unnecessary trouble. If you do not use the password often or wantonly, or pass it on to others, you are probably okay.

SUMMARY

The root password is set deliberately to confine the number of users to a few properly trained individuals. When you do something as root, there is generally no undo command available. Restricting access enables system administrators to maintain basic control over their computer networks. There are many times when well-meaning end users accidentally mess something up in the system. By sharing the fact that you overheard the passwords, the administrators are likely to be more careful in the future.

Using Shortcuts – If the Back Door is Faster, Should You Use It?

As a mechanical engineer, you join a team that has been working together for over a year. In order to do your design work, you need access to the product's existing drawings; however, there is an elaborate process to check them out of the database. Your new workgroup routinely circumvents this process because they have found a fast, back-door way into the database that gets the same results. Should you participate in the alternate way?

Conservative Absolutely not. This activity negates the value of the database. Even though you are working with existing drawings, you cannot know all the repercussions of not checking them in and out properly. By circumventing the database, you are not allowing the speed problem to be found and resolved.

Liberal You are probably okay because the drawings in question are existing drawings, not in the revision process, and the rest of the group is doing it. It could take significantly longer to follow the formal process.

SUMMARY

You need to use the database as the company has implemented it, or let management know why you cannot. Databases cost tens of thousands of dollars and the company has invested in one partly to maintain control over their documentation. By going around the system you are not letting it do what it was designed for—monitoring who has what files when.

Viruses

Most of us at work are well protected from virus invasions; we have system administrators to call in the event we contract an infection. Virus and worm issues are much more noticeable outside of the work environment, where we have to depend on our ISPs to be the line of defense for our home computers.

Potential False Alarms – Do You Send out Warnings of an Unconfirmed Virus?

Your brother says his computer has a virus and he thinks he has spread it to your computer through his e-mail. He e-mails everyone in his address book and tells them to immediately warn everyone in their address books of the problem. He learned of the virus when he opened MSWord and his computer started deleting files in the "My Documents" directory. You have been on your computer for the last few hours, including using MSWord, and you have no evidence of the virus. Should you immediately notify everyone in your address book of the potential hazard?

Conservative No. Before disturbing others you should make the effort to verify that you indeed have the virus. If you do not want to take the time to determine the validity of the threat, why foist this task on others? Even if there is only one person in your address book, you (or your brother) should take ownership of the situation to see what needs to be done. You should be knowledgeable enough to determine if your computer has a virus; if you are not, this is the time to become so.

Liberal Yes. It is an easy matter to alert people and let them be on the lookout for symptoms. Write them an apology for any infection they might have incurred, and get the message out as quickly as possible to contain more damage.

Summary

Being on the Internet and on e-mail servers exposes everyone to viruses. Being ethical in the matter of viruses entails operating in a proactive manner to:

1. Install an industry-standard virus protection program such as McAfee or Norton System that works on all of your computers.
2. Maintain updates for the virus protection software by visiting their Web site weekly or signing up for their auto-update service.
3. Verify that you have the latest version of your operating system from your supplier.

After taking all three of these steps, you can run a virus scan on your computer and find out if you have a virus. If you do, you can then notify everyone in your address book so that they can scan their systems.

@#&!?!

Electronic Venereal (Etherial) Diseases

One morning there was a particularly intense meeting; the type where flamethrowers were wielded and aspersions were cast. A short while later the meeting's participants received an e-mail from their group leader. The subject line was "ILOVEYOU" and the message contained an attachment. Thinking that their boss was trying to smooth over all the ruffled feathers, they ALL happily clicked on the attachment. Very few of these people had virus scanners and/or up-to date virus definitions. NONE of them had desktop backups. Amazingly, these folks are all computer professionals.

On the plus side after this event, the resources for central virus scanning, which my group had been pushing for, suddenly became available, thereby mitigating the damage caused by more recent threats.

Jason Soverland - System Administrator

Virus from Your Actions – What if it is Your Fault a System is Contaminated?

At a deli lunch spot you find a disc left on the counter with a handwritten label that says "Summer Secrets." Curious, you take the disc to work and insert it into your computer, which is on the company network. You do not find any files on the disc so you start working and forget about it. As you work, random windows come up on your screen, flashing in different colors. You suspect a virus from the disc, but do not want to tell system administration because you are embarrassed about what happened. You have antivirus software installed. Should you try to get rid of the virus on your own?

Conservative No. By all means report the behavior you are seeing. You should turn over your computer and the suspect disc to your system administrators. They are professionals at dealing with these situations and need to take charge, since the virus may perpetrate through the company network.

Liberal It would be better to call in system administration, but it is understandable why you do not want to tell them about your actions. You could try figuring out what is gong on first, and at least try to find out if you have a virus. If so, it seems to be just a playful one. Maybe you could clear up the problem and then check with some coworkers on your network to make sure they are not seeing unusual behavior.

Summary

Though you saw no files on the disc, there was quite likely a virus on it stored as a hidden file. An innocent-seeming virus can be a wolf in sheep's clothing, and this one could be quietly destructive. In any event, you cannot control how it may spread through the network, and harmless or not, it needs to be removed. Call the administrators to do the work.

Data Destruction – Is There a Reformat Process?

While using the undelete function of Norton System Works on your computer, you recover not only your files but also some from the previous owner of the computer, a group manager. Within those files you notice files with personnel information about people in the organization. What should you do?

Conservative Delete the files without looking at them. Then notify system administration about the episode so this will not happen to someone else in the future. If they do not respond, inform the previous owner about the issue and your actions, letting him know the potential exists for it to happen again.

Liberal Delete the files without looking at them. Do not discuss the matter with anyone as it was an innocent occurrence; talking more about it will only raise curiosity about the matter.

Summary

Someone's data is their proprietary information, which they rightfully expect to be maintained as private. It is imperative that you do not look at the files, and it is unacceptable that you received a computer containing previous files. The company's computer administrator needs to install processes to reformat the hard drive of used computers still in the computer pool.

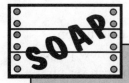

Surplus Computers

Computers and peripherals are expensive and many organizations recycle hardware internally in order to squeeze every penny out of their investment. Eventually a machine reaches the point where it cannot support another memory or hard drive update, so off it goes to the trash or perhaps a surplus yard. But what about the data that has accumulated on those drives? Even while the computer was being moved around inside the organization, sensitive data from one employee was potentially visible to another. Do your employees know what to do if they stumble over files left behind by the previous user of the computer?

During the dot-com boom a few years ago, companies flourished and died almost overnight. In their wake were thousands of computers that eventually found their way to online auction sites, repossession sales, or discount warehouses. Many of those small start-ups supported larger, more established companies. Most were storing information from the larger companies on their local hard drives. After those computers were sold and repurchased, the new owner might find very sensitive corporate data files, valuable intellectual property, working copies of expensive software, personal e-mail, or even data that might be used as evidence in a criminal trial.

The lesson learned is that prior to releasing a computer to a reseller or surplus facility, every effort must be taken to ensure that the drives are completely empty and have been scrubbed with a tool that cleans it as best as possible. Computers that are donated to churches, schools, or charities are also vulnerable to data leakage if the drives are not sanitized first.

Marcus H. Sachs
The SANS Institute

Networking – Should You Ever Circumvent a Firewall?

You have signed up for online interactive training for cold fusion Web development software. Twenty minutes before the training, you attempt, as scheduled, to logon to the cold fusion Web site. You learn you cannot access their server because of your company's firewall. To request a change from your Information

Technology (IT) department will take one and one-half days. The cold fusion training will not be held again for six weeks, and you need it to do a new project you have been assigned. Scotty, your coworker, says not to worry, he can set up your computer to go around the company firewall, just do not let IT know. What should you do?

Conservative Postpone the training and submit a request to the system administrators to resolve the issue before the next session. You could do incredible damage if your computer is not firewall-protected while you are still on the company network. Even if you temporarily disconnect from the network, you could get a worm in your computer that would later infect the rest of the company when you reconnect. The potential consequences are too high.

Liberal It is probably okay to go forward with the training. It is unlikely any damage will occur in the time your computer is not firewall-protected. To be safer, you should disconnect from the company network during the time you are outside the firewall. Then, before going back on, run a system check with your antivirus software to see if it can detect anything wrong with your system.

SUMMARY

The purpose of a firewall is to keep out unknown intruders. By the nature of how it works, it keeps you from accessing the full power of the Web. Damage from a hacker or a worm only takes a split second and can be devastating. Your opening could be just the moment some piece of spyware has been waiting for. Do not take the chance.

Physical Security

Physical security has increased in high tech companies over the last decade. Corporate spies used to be unheard of, and the modern culture led to lax environments where employees freely wandered around while musing on complex problems. But after several incidents of information leaking out about new products, the environment changed. Now almost all companies have strict entrance controls at every door, and employees must have photo badges visible at all times while they are at work.

Lock and Key – What if You Loan Your Key to Your Coworker?

The company's computer lab is kept locked and you have one of 15 keys for it. One of your coworkers, Sam, who also has a key, periodically forgets his and asks to borrow yours. Is this acceptable?

Conservative No. You should not be lending your key to anyone, even a fellow legitimate user. If you lend the key to Sam, you cannot be sure of what will happen to it or to whom he might give it to. You are the one responsible for it. One time might be permissible, but the fact that Sam is making a regular practice of it demonstrates a careless attitude on both your parts.

Liberal There is probably nothing wrong with lending your key as long as Sam does not give it to someone else. The purpose of keeping the room locked, is to keep out unauthorized people while letting those of you who are supposed to use it have access. Since you and Sam are both in that group, it should be fine to give him your key?

SUMMARY

The right answer here depends upon how strict your company's security policy is, and how big the threat of intrusion. But clearly, it is better if your coworker keeps track of and uses his own key.

Convenience over Security – Is Okay Once in Awhile?

You work in a secure building with one entrance about a ten-minute walk from where you sit. Your desk is near an emergency exit door to which you do not have a key. While working late one evening you notice it is starting to rain and you realize your car windows are down. You are tempted to go out the emergency door and block it with a nearby brick, just long enough to roll-up your windows. Is this okay?

Conservative No. The whole point of having a secure building is to keep all entrances locked or guarded.

Liberal It is very unlikely someone would be able to capitalize on the open door during the brief moments you are outside. Your biggest problem would be if you got caught; only take the chance if you can be sure no one is in the area. You are probably fine if you do not use this door very often.

SUMMARY

A security system is only as strong as its weakest link. Your company spent hundreds of thousands of dollars to be able to maintain security; all to have you potentially negate its value.

Securing Your Responsibilities – What if Your Coworkers Help Out?

You work for a Los Angeles area defense contractor on a secret project for the government, and therefore have "secret clearance." At the end of each workday you lock all documents, files, and drawings in a safe in your office, according to the job requirements. One day after you are almost home you realize you may not have locked your safe. Returning to the office requires a 45-minute or more drive each way through traffic. Although the rules of secret clearance require you to personally lock your own safe, you are thinking of calling one of your coworkers who is still working to have him check the safe for you.

Conservative Unfortunately, you have to drive back to the office and check on your safe yourself. Doing so should help reinforce your memory to always check the lock before leaving. If you do otherwise you may risk not just your secret clearance but also your job.

Liberal You could consider calling the coworker, if they are someone you would trust completely to take care of the matter without discussing it with anyone else. Hopefully, your habits will improve and you will not need to use this method again.

SUMMARY

Rating a secret clearance is a valuable achievement, one that you should take very seriously. One of the fundamental aspects of operating under secret clearance is to do what is right, what is required, regardless of how much trouble you have to cause yourself or others. You need to immediately drive back to the office to check your safe.

Missing Material – What if Material is Lost Under Your Watch?

Failing to properly watch your company computer equipment in an off-site conference, you later realize that some of the gear is missing. Should you report this incident or let someone else make the discovery?

Conservative You need to report everything you know about the theft as soon as possible. In doing so you may be able to help figure out who stole the equipment. Owning up to a mistake like this one is a basic character-forming experience.

Liberal It is understandable that you would be reluctant to report the theft, since you are directly responsible for it. It probably will not hurt to let someone else discover the loss, since the damage is already done. Perhaps no one will notice and you will realize that the gear is not so important after all.

SUMMARY

Keeping quiet will do nothing to help the situation, and will only compound your embarrassment when someone else raises the alarm. By cooperating fully, you may help prevent something like this from happening in the future, and others will learn from the experience.

Money Matters

Most ethical issues in the business world revolve around money. While those of us in high tech have additional complicating challenges, money underlies many a dilemma. Here are a few representative issues about payroll and travel expense reports.

Payroll Problems – Bonus or Bogus?

Payroll accidentally paid you twice for the same pay period. Do you keep the money?

> **Conservative** No. You need to report the overpayment.
>
> **Liberal** This hardly ever happens, so if you do not say anything perhaps you can keep the bonus income. That way you will feel more generous the next time you think the company demands too much from you.

SUMMARY

There is more going on here than just the bonus pay. Someone or something in the system made a mistake. If it is systemic, it means a serious problem for the company. You are in a unique position to uncover this problem. By returning the second paycheck, you may be contributing something of far greater value to the company, which hopefully will appreciate it.

New Company, No Pay – What if Time is Not an Option to be Paid?

You are working for a start-up company and have not received any salary in over a month. The company promises to pay you as soon as they receive some funding. Do you stay with it? How long do you stay if you have not been paid— two months, six months?

> **Conservative** It is time to leave. The reality is that most start-ups fail. Employees who were paid put in long hours for the amount of money they received. A month is long enough. Get packing.
>
> **Liberal** It depends on your personal finances. People who succeed in start-ups usually have rough spots in the beginning. Though the great majority of new companies go belly-up, the ones that make it in the computer industry can give phenomenal compensation. If you can afford it, give yourself another month and then reevaluate.

SUMMARY

Unfortunately, this scenario has become more commonplace since late 2000 and the demise of the Internet extravaganza. Many young people especially are working for no pay, living on credit cards and hopes for the future. Each month they tell themselves this will be the last one they will work for free. CEOs are paid to instill great optimism, but if the company folds, there is no worse feeling than having worked for nothing. Your working for free creates the illusion to the stakeholders the business can be run this way, and they become dependent on it. It is time to leave.

Retirement Plans – Should You Withdraw It?

Your company is about to go into bankruptcy and you will lose your 401k plan. Since you have advance knowledge of the company's failure, do you withdraw the money?

Conservative Withdraw the money but without telling anyone else. You do not want to be responsible for a stock run.

Liberal Yes; withdraw the money. You have the right to do so. If your fellow employees are not in the know, tell them so that they can choose to withdraw their money.

SUMMARY

Being in this situation gives you an inside line into how it feels to be classified as an "insider" by the Securities and Exchange Commission (SEC), and hence restricted on when and if you can make stock trades. The pressure to cheat is enormous. Those of us on the front lines do not have to worry about the legality of the situation, only our ethics. Share your intended actions with others in the same boat, and then go ahead and pull out your money.

Expense Reports – Should You Follow the Leader?

Everyone at the office throws a few personal expenses into their expense reports; even senior management does it. Is it okay for you to do so also?

Conservative No. "Just because everyone else does it" is no way to form your ethical creed. You need to answer to your own calling, one that recognizes that the company should not be paying for your personal items. You can carry a strong ethic wherever you work, through different times and companies, without having to spend time reevaluating what to do.

Liberal It is certainly okay to include the expenses because it is so much a part of your company's culture and perhaps policy. Be sure to stick with items you would need on the trip, such as toothpaste, deodorant, and a newspaper. Buying a present for your spouse would be out of line.

SUMMARY

Doing what everyone else does may make sense in this situation. It is not necessary to form an ethical high ground, unless it is intrinsic to who you are. If you go this route, you will need to learn exactly what is and what is not permissible, and keep up-to-date as the rules and conventions change. If, on the other hand, you are one who conducts yourself with a strong ethical creed, you do not need to learn all the rules, as your normal behavior will fall well within bounds.

Paid Vacations –Include Them on an Expense Report?

You are going on a business trip to England and arrive one day early to enjoy a personal vacation. Can you put your vacation expenses on the corporate card, lumping them in with your business charges on your expense report?

Conservative No. The company should not be paying for your personal time. You received a free trip to England; you should not take advantage of the opportunity.

Liberal You can justify doing this because you spent a good deal of your personal time traveling to and from England. Your employer could pay for a hotel night, food, and day of rental car in return. Just do not get carried away and add sightseeing costs. You can mingle the funds on the report, because most managers do not examine expense reports thoroughly.

SUMMARY

On a travel expense report, you must be completely honest about what are vacation expenses and what are business expenses. Though you can go for many trips without getting caught mingling the two, at some point someone will notice and you will be called on it, which will not be pleasant. Endeavoring to have the company pay for your vacation costs constitutes a form of stealing from them, and it will be treated as such.

Company Supplies

The company supply cabinet is full of supplies. You need a few items for work, but could also use a few supplies for your home office, which is not used for company business. The company is making plenty of money but underpaying you. Is it acceptable to take a few pens, pads of paper, and reams of copy paper for your office at home?

Conservative No. It is theft to take company resources for personal use. If you get into the bad habit of helping yourself to a few things, it will tend to grow with time to include printer cartridges and batteries. Do not cross that line.

Liberal It cannot hurt to take a few things, as long as there are plenty of those items in the cabinet .

SUMMARY

Whether or not employees take a few pens from the supply cabinet varies not only by company culture but also by groups within the company. Marketing and sales run much looser than does the IT group. You would do well to form your own policy that stops at taking anything for personal use. That way you will not need to re-question your behavior as you switch positions. The amount of money you would save does not really add up to much. If you feel you are being underpaid, address that issue head-on with your manager. Do not try to counteract it in other ways. It is bound to backfire.

Helping Your Fellow Employees

Many ethical issues arise vis-à-vis coworkers. An entire chapter of this book is on the topic of when to be your brother's keeper when they are being unethical. Another question of interest is when to volunteer to help your coworkers. Companies and the organizations within them have strong cultures regarding this matter. In some places you would not consider sticking your neck out to help another, whereas in others there is a strong sense of teamwork. High tech companies want their employees to work well together, yet typically people in a workgroup are performance-ranked against each other. Microsoft was known for its competitive atmosphere from its early days, and a few years back made a conscious effort to change its culture. In 2002, they added a section called "Distributing Knowledge" to their employee's performance reviews to try to foster collaboration within the company.

List-serves – Should You Help?

As a regular reader of your company's list-serves you see requests you could help with such as "I'm having trouble configuring my noteserver [from Lotus]" or "What is domain-sharing violation?" You have some knowledge in these areas. Should you help?

Conservative Are you sure you have done all the work you need to for your own job? Some people are chronic rescuers, and you could become one of them. If you solve other people's problems for them they will not learn for themselves. Maybe your group competes against this person's for resources. Even if you should help out, knowledge is different from expertise and you might take more time than another person would to compose an answer. Better to hang back and let someone else reply.

Liberal You could take the lead in replying to questions like this, setting a cooperative tone for the organization. After you have responded for six months or so, you could back away and let others fill the role.

SUMMARY

It is difficult to generalize what is right or wrong here as there are many value judgments that go into it, such as how much time it would take you, how certain you are of your answer, and how important it is for the requester to receive assistance. Certainly, if there is a customer situation involved you should help with what you know. Also, if your manager asks you to get involved, you should do so.

Some people ask simple questions that can be answered quickly. Some requests, such as how to do a configuration, generally have follow-up questions that can take a few hours of your time. It matters how busy you are; offer help only when your own workload is under control.

Dealing with Management

Ethical issues with one's boss is something that all employees can relate to. Management is a two way street. We are all familiar with directives coming down from the boss, but as employees we have a responsibility to communicate back to our managers.

New Management – What if Your New Manager is Sub Par?

After a reorganization you are assigned to a manager, Don, who is younger than you and famous for his technical knowledge. You have been in management yourself and are accustomed to a trusted relationship with your manager. You have been kept apprised of the group strategy and served as a wise adviser to your team. Don does not seem to understand your role and is quite closed as to his priorities. You see inefficiencies in the new organization and want to help him figure it out, but he will not engage in conversation and gives you mundane assignments. What should you do?

Conservative Your primary role is to make your manager look good, wherever you are in the organization. If he says jump you should do it and not question his methods.

Liberal You could talk to Don one-on-one and tell him your concerns. If this does not work, you ask the Human Resources department to help you with your frustrations.

SUMMARY

In order for Don to accept you in a more advanced role, he has to see you successfully operate in it. You must first meet your objectives and then look for ways to demonstrate your strategic ability to him. People often underestimate their manager's ability to recognize shortcoming and change. Managers are motivated by the success of their group, so your interests naturally align. If you are truly concerned about the good of the organization and not just trying to get ahead, he will gradually see what you are capable of.

The Manager's Assistant – Should You ask the Assistant for Your Manager's Opinion?

You join a group where the manager's personal assistant has full access to his computer system. Others in the group use this fact to seemingly innocent ends. Asking her to find out when he is available. Did he hear back on the e-mail he sent to the General Manager? Did he send the e-mail to the group in the West Indies yet? You sent an e-mail to your manager with concerns about how little authority he allows you for your assigned project, and you copied his boss. Your manager has arranged to talk to you this afternoon about your concerns. Before you do, it would be very useful to know if his boss sent him any correspondence about your message. This would give you insight as to how much support you have for your position. Should you go to your manager's assistant for help?

Conservative No. Do not get into this pool of potential problems. You are liable to get the assistant in trouble as well as yourself.

Liberal It probably will not hurt anything as long as you are quite careful that your manager does not learn of your actions.

SUMMARY

As tempting as it can be to find out inside information about your manager's intentions, you should resist doing so. For one thing, it can become addicting. For another, it undermines your ability to form an open, direct relationship with him. And finally, you are putting his assistant in the awkward position of compromising her boss's privacy.

Impossible Deadlines – What Happens When Your Manager Does Not Realize It?

You are working on a major project for a software company that is under a lot of competitive pressure. You can see the schedule is unrealistic by at least a quarter. You raise the issue to your project leader, Amy, who does not respond. Should you take the matter to higher management?

Conservative　Yes. Management needs to be informed about what is happening even if they do not like the news.

Liberal　Your project leader is charged with making management aware of the schedule issues. Her lack of response indicates management does not want to know more. Let it lie for a while.

SUMMARY

It is usually wise to let your boss, in this case Amy, do her job without you trying to overstep it. However, there are certain issues that merit making them widely visible, such as a project that grossly misses meeting its schedule.

Competitive Managers - What Happens When They Take Credit for Your Ideas?

You work at an Internet start-up where the dynamics are cutthroat. Your manager Ruth, who is five years younger than you, is taking credit for work you have done. You expected this, and did the work gladly for her and the team, but now she is implying that she thought of the idea, she took it from soup to nuts, and that you were not even involved. What should you do?

Conservative It makes sense to call Ruth on her behavior, first directly and then to her manager if she does not change. Letting this continue will inevitably create more problems for you.

Liberal This happens all the time in the business world and especially in fast-growing companies. Take your solace from your trusted teammates who really know who did the work. If it continues to happen, look for another position.

SUMMARY

This is a classic situation that can arise with one's manager. How you respond depends on many factors such as your company's corporate culture, your length of time at the company, and your boss's reputation. Generally though, cream rises and ill-gotten gains do not last. If you remain true to yourself and produce good work, it will become known without you tooting your own horn.

Roles Within the Company

The following sections capture some of the different roles in the computer world and the various issues that arise unique to that particular position. Each of these roles could provide a chapter of a book themselves with the range of nuances in all their ethical issues. We cover some of the major ones that can happen to most people in this position.

Marketing Roles – What if You Have Insider Knowledge about Your Competition?

You work in marketing for a database management system in charge of training the sales force. You are in a tough market against two other players, one of them named Zyged. One of your resourceful salesmen has gotten a hold of Zyged's sales training manual from a crony who recently left there, and your sales representative immediately sends it to you. This manual is full of useful information, including tips on how the Zyged's sales force should successfully sell against your system. What should you do with this information?

Conservative You can use the information to create your sales training material, as long as you rewrite it so that the source is not revealed. It is surely against the competitor's company policy for the ex-employee to distribute the information, but you are not in ethical violation to use it as reference material.

Liberal You should copy the sales training manual and distribute it to your sales force. They will best know what to do with the information without you trying to re-process it for them. You have done nothing wrong in having and distributing the material.

SUMMARY

Be careful in what you give your sales people. They have a different set of ethics from others in the company, and usually have several friends who work elsewhere in the industry. Figure anything you give them could get relayed to the competition. What goes around comes around.

Product Managing – What if What They Want is Not What is Best?

As the product manager for a computer-aided design system you are responsible for recommending what changes development should make to the product in its next major release. It is clear that the current user base is unhappy because the system does not support all drawing standards. However, to sell the product better, the sales force is demanding a flashy user interface and wizard-style help system to use in demonstrations. What should you recommend?

Conservative Go with what the current users want, whatever it may be. If you do not have happy users, you are in peril of falling apart from the inside.

Liberal You could focus on the sales force flash and throw a few bones to the users by fixing a few of the shortcomings to which they refer. As long as sales are rolling in, you have a lot of room to maneuver.

Summary

This is a product manager's major dilemma: whether to do what they know is right versus what will sell. Unless your sales are so down your product is in danger of surviving, it usually pays to fix the more mundane parts of the system needed by the current users. They are your best source of future business, and provide valuable reference sites. Whatever you do, do not try to do both improvements at once to please all, as you will likely leave everyone unhappy. It is time for a strong backbone.

Product Marketing – What if You Give Your Friend Insider Information?

You work in product marketing for a major computer manufacturer, and have access to every kind of market research imaginable in the technology field to help you get your job done. You have a friend who is starting her own company with her husband, selling software that edits visual media. She has asked you as a favor to get her several reports from industry analysts in the visual media field. She says the reports would really help her in her new business and her start-up company could not begin to afford to pay for them. Your company is in the visual media field and it would be an easy matter for you to get the reports. Should you?

Conservative No. This is another form of stealing, though not as obvious as most. It would be an inappropriate use of company resources. Also, obtaining the reports will take up some of your time, as well as the time of those in your company charged with maintaining the market research.

Liberal You could do this favor to help your friend as long as she does not expect it to be an ongoing deal, and of course you should not receive any money for it. Start-ups have a hard time competing against big companies, and this is one way you could balance the situation. Your friend would not be a purchaser of the reports anyway, so the research firm is not being deprived of any revenue that it would otherwise receive. It is likely no one would ever know of your actions, as the information she is requesting is fairly obscure.

SUMMARY

This is an interesting issue in that the ethical relationship in question is between your company and the market research firms. Though the information may not seem important to you, these types of reports cost thousands of dollars. To someone in the field, they are as valuable as a company profile is to a stockbroker. Someone at your company signed an agreement saying it would safeguard a research firm's intellectual property. Passing the information would likely be a violation of the report's copyright, and hence against the law. While such an action is not likely to be caught or even noticed, it is still unethical.

Sales Person – Should you Make the Sale?

As a trained and knowledgeable sales person for networking software, you realize your product is not right for one of your new prospective customers. Due to their specific needs, they would be much better off with your top competitor's software. This prospect seemingly has a lot of trust in you and does not know much about the competition. Should you sell them your system anyway?

Conservative It is always difficult for a sales person to do, but the right thing to do is to pass on this sale.

Liberal You could sell the customer your product and figure it will change to meet their needs over time. It is always good to have sales, and expanding your installed base generates more sales, even if a little off-target. In going forward with the sale, you should allow for extra time and effort to see that this customer is successful after the system is delivered.

SUMMARY

As an individual sales person of a system of this scope, you cannot put in enough energy to compensate for a product misfit. If you want to pursue the sale, you need to marshal the necessary company resources ahead of time to ensure the customer's success. It is a rare sales person who can resist a sale. You will gain great esteem for you and your company if you recommend the competitor's product. On the other hand, having a dissatisfied customer could lead to great harm. If you lose a lot of sales in this manner, let marketing know of your product's shortcomings rather than force-fit a solution on the customer.

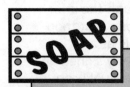

Trade Show Trinkets

It seems like in every organization there is always that one person who gets to go to the trade shows and conferences. They travel several days each month, and they usually come back with a suitcase full of brochures, free product samples, pens, mouse pads, and other advertising paraphernalia. They might also return with t-shirts, ball caps, golf balls, or other items of value. In many cases the employee knows what the ethical limits are, and at most trade shows the people in the booths are also sensitive to the limits of what they can give away.

But what happens to all of that bounty, especially when an individual is a frequent traveler to these types of events? Should the employee bring it home for the kids? Or does it belong to the employee's company if the company paid for the trip and expenses? In many companies, employees who travel frequently are encouraged to donate the bulk of the "loot" to a company storage locker rather than letting it build up at home or in a cubicle. Then, when the company has an internal office party or social event, the accumulated items are given away as door prizes, raffle prizes, or just simply laid out on a table for those who do not get to travel to take home. For the frequent traveler, this is a great way to express gratitude to their support staff that rarely get to attend conferences and shows, or travel on the company's nickel.

Marcus H. Sachs
The SANS Institute

Sales Team – What About Those Conferences?

As a sales team member you are responsible for setting up and demonstrating a few of your IT company's latest (expensive) products and services at conferences around the country. If during the afternoon the flow of customers slows to a trickle, your fellow sales folks typically pack up and leave their displays early. It is early afternoon at a trade show, and the floor traffic has slowed down. A group of friends invite you to lunch at an old Italian restaurant down the street. It is too early to close, but you have been on your feet since the show opened and you want to go with them. Should you leave your post unattended for a couple hours to join them?

Conservative You cannot leave your station unattended. You do not know who will come up to your booth to learn about your products. This is especially important considering you are responsible for newly released products. A quiet intruder posing as a customer may even sabotage your demonstration. You need to schedule your lunchtime to be brief, and arrange for someone else to cover your station while you are gone.

Liberal Depending on your company's habits in this regard, you should be all right to go. You deserve some kind of lunch break. A couple of hours is a long time to be away, but if you take a longer lunch time just one day it is okay.

SUMMARY

You should never leave a trade show station unattended even for a short time. Your competitors are at the show, and you can be sure that one of their people is willing and able to take advantage of the opportunity to freely operate your company's latest product.

The nature of the sales job provides some of the easiest access points for corporate spies to gain competitive information in the computer industry. Sales representatives tend to believe it does not matter anyway—that competitors will find out what they will, and the real issue is keeping your company's products two steps ahead of the rest of the industry. You must do all you can to help prevent knowledge of how your company's products work from being widely known.

Software Developer/Programmer/ Engineer – Should You Do More?

As a software developer in printed-circuit design software, part of your role is to fix bugs in the software. The quality group sends you a Change Request to correct a defect in the board layout program. You realize that this is a great opportunity to clean up some other parts of the code you have always wanted to improve. While fixing the defect will only involve changing two lines of code, your more extensive changes will impact about 50 lines. Should you make the improvement?

Conservative No. You should stick to what you were asked to do or you could really make a mess of things. At the least you will create a false impression of your programming effort, since you will be doing untracked work. What if you were to introduce more bugs while making your improvements?

Liberal It might be a good idea to do the improvement if you are careful. Too often one does not get around to cleaning up inefficient code and this seems like a good opportunity since you are familiar with the problem.

SUMMARY

Good quality management depends on programmers only doing what the change request requires them to do. If you create another defect during your improvement efforts, you will cost the company far more than any benefit from your efforts.

Development Team – Is it Okay to Infiltrate Your Competition?

As a developer in the CAD Solid Modeling Software group you have an intimate knowledge of your product. The marketing manager gets the idea to have you attend your top competitor's software training as a spy, to learn what their solid modeler really can do and uncover its weaknesses. You would pose as a CAD user from a small company evaluating whether to buy the competitor's system. Your manager goes along with the idea. Should you?

Conservative Lying about almost anything can get you into trouble, and this is no exception. If you are "caught" at the training you will be the guilty one.

Liberal Since your manager has agreed to the idea, you should be fine. Just be careful not to show off your in-depth knowledge of these types of systems.

SUMMARY

When your company wants to take an ethical risk of this nature, it is legitimate for you to go along with it. However, if doing so would violate your sense of honest, by all means you should refuse.

Sales Representatives – How do You Deal with Them?

Due to your knowledge of computer systems, you are brought into the selection process of a major computer purchase for your company, including two servers and a series of PCs to connect to them. A sales representative from one of the providers gets chummy with you and takes you to lunch. There he offers you two free tickets to an upcoming NFL game. What should you do?

Conservative Politely decline the tickets.

Liberal You could accept the tickets if they did not influence your recommendation.

SUMMARY

According to most companies' policies on this kind of situation, the tickets need to be refused. Employees may accept gifts only of nominal value such as a basic pen or coffee cup. People who work in procurement and are involved with suppliers for a living, receive extensive training in what is acceptable in the receipt of gifts, and become sophisticated in how to handle sales situations. However, those in other departments, particularly engineering, can be buffaloed by sales people and are susceptible to undue influence.

Finance - What Should You Do?

You are the financial analyst in a group that has gone through a lot of upheaval, power struggles, and reorganization. Two of the managers that emerged on top, Paula and Sam, are apparently trying to blame a third, Jerry, for past financial troubles and get him fired. Paula asks you to determine how much money was lost in a failed special project that Jerry took the blame for. You do not like the tone or reasoning for the request. Is there anything you can do about it?

Conservative You are being asked to do work within your role. You should provide the information as best you are able and stay out of the reasoning behind it.

Liberal You have some leeway as to how badly the project failed financially. Discuss the situation with your manager to see if you can minimize the financial impact from the project's failure.

SUMMARY

The finance person has a unique role in high tech groups in that they are responsible for the financial reporting of an organization, yet they themselves are not part of the group. Many times their own manager does not even know about the business and people issues they are facing. They serve as an external auditor who can sometimes get pulled into disputes and care about the people involved. Similar to the use of statistics, the financial analyst has a lot of discretion about how good or bad a project can look, depending on what expenses they load upon it.

In situations like this one you are best off to fulfill the request but without spending too much time on it, nor using any extra accounting methods other than to report the expenses directly tied to the project.

Procurement

Those working in selecting parts and systems for high tech companies are subject to outright bribes from vendors trying to win your favor. We know of an instance where a vendor offered a procurement engineer $5000 during a private meeting to select that company as a supplier. While it would obviously be unethical to accept such a bribe, we wonder about the stories we do not hear. Besides out and out bribes, suppliers often wine and dine their clients and it gets to be a gray area as to what is acceptable. There is an economic benefit to having a long-term relationship with your suppliers, who may need to jump through hoops for you if a problem arises with one of their parts. People working in procurement get a lot of training about what are and are not acceptable levels of gifts and services according to their company policy. Following are some other kinds of issues procurement people encounter.

Supply Management – What Happens when Your Supplier Falls Behind in Innovation?

You are responsible for selecting the suppliers for a variety of printer components. As part of your job, suppliers tell you about the latest innovations they have made in their product. You have a long-standing relationship with Byran Sheet Metal, and now you have learned of innovations from two other suppliers that surpass what they offer. Can you tell Byran Sheet Metal about the innovations so you can still work with them?

Conservative No. What the other vendors have told you should remain secret, as you need to protect their rights just as you would want them to protect yours. The only technical information you can share with Byran Sheet Metal is what you know from your own company's research and what you find in industry publications.

Liberal Yes, unless you have signed something to the contrary. You should look after the interests of your own company first and not worry about third parties. It is useful to keep your long-time relationship and if this is the only way you can still work with Byran Sheet Metal, it will be a benefit to you both if you help them out with what you know.

SUMMARY

You need to weigh protecting the intellectual property of vendors with what is best for your company. The right answer depends on what kind of non-disclosure agreements you have signed with the other suppliers.

Vendors – What if You Choose to go with the Cheaper Supplier?

You have been working with Werner's Precision Parts for years to provide custom machined mechanical parts for your company's copiers. Some of the more complex parts cost $140 each. Now you have learned of companies in China that will make the same parts for $5. Should you switch to the Chinese vendors, knowing that if you do so it will likely put Werner out of business?

Conservative It is risky to move to an overseas supplier, but to compete in the twenty-first century you need to be able to do just that. It is a world economy and the suppliers from Asia have changed the equation.

Liberal You should have some loyalty to Werner, but this is a huge price difference. Talk to them about what you have learned of the Chinese rates and see if you can help them lower their prices.

SUMMARY

You are on the brink of free trade questions that get protesters up in arms. Chinese companies do not have any of the labor and environmental restrictions our companies do. Your father-in-law always preaches to you to buy American. If you have quality problems they will be much more difficult to solve. Then there is the ramifications of your decision that you might not even realize. If you worked with companies in Israel they would consider it screwed up to move some of your manufacturing to China, a place where you have no control. All in all you need to investigate the move because your competitors will and the prices of technology products keeps lowering primarily due to Asian labor rates.

Offensive Issues

These are the times when you know you are not behaving ethically, but feel you have a justified reason for doing so. The following issues make for interesting reading as you try to imagine yourself facing them.

Settling a Score with a Coworker – Should You Do it?

Your team has been hired for a job with the Department of Defense Mapping Agency, work that requires top security clearance. The agency puts your team through an intense training course in mapping. Your group grows quite competitive in the training as future job opportunities are at stake; those who do the best receive the best positions. As part of the experience, members of the security investigative team visit you with very pointed questions about your drinking days in college. During the questioning you surreptitiously notice the name Sally Andrews, one of your coworker's, on the security team's background sheet about you. Sally knows of your college party experiences, and apparently told the security investigators in an effort to pull you down in the competition.

A unique opportunity for retribution comes your way. During the training the team is split into groups for accessing the mapping system computers, comprised of six terminals with a central server. Throughout the weeklong training you are assigned to the same evening shift as Sally and four other trainees. As the training starts each evening, you find it a fairly easy matter to reset the response time for Sally's terminal down to 2400 baud, thereby quietly crippling her ability to perform up to par at the training. She mentions that the computer seems slow, but others do not realize she is operating at a different speed. At the close of the evening you reset her terminal performance to that of the others. By the end of the week she has significantly fallen behind the class. Was this okay to do?

Conservative   Your action is totally inappropriate. You do not have the right to design your own consequences for what you believe your team member did to you. And what if you are wrong in your suspicion of her?

Liberal   Your behavior is not admirable, but understandable. At least you found a way to get revenge without creating a scene or implicating others. Your choice of a way to settle scores is at least a very clever one.

SUMMARY

When someone has hurt you at work enough to make you feel spiteful, it is a time of strong ethical testing. Another person's actions gravely weaken your normal sense of what is right and decent behavior.

Chapter Summary

In this chapter we covered the various assortment of ethical issues you encounter in the workplace, where you are considered an end user of computer systems. We started with a discussion of work/life boundaries, which sets the stage for talking about your ethics. Some of us lead a home life that is very intertwined with our companies, and some make very clear boundaries.

We next delved into the many issues caused from your computing environment, including what is normal to access on the Internet while at work. You learned about how to handle the tricky situation of looking for another position at work. We covered what rights you have to change settings on your work computer, and the reasoning behind restricting your full access it. We touched a bit on the topic of viruses and how to avoid them, though these are covered further in other chapters. You learned about the limitations and ramifications of being on the company network, and discussed the impact on the high tech world due to building security changes.

We went on to a discussion of money issues, always a fruitful subject for ethical interest. This led into some of the most common ethical issues for individuals, namely deciding when to jump in to help a coworker, and what to do with problems with your manager.

Several of us are in specific roles that have their own ethical quandaries. While several of these roles are important enough to warrant their own chapter such as database administrators, here we offered a glimpse into some of the other players in high tech, such as those in marketing, sales, and finance.

Finally, we looked at a situation where the person deliberately acted unethically, something that happens all the time. We got a peek into why this occurs and in this instance how it unfolded.

Frequently Asked Questions

The following Frequently Asked Questions, answered by the authors of this book, are designed to get you thinking about the ethical circumstances you may face in your position at work. Unless legal issues are involved, then answers in the FAQ may not be the right answer for your organization.

Q: How do I know what is permissible on my workplace personal computer. The acceptable use policy is vague in a number of areas?

A: An acceptable use policy cannot cover all the bases, but there are a couple of principles to keep in mind. First, it is not a personal computer if it is at work; it is a business computer and you should be using it for business. Second, if you feel entitled to steals bits of time away from your boss, depending on your culture that might be okay, but be certain to never be the person that allows malicious code to enter your organization. If you are going to do a lot of surfing, you probably should invest some time in reading about malicious code first.

Q: Which kinds of positions have the most challenging ethical dilemmas?

A: It is difficult to generalize across different corporations, but those roles that interact a lot with people outside of the company typically have the most issues. Outsiders bring in situations that the company has not prepared policy for, and situations where no one is watching you. These roles include all of sales (a whole book in and of themselves), those who purchase parts, and people who work with partner companies.

Q: Have ethics gotten worse in the last few decades?

A: It would certainly seem so from the press on Enron and other corporate scandals. It is like domestic violence that went on for years and seemingly came on the rise with the increase in reporting of cases. Similarly, we suspect that there were significant ethical travesties for years that went unknown. Most people today behave very ethically, yet we do not hear about them in the news.

Q: What if you have an ethical dilemma and you really do not know what to do?

A: The first choice is to talk it over with your manager. If they approve, you are in the clear regardless of which way to go. If that is difficult due to situational constraints, try to postpone action until you can think more about it or reach them. If you do not want to go to them because the problem involves them, you probably need to go to their manager.

Q: If I am being treated unfairly as an employee, what should I do?

A: There really is no possibility that anyone will be treated according to their definition of fair all the time. You know the saying, "you cannot please all the people all the time," well it starts with you. That said, if you are being treated really unfairly, consider giving a labor lawyer a call.

Chapter 12

Customer Ethics

Ethical Dilemmas in this Chapter:

- Customer Rights
- Customer Complaints
- Automated Customer Service

Introduction

If you are like most of us, you received your indoctrination into customer ethics at your first high school job waiting tables or pumping gas. One day a customer began to complain about your job performance. Your manager entered the picture to sooth her over and gave her a discount off her order. After the customer left, you turned to your manager and said, "But Mr. Wilson, she was terrible, she didn't even try the food, she disturbed the other tables around her, and she wouldn't let me explain anything." Your manager said, "None of that matters, the customer is always right."

As we moved into salaried employment and became customers ourselves, we learned that that adage still holds true for successful companies. It is a value we must deliver to the customers our companies serve, and it is what we expect to experience from companies that serve us.

High tech brings its own aspect to the question of how we treat customers. First, much of high tech selling is individualized; the provider adapts the product and sale to the customer. It is not like selling a car where the prices and features are published for all to see. Secondly, unhappy buyers can air their complaints over the Internet, bringing more visibility to them. Gone are the days when you wrote a scathing letter to an airline, received an apologetic letter back from its president, and the matter ended there.

This chapter focuses on the matters of customer rights and complaints. We also discuss the infuriating topic of automated customer support.

Customer Rights

Many high tech customer issues stem from software companies. This section shows four examples of the kinds of issues software companies generate by factors unique to their industry. We forget that the more high tech we become, the more we have to engineer "touch." There is a tendency to "one size fits all" thinking in the software business that can lead to decisions that are touchy from an ethical perspective. And yet, it is in the best interest of the industry to carefully consider the needs of the consumer. On average in the software business, 50 percent of the cost of producing a software product is marketing. And, if enough people write negative reviews, all the marketing in the world will not save the product.

End-user License Agreements – What is the Company's True Responsibility?

Some software vendors create End-user License Agreements (EULAs) that actually take away the rights of the customer. If the software is faulty, you cannot sue the company or complain. When you buy the product from the store, these agreements are usually inside the box so you cannot see them before purchase. When you purchase the product over the Internet and download software, they present the agreements at length on your browser in one long stream, and you go along with a one-sided, click-through license. Is it ethical for a software company to write a EULA that absolves it from all blame?

Conservative The practice of writing EULAs that strip end-user rights is completely unethical. The vendor should take responsibility for their product. The fact the licenses are difficult to read and access shows that the vendors are not being fully honest with their customers.

Liberal Software companies have the right to legally protect themselves. It is difficult to know how a program will function on anyone's computer, because each configuration is unique based on the software already installed, the operating systems, the Internet connections, and so on. Limiting their liability in a EULA is a reasonable response for vendors to the unpredictable computing environment. Customers do not want to read these kinds of details and negative pronouncements at the time of purchase, so as long as the EULAs do not really affect them, it is understandable that they are a background aspect of the sale.

SUMMARY

When you purchase software online and see a license agreement, your tendency is to click and bear it, thinking that enforcement of the terms of the license will never occur. You should know that acquiescence implies consent; at least you had a chance to see it. Software vendors should also give store shoppers the opportunity to review the license terms and conditions by printing them on the outside of the software packaging.

EULAs are troubling when they absolve software companies from blame if there is a problem with their product. If vendors want to limit their liability in this manner, they should do so in large bold print. Most consumers would readily agree to the rest of the license agreements that protect the vendor's intellectual property without needing to read the fine print.

This will probably come to a head in the next few years and the software companies will probably take a beating. People are becoming angry enough about bad software and bad operating systems to actually do something about it.

Unfair Product Pricing – Is it Extreme?

You own a landscape architecture business and have several computers on a network. You would like to buy some scheduling software you heard about from your sister, who uses it at Boeing. When you go for a price quote, you find out that the software will cost you over three times what your sister's department paid for it. You expect big corporations to get a discount for large purchases. Is this extreme?

Conservative Companies have the right to sell their product for whatever they choose, which is usually whatever the market will bear. You as a consumer do not have the right to know what others are paying so that you can compare price quotes.

Liberal It seems unjust that you have to pay more for software just because you are a smaller company. It is the same product either way and it does not cost the vendor much to make. Software vendors seemingly overcharge for their products just because they can get away with it.

SUMMARY

Software companies have the distinctive feature that their product costs are practically nil compared to the rest of their expenses. They need to recoup their relatively large development and marketing costs. It is not like selling a computer or printer where the consumer can plainly see material costs. Software pricing is variable according to the size of the sale and how much the company wants the business.

Reselling Customization – Is it Detailed in the Sales Agreement?

One factor in major system sales, such as for database management products, is the amount of customized software sold with the system. The customer pays for these software enhancements, which can cost tens of thousands of dollars, and key technical representatives from the vendor selection team get very involved with the software specification. When the deal is closed and the system is in place, the software vendor retains these customized pieces of code. The developers frequently write the code in such a way that the enhancements can be re-sold. Is it ethical for the software vendor to sell this code to other customers?

Conservative The code should belong to the customer who paid for it. This must be outlined in the sales contract and adhered to.

Liberal As long as the customer has not signed an agreement specifically forbidding it, the software vendor should be able to resell the code to other smaller customers who might not otherwise be able to pay for such enhancements. Even if others benefit from the software, the first customer had the benefit of specifying it and getting it before anyone else did. Besides, major customers who pioneer such customization often have an exaggerated view of their own contribution as compared to what the vendor and its development team was planning to do anyway.

SUMMARY

There are two ways software vendors can resell customized enhancements. One, quite visible to the original customer, is when the improvements show up in the next revision of the software. The sales contract for the customization should clearly spell out when and if the code will be re-used in this way. If it will become part of the mainstream product, the customer should expect to pay far less for it. Secondly, the code can be re-used in customizations for other customers, especially for those in the same industry. For example, in the case where the vendor sells, develops, and delivers a customized database to an office furniture manufacturer, there is an immediate opportunity to approach other makers of office furniture and offer to do the same at a reduced cost. The original customer would have little way of knowing this had happened, except through industry leaks. While they did get the first benefit of the software, they also had to deal with the initial bugs and problems in the

new installations. Moreover, they might be very angry to find out that
the innovations they helped design are now going to their competitors.
On the other hand, it is not reasonable to expect the vendor to withhold
all improvements in this area once they have done the work.
Undoubtedly, their customization team learned some things of use that
could come into play in other deals. The sales contract should detail
exactly where and how soon the vendor can use the new code.

Known Product Defect –
Do You Notify Your Customers?

In testing, software vendors learn of product defects that they cannot or do not
choose to correct immediately. Research and Development (R&D) managers perform triage on what can be fixed, because only so much can be done in any one
release. In addition, marketing is left to figure out what to say about the situation.

You are a product manager for a 3D Solid Modeling CAD system, sold primarily to companies that design small mechanisms such as cameras and printers.
A member of the software test team has wandered off from the standard tests to
create models of doughnuts and intersecting doughnuts with the torus shape. He
finds many tori operations work, but when he uses them to make a model of the
Olympic rings, the system crashes and all unsaved work is lost. The development
team confirms the defect, but says it involves rewriting code in the kernel of the
system, which they will not be doing for at least a year. Your promotional material says the product handles the torus shape, but your customers rarely if ever use
it; it does not come up in machined metal parts. What should you do now that
you have this knowledge?

> **Conservative** You should notify your customers of the problem through
> standard user bulletins or via a special letter. You cannot control to whom
> your sales people sell your product and for what application. Therefore, you
> need to change your brochures and other promotional material to remove
> reference to the torus until correction of the problem, even if it is an
> expensive change.

> **Liberal** All software has some defects in it and you need to decide how
> probable it is that they will be found. In this situation, what is the likelihood
> of someone else using your software to create a computer model of the

Olympic Rings? If you raise too big a fuss about it, your competition and industry analysts are likely to catch wind of the problem and use it to damage your product's reputation needlessly.

SUMMARY

Software companies often know much more about their product's defects than they let on. It is a joke among developers when their software has some limitation to say, "It is not a bug, it is a feature," or "The system is protecting you from doing that particular action because it is too complex and you should not do it." Development groups have whole databases full of reported bugs, and they do not wait until the database is empty to ship the product.

It is a judgment call on the part of the supplier to decide how much is acceptable, based on reputation.

Customer Complaints

Having dissatisfied customers has been a constant through the ages. The high tech world has made matters more complicated for companies to provide all-inclusive, the customer's always right kind of support. Customer service is expensive as well; a phone call from an angry customer costs $20.00 on average, an e-mail, $10.00 simply to process and that does not account for the cost of satisfying them. With commodity products there is almost no expectation of complaint resolution—when you spend more, you expect more.

Customer Service Reluctant to Help – Should they Offer a Refund?

Your son received a new computer game from Microsoft for his birthday. When he installs it, you are drawn into a chain reaction of events. You learn that your computer is not up to date enough to support the game, but it could do so if only it had graphics that are more modern. You find a suitable video add-on card on the Internet for $30, and justify to yourself that better graphics will also help you when you work at home, so you buy it. The card instructions require you to change a jumper near to where it installs into a slot on the motherboard. You do so, load the new driver according to the directions, and start up your computer, which you have also configured to run Linux. The display seems intermittent, and on subsequent start-ups, the video sometimes will not come on. Suspecting the new video card is bad, you call customer service for the video card company, wade through the phone menus, and reach a technical support person. He listens briefly to your tale and says you probably have a software issue, not a faulty card. He says you could try changing a certain setting in your operating system, meaning Windows, and shows no interest in troubleshooting Linux. He sends you on your way by saying to try this and that and "if you're still having trouble, you can call us back," which you are none to eager to do. You feel somewhat stranded with the mess. Do you think the video card company should provide better support?

> **Conservative** It is understandable that the company can only do so much to avoid losing money. To even be willing to buy and install this kind of product, you must be technical yourself. A certain amount of responsibility lies with you to diagnose what is wrong without taking up the company's support time.

> **Liberal** Yes, customers should expect to buy a product like this and have it plug in and work. They should not even need technical support. The company has not successfully delivered the product until it is working in your machine.

SUMMARY

Several players like this in the high tech industry have reached a bizarre corner of economic reality. Video boards range from $30 to $150, and the cheaper varieties are not much simpler than the complex ones. Video boards have millions of transistors on a complex piece of hardware, and are shipped with custom drivers to tie into complex operating systems. There are settings in the operating system and on the motherboard that affect the card, as well as getting the right driver installed. The video card company's support people must be skilled technically to be of service. With its cost structure, the company cannot afford to pay the technical person to even hear the details of your configuration, much less what you have tried and seen happen. It would be cheaper just to send you a new card. Nevertheless, if your problem is due to some software setting, which is indeed likely, a new card will not fix matters.

The video card company is in a difficult position vis-à-vis support. They might need to change their cost structure, or have a stop-loss policy where at some point the service person offers you a full refund (including all shipping costs) rather than try to solve your problem.

DLL Hell

In the windows environment, modular pieces of code that perform specific functions provide library support for applications. They are called "DLLs" because they end with the extension .dll. For years, software vendors have provided drivers with .dlls that overwrite the one supplied by Microsoft. They do this to achieve the maximum performance and video and sound card manufacturers are the worst offenders. This really becomes a problem when you buy your second sound or video card if it assumes the .dll is from Microsoft, but actually it is a modified one from the first card vendor. Many times in that situation, the new card does not work properly, because the first vendor did not act ethically. And it is the second vendor that has to field the customer support calls.

Stephen Northcutt

Fraudulent Complaints – Which Complaints are Legitimate?

Through the years, food manufacturers have been hit with bogus complaints about their products, because they are known to give free samples in compensation. If you write to say your canned ham was not fresh, you might get an apology letter with a coupon for four new ones. Software manufacturers are also subject to fake complaints from notorious pirates hoping to get something in return.

In an effort to stop software piracy, software manufacturers have developed new systems for creating their product CDs. The copy protection systems alter the CD-ROM so that in some parameters it purposely deviates from specifications. Like genetically altered seeds that grow into sterile plants, the resultant CD can play on most computers but cannot be copied. When a pirate attempts to copy the software, he is suddenly confronted with insurmountable and unfamiliar obstacles and needs information. He tries to get this information from the manufacturer by means of a complaint cleverly veiled as real. Additionally, certain software pirates try to get their money back this way, since the copy protection system denies them their profits. For the manufacturer it can be difficult to discern a fake complaint from a real one. How should they handle the situation?

> **Conservative** They should give clear and standardized instructions to use when dealing with complaints. If the support person ascertains as precisely as possible the error symptoms with each complaint, they should be able to tell if it is legitimate or not.

> **Liberal** Manufacturers should treat all complaints as real until they learn otherwise. By supporting personnel working with fake complaints, they will learn and become better equipped to help the next customer.

SUMMARY

The manufacture should inform its customer service team and its stores about possible complaints before delivering the copy-protected product. For example, complaints may be legitimate from people with PCs having outmoded drivers or drives, which do not accept copy-protected CDs. In addition, false complainers deliberately word their story to appear real. Fraud is a multi-billion dollar problem and it is not getting any better. Companies learn to detect some signs that they are being played. For instance, complaints that are not legitimate often express extreme dissatisfaction. One of the classic flags is the phrase "it was totally unusable." However, a very angry customer that has just lost a lot of work might use extreme language to point out his distress. This poses quite a problem for manufacturers. Fake complaints can really gum up support services, which are already strapped to provide enough help. The result to the consumer is more stock answers and less sympathetic help desks.

E-mailing Complaints to the Public – Would You Have Been More Cautious?

You hear tales of someone who was so unhappy with a product that she e-mailed thousands of people to tell them about it. However, the missive will only carry as far as the quality of the story will take it. If it sounds like too much of a rant, you as the receiver will just consider it spam and delete it. Another approach is for the unhappy customer to write something catchy and send it to a few. When you receive a compelling tale to which you relate, you want to share it with others and the Internet phenomenon of exponential spread takes hold.

About 2:00 AM one morning in mid November 2001, Tom and Shane arrived at a Doubletree hotel on a business trip, where they had guaranteed reservations on a credit card. However, not only did the hotel not have rooms for them, the night desk clerk, Mike, was decidedly unapologetic about the mix up, seeming to think it was the customers' problem for arriving at such an unreasonable hour. Mike reluctantly found them another place to stay, in smoking rooms at a motel six miles away. To add insult to injury, he failed to ask the day shift to relay an explanatory message to Tom and Shane's associate, who was to meet them at the Doubletree first thing in the morning.

Mike chanced on the wrong two men to irk that night, as they were very upset and have great talent with graphics. They created a cutting and humorous PowerPoint presentation entitled "Yours is a Very Bad Hotel" to send to the hotel management. The title sets the tone of this satirical slide show, which resembles a bad dream of a business presentation complete with charts and graphs of the hotel's failings. Tom and Shane also e-mailed a copy to their friends, telling them to spread it freely. People who over the years had learned "guaranteed reservation" means it is guaranteed you will be charged, were delighted to find a real life story where the hotel goofed up, with real names and facts, beautifully documented. The presentation soon traveled far beyond the original group of e-mail contacts. Before long someone posted it on the Internet where untold numbers of people all over the world have seen it. The hotel and the authors of the presentation received hundreds of e-mails from five continents either scolding (primarily to the hotel), or supporting (primarily to Tom and Shane) the story and its unfolding. Were Tom and Shane wrong to have publicized their story?

> **Conservative** Yes; they should have complained to the hotel management first and let them respond accordingly. By creating and publicizing this presentation, they are like the Sorcerer's Apprentice, doing something that starts out mischievously playful, but which multiplies out of everyone's control. There is no sorcerer here who can stop the presentation from being copied and forwarded.

> **Liberal** No. They were right to go for it. They were mad, and you cannot control what a justifiably angry consumer will do, as is shown by how much

effort they put into creating the presentation. Their revenge exults in the power of the Internet and shifts the power dynamics. This type of action gives the little guy a strong voice he would not have had in the past. The result was a learning opportunity for everyone at how far you can go when you set out to stir things up.

Summary

The Internet provides variable but unprecedented access to an audience all over the world. It is like a labor union for consumers, one without dues or strikes, where they can join forces and get their complaints heard. But it also lacks a union boss to exercise restraint or to develop an overall strategy. In this situation, the hotel manager, and even the authors of the presentation, have made efforts to get it off the Internet to stop the maligning, saying that the incident has already caused enough reputation damage. However, it is very hard (impossible?) to get something completely off the Internet. Later, when cooler-headed, the authors may wish that they had not included the names of the hotel managers, but once it is out, it is too hard to erase them from the story.

Therefore, when you are looking for revenge, caution is advised. At first you may think you do not care how far something spreads, but bad press can be very long-lasting; it is human nature to think after a while that enough is enough. Perhaps the best ethical guidance is go ahead and write up your story, but let a weekend pass and take a close look at it before you send it to anyone.

@#&!?!

The Heavy Burden of Breaking People's Privacy

During the investigation of a series of unexplained and difficult-to-trace compromises at a customer's site, we decided to start supervising all network traffic, paying special attention to Internet Relay Chat (IRC) (which seemed to be the covert commanding channel). It wasn't the first time that I had to supervise potentially confidential or personal information so, following my self-imposed code of ethics, I used a set of techniques that usually helped me avoid accessing it. I happened to have a close relation-

Continued

ship with a few people at that site, which only made me feel more uncomfortable.

That evening all odds were against me. Even when I was acting with extreme care, my skimming techniques failed and a chat message from a girl I knew slipped in front of my eyes long enough for my brains to interpret it: she had had an abortion. Even though this happened a long time ago, I can still feel that knot in my stomach; that was a really private and personal issue, and I really didn't want to know (actually, she never made it public). I am of the firm conviction that we must do our best to preserve other people's privacy, but I've come to realize that, unfortunately, discovering and keeping those secrets forever is a heavy burden we must sometimes carry.

Jess Garcia
Security Engineer
National Institute for Aerospace Technology (INTA) - Spain

Note: Facts and characters have being distorted to protect the privacy of the involved individuals.

Automated Customer Service

As companies continue to cut costs, they move to take customer service people out of the loop and let computers handle the customer problems. The Information Technology (IT) department is rapidly becoming the customer service interface, especially for lower-cost items. To avoid the costs of directly servicing customers, they try to do it via a Web interface. Sometimes this works, sometimes it does not. You are freely and often invited to "go to our Web site" where, if you seek help, you are directed to a list of Frequently Asked Questions (FAQs), which never seem to be the questions you are asking.

Automated Billing – Account Out of Control

You set up your wireless cell phone bill for automatic payment on your credit card, and sign up for e-billing with e-mail notification. About six months later your post office informs you that some credit card offers were found stolen from your mailbox. Therefore, as a precaution you request Visa to issue you a new card, just as you are leaving for an extended trip. While traveling, you receive your normal wireless e-mail notices over a dial-up connection, but cannot successfully access your bill. You are not too concerned, because you are on a flat rate plan and your charges are always the same. A month later, you realize you have not seen a wireless phone charge on your credit card statement, and remember the change of Visa number. You go to a friend's place to get on a high-speed Internet connection, but still, when you select the e-mail link to your bill, you are denied access. Determined to find the underlying cause of the matter, you call the phone company and are routed around until you finally get to someone who understands how the Web site works. It turns out the e-mail link has timed out, and to get to your account you need to go in through the company's home page. There you find your account is two months in arrears and lined up to go to a collection agency! Are you to blame?

Conservative   You are responsible for your bill no matter how it is set up. If your circumstances do not lend themselves to e-billing, you should not use it.

Liberal   It is understandable that you did not keep up with your payments, and hopefully the company will be forgiving when you explain the situation to them.

SUMMARY

When you switch over to e-billing and automatic payment, computers take over and things can go wrong without your knowledge. Electronic monthly statements can have glaring issues you would notice if you were to receive them in a mailed statement, but are silently waiting for you to come find them. Customer Service Representatives are often unfamiliar with how their Web site works and do not know any more than you do how to troubleshoot issues.

Automated Billing – Account Access Lost

Jim and Sally Clyde recently received a call from their credit card company's anti-fraud unit, asking them to verify several charges including one called "computer service." Jim figured it was from their high-speed Internet connection, where their payments are fully automated. He went to the company's Web site only to learn that the company redid the site and his password no longer worked. The site instructed him to enter his account information to re-set up access. However, the Clyde's account information is on the Web site, as they no longer get paper bills. They also had trouble figuring out how to call the company, since they did not have the phone number handy on a bill, which they would have to logon to see. Jim persevered, with difficulty, as we will see in the next issue, but was already quite annoyed with the company. Do you think the Clyde's were partially responsible for using e-billing and not keeping paper records?

Conservative Adding e-billing should be an extra convenience, and not replace a customer's method of contacting the company.

Liberal People who make the electronic leap need to be prepared with all the backup necessary to maintain their accounts.

SUMMARY

This is a classic Catch-22 situation, where the information you need is on the system you can no longer access. For a moment you feel powerless, and feel that the company has negligently wronged you. It is unlikely that the company knew of the consequences of their Web site change, and it will likely not reoccur. Still, the experience reminds us of the value of back-up information; in this case, an electronic copy of a past bill stored on your computer would suffice.

Automated Phone Systems – Are They Helpful?

Frustration rising, Jim finally found a phone number to call and was routed through a phone tree. The company automatically detected his phone number and gave him his account balance and other information he was not interested in now. It took him several tries to figure out how to get through to a person. He finally did and told the service representative his situation. The representative listened to the full story and then said, "Let me transfer you to someone who can help you." Jim then found himself back at the top of the phone tree. Stepping down through the options again he eventually reached a representative and immediately asked to speak to a supervisor. Jim managed to learn his account information and verify the charge in question. When he was done over an hour from when he started, the normally mild-mannered Jim was tense and frustrated, yet did not have any one tangible overriding complaint to take anywhere. Was the company out of line in its customer service?

Conservative Companies try to get so slick with their electronic interfaces that you cannot get to them. When one enters a phone tree trying to speak to a person, it is seemingly impenetrable. Companies should offer the opportunity to speak to a person as one of the first four menu choices. Moreover, a representative should never route you back into the menu maze.

Liberal The company is behaving normally, trying to route its calls more efficiently to keep its costs down. It is a pain for consumers to deal with, but with time you get used to their system. If you need to call the same company repeatedly, make a note of what options to select so you do not need to listen to the whole list every time.

SUMMARY

In the early days of automated phone systems, companies took great care to make sure you could easily get to a person if you needed to. A nice informal standard developed where they said something like "at any time you can select 0 if you need to speak to a representative." No longer does pressing "0" work on many systems, and it takes a brilliant person with perseverance and anger to get through to a person. If you are at a party and the conversation is lagging, try bringing up interacting with automatic phone systems; you are sure to get things sparked. People have tales from entities of all sorts, though those dealing with the telecommunications industry seem to be particularly bad. Others such as a credit unions may annoy you by beginning with a welcome message about a cause they are supporting, like Special Olympics, which you hear each and every time you call. These messages are left on their system for a year or more, long after they are newsworthy to the customers.

The company described is not at all unique; they are well within today's norms for customer service. Customer service representatives usually make good effort to respond to customer needs, but they are limited by their own knowledge. Explaining items on your bill is what they know best, but they are starting to bow out when it comes to helping with their Web site.

The Customer is Always *First*

Anyone who has done time in the world of retail has come across the kinds of situations we mentioned in the introduction to this chapter: an unreasonable customer walks in and makes life difficult for everyone around them. Now, in many cases the customer really does have a legitimate gripe: a hotel reservation was lost, a product order is late, or a billing snafu has occurred. Since they can't vent their frustrations against a faceless corporation, they'll yell at the customer service rep sitting across the desk or on the other end of the telephone instead. This is especially frustrating when working with technology, because there are some cases where you simply *can't* satisfy the customer's request: either they're asking for a feature that your product doesn't deliver, or they're asking for something that violates a security or usage policy. (Think "Why won't you give me my password over the phone?")

It's your job in these situations to provide excellent customer service. What does that mean, really? You should do everything within your power to give the customer a good resolution to their problem. But that doesn't mean that you should subvert your company's security policies, nor does it mean that you should just "sit and take it" if a customer becomes verbally abusive towards you. Being "the customer" does not absolve anyone of the responsibility to treat you like a human being.

Laura E. Hunter
Network Engineer and Technical Trainer

Automated Support – Can They Provide Custom Help?

The Blaster worm invaded your computer. After removing it, you realize you should install a firewall on your laptop. You try the ZoneAlarm product because it has a good reputation according to the reviews. The supplier, Zone Labs, offers a free demo version. All goes well with the installation and your first days of using the firewall. It tells you of cookies about to be put on your computer, and of other machines trying to access it over the Internet. However, after you download a small update to Windows from the Microsoft site, your computer can no longer access the Internet. You suspect the firewall, turn it off, and sure enough you are back online. You read the troubleshooting information on the Zone Labs Web site and do a little testing. You discover everything works fine if the firewall does not launch at startup, but instead after you have accessed the Internet. This order of loading is not a good way to work, however, as you are briefly unprotected on the Internet. Plus, every time your system goes into standby mode, you have to stop and restart the firewall to be able to go online. Because the firewall worked fine before you did the Windows update, you believe you have found a software defect that Zone Labs would like to know about. Their Web site offers Instant Support where you can "Chat online with a Zone Labs Virtual Technical Support Agent." However, when you do so, you soon realize you are dealing with a computer that is automatically referring you to pages on their Web site you have already read. The computer keeps assuming your Internet connection may be down. The Web site also offers Premium Telephone Support where you can talk to a technician and have your credit card billed. Nevertheless, you do not feel you should pay to diagnose what is seemingly a defect.

Feeling frustrated, you compose a long clear explanation of your experience, including details of the module you installed from Microsoft, and send it via e-mail. You get a very long e-mail back, which is a concatenated version of all verbiage on their site about how to install their product, how to verify your Internet connection, and saying that maybe anti-virus software is interfering with the firewall. Nowhere does it refer to the Microsoft module you installed, and hence it seems also to be computer-generated. Now very disgusted with them, you purchase a firewall from Norton, because you have their anti-virus software. Should you have expected better support from a company when you were working with a free demo version?

> **Conservative** A company should save its best support service for its real customers, not browsers. They cannot afford to diagnose every problem by everyone installing their software. A good computer response is better than connecting you to a person who does not know enough to be useful.
>
> **Liberal** The company will hurt its reputation if it cannot help people even get started with their product. It already says a lot about their support that on their Web site they suggest charging you to speak to a technician.

SUMMARY

A firewall has some of the characteristics of the video card described earlier: being very complicated to diagnose because of its interactions with other systems, in this case other software on your computer. The manufacturer cannot hope to provide custom technical support for each configuration issue you may have. Their best bet is to have a superlative help system that guides you through whatever issue you have, and educates you as to the use of firewalls along the way. Unfortunately, the automated computer response puts off existing or evaluating customers, who always prefer, if not require, speaking to a person.

Chapter Summary

People want to be listened to and they want their problems solved. It is difficult if not impossible to really meet people's needs without some human involvement. Is this ethics or just good business? Certainly, it is unethical if someone intentionally designs a company's information flow so that sales support is impossible to get. If you create a license that is abusive of an individual's rights and force them to agree in order to buy your product, again, you need an ethical tune up. In many other cases, it comes down to a business philosophy; the closer your product is to a commodity, the less service you are going to get. Over the years, you have seen businesses cycle from more to less customer service, but the businesses that dominate often provide good service in an efficient manner. This chapter discussed the ethical considerations of customers, starting with their rights with respect to software companies. We then went through a series of customer complaint profiles and the handling of them. The profile of the unhappy hotel guests was rather interesting in its unfolding, with much greater results than expected. We ended with a section on automated customer service, why companies do it, and how customers react to it.

Frequently Asked Questions

The following Frequently Asked Questions, answered by the authors of this book, are designed to get you thinking about the ethical challenges you as a customer may face in the high tech world. Unless legal issues are involved, then answers in the FAQ may not be the right answer for your organization.

Q: Do companies provide poorer customer service than they used to 50 years ago?

A: It can seem that way, when we think of the corner gas station of the 1950s compared to today's gas-n-go stations. In the high tech world, there is a compression of range. The best cannot afford to provide the kind of customer service they used to, and the worst are gone, as a company can no longer get away with not delivering basic products and services.

Q: Does the Internet make customer interaction more aloof?

A: One would think so, but in fact just the opposite occurs. Companies have a natural concern for their reputation as providing good customer service, and this desire is heightened by knowing unhappy customers can get much more mileage than they used to out of their ire. Also, customers now have so many ways to reach companies, with 800 numbers, faxes, Web page interaction, and e-mail, which can be sent any hour of the day or night. The culture of the Internet is very personal, as individuals are heard and known wherever they may be.

Q: What can you do if you hate automatic phone systems, but you need to regularly call your cell phone provider who has one?

A: There are several strategies here. If you reach a person who helps you with a particular problem, ask for their extension so you can call directly with any follow-up questions. Barring that, write down the sequence of keystrokes you need to jump through the menus so you do not have to listen to all those annoying choices that do not pertain to you. If you are still having trouble, consider changing cell phone providers. If you are locked in a contract and really stuck, you might consider creating a really vivid description of your experience with their service center, and send it to the company, saying you thought about putting it on the Internet, but thought they would like a chance to respond first.

Chapter 13

Trusted Assistant

Ethical Dilemmas in this Chapter:

- **Communicating on Behalf of the Manager**
- **Taking Advantage of Your Position**
- **Using the Manager's Names**
- **Access to Company Resources**
- **Conflicts of Interest**
- **In-house Politics and Secrets**
- **The Loyalty of the Trusted Assistant**
- **Handling Sensitive Information**
- **Boundaries of the Trusted Assistant**

Introduction

In the past, a trusted assistant was referred to as a "secretary." In this information age, secretaries are trusted with very sensitive information and computer access; therefore, we refer to them as "trusted assistants" in this book

The relationship between the trusted assistant of a manager and the staff and colleagues of that manager is very different. Prior to e-mail, if a trusted assistant told their manager's team what to do, they probably would not listen unless it came directly from the manager. Today, trusted assistants control the e-mail and other communication mechanisms of the manager. In short, there is a lot more power in the hands of trusted assistants in the information age.

This chapter discusses the ethical issues associated with the role of the trusted assistant, including reaping benefits from your manager's position. It also considers conflicts of interest such as working with your spouse, family, and friends, and the old cliché of having an affair with the manager. Politics and secrets are issues that trusted assistants deal with daily. Toward the end of this chapter, we talk about boundaries, blame, and the repercussions managers and trusted assistants face when they make mistakes. Also in this chapter, we raise questions regarding what are the appropriate boundaries for a trusted assistant. Deciding whether to confine work to office-related tasks and not do personal chores for the manager is a huge ethical decision. Finally, this chapter concludes with the issue of using the trusted assistant as a scapegoat for blame.

Communicating on Behalf of the Manager

In the information age, it is common for trusted assistants to speak on behalf of their managers through e-mail or other electronic means. This brings to light many different ethical dilemmas. Managers do not always have time to check everything their trusted assistant communicates via their e-mail, which may lead to mistakes or serious miscommunications. How does a trusted assistant handle being the electronic manager? What do they do when they make a mistake? The following issues address the ethics of these questions.

Communicating via E-mail for the Manager – A Primary Role?

You are a trusted assistant that responds to your manager's e-mail under his name. There are literally hundreds of e-mails everyday. Is it ethical to speak for your manager through his e-mail if that is what he requests from you?

> **Conservative** There are many dangers inherent in speaking for the manager if you do not possess their expertise. Senior management should handle their own communication to the best of their ability to avoid inaccurate information.

> **Liberal** Handling routine e-mail is acceptable for a trusted assistant. When the e-mail is more complex and specific, it is best for the manager to respond to ensure accuracy. One of the primary roles of a trusted assistant is to respond to the plethora of e-mail that bombards their managers e-mail inbox. This is common ethical practice.

SUMMARY

Handling the manager's e-mail can be scary for the trusted assistant, especially when it requires them to communicate with senior management and there is the risk of making a mistake. Most people would consider this task part of the role of a trusted assistant. As long as the assistant knows the manager well and does not send miscommunications, this practice is ethically acceptable.

Making Mistakes when Speaking on Behalf of the Manager – Should You Confess?

You are a trusted assistant trying to respond accurately to an e-mail about a high tech subject you know little about. The hazard of responding to your manager's e-mail is making mistakes and your response contained glaring errors. Upon error exposure, how do you handle this circumstance? Even worse, what if you respond to the wrong person? For example, your manager instructed you to write to "James Smith," and you thought he said "Jamie Smith?"

Conservative   This example requires you to confess that you responded to your manager's e-mail. Otherwise, your manager will suffer the consequences. You were over your head addressing complex technical issues. In addition, you made an error by sending the e-mail to the incorrect person.

Liberal   Mistakes are inevitable. Check with your manager regarding the correct answer. Then, verify the name of the recipient. Do not tell anyone you are the one behind the e-mail. This will take the effectiveness out of the communication. Apologize to your manager for sending the e-mail to the wrong person and move on. People forget easily.

SUMMARY

Human beings make mistakes. The best thing to do when you make a mistake communicating for your manager is to tell them and let them decide how to handle the situation. Whether they choose to divulge that you were the author of the e-mail or not is up to them. Allow management time to remedy the situation.

E-mail Lists and Distribution of Information – When to Say No?

You are responsible for e-mailing details of sensitive information to a senior management distribution list. Other employees at the company want this information sent to them as well. They do not understand the confidentiality of such data. It cannot go out to anyone who is not on the list approved by your manager. If a senior executive who is higher-ranking than your boss requests the information immediately, do you send it to them or do you wait until you can ask your manager first?

Conservative   Senior management has the authority to override the word of your manager. Provide the information requested and send a communication immediately to your manager explaining the circumstances.

Liberal   Following procedures concerning confidential information must be exact. This example is a risky situation since the person in question is senior to you and your manager. However, you must follow your manager's request and not give out the information until you can speak with them directly and obtain formal approval.

SUMMARY

This is an example of a high-risk circumstance where, regardless of the choice you make, you run personal risk. As the trusted assistant, you may find yourself in a tight spot occasionally when you are in control of the distribution of sensitive information. Others want access to the data you control. If someone junior to your manager requests the information, the answer is obviously "no." However, the issue is complicated when you must field requests from management senior to your boss. Both the liberal and conservative responses are within an ethical range of acceptability.

Taking Advantage of Your Position

Trusted assistants have gained a lot of power since the advent of technology. They have the most information because they access the majority of the information that the manager accesses. With this power comes responsibility and abuse. Trusted assistants can take advantage of their access by using the manager's name for personal advantage or tossing their manager's name around like an all-powerful mantra. Another ethical pitfall trusted assistants can get into is when they try to influence their boss for personal or professional reasons. Following are examples of the ethical issues faced by the ego-inflated trusted assistant.

Getting Ahead by Association – Does it Work For or Against You?

You are the trusted assistant for the CEO of an information technology organization. Due to the workload, break time is limited. You are hungry so you run to the cafeteria and get in line in front of everyone else that is waiting. No one says anything because you are the trusted assistant of the CEO. Is it ethical to cut in front of everyone in line because of your role at the company? Should employees and management allow you special privileges by association?

Conservative It is never appropriate to presume special privileges. This may work in your favor at the cafeteria but will work against you later. People will grow to resent you over time. If you are ever demoted you will find yourself isolated. When you are in a position of potential privilege it can get to your head, but reality is just around the corner.

Liberal As the trusted assistant of the CEO, you have incredible demands on your time and others understand that. Utilize the pull you have to make your life easier in the face of such a hectic schedule.

SUMMARY

Using your status can work for and against you. You may find sincere sympathizers and people who want to kiss up to you because of whom you work for. These types will be supportive and helpful to you. On the other hand, there may be a lot of "behind your back" talk and you will have to deal with some serious resentment from the other employees. Using your power as the trusted assistant to the CEO ultimately falls into your hands. Remember, when you abuse power or show off, it generates resentment that will eventually come back to haunt you.

Using the Manager's Name – Should You Play the Game?

You work for the high profile president of an information technology business. This business specializes in complex mathematical trading floor calculation systems. During the average day, you drop your manager's name many times to get the job done. You toss it around when you speak with hotels for reservations and when setting up conference calls. The reason you do this is to get the best deal for your manager. His status impresses others. Is it appropriate to name drop to get the job done? Do you have an ethical responsibility to allow your boss more privacy?

Conservative In addition to getting the job done, one of the key roles of the trusted assistant is to ensure privacy for your manager. If they are famous in the public eye, privacy is critical for protection against unwanted media. You should be able to get the job done on your own merit rather than pushing your manager's name on everyone you meet. Maybe you do this because it gives you a sense of power and control over others and not because it is necessary to get the job done. This is not ethical behavior.

Liberal There is nothing wrong with playing the game to get your manager the best. If mentioning his name will provide a better room or a vacancy when there was none, do it. Just be cautious of being a beacon for the media. Try not to broadcast his whereabouts when possible.

SUMMARY

Name dropping does open doors that are closed. For example, if your manager is traveling unexpectedly and you must get him the Presidential suite at a posh hotel, dropping his famous name alerts hotel management and may provide additional options. However, keep this practice to a minimum in order to respect your manager's privacy. In addition, do not power trip on your manager's name. That demonstrates a lack of professionalism and is just plain childish.

Influencing the Manager

You do not like one of your coworkers; therefore, you try to influence your manager to fire him. You do it in a nonchalant way by dropping hints. If something goes wrong on a project, you mention that person was involved even if they were not. Eventually your manager fires him. Is this type of behavior ethical?

Conservative This type of behavior is unethical. Abusing your position as a trusted assistant for petty personal reasons is ridiculous and immature. That person might have been an asset to the company or your manager's friend. Your manager will be on to you soon and you will be gone just like the man you did away with.

Liberal Trusted assistants are in a position to make other employees appear a certain way to their manager. They may do this for personal reasons. However, if your manager fires someone because of what you told him or her that is up to them. You are human and have feelings about people who you deem mistreat you. You are entitled to communicate those feelings. When someone loses their job under false pretences due to your communications that is your manager's fault for not taking the time for a full investigation.

SUMMARY

What human being does not try to influence the opinions of their friends and superiors when they face someone whom they find distasteful? There is nothing wrong with communicating your feelings to the manager. However, lying about the failings of another is a different story. This will not only cause an innocent to suffer, but once the truth comes out, you will lose the trust of your manager.

Wormtongue

As a senior manager, I have had to learn to be very careful to take the statements of anyone, even those that are close to me, at face value when they deal with another person. I call it the Search for Truth. It is a fascinating problem that every manager faces; good employees, sane individuals will actually give you a different answer to the same question twice in one week. So what do you do when an employee, especially a trusted employee, says something that affects your perception of someone else in the company? I try to get at least three valid statements from three trustworthy individuals before taking any action. If I find the trusted assistant has misled me, I explain the results of the fact finding and point out that their statement was leading me to incorrect assumptions and action.

Stephen Northcutt

Access to Company Resources

Managers often grant their trusted assistants full access to corporate resources, including corporate credit cards, telephones, office supplies, data, and much more. The trusted assistant performs all of the logistical legwork for the manager; therefore a great deal of access is required. Having blanket access is a dangerous temptation for the trusted assistant. In addition, when a temporary assistant is on the job it can be even more dangerous.

This section discusses the use and abuse of company resources by the trusted assistant. We address questions such as what is right use, what is abuse, and should temporary employees have the same access as full-time employees?

Free Long Distance – Do You Think Twice About It?

Your manager travels most of the time and you remain in the office to answer his calls. It can get quite boring. You have full access to the phone lines and no one checks if you make personal calls. Since you are completely bored, do you take advantage of this phone access and call your family and friends long distance?

Conservative   Abusing company resources is never an ethical choice. Attempting to justify this behavior by claiming you are bored is a joke. This type of activity is stealing whether it appears innocent or not.

Liberal   Everyone makes a personal call or two from work. Using the company phone is an every day occurrence for most employees. There is no need to get righteous about it.

SUMMARY

Even though the liberal point of view is true to some degree, it does not make it ethically correct. Using company resources for personal means is unethical. However, that does not change the fact that nearly everyone does it and does not think twice about it.

Corporate Credit Cards – Should You Presume?

Your manager uses the corporate credit card to purchase his lunch. He has the approval from senior management to do so. He usually buys you lunch when he is in the office, because you never get away from your desk to get to the cafeteria. Since you have full access to the corporate credit cards, is it appropriate for you to use them to buy yourself lunch when your manager is out of the office?

Conservative   If your manager decides to take a risk and purchase your lunch with the corporate credit card that is his business and his ethical choice. However, presuming you may do so on your own is not a wise move, neither is it an ethical one. One would presume that when your manager is not in the office you have the time to go to the cafeteria, which is what he probably assumes.

Liberal   Your manager has set a precedent and he can hardly blame you for following it. As long as you can get away with it, buy your lunch on the corporate credit card. Once someone notices you can explain that your manager does it for you so you presumed it was acceptable. Anyway, you are entitled to lunch on the house because you are overworked and underpaid. The company has to make up for it somewhere. You are just making things fair.

SUMMARY

This issue is on the gray side compared to the ethical issue of using the company telephone for long distance calls. Your manager has the approval to purchase lunch on the corporate credit card and buys you lunch as well because you are too busy to leave your desk. It could be easily justified that if you are equally busy when your manager is away from the office that you can use the credit card to buy yourself lunch. On the other hand, it is not your money, which is a glaring ethical issue. It is best to ask formal permission than presume authority in this matter.

Temporary Employees in the Role of Trusted Assistant – How Much Access Should They Have?

You are a senior manager and your normal trusted assistant is on maternity leave. This circumstance requires you to hire a temporary employee for six-weeks. For proper job performance, the temporary trusted assistant needs to have a significant amount of access. Should you grant the same level of authority and trust in the temporary employee?

Conservative A temporary employee is not as invested in you or your business as a permanent trusted assistant. There are security risks with providing them with too much information. You may have to suffer through a few weeks of doing more work yourself, but this is better than needlessly putting the company at risk. Supplying a temporary employee with too much confidential information or credit cards increases the risk factor. After all, the temporary employee may be a spy for the competition; you never know.

Liberal If you want the temporary employee to get the job done in a manner similar to that of your trusted assistant, you must supply them with the necessary access. Limiting access will result in lower work performance and support.

SUMMARY

Utilizing temporary personnel is a very common practice in big business. Everyone handles temporary employees differently. Some managers grant them the same access as their personal trusted assistant. Others significantly limit access and power to the temporary employee. Unfortunately, senior management learns the ethical lessons of temporary workers on a case-by-case basis. The results of the work accomplished reveal the accuracy of the access decision.

Conflicts of Interest

There is evidence of conflicts of interest in the work place through the highly publicized lawsuits and big business media circuses. Trusted assistants' face a plethora of conflicts of interest, including relating to friends and coworkers when their loyalty must remain with the manager, or working at a company where their spouse works in another department of that company. Finally, there is the old cliché of the affair between the trusted assistant and the manager.

This section addresses the ethical dilemmas of each of these scenarios. You will see that they are not as cut and dry as one might expect.

Working with Your Friends – Do You Tell Them?

You are a trusted assistant at a very small high technology Internet start-up business where everyone in the office are friends. From time to time, someone asks you what the manager thinks of them, or the manager communicates an opinion about one of your coworkers to you. How do you ethically handle these circumstances? If you do not tell your friends of the manager's problem or opinion regarding them, you are betraying your friendship. However, if you tell them, you are betraying the trust of your manager and your role as trusted assistant. What is the ethical response to this fragile situation?

Conservative Your loyalty remains with your manager. If your friends are true friends they will understand that you have to keep some work-related discussions private. Therefore, friendships must remain outside of the office business. You cannot ethically tell your friends what your manager thinks of them or reveal information he said about other coworkers.

Liberal Providing warnings to friends whom you work with is true friendship. You would not knowingly let your friend drive a car without brakes. The same is true if you know something about them and a warning on your part will help them out. It is unrealistic for your manager to expect you to refrain from developing friendships with people at work.

SUMMARY

Matters of privacy are one thing, but friendship in the workplace is another. All trusted assistants must make a personal choice as to whether to divulge information to their friends. Unfortunately, it is a no win situation, because the manager will be upset if information is divulged and the friends will be upset if they are not forewarned.

It's Lonely at the Top

My favorite course to teach is SANS Security Leadership, a course designed for CxOs, VPs, and upwardly mobile managers. One of the first things I try to get them to understand is once you reach VP level, you have no friends in the organization that are not VP or above. This same rule holds for the trusted assistant of a senior manager. No employee can be your friend, if you were friends before you are acquaintances that respect one another now. The military has a name for this, fraternization. It is a critical concept because from now on, the corporate good has to be your primary responsibility and relationships can confuse and confound that responsibility.

Stephen Northcutt

Working with Your Mate – Where Should Your Loyalty Be?

You are the trusted administrative assistant of the senior vice president at a marketing company. Your wife also works at this company and is a marketing sales representative. She asks you what the senior VP is planning for the next proposal so that she can produce something that will wow him but also keep in line with the marketing theme he has set. Should you help your wife and provide her with the marketing information?

Conservative Under no circumstances, even to aid your spouse, should you release information that is trusted to you, especially about business marketing ideas. Your wife must understand that this is a requirement of your employment.

Liberal Your manager must be aware that if your wife succeeds and makes more money you will benefit. After all, anyone can guess your loyalty will lie with your wife first. You took a marriage vow with her, which indicates loyalty to her above everyone else. Expecting someone to withhold information from their spouse is unrealistic. If your manager hired you knowing your wife works for the company, they must have known that you would be talking to her and your loyalty would lie with her first and your manager second.

SUMMARY

Working with your spouse is a serious conflict of interest when one of them is a trusted assistant and the other gains benefit from knowledge the trusted assistant can provide. On the one hand, some may consider passing on business information completely inappropriate regardless of whether it is between husband and wife. Others will argue that if the manager hired the husband, he must expect that there will be some level of information exchange between the two.

Dating the Manager – How Does This Change Things?

This is very cliché but it does happen. Job intensity, long hours, and the corresponding intimacy may result in dating the boss. What is your ethical responsibility as the trusted assistant if you end up dating your manager, assuming your manager is single? Would you feel differently if your manager were married?

Conservative Good business sense dictates that the trusted assistant (and any employee for that matter) should always avoid any type of intimate relationship with their boss regardless of whether they are married or not. If you want to get ahead in business with ethics, you must keep your personal feelings out of the job. It is that simple. In addition, having an intimate relationship with your manager for the purposes of power or status is completely unethical.

Liberal Dating your manager is fine as long as they are single and it does not interfere with your work or break any rules of conduct at the office. Having an affair with your married manager is obviously unethical behavior.

SUMMARY

Having an intimate relationship with the manager changes the trusted assistants reputation and status or power within the organization. This matter is more complicated if others at the office are aware of the relationship. If you fall in love with your manager and they are single, one can hardly help love. You may need to seek employment elsewhere to maintain the relationship. Nevertheless, be aware that you could end up losing the respect of your coworkers. This is especially true if your manager is married.

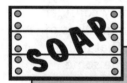

This isn't grammar school, people...

The ethical issue of romantic liaisons in the workplace is one that we're all familiar with. Some companies have adopted a zero-tolerance policy towards this phenomenon, firing people outright when their relationship is discovered or transferring one person (but not the other) to an office in another city. In other cases, the repercussions are more subtle, but no less damaging in the office political struggle. But why does it really need to be this way? The reality is that most of us (especially in upper-level or highly technical positions) find ourselves working extra-long hours that leave us with little time to travel to "acceptable" social gatherings and meeting places. Gone (for most of us, anyway) are the days where you married your college sweetheart and embarked on your journey up the corporate ladder; companies are becoming more and more populated with single and divorced employees at all levels of the org chart.

Continued

Now, I'm certainly not advocating turning the workplace into a dating service, since that's not what *any* of us are here for. But these kinds of zero-tolerance policies are rather anachronistic, and do not allow employees the ability to behave like adults. Better to address individually those situations where behavior becomes inappropriate – holding hands by the coffee machine, hanging out at each other's cubicles, and taking long lunches together? Absolutely not; professionalism still needs to win the day.

Laura E. Hunter
Network Engineer & Technical Trainer

In-House Politics and Secrets

Politics, politics, politics. Big business thrives on politics. How does the trusted assistant succeed at the game and stay ethical? Trusted assistants are often highly underestimated in terms of their power within the organization. This section deals with the inside scoop trusted assistants are privy to, as well as the political games trusted assistants play.

Giving the Inside Scoop to Coworkers – Is It Ever Appropriate?

You work for an information security company and your role as the trusted assistant is highly secure. Coworkers are always asking for the inside scoop, wondering what it is like to work for your manager, what exactly you do for him, what kind of information comes across your desk, and so forth. Is it ever appropriate to tell anyone this information?

Conservative As mentioned previously, providing any information about your manager is unethical. All of the information your coworkers are questioning you about is just some sort of fascination and should be discarded as such. Do not respond to these questions.

Liberal It is natural for people to be curious about a top-secret job and try to find out more information from the trusted assistant, especially if their manager is prominent in the industry. It is ethically acceptable to satisfy some of their curiosity by communicating non-confidential information about your work and your job.

SUMMARY

The safest route for a trusted assistant is to lean on the side of confidentiality in all matters, even if they appear to be harmless. However, this may agitate more curiosity. If it will reduce the questioning, you may want to provide some tidbits of essentially useless non-confidential information about your job.

The New Girl – Do You Sabotage Her?

Your manager hires a new trusted assistant designated to your care. According to your boss, she is to assist you and make your life easier since the workload you carry is burdensome. However, you suspect that your manager is bringing her in to eventually take over your job. Is it ethically acceptable to sabotage her career for job security?

Conservative   There is no reason to presume the new assistant will take over your position. Sabotaging someone else's career out of your own insecurity is unnecessary unethical behavior.

Liberal   Ensuring job security is a major political game played in corporate America. Many times when management introduces an additional trusted assistant in the mix, it is to replace an existing one. You would be stupid to fall for this ploy and not do something to protect your position.

SUMMARY

Politics in the office is not going to go away anytime soon. However, ethical standards require preventing innocent people from being wrongly punished. If you are insecure about your position with your manager, simply ask them about it. Not getting a straight answer may force you to guess. Always take into account that your assumption may be wrong and that you could be hindering the efforts of one who is simply there to help you. Seriously consider if you can ethically damage someone else to ensure your job security. You cannot get away with that type of behavior without being discovered eventually. Do you really have to take someone down with you?

Interrupting the Manager – Should You Wait It Out?

Your manager has assigned you numerous tasks, one of which is labeling personnel files. In prioritizing tasks, you put this task on the back burner. Some of the unlabeled personnel files make their way to your manager's desk right before an interview with a potential employee. You know he is a stickler for details. Should you interrupt the interview to retrieve them?

Conservative In this case, it is better to be correct than for your manager to get upset with you. As politely as possible, interrupt you manager and provide him with the correct information. You may have to take a little heat, but this is better then providing your manager with incorrect or incomplete information.

Liberal Missing labels are not a reason to interrupt your manager during a job interview, regardless of the political consequences. He can open them himself and find the right one.

SUMMARY

The response to this question differs based on the trusted assistant and manager relationship. Some may opt for the more conservative approach knowing their manager would prefer that, whereas others would just wait it out.

The Loyalty of the Trusted Assistant

Management expects loyalty from the trusted assistant. Moments will arise to test loyalty on the job. In some cases, it is ethical to be loyal to your manager, but in others it is not. How would you handle senior management checking up on your manager? What about telling on others to your manager? Then of course, there is the famous whistle blowing. Finally, how would you respond to an attractive bribe?

Senior Management Checking in on Your Manager – Where Does Your Loyalty Lie?

The owner of the company you work for calls you to obtain inside information about your manager. You are the trusted assistant for the Chief Operating Officer (COO) and the questioner is technically senior to your manager, although your manager essentially runs the company. Does your loyalty remain with your manager or the company owner?

Conservative   When addressed by senior management, you must respond accordingly. You may be conservative in your response when the owner of the company asks you questions, but by no means jump on a soapbox and communicate that you will not speak about your boss. It is possible to remain loyal to your manager while answering the owner's questions simply, kindly, and truthfully.

Liberal   Your loyalty is with your manager, not the owner of the company, who is just a figurehead. Do not reveal any information about your manager or your experience working for him.

SUMMARY

When the owner of a company or someone in senior management contacts the trusted assistant to get the scoop on their manager, the issue of where to place loyalty is in the forefront of the conversation. If you have a serious gripe about your manager, can you tell the owner and trust it will not get back to your manager? This is the type of decision a trusted assistant must make.

Tattletale Trusted Assistant – Should You Tell?

In some cases, there is an expectation of the trusted assistant to be a tattletale on others at the company. Their manager encourages them to find out as much information as possible regarding everyone in the office and then questions the trusted assistant about other executives and employees. Is expecting a trusted assistant to be the eyes and ears for the manager an ethical job responsibility?

Conservative The trusted assistant should avoid being a spy for their manager. This is an unethical request made on the part of the manager. It is way beyond the job description and places the trusted assistant at odds with the rest of the office.

Liberal When a trusted assistant is loyal, they will automatically support the career of their manager, and if they come across any useful information will pass it along. The manager and the trusted assistant are a team aimed at mutual success.

SUMMARY

Requiring a trusted assistant to gather intelligence and spy on others in the workplace is going too far. However, there is a dynamic that occurs with well-matched trusted assistant and manager scenarios. They may join forces to further both of their careers. If the manager goes far, the assistant will go with them. In this case, the trusted assistant becomes an extension of the manager.

Whistle Blowing – A Difficult Decision

You are the trusted assistant for an oil company executive and discover that he is involved in illegal activity, essentially stealing millions of dollars from the company. Do you blow the metaphorical whistle or keep silent due to your loyalty to the executive?

Conservative You must immediately contact the appropriate authorities regarding the illegal activity. Failing to do this is both morally and legally wrong.

Liberal Although most people would consider the right answer to be report them, in reality, the trusted assistant is familiar with the current power structure and may be too intimidated to do anything different. This is unfortunately true even if the manager is ethically or legally wrong. This is why most whistle blowers are peers rather then subordinates. It is very difficult to go against the manager, especially when the trusted assistant knows the result of reporting them will at the very least cost them their job.

Summary

It is unusual for a trusted assistant to be a whistle blower; maybe because of the power structure or because they are not privy to the information that other executives have. When illegal activity is occurring in the work place, the ethically correct action to take is to report it to the proper authorities. Some trusted assistants may not be able to do this because they are blind to their manager's actions or will struggle financially if they lose their jobs.

Taking a Bribe from an Interviewee – Is It Ever a Good Idea?

It is hiring time in the department and plenty of people are kissing up to you, the trusted assistant, to get on the job interview list. Is it acceptable to put some resumes at the top of the pile or recommend others because those people paid special attention to you? Would you feel different about this issue if an interviewee slipped you some cash or a gift?

Conservative   It is never ethically appropriate to respond to flattery or bribes in the workplace. Most job interviewee's will try to make friends with the trusted assistant because they know it may help them get the job. Ignore this type of behavior and remain impartial to all applicants.

Liberal   You might as well play the game since you will have to work with whomever your manager hires. If you see someone that you can work well with and is nice to you, put that resume on the top of the list and advocate for them. After all, you do not want to end up working with someone who is not friendly to you.

Summary

Taking bribes is one thing, while feeding on job applicant praise is another. As discussed, accepting a bribe is a bad idea both legally and ethically. However, helping out a job applicant because you approve of them is completely up to you as the trusted assistant.

Handling Sensitive Information

The trusted assistant is privy to an incredible amount of sensitive information. This data often includes both personal and corporate information. The trusted assistant must handle information in a sensitive manner. The following ethical issues address intellectual property, personnel information, and vendor requests for information. We also discuss how owning responsibility for this sensitive information may lock a trusted assistant into one job. The trusted assistant may find they are unable to receive promotions and move on because they possesses too much sensitive information about one executive or business area.

Intellectual Property – What Can You Share?

The trusted assistant maintains records regarding incredible amounts of intellectual property. Must they submit to a life of silence because that information is private? Does the fact that you are a trusted assistant forbid you to speak about your job? What should you share or not share in terms of intellectual property? Will your manager perceive you as a person who does not care about the rights of the organization's intellectual property if you talk about your stressful day to a friend and mention some of the business?

Conservative Under the circumstances, intellectual property must remain private. This means that the trusted assistant cannot go home to her family or friends and vent about her day. In one sense, the trusted assistant submits them self to a life of silence regarding intellectual property and confidential information.

Liberal Expecting another human being to remain silent about their job is relatively unrealistic unless you are dealing with issues of national security. As long as you reveal information to your loved ones or close friends and not to the competition, there is nothing ethically wrong with letting off a little steam.

Summary

There is a fine line between protecting intellectual property and receiving a sentence to a life of paranoia and silence. If legal agreements are in place forbidding the trusted assistant from communicating about secure matters, they are due proper respect. However, expecting someone to remain silent concerning all aspects of their career is simply unrealistic.

Personnel Information – Is It Confidential?

You are the trusted assistant of a senior manager. One of your responsibilities is to submit payroll to the accounting department. Frequently, employees ask you how much compensation one of your coworkers receives in comparison to the rest of the team. Your manager has never communicated any direction you should take in regard to these pointed questions. Do you provide the information or remain silent about employee wages?

Conservative Payroll data is confidential and must remain so. The only reason your manager did not provide you with any direction about handling this sensitive information is that it is common knowledge that this type of data is not made available to the general staff. Revealing payroll information creates a mess of competition and arguments of unfair treatment among the team.

Liberal You may decide to reveal or hint at payroll information because you feel that your manager or the company is unfairly under-compensating an employee for their work. Make these revelations based on your personal ethics of fairness.

SUMMARY

In most cases, payroll information is confidential. If your manager does not directly indicate this, presume it. There may be instances where your personal ethics concerning the treatment of a particular employee press you to communicate some information to them. That is a personal choice that will have consequences in your life, your manager's life, and the employee's life. If those consequences are worth your personal morals, then do it.

Requests for Information from Vendors – Should You Pass Along Information?

You arrange for conference rooms for your manager at well-known hotels. On occasion, the hotels inquire about the nature of the contracts of competing hotel chains. They request to see the physical contracts submitted by other hotels. Is it ethical to pass along vendor information to their competition?

Conservative   Information, whether it is internal to your organization or external vendor contracts, should remain confidential. There is no ethically good reason to supply information to competitors regarding the vendors you utilize.

Liberal   If the vendor wants to see a competitor's contract in order to give you a better price or deal, by all means show it to them. This is a simple negotiation practice that is within the boundaries of good ethics.

SUMMARY

In most cases, confidentiality is a highly respected ethical principal, even if your company does not benefit from it. However, saving your company a lot of money by quoting from a competitor or providing documentation from a competitor is within the range of ethical possibility as long as it is legal activity.

Getting Stuck as a Trusted Assistant – When is it Okay to Leave?

You have worked for your manager for 15 years and have been privy to a wealth of intellectual property and highly sensitive information. Your manager is a senior vice president of an investment firm. She would never accept you working for anyone else in the company because of how much you know about her personally and professionally. You would like to do something else with your career, such as become a project manager. If you leave the investment firm, you will lose all of the seniority you have earned through the years. How do you get out of being a trusted assistant and speak to the manager about your future? What do you do if you find yourself locked into a job because you are so valuable, or know too much to go anywhere else?

Conservative   If you really feel it is time for you to move on to something better for yourself, the best option is to sit down and have an honest conversation with your manager. Maybe out of loyalty to you she will help you find a project management role at the company. However, be aware that you are taking a risk when communicating these feelings to her. This will be a warning sign that it is time to find someone new. Busy executives have little time for a huge disruption such as their trusted assistant leaving. Your manager may create a backup plan for herself.

Liberal   You will probably have to go to another company to find a new job that provides you with the career opportunities you are seeking. Perform the job search on the sly, because as soon as your manager finds out, you can be sure there will be a replacement for you brought in to train, which will limit your job search time significantly.

SUMMARY

Honesty is always the best policy in terms of ethics. In most cases, communicating directly with your manager is the optimum solution to this ethical dilemma. There are circumstances, however, when you cannot talk to your manager because, as their trusted assistant, you are so crucial to their lives that they would never accept you doing anything else. You may need to break yourself free and find employment elsewhere for your own growth.

Boundaries of the Trusted Assistant

Since management often grants trusted assistants with access to personal and professional information, questions of personal boundaries arise. Even if the information is not freely given, reviewing credit card records for expense reports and simply answering the phone provides a great deal of personal information. How far does the trusted assistant take such privacy matters? There are professional expectations that are more obvious, but what about the personal expectations? The line gets blurry once trust is established.

At some point, trusted assistants may find themselves over their heads in terms of ethical confidentiality and the need to set some boundaries. For example, how does the trusted assistant handle knowledge of personal information about their manager, such as an illicit affair? What do they do about inquiries regarding their own personal life on the part of the manager? This section addresses those issues as well as others including performing non-work-related chores for the manager, taking the heat for the manager's mistakes, and being an alias for the manager.

Personal Information About the Manager – Should You Intervene?

It has become completely obvious to you that your manager is cheating on his wife. He has even joked about it to you. You have gotten to know his wife through the years and sincerely respect her. You feel infidelity is immoral so this action on his part goes against your personal ethics. How do you handle this circumstance? Do you tell his wife or should you keep is confidential?

Conservative When faced with personal issues at the workplace that conflict with your morals, you must not destroy your own beliefs to protect your manager personally. You may want to communicate your feelings directly to your manager rather than to his wife. If this is ineffective, you will have to speak to his wife directly about the matter. This is a no win situation. Communicating anything about the circumstances will intertwine you in this personal mess. On the other hand, you are already in the middle of it.

Liberal Even though your manager has brought his personal choices into the office, there is no reason for you to meddle and get directly involved. It may be painful for you, but remember that work is work and your personal morals and feelings should not destroy your working relationship with your manager. There is nothing wrong with people having different values and beliefs.

SUMMARY

Maintaining your own personal boundaries and morals in the workplace may be very challenging when your manager has brought personal and questionable morals to the office. You have two options: stay completely out of the matter or get directly involved. Both are not much fun if you have strong moral opinions in either direction.

Professional Distance – What is a Good Balance?

Your manager speaks about her personal life to you. She never asks you about yours and is offended if you mention something about your life outside of the office. Is it ethically appropriate to have a one-way relationship on a personal level with your boss?

Conservative Be grateful that your manager does not want to know about your personal life. Since she is your superior, just listen to what she has to say and try not to retain anything. Maybe she just needs to vent occasionally due to the stress of his job.

Liberal This is not a balanced relationship. However, since she is the one with the power she can dictate the nature of the relationship. It is not ethical but a potential reality for a trusted assistant.

<u>**Summary**</u>

When you are dealing with a power structure, you cannot expect balance between the trusted assistant and the manager. Whether you feel the relationship is fair or not is irrelevant to the role you must play as the trusted assistant.

Performing Non-work Related Chores – Are You Setting a Precedent?

You are a trusted assistant for an old fashioned senior manager at a construction company. He frequently asks you to bring him coffee or do chores for him such as picking up his laundry at the dry cleaners during lunch. Is it ethically appropriate for the trusted assistant to do personal chores for their manager?

Conservative You need to remind your manager that you are there to perform a job for him in relation to corporate business and not his personal needs. Recommend that he get a housekeeper if he needs help with his personal chores. You should not perform these responsibilities.

Liberal It really depends on how you feel about the chores and the nature of your relationship with the manager. If you like getting out of the office and can handle some of your personal errands at the same time it might be convenient for you.

SUMMARY

Whether you agree to handle your manager's personal chores or not, remember that you are setting a precedent for your employment. He may expect more and more from you as time goes one. Once the precedent is set it will be more difficult to change later on. Keep in line with your personal morals. If it makes life easier for you to do some personal favors for your manager then do it. If you feel demoralized by doing them, then do not do them . Remember to keep it fair in terms of company money. If you are running personal errands for your manager on company time, you are dealing with additional ethical matters.

Taking the Blame – Should You Be a Scapegoat?

When your manager makes a mistake, he publicly blames it on you; you are his scapegoat. Is it ethically correct for the manager to pin his mistakes on you or should he own up to them?

Conservative Morally speaking, everyone should own up to their mistakes and not cover them up by targeting another.

Liberal If you and your manager have an agreement that you will take the heat for his mistakes, it is your choice and a means by which you are strategically supporting your manager.

SUMMARY

Taking the heat for the manager happens in many circumstances. Clearly communicate what level of heat you are willing to accept to protect your manager and what your threshold is. Some trusted assistants will not do this at all.

The Manager's Alias – Should You Be a Buffer?

Your manager asks you to give feedback to other employees and make it seem like you are the one providing it. In truth, they are your manager's words. Is this responsibility on the part of the trusted assistant ethical?

Conservative It is common practice for a manager to test the waters prior to jumping in. Your manager may be trying to get a feeling for the employees and tactfully using you as the means to better manage the situation. This is ethical behavior.

Liberal In this case, the manager may not want to alienate himself from coworkers and subordinates by providing negative feedback. He is using you as a buffer. However, most coworkers know that the words of the trusted assistant are that of the manager.

SUMMARY

When a trusted assistant is trying to pass off feedback from the manager as their own, it is usually obvious. The benefit of this type of communication is that coworkers and subordinates may find it less offensive or threatening coming from the trusted assistant rather than the manager.

Chapter Summary

You are now acutely aware of the complex role of the trusted assistant in the information age. The relationship between the trusted assistant and their manager is significantly different with the use of computer technology. You learned the means by which the trusted assistant controls e-mail and other communication mechanisms. Today, the trusted assistant wields a great deal more power than in the past. This power may lead to temptation if ethics are not brought into the mix.

This chapter introduced you to the ethical dilemmas facing the trusted assistant in the information age. Among them is the age-old issue of access to company resources such as making long distance telephone calls, utilizing corporate credit cards, or taking supplies from the office.

We also discussed potential conflicts of interest and how friendships and intimacy in the work place is much more complicated than most people realize. They can jeopardize the confidentiality of information.

In the sections on politics, loyalty, and handling sensitive information, we delved into the complex web of privacy expectations. We talked about the dynamics of how trusted assistants and their managers use and abuse their power and influence over each other.

In response to all of the ethical considerations of this chapter, we discussed boundaries. Boundaries arise when an individual's moral beliefs starkly contrast with their work expectations. You learned when and why trusted assistants must set them.

Finally, this chapter concluded with business strategies that transfer blame onto the trusted assistant from the manager. We discussed whether these strategies are ethical.

Frequently Asked Questions

The following Frequently Asked Questions, answered by the authors of this book, will get you thinking about the ethical circumstances you may face as a trusted assistant. Unless legal issues are involved, then answers in the FAQ may not be the right answer for your organization.

Q: When you speak for your manager through electronic means such as e-mail or on-line chats, what are the possible dangers of this type of power and communication?

A: If you make a mistake while you are speaking for your manager, it will affect their reputation. There is also the tendency to abuse this type of power for your own personal means.

Q: Is it appropriate for a trusted assistant to influence the manager in any way?

A: The trusted assistant and the manager are a team in a sense. It is appropriate for the trusted assistant to provide feedback to the manager about a job interview candidate or other employee if the intention of that information is to benefit the company and not based on personal motives.

Q: Are there any company resources that the trusted assistant is justified in utilizing for personal purposes?

A: For the most part, corporate resources are for business purposes. When a manager or senior management suggests that the trusted assistant may utilize corporate resources to purchase a meal because you are working overtime, that is an ethical example of using corporate resources for personal means. Any utilization of company resources that is out of relationship with your manager is inappropriate use.

Q: What are the different types of conflict of interest for a trusted assistant?

A: There are many different examples of conflicts of interest when it comes to information confidentiality for the trusted assistant. Among them is providing information to coworkers that you have a unique relationship with, such as working with your spouse.

Q: What part does corporate politics play in the role of a trusted assistant?

A: Due to corporate politics, the trusted assistant may find themselves in the role of a spy for their manager. They may also play politics themselves and try to influence their manager in one direction or another for personal gain.

Q: What are the loyalty obligations of the trusted assistant?

A: The trusted assistant is expected to keep all confidential work-related information private. That is the bottom line. Anything beyond that is the ethical choice of the trusted assistant.

Q: Is there ever a circumstance when the trusted assistant can empower themselves to pass on sensitive information entrusted to their manager to someone else within or outside of the corporation?

A: The only acceptable circumstance when a trusted assistant may choose to pass on sensitive information is to management senior to their boss.

Q: The trusted assistant often knows far too much personal information about the manager. How can they abuse this knowledge?

A: Blackmail is one means by which a trusted assistant can abuse personal information about their manager.

Q: Are personal ethical boundaries important for trusted assistants, or should they submit to the ethical boundaries of their manager?

A: Blindly submitting to the ethical boundaries of the manager is a mistake. If you partake in illegal activity, the law will hold you accountable even if you are simply going along with it. Submitting to another's ethics when they are contrary to your own may wear away at your self respect.

Chapter 14

Ethics and Contractors/ Consultants

Ethical Dilemmas in this Chapter:

- **Strategies for Obtaining Contracts**
- **Pushing the Limits**
- **Withholding Information**
- **Work from Previous Contracts**
- **Vague Areas in Legal Contracts**
- **Making Use of Available Resources**
- **Consulting Agencies**

Introduction

This chapter discusses the major ethical issues pertaining to contractors and consultants. When referring to contractors and consultants we are talking about non-employee individuals hired by a company to perform a specific role for a specific period of time. The title "contractor" derives from the fact that you are under legal contract with a given company. For example, you are a business analyst consultant hired by a company to define specifications for their new accounting system. If you are an independent consultant you probably have your own corporation, are a sole proprietor, or are a 1099 contractor. Upon hiring, you are provided with a contract from the hiring company that states the terms of your employment. The terms include the rate of pay, which can be a daily, hourly, weekly, monthly, or fixed-bid rate. The contract will also include the start date and end date of your employment. When the end date arrives, you and the hiring company are no longer under obligation to each other. At this point they may renew your contract, which you can accept or not.

Contractors are usually experts in a specialized area of Information Technology (IT) or business. They are paid at a significantly higher rate than full-time employees because of their valuable knowledge.

In addition to the types of independent contractors mentioned here, there is another type, the "big six consultant," who is an internal employee that is farmed out as a consultant to an organization on a contract basis.

Ethical issues in contracting and consulting work vary from over billing customers, contractors that are under qualified, and working around the legal contract itself. This chapter begins with the ethical issues of getting your first contract or maintaining your contracting status through networking.

Strategies for Obtaining Contracts

Whether you are just breaking into contract work or have been contracting for a while, you may choose to implement various strategies for developing relationships that will produce more contracts for you in the future or land you that first job. Networking plays a key role in contract work. In the following issues, we will discuss the means used to develop relationships and the corresponding ethical circumstances you may find yourself in when pursuing these means.

Networking for Contracts – Should You Help Your Friends at the Expense of Others?

Networking is a big part of being a contract worker. Building relationships and maintaining them keeps you alive in the industry and is essential for continual consulting survival. You are a management consultant and one of your contacts provides you with an excellent contract lead. In exchange for the lead they request that if you are hired you must hire them. You get the job, but the team is already in place. The only way to get your friend on it is to fire someone. What do you do?

Conservative You should not have made that type of promise to begin with. You need to go back to your friend and explain the situation. Tell him that as soon as an opening comes available he will be the first one on your list to call into an interview. You cannot simply just hire him because he got you the job; you need to know he will be a good candidate for that job.

Liberal Your network of contacts is crucial for finding future work. Your friend helped you out; now it is your turn. Fire the least competent person and bring your friend in. Anyway, if you are in management it is always good to fire someone your first week on the job; it makes people respect you.

SUMMARY

Whether you decide to trade favors with people within a network of relationships you maintain in contracting or not, this example is an important issue to consider. Keep in mind the job at hand and remember that if you bring people in because you owe them one but they cannot get the job done, you as the management consultant will be to blame. On the other hand, if you break promises to people within your network that helped you find work, you may not have much of a network left. Be careful what you promise and to whom. Take some time to think before giving an answer to anything. Every choice you make as an independent contractor will take you down a different road in your career.

Another factor to consider when trading favors is how deep to get into it. Do you really want to end up like a politician who cannot make their own decisions because they owe everyone so many favors they are ruled by paybacks?

Free Contracting – How Far Should Free Assessments Go?

Consultants breaking into the contract market will occasionally offer free work as a means to attract new clients or catch that big client's attention. The most important thing to consider when performing a free assessment is whether the company can afford to hire you to do the job. After all, you do not want to do a lot of work for a company you know cannot afford to hire you. Perform research prior to putting yourself out there in this manner. Consider the following issue.

You are trying to make a name for yourself as an independent consultant and offer a free assessment of a potential client's contingency plan in hopes they will hire you to create a new one. They like your assessment but decide to implement the changes you mentioned with their full-time staff. You never signed a legal agreement with them stating you would do the assessment free. Do you have the right to go after them for the assessment?

Conservative   You took a chance and lost. Let it go and move on. A verbal agreement is still an agreement. You have no right now to go back and change it since it is not in writing. Learn from this and handle yourself in a more structured manner next time.

There is no sense getting into a personal or legal battle over it. That would defeat the purpose of offering the free work to begin with. You did it to attract new clients. If you go after one legally or personally, it will display you in a poor light whether you are right or wrong.

Liberal   You have been scammed. It is one thing to offer a free assessment and another to take that assessment and have someone else implement it. That is just bad business. Speak to them about getting some compensation for the assessment or tell them they do not have your permission to use the assessment.

If that does not work, threaten legal action and be ready with your lawyer for a battle. You need to show your strength.

SUMMARY

You may want to outline things in a more detailed manner the next time you use this type of strategy to attract clients. Generate a written agreement that states that if they want to implement your work they will hire you to do it. Again, do research in advance to make sure the company you provide free services for can actually afford to bring you on.

Pushing the Limits

Some contractors try to push the limits in terms of their skills to make an extra buck. In some cases, they push the limits by exaggerating on résumés or using strategies such as "bait and bail." In other cases, they push the limits when it comes to billing for the work they have done.

Consulting work is lucrative and there is a strong demand for contractors, therefore, it is tempting to try to break into it without experience or before your time has come. In the industry, you may find that some big six firms and placement agencies try to pass off unqualified people as IT consultants.

Another big issue is over billing. Pushing the limits in terms of billing can be very tempting for contractors. Adding an extra hour here or there can mean a lot more money in their pocket if they are not caught.

Fake IT Contractors – Contracting Unqualified Clients

A common problem for big six firms and independent consultants alike, is unqualified consultants. Since the need for IT professionals is greater than the number of people in the market, unqualified individuals are billed out as consultants. Big six firms are known for hiring people straight out of college and billing them out at a much higher rate than they are worth. The following is an example of this dilemma.

You make social conversation with a big six consultant contracted at the brokerage house you work for, and find out she just graduated from junior college as a graphics artist but is being billed out by the firm as a senior management consultant. What do you do?

Conservative Under no circumstances should a person without a college degree in IT and the appropriate work experience be billed out as a consultant, even if they work for a big six firm. Immediately speak to senior management and encourage them to let this person go since they are not qualified for the work.

Liberal It really does not matter what background she has as long as she can do the job. Keep quiet and let her do the job. If she cannot do the job she was hired to do, it will be revealed in time. There is no sense in getting yourself involved in this situation.

SUMMARY

IT consultants represent different skill levels. Due to the demand in the marketplace, you will find people who have changed occupations doing well in IT. It is really a decision on the part of the hiring company if they are willing to accept someone who has little or no experience. Responses to this matter will vary depending on the organization.

Hired but Cannot Do the Job – Should You Take the Job?

Yes, it happens—contractors are hired for jobs they cannot do. Either a non-technical hiring manager just liked their personality or they bluffed their way through the interview. Consider the following issue.

You are hired for a job that is way over your head. You were a system administrator on your last contract, which meant you had to physically set up workstations and install new software. For this contract, being a system administrator means controlling all of the system files, resources, and security. Job definitions at different companies vary; since this is only your second contract you were not aware of this. Do you take the job and learn as much as you can or decline?

Conservative   Be honest with the hiring manager and tell them you are not qualified for the job. This is better than making a complete fool of yourself and potentially reeking havoc on the IT department. Maybe they will offer you another contract that is more within the range of your skills.

Liberal   Take the job, study at night, and find some experienced system administrator friends that you can call during the day when you are stuck. Go for it. If you can do it, great. If you cannot, the worst that can happen is they fire you.

SUMMARY

Balancing your personal goals and desires against the needs of an organization is primary to this issue. As a consultant, you are expected to think beyond yourself at a higher level. Who does not want to advance their career and go for something new and more lucrative?

Résumé/Portfolio – Should You Use Exaggerations and Lies?

Résumé exaggerations and outright lies are factors in all industries. There are three types of consultants: the super straight, highly educated, and experienced, the exaggerators, and the outright liars. The liars are relatively easy to spot and are usually caught during the interview process. Sometimes it is hard to tell the difference between the straight shooters and the exaggerators. The following is an example of that scenario.

You are a full-time employee. You have noticed the big money that independent contractors make and want a piece of the pie. You know you need another five years of work experience to break into consulting, so you re-word your earlier work as an administrative assistant to look like you were doing IT work instead, which gives you enough years to put yourself forward as a consultant. You are just as good as the consultants you have seen, but do not have as much experience. Is this acceptable if your skills are equivalent?

Conservative It is never appropriate to lie on a résumé to get a better job or more money. This type of person cannot be trusted. Many companies have a background check performed on every new contractor to validate their information. Be prepared to get caught in a lie and damage your reputation.

Liberal Sometimes it is hard to break into contract work if you do not have ample years in the business. In some cases, it is okay to exaggerate a little bit to get your foot in the door. As long as the talent is there and you can perform the job at hand, who cares if there was a little exaggeration?

Even in the case of outright lying, everyone has to start somewhere and breaking into the industry can be very difficult. So what if you make up a few companies and a little job history to get yourself that first gig. You can take the lies off of your résumé once you have some actual work experience as a contractor. You are not hurting anyone.

SUMMARY

Breaking into consulting is not easy unless you have had a lifetime of contacts. Sometimes you may come across people who exaggerate their résumés and in some cases lie about work experience. Standardized testing during the interview can help hiring companies determine if a person can do the job regardless of work experience.

In some cases, hiring is done by non-technical managers. In this case, they may not be able to detect exaggerations and lies on résumés or during interviews. It is important to be aware that this occurs.

"Bait and Bail"– Should You Risk It?

In the consulting industry, independent contractors sometimes help each other out by using the "bait and bail" strategy. Bait and bail occurs when a talented person with great interview skills goes on an interview for a job, gets the job, and then informs the hiring company they cannot take it. They immediately refer their friend who they say is just as qualified as they are. Since the hiring company sent everyone else home and is probably tired of interviewing, the client takes the friend who in most cases is not as qualified or talented as the person they originally selected. For example, you are a junior consultant and want to break into senior consulting. You feel you are ready. You ask your friend to interview at a senior consulting position and then refuse the job and recommend you. You have heard of others being successful at this bait and bail strategy. Is this ethical?

Conservative   Attempting to trick a potential employer is never a smart move. Contact your friend and tell them you will try to get the job on your own merit. Work your way up the corporate ladder and do not try to skip steps; if you cannot get a job on your own merit you probably could not do the job anyway. Do not rush it!

Liberal   It works like a charm. There is nothing wrong with using a little strategy to get your foot in the door when you are looking to move up. Make sure you take your friend out to dinner to thank them.

SUMMARY

The choice to use edgy strategy when moving up the ranks in contract consulting is a personal matter. If you use the "bait and bail" strategy some companies may not even notice; others will and will blacklist you and your friend. Whenever you push the envelope, you are risking your reputation. Then again, you need to take risks as an entrepreneur.

Over Billing – Doing What You Think is Right

Over billing is more common in large impersonal companies, probably because consultants cannot see who gets hurt by this practice. Common over billing practices include leaving early and still charging for the full day or sneaking out of the office for coffee with coworkers and charging for the time. Another example is contractors working from home and billing for hours never worked, and contractors who play games or surf the Web during work hours and bill for that time.

In the case of large businesses, the money comes out of the overall IT budget and can really add up depending on the size of the department. If detected, the manager of the IT team is held responsible and potentially fired for failing to properly manage the consultants. If undetected, the IT department as a whole suffers because money that could have gone to additional consultants, equipment, and facilities has been wasted.

Over billing is less common in smaller companies because the consultant knows whom they are ripping off. However, it still happens for many reasons. Some people do not want to work a full day but feel they need to make it look like they did. Others are simply out for themselves and want to make as much money as possible with as little effort as possible. Since many IT managers are not technical and do not know how long it takes to design a database or write a program, this type of practice tends to go undetected.

Rogue Router at Customer's Expense

Several years ago, I noticed a contractor spending quite a lot of time and effort getting himself ready for his day of work at his customer's site. I noticed that both Ethernet and telephone jacks were being used to make connections to his laptop and asked what he was doing. I was told that the Ethernet connection was required to connect to several systems he was working with on the local network, while the modem connection was used for both accessing his employer's network services and supporting remote (Telnet and FTP) access from his colleagues.

His long-distance dial-up modem connection was maintained all day and every day during his stay, adding a significant overhead cost to his

Continued

> professional services. Worse, his laptop was an unrestricted and unsecured extranet router between two large multinational companies.
>
> *Algis Kibirkstis*
> *System Designer (Security)*
> *Ericsson Canada*

You are a contractor and your manager has allocated one month for a project you know will take you one week to complete. Do you keep quiet and bill for a three-week vacation or ask for a new project to begin?

Conservative It is never okay to be paid for time when you are not working. As soon as you have down time, report to the manager and say that you have completed the project and can begin something new. They will appreciate you for the expedience of your work.

Liberal It is management's job to allocate time and resources. If they misallocate, that is not your problem as a consultant. Work the one week then take a break. You earned it.

SUMMARY

These points of view reflect the good boy versus bad boy strategies. You may find an abundance of bad boy strategies in consulting because often consultants do not feel they are responsible for management of time. In some cases, there are very young consultants who may still be going through a rebellious phase such as genius kids in the arena of Web development and computer graphics.

The following discusses the over billing issue with a slightly different twist. In this case, over billing has been happening for a long time at a company.

You know that all of the consultants over bill in your department. They justify this by saying it is a huge impersonal company and it does not hurt anyone if they make a few extra bucks. Their managers do not care because it is not coming out of their pockets. Do you over bill or keep it straight?

Conservative If everyone were going to jump off a cliff, would you do it too? Better to bill for exactly the amount of time you work. You should consider turning in the consultants that are over billing. The company will appreciate it.

Liberal Everyone does it, so stick to the norm. Big businesses these days have huge IT budgets that they waste most of the time anyway. You do invaluable work and should get as much money as you can.

SUMMARY

This matter of over billing is a little trickier than the previous one. If you bill correctly you could target the entire team, which sets you up in opposition to them. In addition, who would not want a few extra bucks if they feel they are doing a good job? This comes down to personal ethics and having the courage to do what you feel is right whatever that may be.

Withholding Information

Consultants are known for hoarding information. Sometimes they are being protective of their hard work and experience. Other times they are being security conscious. However, in many cases, they are trying to ensure job security.

The following are different ways in which consultants withhold information. There is the mumbo jumbo talk, the old "let's make it hard for everyone else to do their job," and then the more honest reasons for withholding information such as getting the money owed to you and saving your own butt.

Honesty and Clients

A common ethical dilemma for consultants is being asked by a client, 'How do you do <insert technical task here>?' Many times the first reaction is not to provide an answer, but rather to question the motives of the person who is asking the question. Are they asking because they hope to do some task without incurring the costs of having you there to do the job? Are they testing you? Or are they simply curious?

The negative side to providing the information can seem to be a loss of income due to fewer billable hours or even the possibility of someone completely taking over the job and the loss of a client. It comes down to:

Continued

'If I tell this person the true answer, am I cutting my own throat?' Positive reasons for giving the information seem to be fewer or even non-existent. However, over the years I found that a straightforward answer is the best strategy.

First of all, few people are testing you and most are simply curious. Sitting in front of their PC day in and day out, they are inquisitive about what's 'under the hood.' Just explaining an overall procedure is usually more than enough for those people.

For those clients who are seeking to make some task of a more 'Do It Yourself' chore, my experience is that they generally fall into two classes: The first is the client who, having learned the complexity of a job, realizes that they will be over their head and has you do it. The second class of clients are those who don't realize their own limitations and botch the job. These people usually end up calling you back to do the original job AND fix their mistakes. Either way, there is little chance of loss of income over the long term.

There is a third, very small class. These are the people who pick up the small task and can run with them. There can be a small amount of decreased billable hours with this type of person, but I find they generally are much quicker to recognize their own skill limitations and are quicker to call you in for the bigger jobs. Again, in the long term it usually doesn't mean a loss of income.

Finally, by giving a straightforward answer, and not being evasive, you enhance your reputation for being honest and ethical with clients.

Frank Thornton,
Technology Consultant
Blackthorn Systems

Using Mumbo Jumbo – Does it Provide Job Security?

You are doing contract work at a telecommunications company. One of your strategies on the contract is to make yourself indispensable by creating procedures that are more complex than necessary. If a new consultant enters the department, you try to mystify them with complicated mumbo jumbo talk that even you do not understand. Is this acceptable behavior for job security?

Conservative   This is not acceptable behavior. This behavior demonstrates simple insecurity. Although a lot of technology professionals do such things, you do not need to do it. If you are good at your job, it will show. There is no need to mystify everyone else and make things more complicated than necessary.

Liberal   Whatever you have to do to ensure job security is what you need to do. In addition, if the new person does not realize that you are talking mumbo jumbo, they are not qualified anyway. Moreover, if they do know that you are just trying to stump them and they are simply too afraid to say anything, they do not have the strength of character for the job.

SUMMARY

Jockeying for job security or superiority is found in every workplace. Consultants have an edge in some ways because they tend to be more knowledgeable than internal employees simply because they are hired for their expertise in a specialized area. That power can be used or abused.

Making It Hard for Others to Do Their Jobs – Should You Play This Game?

You are a consultant in system administration working at a fiber-optics company. You work with a team of three administrators including yourself. You have been at the company longer and refuse to provide the root password to the other workers. When asked, you say this is for security purposes, but the real reason is so you can keep control of the department. Instead, they cannot do their job without you. Is this strategy okay to take?

Conservative   It is important to test out newer administrators prior to giving them the root password, but you should set up a testing timeframe in advance so they are not left up in the air regarding proper access to the resources they need. After they have proven themselves, it is your responsibility to give them the root password.

Liberal   You were there first; you do not need two other people to work with you. Just choke them out of there so you can have full control again and so none of them tries to take your job. After all, as they say in system administration, "There can be only one!"

Summary

The hoarding of passwords, development libraries, and other forms of information occurs quite often. Sometimes people are protective or insecure about their work. Other times they view you as the competition and want to give you a hard time. Whatever the case may be, it is good to come back to the job at hand. Will your behavior get the job done or build in time and complexity? Maybe you are working at a highly political company and everyone is playing these games. Do you have to play them just to stay at the company? Is it worth it to you? There is a lot to think about when it comes to balancing perceived job security against getting the job done. In the end, it is up to you.

Withholding Information for Pay – Should You?

You created a detailed business plan for a Wall Street brokerage company and they have not paid you yet. You decide to hold the business plan until you receive payment. Is this fair?

Conservative   You were hired to do a job, so do the job. They will pay you for your time. Do not get into game playing. Even if they do not pay you, they have the power to blacklist you.

Liberal   The agreement was payment for work. If you have not received payment for your work, do not provide the business plan. Use the business plan as leverage to get your money. After you hand it over you may never see your money. Be smart; do not let anyone take advantage of you and your hard work.

Summary

In the previous issue, "Making it Hard for Others to do their Jobs – Should You Play the Game?," the contractor was making choices more out of personal insecurities and emotions. This issue is more about business strategy. Now that you have seen the same general issue from two different points of view you can see that every issue is very specific to the circumstance. If your company has a general policy of never with-holding information, that policy itself may not be ethical. In the world of ethics, generalizations cannot be made.

Owning Mistakes –
Is Honesty the Best Policy?

It is difficult for people to own up to mistakes. In some ways, it may be more difficult for consultants because they are brought in as the experts in a given area. Sometimes their egos are inflated since they are the high paid "star" and it is easier for them to pass blame then own up to the mistake. This especially occurs in management consulting. When faced with your own mistakes, which road will you choose?

You make a mistake while contracting at a company. You did not allocate enough time in the project plan for programming. Your mistake results in the firing of a full-time programmer who took the time to create solid code that will work well. However, this set the project off by one month. If you acknowledge the error on your part, it will affect your reputation in the consulting industry. What do you do?

Conservative Honesty is always the best policy. A consultant should demonstrate maturity and integrity. Acknowledge your mistake and face the situation.

Liberal Save your butt. If someone else is going down for you, they must have been in the wrong place at the wrong time. Be glad for your luck. It is a good thing they did not find out it was you.

SUMMARY

Choosing between your own job and the truth can be difficult for some people. If someone is taking the fall for something you did, it takes courage to speak up. This issue can be expanded in its complexity depending on the circumstance of the consultant. What if the consultant had a newborn baby and could not afford to be out of work? What if the employee was about to retire and took a settlement package that he was happy with. There are always many dimensions to any given issue. Consider them all fully when making your own choices on the job.

Strong Finish

When I am given a copy of a final report that is someone else's part of a large project, and have to consider redoing sections of the work because critical information is inaccurate or the data is erroneous or missing, I get frustrated. As a contractor, you are left with two options:

1. You need to redo part of the work to accurately complete your contract

2. You fudge or 'guesstimate' part of your final report

The issue is ethical, because you want to provide the client with the best possible service, accurate, useful and usable information. You must advise the client of the need to redo portions of the parallel contract to meet the objectives.

Guy Bruneau B.A. GSEC, GCIA, GCUX
Senior Security Consultant
InfoPeople Security Solutions Inc.

Work from Previous Contracts

Many consultants save their work from previous contracts. In some cases, this material is confidential, in others it is not. The laws are clear for confidential material. In the case of non-confidential material, ethics come into play. The next two issues address the saving and reuse of previous contract work.

Saving Work from Previous Contracts – Adding to Your Portfolio

IT consultants often save their previous work as part of their portfolio. Some of it is confidential, some of it they have permission to use. Does a contractor have the right to save any of this material?

Conservative Contractors should leave all work behind whether it is confidential or not. That work belongs to the company the contractor performed the services for. If you are asked for samples of previous work, state that it is confidential. New employers will respect you for your integrity.

Liberal If you worked hard on a particular project, you should have the right to save that material as long as it does not go against your contracting agreement. Even if it does, if you do not show it to anyone it might be good to save it for future personal reference. It would be impossible to build a personal portfolio if you did not save your work. New employers often ask you for samples of previous work, so saving work is obviously a necessary part of building a career.

SUMMARY

This issue is a classic case of balancing your personal career with the privacy of your previous clients. How far you lean towards conservative or liberal on this issue is up to you. Some modify previous work for their portfolios so that it does not easily identify any particular company. There are many options in this area.

Re-using Work from Previous Contracts – What Makes Sense?

You wrote software for one company that is now re-usable at a different company. The two companies are not in the same industry. Is it okay to re-use your work?

Conservative This depends on the agreement with the first company. If you set up an agreement in advance that you can re-use your work, it is okay. Otherwise, start all over again. Since you have already done this type of work in the past, you will get through it quickly and easily. Be glad you had the previous experience.

Liberal If you wrote the code, there is no sense rewriting it, which will waste time and money. With a programming language such as C, it is especially common practice to build re-usable code libraries. In the case of code that builds graphics, you may want to tweak it a little so you do not create something identical to what you did in the past.

SUMMARY

Reusing code has strengths and weaknesses in both the conservative and liberal points of view. Choosing the ethical solution in this case is a matter of common sense.

Code Re-use for a Different Customer – Should You Charge for It?

Following the previous issue, if you are within the terms of your agreement with the previous company and choose to re-use the code, can you charge the second company for the time it would take to develop the code?

Conservative The answer is absolutely not. You cannot charge for something that you have already received payment on, even if it is for another company. It will take no time at all to implement code that you have already used, therefore requiring payment for that work is wrong. Just add the code and move on.

Liberal You should definitely charge for the code. The company that hired you did so not just for the hours you put in but the intellectual property you provide as an expert in your area. Your code is no different from a software product and is worth money at each location it is used.

SUMMARY

Charging for re-using old code is a personal choice. This issue will probably not be a hot topic for the company you are consulting at because either way they are getting the work they require of you.

Re-using Code – Should You Credit Your Previous Company?

The final question concerning code re-use is crediting the previous company that paid you to build the code in the first place. Should you credit the first company somehow?

Conservative Applying credit where credit is due is standard behavior when using something from another business, resource, or technology. Consider a way to credit your previous company.

Liberal You wrote the code; the only one who deserves the credit is you. If you credit them, then it will only draw more attention to the fact that you are re-using their code and may create issues between your current employer and previous employer. There is no sense in making waves. Just use it.

SUMMARY

Allocating appropriate credit when it comes to code is tricky because unlike writing, code can be very methodical and exact. Several people can write the same code library in exactly the same way. Therefore, it is difficult to tell the re-use of code from a previous contract. From one contract to another, you would probably write the same exact code. Therefore, this comes down to a matter of personal preference. Factors that influence these decisions are how you feel about your previous contract in comparison to how you feel about your current contract.

Vague Areas in Legal Contracts

A consulting contract is a binding agreement between an independent contractor or consulting firm and a corporation. This contract outlines the expectations and terms of work expected.

Several ethical issues arise pertaining to consulting contracts, including renewing a contract, completing a contract, and working without a contract. These three matters are discussed in the following issues.

Contract Completion – Are You Obligated?

You are under contract for six months to build a system. The team you are working with fails to complete the system after six months and you are offered a better paying job elsewhere. Do you take it and leave the company hanging?

> **Conservative** No, finish the job you have started. Even if you have finished your time obligation to the company, if the project is not done you have not finished your work obligation to them. If you leave it will be much harder to train someone to replace you and will cost them additional time and money. Never burn your bridges like this.

> **Liberal** Yes, take the higher paying job. You were contracted for six months; you put in your time and now have a great career opportunity. You no longer have an obligation to them. Think of your career and know that you stayed within your responsibility to that company.

SUMMARY

This is a matter of personal goals. If you have a personal goal to advance your finances as quickly as possible, you will take the liberal approach. If you have a personal goal to implement successful systems and thereby obtain a record of job completion, you will probably follow the conservative approach. In this case, neither is obviously wrong. Nevertheless, the choice you make will affect you in the end and will determine if you have the ruthless spirit to make cash and get rich, or the enduring spirit, which will build a business of your own.

Working Without a Contract – Does it Depend on the Client?

You just finished a three-month contract for a company. You are now working without a contract. They say they want to keep you on but fail to produce a new contract. Should you work without one?

> **Conservative** Never work without a contract. If they do not pay you, you have no proof that they were obligated to. It is just plain scary to work without a contract. It is like walking on a tight rope without a net. Do not do it!

Liberal Keep working. It often takes time for the legal department to draw up new contracts. You have been working for them for three months; you know them well enough by now to trust them. Stay mellow.

SUMMARY

In consulting, it is standard procedure to work with a contract, but projects often run over the expected period of time and consultants find themselves working without one. This happens for many reasons: the hiring company does not want to draw a new contract up that binds them for longer than they think the project will last; the hiring company is slow with paperwork; the hiring company does not take contracts very seriously and figures that if the consultant is still on the payroll why worry about the paper work.

Whatever the case, consultants need to assess whether they feel okay about working without a contract with a particular client.

Getting Out of a Contract – Should You Try?

You are contracted through an agency to work at a major corporation (Microsoft). The manager there likes your work but not your agency. He wants you to move to a different agency or go independent and keep working in the group. Your agency contract has some clauses against doing so, but there are loopholes. Do you do it?

Conservative There is no sense looking for loopholes in contracts. Just stay with the agency that found you the job and tell the manager of the hiring company that you signed a contract with them that you cannot break.

Liberal If the manager of the hiring company wants you to switch agencies, do it. There is always a clause that can get you out of a contract. Besides, the agency does not own you. Do what the client wants. If you went independent, you could probably make more money. Make it happen.

SUMMARY

Being asked to do something questionable by a hiring company is when personal ethics are really tested. Alternatively, you can decide it is not up to you in this type of circumstance. Whichever way you go, make sure you stay within the law.

Corporate Insurance – Is it Necessary?

You are an independent contractor working for a manufacturing company. The contract you signed with them states that you are required to maintain a liability insurance policy. Your insurance policy has lapsed and you probably will not renew it. Many contractors will say they have insurance anyway. Is this unethical?

Conservative Working as an independent contractor without insurance is completely unacceptable. Lying about it in addition is down right wrong. Renew your insurance immediately. If you have been working without insurance for any amount of time, notify the company you were contracting at of the lapse and apologize for your lack of prompt renewal in accordance with their policy.

Liberal The manufacturing company you are working for has a full insurance policy so it is silly for you to have one . This is one of those requirements that make no sense. Hardly anyone follows this type of requirement. Save yourself some money and drop the insurance policy for good.

SUMMARY

Making the decision to obtain, keep, or drop independent contracting insurance requires you to consider all of the factors involved. First, there is the relationship with your client and their agreements and expectations of you. Next, consider the industry you are working in. What kind of protection does the insurance provide your client and you? You may want to save a few bucks but are simply placing yourself at risk. Know what the insurance covers and whom it covers. If you opt for insurance because clients require protection for themselves, you may want to add to that policy to protect yourself as well. If you do opt for insurance, read the policy cover to cover and know what you are buying.

Making Use of Available Resources

As a contractor, you often have limitations on resources and privileges. This always leaves the contractor feeling like they are on the outside of the organization and creates a gap between contractors and full-time employees.

The following two issues discuss obtaining access to full-time privileges and resources.

Contractors and Employee Privileges – Should You Receive Them?

Contractors routinely seek out full-time employees to buy items for them at the company store or gain access to other employee privileges. As a contractor, is this acceptable behavior?

Conservative Trying to seek the benefits of a full-time employee while you are a consultant is not acceptable and rather immature. Stay within your professional boundaries.

Liberal It is pretty silly that only full-time employees can use the company store. Finding a way around that rule is perfectly acceptable. If employees are rewarded with special privileges in other areas, why not you too? Work the system the best you can to gain the maximum benefits.

SUMMARY

Consultants tend to make more money than full-time employees and thus often do not need the extra discounts or resources available to employees. However, employee-only access to the corporate gym, could leave the consultant feeling like an outsider when the entire team leaves at lunch to go work out. Pushing the limits on privileges just for the sake of doing so can stir up resentment, whereas pushing the limits for the sake of teamwork can be very important.

Contractors and Company Resources – What is the Policy?

You have a contract at a company and use the company Intranet bulletin board to post ads for your personal consulting firm. Company policy forbids contractors from doing this but it is not enforced. Is it okay that you have posted ads for your personal business?

Conservative Stop immediately. When you work for a client, you should always respect their corporate policy whether it is enforced or not.

Liberal Most companies have endless policy. Few people within an organization even know what the company policies are. You are not hurting anyone and may even help them find better IT solutions. Keep up the entrepreneurial spirit. Sometimes you have to draw outside of the lines.

SUMMARY

Every business has a different relationship with their company policy. The example senior management sets in relation to the policy greatly influences how employees and contractors relate to it. This is a gray area and depends on the factors in place where you are providing consulting services.

Consulting Agencies

There are two primary types of consulting agencies. The first type is the big six consulting firm that has a full-time staff that they farm out to companies. Big six employees are considered consultants at the contracted company.

The second type of consulting agency is a go between for the independent consultant and the client company. This agency provides placement services for contractors. In this scenario, there is a contract between the independent and the consulting agency, and a contract between the agency and the hiring company. The independent contractor does not work directly for the hiring company.

In some cases, an independent contractor works directly for a company with no intermediary, although this is not as common.

Big Six Consulting Firms – What are the Benefits?

Big six consulting firms are companies such as Accenture, Ernst and Young, Coopers and Lybrand, IBM Consulting Group, Price Waterhouse, and Deloitte & Touché that market themselves as overall service providers. They come into a company with a team, either on site or offsite, to provide an overall IT solution. As in any other area of business, they have their strategies for getting in and staying in. Following are some issues that address potential ethical matters of big six consulting firms.

You are an independent consultant and notice that the big six consulting firm that provides contractors for the company you are working at is strategically taking out independent contractors and targeting full time IT employee's as part of their strategy to take over the department and charge inflated prices. Do you report this to senior management?

> **Conservative** Sit down with senior management and explain what is happening. Communicate how they have been applying pressure on you as an independent consultant and how they have ignored the full-time employees and left them out of key roles in the project.
>
> **Liberal** They have every right to be aggressive with their business. It is none of your business. Just do your job to the best of your ability.

SUMMARY

Big six consulting firms are a fixture in IT departments. In some ways they bring a level of organization and competence to large projects, which ordinarily could not be handled in-house. They also bring their own agenda and plan for making money. Balancing the benefits without being wiped out financially or having your human resources wiped out is the key to a successful partnership with a big six firm.

Consulting Rates – Whose Worth What?

Different agencies pay different salaries for similar work, meaning they take different percentages from their employees based on the negotiating power of the employee. As you move from agency to agency you learn more about their practices. You find that some of them treat your fellow contractors in an unethical manner. The agency you work through will give you a bonus if you keep quiet and cooperative. Do you take it?

Conservative It is never good to take a bribe for any reason. However, it is also none of your business how much others who work for the same agency are making. Stay out of it altogether and be glad you got a good rate. Do not take any money and do not tell how much you make.

Liberal You can go two ways here. If you are close to the others at work, you may decide to tell them they can get more money and use your rate as an example. On the other hand, you can take the extra bonus!

SUMMARY

When comparing consulting rates, so many factors come into play that it is difficult to determine what is fair and what is not. Negotiating power, budget expansions and reductions, skills, and personalities are just a few of the factors that affect rates. Some contractors like to be out there about what they make and try to make sure they are on an even playing field with everyone else. Others like to be completely private. Some will take what they know about others rates to drive their own rate up or get bonus'.

Placement agencies consist of a group of sales people so their mindset is often quite different from that of an IT consultant. They may be more apt to cut deals or play the money game a bit more. They are usually being paid a commission on the contractor's rate so they want to get as much as possible. Some are more fair then others. Nevertheless, it is all part of the contracting game.

Failure to Pay the Consultant – How Much is it Worth?

A common problem in the consulting industry is getting your last paycheck. Even if you leave on good terms, you sometimes never see the last check. It is nearly impossible to get this money back through litigation. This happens for various reasons: either they are having money trouble and just do not pay, you got contract work through another agency and they are angry, or you moved to another state and they know you cannot do anything about the money.

You didn't receive your last paycheck from your previously contracted placement company. This has happened to many of your friends who do contract work, but never to you. None of your friends were successful in getting the money owed to them. Is it right that the company blew off your last check?

Conservative Make calls to the human resources department and try to get your last check. This does happen from time to time in contract work and is just part of the business. Once you put reasonable effort into it and still have no response, move on. There is no sense in making a huge deal out of it.

Liberal You are owed that money and you should get that money. Call them a hundred times a day if you have to. Seek legal council. Do whatever it takes to get your money back. Tell your friends not to work for them. Report them to the Better Business Bureau. Go after them for ripping you off.

SUMMARY

You have the choice of putting a lot of energy into the past or not. You may be entitled to the money, but how much energy is it worth to you? That is for you to decide.

Placement Services – Where Should Your Loyalty Be?

Placement services and agencies are an intermediary option for consultants who do not have enough contacts to find direct work.

You obtained a contract at an import/export business through a particular placement service. The import/export business is looking to hire more people and you have a friend that owns a placement service. Is it unethical to refer the company to your friend rather than the service that placed you there?

Conservative Do not bite the hand that feeds you. You are being paid through the service that placed you. Do not refer another placement service to the hiring company. That is a poor business practice.

Liberal There is nothing wrong with providing a friend with a contact. You have to help your friends out when you can.

SUMMARY

Whether you decide it is ethical or not to refer an agency to the hiring company, try to keep in mind the goals of everyone involved and how you will be perceived by both the hiring company and the placement service. If you can help your friends out without burning your own bridges, do so. Try to keep everyone feeling good about you, your business relationships, and your work.

Shady Consulting Gigs – Follow Your Instincts

From time to time in the consulting business, you may come across a work environment that just does not feel right to you.

You just started at a new contract and something is just not right. You are privy to information that makes you believe the company is pursuing illegal means of business. Do you stay with them since the money is good or get out?

Conservative Get out and report them to the proper authorities. Under no circumstances should you work at a company that you know is doing business illegally.

Liberal If you are not in danger or at risk legally by working for them, what is their business is their business. Since they pay you a lot of money, why leave that kind of cash?

SUMMARY

Determining how to handle shady clients happens from time to time. Depending on the level of illegal activities your client is involved in, you may choose to stay on or go. Make sure you are completely aware of how their actions may or may not implicate you. Obviously, you would react differently to a company that is importing women for a prostitution ring than you would a company that does not report an extra case of copier paper when it is accidentally delivered.

Handling Competition and Politics – What's Your Style?

Everyone handles competition differently. Some people meet it head on, others are more passive-aggressive, and yet others deny it exists at all. Competition is often the root of company politics. In the area of consulting, competition can be between full-time employees or other consultants. As a consultant, there is often immediate resentment towards you from the full-time staff because you make more money than they do and are doing a similar if not the same job. Therefore, dealing with your own competitiveness and the competitiveness of others is an ethical choice in contract work.

When there are budget cuts the competition can get fiery. The following is an example of how competition leads to the game of office politics.

There are several consultants all performing the same function. You have heard from senior management that they may be required to let some people go in the near future because the project budget got cut. Do you simply go ahead and do the best job you can do, or do you play politics and buy the boss a bottle of wine while you mention to them that your coworkers have been slacking off lately?

Conservative As a consultant, the best thing you can do is the best job possible for the company that hired you. Getting into bribery or trash talking will get you nowhere fast. Stay focused in your work and even if you lose your job, you will have your integrity.

Liberal Business is war. If you do not play politics you can be sure the other consultants are and you will be the man left out. If doing a little something extra for your boss (also known as brown nosing) keeps you your job, by all means do it. If dropping a few comments focused on the weaknesses of the other consultants keeps you your job, go for it. You can bet they will be doing the same.

SUMMARY

Politics and brown nosing are rampant in all aspects of business. Some personality types deal better with politics then others. Often the better worker is passed-up for someone who is a friend or is easier to work with. This is an individual matter for each consultant and manager to decide. An entire book could be written on office politics. Nevertheless, it is up to you to decide what type of consultant or manager you are. Do you like a little politics and brown nosing, or do you like to keep it as simple and straightforward as possible?

Communication with Clients – Keeping it Wide Open

Communication plays a key role in contractor/client relationships. The communication responsibility often falls to the consultant because they are the expert in the area of IT in which they are hired, and are depended on to bring the proper solutions to their client.

You were hired to implement a contact management system. You were given general specifications to begin with. One of the specifications was to design a system that can be implemented in-house rather then a third-party solution. The client does not know that there are solutions in the marketplace that will fit their specific needs. Because of the extensive research you have done in the past within this area, you know there is a solution that will save your client time and money if they choose to implement it. Do you tell them about it or stick to the previous requirements?

Conservative   Stay within the boundaries of the original specifications. Do not confuse your client with other options. Just do the job you were hired to do.

Liberal   Set up a meeting with your client and propose alternate solutions including the vendor tool. Explain to them that you understand their needs, have done extensive research in this area, and know that they will save time and money buying a packaged solution. They will be grateful.

SUMMARY

Making calls like this issue is part of the role of the consultant. If you have open communications with your client, you can work with them instead of just for them. Some contractors feel it is up to them to really get to know their clients needs; others just follow what they are told without going out of the box.

Chapter Summary

This chapter discussed the ethical considerations of contractors and consultants. It defined a contractor as a person who works directly for an organization on an independent basis. We tossed around ethical matters such as utilizing work from previous contracts, getting around loopholes in legal contracts, and using employee resources.

We reviewed the business strategies of consulting agencies. These strategies included payment structures and their affect on employees and independent contractors alike. Other consulting strategies discussed withholding information on the part of the contractor, networking, politics, and pushing the limits of job requirements, insurance, and expectations.

You learned about how to ethically break into consulting by providing free contracting and how to handle the competition once you get your foot in the door.

At this point, you should be aware of all of the ethical pitfalls in contract consulting. You know what you are going to face. It is up to you how to handle it.

Frequently Asked Questions

The following Frequently Asked Questions, answered by the authors of this book, are designed to get you thinking about the ethical circumstances you may face when pursuing a career as a contracting consultant. Unless legal issues are involved, then answers in the FAQ may not be the right answer for your organization.

Q: What is the difference between contracting and full-time work? Moreover, why are there different ethical issues for contracting versus full-time work?

A: Contractors are experts in a given area of IT or business and are hired to perform a specific role for a specific period of time. They consequently are paid more money for their specialized skills.

Q: When is it okay to push the limits when applying for a job as a consultant, or trying to keep a job as a consultant? At what point are you going too far?

A: This chapter discussed different levels of pushing the limits. Each individual needs to make their own decision as to what they feel comfortable with.

Q: Is it ever appropriate to withhold information for the purposes of job security? If so, in what cases?

A: Sometimes yes, most of the time no. If you have not received payment for services rendered, you may feel it is completely appropriate to withhold information and work product. If you are just being destructive, you may feel that it is not right to withhold information.

Q: What role does politics play in independent consulting? What about in relation to the competition or big six firms?

A: Politics can be played to whatever degree you feel comfortable. By looking back at the issues in this chapter you can get a sense of whether a particular approach sits well with you or not.

Q: Is it ever appropriate to provide free consulting work? If so, under what conditions?

A: In your career you may want to provide free consulting work to develop contacts. Carefully consider your expectations prior to providing free work. Make sure the plan for developing new relationships does not backfire on you.

Chapter 15

Telecommuting and Mobile Computer Security

Ethical Dilemmas in this Chapter:

- Work/Life Balance in the Home Office

- Tracking Your Whereabouts

- Impact of Instant Messaging

- Telecommuting Access Control and Mobile Computers

- Telecommuting and Mobile Computer Policy

Introduction

Telecommuters approach life in a fundamentally different way than a regular employee who works at an office does. When you work from an office you are productive throughout the day. Even when you stop to chat at a coffee station, you are networking and building relationships with others. You have the opportunity to meet people from across the organization on a casual basis, which starts out socially and may grow to a working relationship. Telecommuters are inherently isolated, and forgo most of these opportunities. They are suspected of not really working. People think, "They cannot really work productively from home. What is wrong with going to work like the rest of us?" And it takes a certain kind of person to be able to work remotely. It requires strong self-motivation and self-discipline.

It is not just their approach to their work life that sets apart the telecommuter; it affects their home life too. Their spouse considers them available to take care of a child home sick from school, or to meet the cable guy who is coming sometime in the afternoon. Somehow their work does not seem very real or important since they are staying home. Telecommuters struggle to fully get away from home chores and issues and establish clear boundaries.

Sometimes the opposite happens and they can never fully get away from work. With a complete office at home, they are wired up to check in at any hour of the day or night. After dinner and putting the kids to bed, they check e-mail one more time at 9:00 PM and find a new issue afoot to which they respond. Their fellow employees, particularly those overseas, have learned that they are available after hours. It is hard to take a vacation day and stay home, since to the office employees who interact with them, the telecommuter's status does not look any different. There is no way to show them an empty desk.

People are most able to succeed in telecommuting if they are the social type who keeps their presence and their projects known. In today's multi-tasking positions, very few people, if any, realize all the work that others do for various projects and remote groups. They need to make this work visible to their managers and to others so that they can understand the telecommuter's value. Yet paradoxically, most of the time telecommuters work in solitude and have little natural ability to socialize and hence share their experiences.

When we speak of telecommuters, we are talking about salaried employees of a company, not independent contract workers (covered in another chapter). Contractor's often operate out of their home office and also have to juggle their time between work issues and home issues. But the independent contractor does not have coworkers or a manager concerning themselves with what they do with their time.

We are also not referring to sales representatives, who also work remotely. It is well accepted that sales representatives' work and personal lives are very intertwined and the sales organization has their own methods for managing this. Representatives are fully compensated for their returns, not their efforts. Sales representatives, while freely accountable for their own time, do encounter the issues of using a mobile computer for sensitive work data (covered later in this chapter).

For the fundamental reason of always having to prove yourself, telecommuting is not for the average person. It has appeal; it seems like it would be great to have all that flexibility, no commute, and work in your bedroom slippers. But many that try it quickly encounter the limits of their own self-discipline.

Despite these caveats and issues, for those telecommuters who succeed at work, life can be truly good. They have great economies of time with no traffic jams, and inherent flexibility. This chapter looks at some of the issues telecommuters face, and how the successful ones handle them.

Work/Life Balance in the Home Office

As an employee working out of a home office, you have to resolve your policy about doing chores and errands during the workday. While companies typically have policies about telecommuting, they often do not get into specifics enough to guide your behavior. You should proactively discuss the issues with your manager before you begin to work from home.

Household Chores on the Job – Is it Okay to Do Both?

When working from home, is it okay for you to also do the laundry, take out the trash, and vacuum the living room during work time? Do the needs of home conflict with your work demands?

Conservative The best policy is to treat the workday as sacred and refrain from any personal activities during that time. Just as in working in the office, you can take a couple of personal breaks during the course of a day, but make those scheduled and brief. Your coworkers will sense your loyalty and single-mindedness if you do not mix sorting laundry with writing reports.

Liberal The ability to accomplish small household tasks constitutes one of the biggest advantages to working from home. You should be able to do some chores during the day and still get your work done, as long as you keep your company's work your top priority.

SUMMARY

This issue really defines the crux of the matter for telecommuters. Working as a telecommuter, you have more freedom and more responsibility for how you spend your time. It takes discipline to stay focused on work, and mixing in chores can lead to many distractions. For some people, there are certain chores, such as starting a load of wash that fit in well as a brief break from work. But being in the laundry room may remind you of a shelf you have been meaning to put up, or a shirt that needs mending, and further pull you away mentally from work. You would benefit more from a work break that provided some meditative time such as going for a short walk.

You are better off to start your telecommuting life doing no chores, and then perhaps after six months add one that fits in well to your work attitude and pace. This will establish a precedent for the rest of your household that during the day you are unavailable for personal tasks. What is important is for you to remember that at all times you are at work, though it feels like home, and behave accordingly.

@#&!?!

Working from Home: Not All That Easy

Telecommuting is one of the true joys that the Internet has brought to us, with the use of TCP/IP you can be virtually anywhere and still be 'at work'. Answer your e-mails, have the same phone number, access all work documents and resources. Sounds just great, and in many circumstances it will aid and increase the productivity of your work life. However, this really depends on the environment you are in; the whole idea of telecommuting is usually to be a better or more stable environment, so what happens when you go home?

You arrive home to get some work done on the "big project," you turn on your computer and log into work's network.. Then quickly remember that you need to put the washing on or you will run out of

Continued

clean clothes, and the dishes need doing, and what are you going to have for dinner? Damn, you should really tidy up this place a little, oh yeah the cable guy is coming by at 3:00 to fix the cable, can't forget.

Soon half the day can be gone, and you haven't even touched your computer.

The tasks seem so normal and average that you don't notice your doing them, and soon the majority of the day can be wasted. On the other side however, is overworking; its far too easy to work if your work space is five foot away from your bed, you can wake up and work till you go to sleep, then wake up at 4:00 AM and work a little more.

We have all done it at some stage. Remember how 'hard' the project seemed after you had done it for a while? You don't notice yourself working so hard that you burn out. In my opinion it comes down to an individual level; you have to be able to detach work from your home life mentally and physically.

If it helps to have a clock or a buzzer to define when you start and stop working, lock yourself in a room, tell your wife/other to leave you alone when you are 'working,' and just work. But when the buzzer tells you that work is over at 5:00 PM, put down the pen, logout and go play some Quake.

Paul Craig
CEO, Pimp Industries

When the Office is at Home, What About Caring for Children?

You have two girls, ages eight and ten, who go to school until 3:00 PM and then to an after-school program at the Boys and Girls Club, because you and your husband work full-time. Your girls complain about the after-school care, saying it is boring and it makes for a long day. Your group has recently reorganized and you now report to someone in another state; therefore, you will be telecommuting. Is it all right for your children to take the bus home from school since you will be there anyway?

Conservative You cannot effectively care for children while you are trying to work. You would not have your kids running around your office and interrupting you, nor should you at home.

Liberal If your children are quiet and responsible, you can probably have them at home while you are working. You should have activities set up for them to do alone, and a clear set of rules about when and how they are to interrupt you.

SUMMARY

There is quite a difference between attempting to take care of children while working and sorting laundry. However, many telecommuters skip childcare and have their children come home while the parent works. Usually, the children live the lives of latchkey children, even though there is someone in the house. The parent cannot meaningfully be there for the child, unless there is a grave injury. The child often feels lonely, watches far too much TV, and seeks another place to go, imposing freely on a neighbor. The other scenario is for you to sacrifice full attention to work and not work a full day. It is pretty hard to be effective at work if you are paying attention to your children.

You could watch your children on an occasional basis, when your normal childcare provider is sick. For those times you should school your children on how to communicate with you while you are working, especially when you are on a work phone call. One telecommuter has her girls, ages five and eight, trained to stand quietly in front of her and signal if they want to talk to her. But this is no way to interact with your children on a daily basis. The bottom line is as a telecommuter you need to invest in as much childcare as you would if you worked in an office.

Handling Personal Finances – Is This Fine in the Home Office?

While you are working from home during the day is it okay for you to manage your portfolio, checking the latest stock prices?

Conservative It depends on what you would do if were in a regular job setting. If you would not do it from the office, you should not do it while working at home.

Liberal You are entitled to a few breaks, and how you spend them is your business. It is good for your overall financial well being to keep up with your investments.

SUMMARY

In today's open office environment, people have little personal privacy and roving eyes can see what you are doing as they walk by your desk. Therefore, many people would not feel comfortable spending time looking up a stock's performance while at work. At home you have a natural privacy, and if it does not interfere with your work productivity, it should be fine to spend a little time checking on your investments.

Personal Privacy for Telecommuters – How Much Should You Have?

Are you entitled to the same amount of personal privacy if you work from home? In other words, does your manager have a right to ask you about the environment of your home?

Conservative Of course he does. At the office, your manager would know the state of your workspace; therefore, he should be able to stop by your house anytime to see how you are coming along with a project. Since it is impractical for him to do so, he can ask you questions to learn more about your set up and what you are doing.

Liberal If you are getting your work done satisfactorily there is no reason for your manager to be concerned about what your office looks like. When you are working with others, how you keep your space can have an influence and set an example your boss may not like. When you are in the privacy of your home, you do not have to change your habits to suit him.

SUMMARY

Your manager has the right to know if your home office is safe and ergonomically set up. After all, the company is likely to be held responsible if you are injured while working from home. Also, your manager has the right to ensure that you are up to date with the equipment you need to be productive. Beyond that, how you arrange your desk and how neat you keep it is up to you.

Proper Reimbursement for Telecommuters – What Are You Charging For?

Do you feel you are reimbursed for all of your expenses when you work at home, such as long-distance phone calls, electric bills, dial-up connections, and so forth?

Conservative You should keep an itemized log of all expenses and submit a regular report that accounts for charges that your company should reimburse you for. For electricity, determine your office equipment's (computer, copier, fax) daily usage in kilowatt hours, multiply it by the local electric rate, and multiply the result by your workdays per month, 20 for full-time work. If you are using the Internet for personal as well as business use, you need to pro-rate that expense as a credit back to the company.

Liberal Determine the cost of all directly related company expenses such as Internet and long-distance calls and bill them accordingly. Do not try to account for electricity and heating charges. Figure that the expenses will balance out.

SUMMARY

Your employer should pay for your major regular expenses such as Internet connections. Who pays for long-distance calls depends on how often you make such calls for work. If you are making more than one or two calls a month, your company should pay for your work-related calls, billed separately. Such expense handling should be determined as part of your original telecommuting agreement. Do not worry about how to charge back your basic home expenses, such as electricity and heating. Your company has invested a great deal to allow you to work from home, and you are reaping many side financial benefits such as saving commuting costs.

Tracking Your Whereabouts

In most companies it is conventional for someone in the workgroup, be it the manager, the secretary, or a coworker, to know when employees leave the office. While this is vital in the rare case of a fire or a security breach, it is also generally useful in case someone needs one of the employees to give an opinion in a meeting, or if their spouse calls with a home emergency. The telecommuter's manager has less knowledge of your day-to-day schedule than that of the other employees. This is appropriate, as you can be accountable for your own location in case of emergency. However, things can quickly fall apart if no one knows exactly where you are during the workday.

Personal Errands – What if You Make Up the Time?

As a telecommuter, you manage your own time. Is it acceptable to leave during the day for personal errands such as taking a trip to the grocery store, if you make up the missed hours during the evening?

Conservative While you are working you should not be taking off to run errands, telecommuter or not. If you go to the store midday, you will lose your work focus and others will quickly realize it.

Liberal Again, the advantage of working as telecommuter is the flexibility. If you are responsible for your projects, then how you spend your time is your affair.

SUMMARY

Your hour-to-hour presence is not tracked as a telecommuter, and realistically should not be unless your work calls for it. It would seem a little silly to call into your manager or the group secretary and say, "I'm going to the grocery store and will be gone for an hour if anyone's looking for me." However, some roles require you to be more accountable, such as when your input may be required for an important decision or to join in an impromptu conference. In those situations, you should avoid being gone during work hours. Also, remember that the successful telecommuter maintains a focus on their work tasks. Leaving your home for errands is likely to disrupt your sense of being at work.

Balancing Time – Are Appointments Okay?

Management has granted you telecommuting privileges. You work long hours above and beyond the normal mandated 40-hour work schedule. Is it appropriate to attend a dental appointment without first informing your manager?

Conservative The policy on how you handle personal errands should not deviate from the office employee to the telecommuter. If your coworkers have the flexibility to go to the dentist in the middle of the workday, you should too. Just make sure you inform your manager.

Liberal As in the previous issues, what matters is if you are getting your work accomplished. If so, there is no reason why you should not go to the dentist during the day. After all, that is when you can get appointments.

SUMMARY

This issue differs from the question of going to the grocery store, in that it is a scheduled time away that, when the time comes, may conflict with a work obligation. As your time is largely your own to manage, you should be able to go to the dentist during the day. For many positions, you would need to inform your manager when you have a pre-arranged personal time commitment that cannot be canceled at the last minute.

Interviewing for Another Job – Should You Tell Management?

You are a successful technical writer who telecommutes. You have become dissatisfied with your level of pay because you have heard of others in your field making much more. You decide to interview at other companies to see if you can get a salary increase. Your time is largely yours to manage. Should you inform your manager of what you are doing?

Conservative Yes. Your manager should be informed of any major work change that you are contemplating. Besides, they may be able to show you why you are fairly paid, or they may be working to get you a raise.

Liberal It is never a good idea to tell management that you are interviewing for another job, unless you have to. In this case, there is little chance that they would find out. If you stay in your position, your manager's attitude toward you may sour.

SUMMARY

While for the normal office employee it is quite challenging to surreptitiously interview for another job during the workday, it is a whole different matter for the telecommuter. There is no reason for you to inform your company that you are looking at another position, as long as you are keeping up with your project goals.

Transporting Your Home Office – Should You Tell the Manager?

Your home office in Portland, Oregon is set up with everything you need to work successfully. Your dad persuades you and your family to come visit him and your stepmother for a long weekend in Seattle, saying you can work equally well from his well-equipped study; they will watch the kids. You agree and join an important conference call at 10:00 AM Thursday morning, where you are scheduled later to present your project's progress. Your father, in his retirement now, avidly collects clocks, which you had not realized the scope and ramifications of, until they start going off every 15 minutes with various chimes and gongs. What is more, your father's phone does not have mute on it, something you consider so basic you neglected to ask about it when reviewing his accommodations ahead of time. As the hour wears on, the chiming and gonging periods get longer and seemingly louder. A manager asks if someone has phoned in from a church. Your time to present is approaching. How do you handle the situation?

Conservative You have gotten yourself into quite a pickle. Best to speak up that you need to reschedule your part of the presentation and get off the call before you cause further disruption.

Liberal Weather through the meeting and your presentation, hoping people have a sense of humor. Besides, they never really need to know who contributed all the background ringing.

SUMMARY

What functions for working from your home will likely not carry over fully to another environment. It is hard to anticipate all that can go wrong, as this case shows. If you had been working as a regular employee you would have requested permission to work away from your office, and so should you have as a telecommuter. It is likely that you will now get discovered, so it is best to confess your true whereabouts to your manager.

Impact of Instant Messaging

A major change to the life of telecommuters came a few years ago with the advent of Instant Messaging (IM). If you use IM, when you logon everyone in your contact list can tell you are working at your computer. This can serve as a fundamental way of improving your visibility in the workgroup. As one telecommuter put it, "It used to be that no one knew when I was working. When I wasn't directly interacting with them they would assume I wasn't there. Now with IM they see me show up."

However, IM itself generates some issues for all of us, including the telecommuter. The next two issues are mirror images of each other; in the first you are an IM enthusiast, in the next management is.

IM and Management – What if They Will Not Use It?

You work as a telecommuter in a geographically dispersed group. The team uses IM frequently as an informal way to keep in touch. Your manager, however, is quite traditional in approach and refuses to install IM software. He continues to question your work efforts, and you believe he would be in better contact if he used IM. Should you insist he do so?

Conservative You cannot tell your manager what to do. You need to make the effort to make sure he knows what you are doing by using e-mail and phone calls.

Liberal You cannot insist that he use IM, but you can be persuasive by participating in important conversations with others. As he gets wind of these, he will begin to feel left out and will join in to keep up with what is happening. Offer to help him download the software and show him how easy it is to use, to remove any potential barriers he may have.

SUMMARY

IM is not for everyone, but it does have its place in the working life of remote workers. It serves a useful function in enabling a geographically dispersed team to keep up with each other on a casual basis with a chat such as, "Hey, how's it going? Did you get a chance to look at my code from last night yet?" The communication should be short, and it should not be used as a forum for decision-making planning or reaching conclusions, because there is no record of the transaction. A typical response to this would be, "Yes, I'm reviewing it now. Looks good. I'll send an e-mail to the team later today about what I think."

It is important to note that IM poses a security risk, as the transmission is sent in the clear on the Internet. Sometimes unaware users discuss sensitive company information. Some IM systems such as Jabber encrypt the transmission to provide secure IM.

As you are chatting, you should be aware to keep the content brief and oblique, unless you have one of the secure IM systems. In the situation where your manager is not willing to use IM, it is important to follow up with an e-mail to make note of what happened in a chat session. If the remote employee takes a lead role in writing such e-mails, it will help your manager follow your work activity.

Availability Status – Should You Always Be There?

Your group has several people who work from remote or home offices. Management strongly encourages everyone to use IM as a way of keeping in touch. However, you find you work best when not online, and moreover you find it distracting having little random windows pop up from people on your contact list. Your manager is in another state and assumes that if your status shows "Away" you are not working. What can you do about this?

Conservative You should talk to your manager to find another way for him to follow your work.

Liberal IM is a great tool. Get more modern; get with it. Use it.

SUMMARY

Some managers like to use IM as a leash to keep tabs on their employees' activities. While it can serve that purpose at first blush, with practice one can use its various settings to subterfuge what you are really doing. IM can be a boon for remote casual communication, but it can also be a big time waster. Regular users of IM develop their own communication etiquette, for example on matters of how frequently to respond and in what length, when and how to add others to the conversation, and how to end the conversation. While you may not appreciate your company management attempting to track your whereabouts using IM, it can play a useful role for people working remotely to keep in touch with others on the team. Establish your own manner for using the system and others will pick up on it.

Using IM as a Shield – Should You Confront Him?

You work in Seattle as part of a small marketing group for an Internet company based in Chicago. You need to frequently interact with the Chicago marketing team and have mutually found IM a good way to develop your relationship. The Director of Product Management in Chicago is a heavy user of IM, and when you are assigned to a joint project you use IM to check in with him about his team's progress. The Chicago director becomes suspicious and jealous of the role of the Seattle group. As the project wears on you find his status more and more set to "away." In conversations with other team members, you learn that this director is really at his desk and is using IM to communicate with them about other projects. Evidently, he has blocked you in IM so that you cannot see when he is available. Should you confront him about this?

Conservative   There is little to be gained from confronting him. Apparently, he does not want to maintain a chummy relationship with you. You should respect that decision and use e-mail to continue your project communication.

Liberal   Confront him and let him know you realize he is avoiding you.

SUMMARY

A feature of IM allows someone to block you without your knowledge. Using it can be a form of a power play, because the person can still see when you are online but you can no longer see them. Being remote from the team can lead to people not wanting to work with you. Since the director has used this IM technique, you have learned something about his personality. In any case, he is not going to be on a friendly enough basis with you to work with IM. Communicate with him in more formal ways and simply drop him from your contact list.

Telecommuting Access Control and Mobile Computers

As is the case with the physical security of a facility, a company's computer network is only as strong as its weakest link. Contemporary telecommuters and other work travelers have the ability to log onto the company network remotely, with all the power and access of being in the office. Encrypted transmission allows telecommuters to use the company network with the same level of security in data transmission that the office computers have. But the office environment carries many reminders of the importance of maintaining security, with access control at every door and system administrators available at your beck and call. At home where family members are present and on the road when traveling with your computer, you have to serve as your own security, at least for the front stage of looking out for leaks, calling for help from your company if you find one.

Personal Files – Should You Store Them on Your Work Computer?

Your company computer has hard disk encryption to protect your data files. Is it okay for you to store personal files on this computer?

Conservative   No, because it is inappropriate to use company encryption software on your own personal files. Files stored on your computer would be encrypted as a matter of course.

Liberal   There is no real harm done to the company if you use the encryption capability of your computer to store your files. Encryption is a company resource that is not limited by use. Your company has likely encrypted the data just because you are working with a laptop. As long as your files are acceptable in other ways, such as size and virus-free, they should not cause any problems if stored and encrypted on your computer.

SUMMARY

Companies use disk encryption more readily on laptop computers, because they are much less physically secure than a desktop machine. While adding your personal files to an encrypted disk would not consume a resource of limited supply, it is a dubious practice for you to do so. It would be like you were a driver of an armored truck and you put a couple grand of your own money in its vault. There is ample room in the truck, but it was not intended for personal funds. Similarly, an encrypted disk carries with it a certain importance. If your company cares enough about its data to encrypt your disk, it is doubtful that they would want your personal files along for the ride.

Personal Use of Company Computer – Should You Use It?

You have an older computer at home that your teenager uses for homework. Your company has now provided you with a state-of-the-art laptop solely for the purpose of telecommuting. Your teen wants to check her e-mail using your slick company computer. Should you let her?

Conservative The laptop computer belongs to your employer; you have no right to use it for personal use.

Liberal It is natural for your daughter to want to check her e-mail on your computer due to its faster speed. You can let her do so as long as you are around to make sure she sticks to e-mail while online.

SUMMARY

The main concern for using your computer personally is the danger of a security breach. Going to an e-mail server is a fairly safe exercise, assuming you already access the Internet in the course of your work and therefore are set up with virus and firewall protection. However, it is improper for you to use your work computer for personal use without permission. You could ask your manager if you can let your daughter check e-mail after hours with supervision, but computers are cheap these days, especially used desktops. Get your boss's permission or upgrade her computer.

@#&!?!

Telecommuting and Corporate Networks

With the prevalence and low cost of broadband Internet connections, telecommuting is an increasingly popular option both for employers and employees. Unfortunately, there is often not enough care and attention paid to securing the method by which the employees telecommute. With the latest rash of worms, most companies have been well protected by firewalls at the company border. Many of the worms have still managed to find their way inside most companies, either through telecommuters bringing the worms straight through the firewall, or by employees taking computers offsite, getting infected, and then re-connecting the computers inside the unprotected corporate network. It is essential that companies place access control mechanisms between any VPN servers and dial-up modem pools and their main network. As well, companies should invest in centrally managed and updated anti-virus software, as well as personal firewall software for any computers that are ever used off-site.

Jens Haeusser
Manager, Information Security Office
University of British Columbia

Personal Use of Company Resources – Which Sites Are Appropriate

You have a company laptop on the company network for your home office, which you can also use for personal use on your own time. You have a secret penchant for gambling and have found some Internet sites that you visit frequently, including during breaks during the work day. Though gambling at work is strictly forbidden, is it okay for you to do so since you are not in the office?

Conservative No. You are still gambling during the work day, which is clearly against company policy..

Liberal It depends on how much gambling you are doing. Gambling has an addictive quality, which could soon interfere with your work productivity. Your company would likely frown on this activity and you might get caught. Find some other recreational activity to do during your breaks.

SUMMARY

The rules of Internet conduct at work apply equally to your home office. What is more, with your computer on the company network, IT security officers can see everything on your computer, just as if you were in the office. Working out of your home gives you an illusion of privacy. Only visit Internet sites that are appropriate according to company policy.

Leaving the Remote Computer at Risk – Should You Report It?

You are telecommuting from home and are in the process of having a copier installed in your home office. You know you must not leave your PC unattended, however, your newborn son is crying and you go to him. When you return to your office, you see the copier delivery person checking out your files on your computer. You should report this incident to management, but do not want to be reprimanded for leaving your computer unattended.

Conservative You must report what happened to IT security or to your manager. It was an error for you to leave your PC without logging off first, but it is surprising that the copier employee took advantage of the situation. Come clean about what happened and you will be in a position to help solve this apparent computer crime.

Liberal Start by asking the delivery person what they were doing on your computer to see how serious an issue this is. If they can give some reasonable explanation for their actions, you might be able to get away with your carelessness this time. Chock it up to experience and be more careful in the future.

SUMMARY

It is strange and very suspect for the delivery person to be doing anything on your computer. You have every reason to consider their intentions nefarious, no matter what justification they give. It seems that the copier company should be informed. But this matter is too big for you to handle and certainly to hide as an individual. Report the incident to system administration and management, providing all of the details .

Users Accounts and Security – Report Violations to IT?

You have just purchased a new laptop and are in the process of setting it up. You have not yet assigned a pass code to your user account, leaving your system wide open. Just before completing the configuration of your ISP, you go to the kitchen for a refill of your favorite coffee. Your teen son wanders into your home office and seeing access to the Internet, begins surfing the web.

Conservative You need to shut down your computer and report the violation to your company's system administrators immediately.

Liberal Log off the Internet and continue to set up your computer properly. Find out what sites your son visited to learn more about what happened. Once you are on the company's network with virus and firewall protection, you can run a virus scan on your computer to see if any damage was done, and if so report it. Give your son a stern lecture about not using your computer in the future unless you give him permission.

SUMMARY

It is absolutely unacceptable for a company computer to be unprotected on the open Internet. Being in your home may make it seem like a minor incident, but it is every bit as dangerous as if it happened in the office. This slip-up may have been just the chance some hacker-created demon needed to infiltrate the company network. Regardless of where your son was navigating, silent activity could have been happening through one of the open ports. You do not know what damage may have happened, and you need to report the matter to IT.

Media Storage – How Important are Backups?

As a telecommuter, you are required to perform periodic backups of the company files you are working on. In a rush to join your old college buddies for a special beach weekend, you forget to perform the mandatory backup and discover on Monday morning that your computer will not boot.

Conservative   Do not do anything more with your computer until you contact your IT department. You undoubtedly will face some time, perhaps days, without your computer and maybe never get your files back. This should serve as a strong lesson to you to do backups in the future.

Liberal   Contact computer-savvy friends who may be able to help you. Computers that will not boot can sometimes be persuaded to turn on one more time with such tricks as turning them upside down, reseating connectors, giving them a strong kick, or holding the power switch on for several seconds. Failing that, see if you can get any copies of the data files from a fellow employee who might have an older version you could bring up to date. It would behoove you to restore the situation as best as possible without letting your IT department know what happened. They probably would take a long time trying to recover from the data loss with little success.

SUMMARY

Unfortunately it seems the best way to learn about the value of backing up one's data is to lose something valuable to a disk crash. Once you have had a calamity, you become a convert and take a few moments to do a backup no matter how pressed for time you are. Better yet, you make the time investment to set up for automatic back-ups to a remote device. While IT departments are not usually adventurous with various rumored techniques to get a computer to boot up, they do have access to the latest in disk rescue software. Sometimes they are able to recover files from a disk that will not boot. Turn the matter over to them and see what they can do for you.

Installing Prototype Software on Your Company Machine – Should You?

Your friend would like to do a demo of his screen-saver prototype software and asks if he can use your work laptop for an hour or two because he does not have one. Do you let him install his software onto it?

Conservative No. You should not allow anyone to use your company computer for any purpose, certainly not to install software, not to mention a homemade prototype.

Liberal It is understandable that your friend needs to test his new software on all kinds of computer hardware. The risk of this program causing harm seems slight since it is only a screen-saver, so if you trust your friend you might as well let him install the prototype and see what he has created.

SUMMARY

A software program, even from a benign source, can do all kinds of damage to a computer operating system. You should not allow anyone else to install software on your work computer thereby risking your computer's integrity. Your company IT department is charged with maintaining your computer in good working order and they would certainly not want to spend time investigating a glitch caused by an unknown source.

Service Access – Should You Allow It?

You are in the process of setting up your home office due to your new telecommuting status. A service man is installing a new cable modem service in your home office, and he needs to configure your computer to accept the new service. Should you allow this technician access to your computer to establish the new communications link?

Conservative You are right to question the propriety of anyone else using your computer, even with a seemingly legitimate- reason such as this one. Contact your IT department and ask what you should do in this situation.

Liberal Yes, it is a normal part of his job. By questioning the matter, you are causing your work to be delayed.

SUMMARY

You are ultimately responsible for this computer and must get used to making sound judgements about its use and access. Assess the service man and the company he works for before making your decision. You are probably fine to allow him to proceed.

Travel Considerations – Should You Work While Traveling?

You are traveling on company business. You are running behind at work and in preparation for an upcoming meeting, you need to review some confidential company files while on the airplane. Even though this violates company policy, is it okay for you to do so?

Conservative Of course it is not okay. The company policy exists exactly for situations like this. You can do the work when you are at your destination.

Liberal It seems unlikely that whomever you are sitting near on the plane will take advantage of anything they may see while you are reviewing the files. It is more important that you are prepared for your meeting. Be careful and do not leave the files open long.

SUMMARY

One of the weakest links of security happens when employees are traveling. Weekday passengers consist mainly of business travelers who know the value and interest in corporate secrets. It is surprising what you can see and hear on an airplane. If it is not useful to the person eavesdropping, they may well know a competitor who would love the information. The snoop would be only too delighted to provide it, having learned it in this effortless and unexpected manner. Do not risk opening the files.

Sending Personal Photos Using Company E-mail – Is it a Good Practice?

While traveling on business you use your company e-mail to check in with your family. You also send them some digital photos from your trip. Is this okay?

Conservative No. You should not use a company resource for personal reasons.

Liberal It is nice to let your family know what you are up to. It ties them into your trip and connects you to them in your absence.

SUMMARY

Downloading the photos onto your company computer is a personal use of a company resource. Digital photos sent via e-mail require bandwidth and space on the mail server. While sending a few photos once in awhile probably will not impact the system, it is not a good practice to promote. Others would likely learn what you are doing, and the e-mail system would be affected if everyone started sending personal pictures. To ultimately decide whether this is okay depends on how much your company allows personal use of its resources, but most companies would frown on this practice.

Telecommuting and Mobile Computer Policy

When an employee works from an office, it is clear when they are at work and when they are not. Such is not the case for the telecommuter. Company management cannot realistically monitor a telecommuter's work hours. Therefore, their work needs to be assessed on productivity. Since a salaried employee's job is never done, the best policy is to evaluate the telecommuter's productivity relative to office-based workers with similar responsibilities.

Studies have shown that for telecommuters to be successful they should meet face-to-face with the rest of the group once a quarter if possible, and at least twice annually. This live interaction is vital to:

1. Establishing social cues. What one can pick up from body language is much more extensive than what you get over the phone. Once you interact with someone live, you subconsciously correlate their mood to voice tone and inflection and then use this ability in future phone conversations.

2. Planning more complex strategies. Being live enables the effective use of charts and graphs and is the best time to discuss where to go in the future.

3. Developing interpersonal friendships. Such relationships bind people closer to their job, making the exit barriers higher.

Setting up a telecommuter implies a great deal of trust in the person regarding their work ethic. Part of the initial set up involves what expenses the company pays for the home office and how those will be billed. Many companies directly receive the bills for the telecommuter's Internet usage and long distance phone line. Whatever the arrangement, it should be determined ahead of time.

Any worker who will be connecting to the company network remotely is engendered with great trust to respect computer security. If this trust is compromised in any fashion, the remote work should be discontinued, inconvenient though it may be.

Chapter Summary

This chapter covered the many issues and pitfalls of the life of a telecommuter. The core issue seems to be how we allow ourselves to act when nobody is watching. The natural tendency is to let things slide when there is no accountability. The worker that aspires to higher principles sees this problem and responds with discipline. One of the big problems of a home office is that the hours can creep up and the next thing you realize you have worked from the moment you woke until you fell asleep. We tell employees that it is a bad sign if they find themselves bringing lunch to the keyboard.

We also talked about the responsibility of having a company laptop computer, including issues concerning connecting remotely to the company network. The danger of this is as much a technology issue as an ethical one; telecommuters are a danger to the network. The overwhelming majority of worm infections do not enter the network through the firewall; they come from users bringing their laptops from home, working from home, and accessing the organization through a virtual private network (VPN). Anti-virus software, content sensors, and security policies are no substitute for a little care, concern, and common sense.

Frequently Asked Questions

The following Frequently Asked Questions, answered by the authors of this book, are designed to get you thinking about the ethical circumstances you may face when telecommuting or using a remote computer. Unless legal issues are involved, then answers in the FAQ may not be the right answer for your organization.

Q: What is the biggest issue that faces telecommuters?

A: The most difficult challenge is developing and maintaining your boundaries between work and home, especially exacerbated for those who have a family. One telecommuter we know manages the situation by wearing shoes when he works in his home office. When he is at that same office busy handling personal matters, he takes his shoes off. Employ whatever means you can find to draw your boundaries and stick to them. In time your fellow employees and family members will learn to respect your role switches.

Q: What kinds of people and jobs are most successful at telecommuting?

A: Programmers are well suited for telecommuting, since they typically have the necessary IT infrastructure to allow them to do it. Writers do well because their work requires little online interaction with the company. Both of these professions have fostered very successful telecommuters, who have worked remotely for years. A key reason is one can assess their work solely by evaluating their output, as opposed to more intangible responsibilities in marketing or in management.

Programmers and writers each can benefit from working at odd times of the day and night, getting into a zone where they go for hours on end. If these same people were to work from an office, they would face many distractions. For any telecommuter, a vital ingredient for success is having well-defined goals. Successful telecommuters work well independently with self-discipline, yet can interact in a good way with a team on a regular basis, so that people constantly remember them.

Q: What are the benefits of telecommuting?

A: Primarily flexibility to be able to work when you want and how you want. You have more of a sense of being your own boss, with some control over how you spend your time. And it is really great to work without any commute.

Q: Does a telecommuter have the same opportunities for advancement as someone who works from the office?

A: Honestly no. Many managers today work remotely as companies grow more decentralized and work internationally. It is not surprising for one or more people in a typical work group to telecommute, including the manager. But it is rare that someone who has been a telecommuter for any length of time gets promoted. It takes the visibility and connections that you can only get from working in the office to get recognized for growth in the organization.

Chapter 16

Personal Computer Users

Ethical Dilemmas in this Chapter:

- Computer Addiction

- Newsgroups and Web Logs

- Chat Rooms

- E-mail Etiquette

- Viruses and Worms

- Web Site Browsing and Usage

Introduction

We use computers for many aspects of our daily lives and many of us are online for much of the day or evening. This chapter examines some potential situations you may encounter while using your computer at home or on vacation.

The most basic question you should assess in your personal computer use is whether your actions are causing harm to other users. In addition to the more obvious impact of sending others a virus or in other ways damaging their system, harm can take the form of infringing on their time. Beyond this basic ethic of not harming others, one's computer and Internet use can lead to compulsive behavior where you spend inordinate amounts of your day or evening on the computer.

Additionally, there is concern about how we use the information we find on the Web; we make assumptions that what we read and see on the Internet is authoritative, current, and sending the intended message. And people are meeting each other and doing business over the Internet in ways unimaginable only a couple decades ago. In this chapter, we discuss issues regarding individual conduct while online.

Computer Addiction

Addiction is when a person becomes obsessed with an activity to the detriment of everything else. The computer is a great tool and the Internet is a fantastic resource; unfortunately, some employees burn work hours doing things like playing computer games, entering chat rooms, and surfing the Web—hours that could have been invested productively and that may now harm their future career potential. The next section examines some of the addictions people develop for computer activities.

Computer Video Games – Are They Really Addictive?

You have developed a penchant for the computer game "FreeCell;" it taps into your card-playing experiences from college. The game seems like an innocent distraction at first, but you find yourself playing it more and more. When you are supposed to be working on financial records, you start a game, which may not even be gratifying, but you see it through to the end, because you have developed the knack of winning almost every game you play. One day you stumble into a particularly challenging game and try it over and over without success. Your husband asks that you come to bed and not play past midnight, a reasonable request you cannot seem to abide by. Can games on the computer truly be addicting?

Conservative When your behavior is starting to affect your family, it is an addiction regardless of how simple the source. You should treat your actions as you would any other addiction—stop playing the game immediately, and seek support from those around you.

Liberal Playing multiple games of FreeCell is not in the same league as drinking, gambling, or other major addictions. Some kids have developed Repetitive Strain Injury in their wrists from their time spent on the computer, but as long as you are not having those symptoms there is no real harm in a little light diversion.

SUMMARY

Playing FreeCell is no more or less an addiction than playing video games. The computer can be quite habit-forming and as we use it our attention spans keep shrinking—check e-mail, check the market, surf aimlessly, and repeat. If you have a slow Internet connection at home, you may interweave playing FreeCell with Web browsing while waiting for a site to load. Indeed, whenever you begin to feel at a loss you open a new FreeCell game. Increasingly, you consider life as a series of computer operations to feel plugged in. Whether one labels your action an addiction is not as relevant as the need to bring matters under control, so you consciously decide when and how often you want to spend time recreationally on the computer.

Surfing – How About a Schedule?

You have become a chronic Web surfer. One typical evening, you go onto the Internet to search for a certain coat you have in mind for your grandson. One link leads to another and the next thing you know an hour-and-a-half has gone by and you have been looking at Web sites on warm clothing, European imports, travel in Switzerland, and Italian recipes the entire time. More and more of your time goes into browsing the Internet. A few years ago you did not understand what all the fuss over the Internet was about, and now you are hooked. People ask what you have been doing lately and you cannot remember anything significant. Is this a problem?

Conservative You should schedule your time on the computer as you would any pastime, and then adhere to your schedule.

Liberal How you spend your free time is not the concern of others. There is nothing wrong with browsing. In doing so you can learn all kinds of interesting things and can get immediate answers to whatever questions you have. The more you surf the Web, the better you become at it so you can more readily find informative sites.

SUMMARY

The Internet has a vast amount of important information, but that does not mean it is all important to you. It also hosts junk of little consequence to anyone. To use it effectively, you have to stay focused so that the computer is not leading you but rather you are leading it. This requires a good deal of discipline, the ability to stay centered while browsing and using the computer, and the ability to limit your time so you do not squander it.

Newsgroup and Web Logs

A significant part of Internet use is the emergence of newsgroups and chat rooms where people with common interests can learn from each other and share experiences. It is now possible to learn who in the world has grown the largest pumpkin or who currently has the longest hair! The world gets smaller as we meet one another across the globe.

Virtual Friends – How Do They Fit into Your Life?

You love horses, own two, and would have more if your husband would allow it. You have tried to get your kids interested in riding with you, but they are not responsive to the care, feeding, and all of the other associated concerns. You have joined the horse newsgroup and have become a regular contributor. It is rewarding to have new friends who share your passion, some from other countries. You spend most evenings on the computer chatting about issues ranging from hay to hooves. For once you have found people who do not tire of the subject. Is this a problem?

Conservative You should quit spending so much time communicating to others remotely, and spend more time with your husband and family.

Liberal It is great that you have made new friends from afar with whom to learn and share stories. There is no problem as long as your marriage is not in danger.

SUMMARY

With a newsgroup you can develop camaraderie by sharing information, telling and listening to stories, and asking questions. It can give you tremendous support when you are having horse-related problems, leading to new friendships. While browsing introduces an ever-broadening array of information, with newsgroups you become more and more focused into one issue. But the question here is not whether you should be browsing, but how this newsgroup fits into the rest of your life. If you are on the computer instead of watching TV, you are replacing a passive activity with a more active and social one. If, however, the newsgroup is replacing interacting with family and friends, you should take a hard look at its value.

Exploiting Virtual Friends – Should You Issue a Disclaimer?

You are an avid musician and a frequent visitor of a piano newsgroup where you participate in numerous discussions on the merits of various types of pianos, entertain questions on music theory, and learn about piano care from some of the piano tuners who are regulars on the site. Of late, you have joined in a long discussion about the merits of the Damp Chaser Unit, a device that maintains the humidity of the instrument to an even level. A heated discussion ensues and you become one of the strongest advocates for the product. You have installed them in the past, and still do it occasionally. Should you reveal this fact to the group?

Conservative By all means. People need to know where you are coming from.

Liberal It depends on whether you stand to financially gain if the participants start to use the product. If not, you do not need to share your background, as it may discount people from listening to you.

Summary

When information is shared in newsgroups, you do not know what is behind a participant's posting, be it deep expertise or an aspect of salesmanship. It is hard for participants to calibrate themselves as to the relative amount of their expertise or the impact of their biases, so oftentimes they will not say much about their credentials. In a situation where you are involved in a specific topic that you have knowledge about, you should explain your background and how it is impacting your views. If you handle it right, when you issue a disclaimer people will often like you for it and trust your opinion even more.

Flaming Newbies – Should You Go Easy?

You love to snowmobile and have found the snowmobiler's newsgroup to be a wonderful place to converse with your fellow enthusiasts. You form a real affinity for the group and its culture. When you make a new posting asking for advice on the best trails in Idaho, you find yourself hoping "Harry B" will respond as he always has such good insights. A "newbie" arrives and soon puts up a snowmobile for sale. Your group does not list items for sale, as there is a separate group for such activity. Should you flame him or just give him a gentle chiding to explain the group's protocol?

Conservative The group's rules should have been clearly stated as he entered so that the new fellow would not have transgressed in the first place. If the rules are posted, by all means give him grief with both barrels, a rip-roaring flame. He will then decide if he wants to participate in the future and do so more carefully.

Liberal Take it easy on him—he is a newcomer. If you are rude, you are liable to lose him permanently.

SUMMARY

Each newsgroup has its own culture, which the regulars preserve. A well-run group often has a moderator who assists newcomers, keeps the group on topic, and manages the rules. It is a full-time activity for someone who has the time and the interest. You have to hope it is someone patient, calm, with good judgement, and not too large an ego.

Sharing Your Deep Feelings in a Newsgroup – A Good Idea?

You have a new pet cockatiel and you have just joined a newsgroup about these birds. A posting just came in from a "Davie K" questioning the morality of maintaining birds as pets. You did a lot of searching about that question before getting your bird and want to share your concerns and your wisdom. Should you?

Conservative It is not for you to be the one to address Davie K's points. Leave this to the more experienced members of the group who may or may not choose to challenge him.

Liberal The ground rules of a newsgroup are for anyone to join in who has something to add to the conversation. Feel free to speak your mind, as long as you do not use profanity.

SUMMARY

Davie K may be a "troller," one who makes a sport of disrupting newsgroups. The well-constructed troll posting induces newbies to look clueless while subtly conveying to the savvy that it is in fact a deliberate troll. Additionally, trollers like nothing better than to get a newsgroup fired up about an argument they have been through before. Before long, the regulars are wondering what has happened to their beloved newsgroup. A moderator would greatly help the situation by spotting trolls and keeping them out. As a "newbie" or newcomer to the group, you are better off reading for a while before posting anything. Otherwise, you might inadvertently fall for this "flame bait" and kindle a newsgroup war.

Web Log – Public Diary?

Your 44-year-old cousin has begun putting her diary online in a Web log. Your family cannot understand this idea: what happened to the days when women did not want anyone reading their diary, much less the whole world? How should you weigh in on the situation?

Conservative There are a lot of kooks out there and you do not know who will read her diary and do what with it. Your cousin is free to do as she chooses, but you should advise her against it.

Liberal Little harm is likely to happen from your cousin creating her own Web log. Maybe someone will read it and discover her as a writer.

SUMMARY

Web logs or "Blogs" are a growing phenomenon where people maintain a running commentary on what is going on in their lives, from the mundane to the reflective. Groups form where people read each other's Blogs and comment on them. Blogs have elements of a chat room in that they are more personal than informative, and elements of a newsgroup in that the postings are longer and more thought out. Each person maintains their own Blog, often with nice graphics, references to back issues, maybe some photos, and sound clips. Politics and the state of the world are common topics, as well as people relating the events in their daily lives. Other people maintain such an eloquent running commentary that others get hooked on the storyline and follow that person's writing from then on. Think of it as reality T.V. in very slow motion.

Chat Rooms

While chat rooms have many of the qualities of newsgroups, they have a fundamentally different feel because they are live. They often have a more frivolous feel, with people spouting off on a topic. One regular frequenter to each says he considers chat rooms a diversion in the league of video games, and he will go to a newsgroup if he has something of consequence to say. Chat rooms serve as a meeting ground for those who would not otherwise find each other.

Ad Hoc Business Agreements – Should You Trust Them?

You are a regular in a programmer's chat room where people sometimes wander "in" looking for technical help with, say, Internet Explorer. While this is not really on topic, participants will normally respond with information. In one evening's chat, you are talking to "Ian" who is 20 years old, wants a specific program written to retrieve files from the Web and is willing to pay for it. You become intrigued, realizing you could put together something in a couple of hours, by looking up a couple of application program interfaces (APIs) and stringing them together in a little program. You switch to e-mail to further the dialog, perhaps thinking perhaps about making a little money. Is this kind of deal appropriate?

Conservative You do not know anything about this person and you are considering doing a business arrangement with him? It is certainly a bad idea—likely a waste of time and maybe worse.

Liberal You do not have much to lose other than your time. It might prove an interesting experience. Have some trust in your fellow man.

SUMMARY

Chat rooms provide a forum where people with complimentary needs can find each other quickly and easily. This can lead to diverse direct interactions outside the scope of the chat room. Any endeavor, be it a meeting or a work contract as portrayed here, is fundamentally between two strangers with no guarantees or recourse if issues arise. Unlike eBay, where strangers successfully do business together all of the time, chat rooms offer no systems to file a grievance or to check out another person's reputation. Maybe everything will work out great, maybe it will not. Your time may feel expendable to you now, but you may feel differently later if you are taken for a ride.

Internet-based Activism – Is it Effective?

You are a political activist who wants to see a major change of government so you start to partake in chat sessions at talkopolis.com. People come in with views from all over the map, with rants and conspiracy theories you find quite intriguing and somewhat alarming. You are struggling with if and how you can be effective. Is this a waste of time?

Conservative Most decidedly. If you really want to do something useful get involved with the political process the traditional way and attend caucus meetings.

Liberal There is no harm in participating as long as you do not take what you read to be necessarily true. You might expand your views and make some new friends.

SUMMARY

If you consider the chat room a social experience in which to practice sharpening and clarifying your viewpoint, then it has its place. A political chat session such as one conducted by the New York Times might give you some idea as to the current pulse of public opinion. However, realize that people talk more than they read or reflect, there is a lot of non-sense out there, and you might end up getting very fired up in a way that puts off the average citizen. You should view the chat room as a social experience, rather than a primary source of information.

Meeting the Right Virtual Woman – Is it Possible?

You are an engineer, single and quite shy, living in Seattle. You always found nightclubs loud, unpleasant, and certainly not conducive to you meeting a woman. Lately, you have started going to the local singles chat room looking for romance. Is this a good idea? There are postings from all kinds of people ranging from someone who says, "come see my photos," to a surprising number of women from the Philippines eager to meet a Seattle man.

Conservative No, this is not a good way to meet a woman. What kind of woman would contact strangers over the Internet? Ask some friends to introduce you to a woman they know. You will find they will be glad to help.

Liberal Why not go for it? You do not have much to lose. You could at least get more used to conversing with a woman who is a stranger and build your confidence up. It is good to know some of the basic lingo of chat rooms as you get started: LOL is laugh out loud, NP is no problem, and ASL means age, sex, and location. Good luck.

SUMMARY

Chat rooms can provide a way for people to get to know each other who would not ordinarily meet. The mere fact of meeting someone over the Internet changes the whole typical dynamic, where people meet in a bar and form their first impressions of each other from physical appearances; the personality and character relations follow only if they are attracted physically. On the Internet, people have their first encounters according to their interests and how simpatico they are, and then introduce photos and even meet to see if they want to go further with the relationship. On occasion, they find and connect with people they never would have noticed on the street or in a nightclub.

Interestingly, recent studies have shown that most Internet dating occurs between married or otherwise committed people having affairs. Chat rooms and single services seem to provide an outlet for people trying to get out of an unfulfilling relationship.

Postings from participants can get quite raunchy, especially late at night. Additionally, chat rooms are thick with ads for porno sites, including postings from a bot or robot posing as a participant, such as the one offering to come see photographs in this scenario. The unsuspecting responder is led immediately to a porn site and gets an onslaught of cookies and porn ads. And there are foreign women looking for U.S. husbands, sometimes targeted to a specific geography such as the situation here where Filipino women are looking for Seattle husbands to connect to the existing Filipino community.

So, it can be a wild ride to frequent such chat rooms, but people do meet and form lasting relationships there.

E-mail Etiquette

We have learned over the years that the tongue is the most dangerous organ, but with computers the fingers are just as deadly. A relationship that took months or years to build can be damaged in seconds with a few hateful works. To a lesser extent, ignoring the rules of the road for e-mail can affect the way people think about us. We have talked about e-mail issues in several other chapters and do not want to belabor them here, but it is worth noting what the etiquette is for e-mail in your personal life.

Useless Forwarded E-mail – Delete It?

Your sister sent you and others on her list an e-mail of drawings of dancing potatoes, with a message to turn up the sound and listen to cute puns about types of potatoes. At the end of the message, it says to pass it on to your friends. You can see from her list who she has sent it to. You do not really like getting these cute little messages from her. Should you say something?

Conservative   No. You are likely to hurt her feelings. Better to just delete them as they come in and forget about it. A good rule of thumb is to delete any e-mail that has been forwarded more than once.

Liberal   It seems your sister wants contact with you and the best way to handle the situation is to write her more regularly. After you do so for a while, you could gently bring up that you do not like getting group e-mails from her.

SUMMARY

It seems there is always someone in your life who, without you ever asking, sends you jokes, cute wisdom from kids, and greeting card e-mails. The main issue comes when they have not learned to hide the "To" list, and everyone else can see who is on their e-mail list. This can become a privacy matter in unexpected ways, as some people are very closed about sharing their e-mail address. Also, you can learn who your contact likes for what kind of missive. Educate your sister about sending lists to undisclosed recipients using bcc or by forming an address list. Whether or not you ask her to stop sending you these types of e-mails is a matter of your own discretion.

"Yes, I know it's a work machine, but..."

Another controversial topic is the use of office or professional computers for personal use. Most companies have an Acceptable Use Policy that defines how corporate assets are (and are not) to be used. Many companies allow for a "reasonable" amount of personal computer use, like sending e-mail or surfing the Web for a few minutes during a coffee break.

But what about companies who have taken a more hard-line approach, who don't allow any personal use of office computers whatsoever? Now, you can maybe see where they're coming from: someone in their Accounting area said "We have 40,000 employees with an average salary of $30,000/year. If we can stop every person in the company from spending 15 minutes a day sending personal e-mail messages, we'll save a gazillion dollars a year!" However, there comes a point where you need to treat a grown-up...like a grown-up. What about the account executive, whose only grown child has moved across the country? By preventing him from sending her a "Hi, how's it going, just checking in" e-mail when he gets to the office in the morning, the company may well be saving money at face value. But how much happier will this man be, knowing that he can check in with his kid and know that she's alright from day to day? Forcing someone to give up that kind of peace of mind, especially when it costs so little, in favor of a number on a balance sheet is rather short-sighted.

Now I'm not suggesting that companies should give up striving for peak productivity and encouraging a strong work ethic. But I think we can all agree that there's a difference between addressing the chronic Web surfer (who misses their deadlines in favor of searching eBay for vintage New York Giants trading cards), and allowing otherwise responsible adults the freedom to manage their time in their own way.

Laura E. Hunter
Network Consultant & Technical Trainer

The Neiman Marcus Cookie and Other Urban Legends – Should You Forward It to Others?

You receive an e-mail with the following tale:

A woman ate lunch at Neiman Marcus and liked the chocolate chip cookie she had so much she asked for the recipe. The waitress told her it would cost two fifty and the woman agreed to buy it, thinking it would cost $2.50. But when she got her credit card bill at the end of the month, they had charged her $250. She complained but the company stood firm, saying that was the cost of their recipes. The woman is so incensed she copied the recipe in revenge, and asks all who received this message to send it on to everyone they know.

What should you do?

> **Conservative** If you care about the person that sent the note, invest in the time to educate them about urban legends and gently explain how sending these types of notes puts them in a poor light.

> **Liberal** It would not do any harm to just delete this e-mail. The sender of the note will learn better eventually.

SUMMARY

This particular e-mail hoax has been around for years, and it goes around and around without stopping. As new people receive it, it seems like a new story to them and they pass it on with relish. Neiman Marcus did not even have a chocolate chip cookie recipe until this epistle generated so much mail that they developed one and posted it on their Web site for free. There are e-mails to help women in Afghanistan or help a cause for the UN, that if you investigate further, ended in the year 2000. There is hardly ever a time that you should forward an e-mail to everyone on your list. It is a favorite ploy of hoaxes to ask you to do so. Those very words should be enough to make you want to delete the e-mail right then and there to try to break the chain.

Viruses and Worms

When you are operating on your own outside the auspices of your company's information technology (IT) department, you are liable to encounter the big bad world of computer viruses. To be online these days you should have virus protection software running or you are likely to catch a virus. Even that is not foolproof, as shown in the following situations.

When Anti-Virus Fails – What to Do?

You are traveling on an extended vacation and use your laptop for e-mail, Web browsing, and doing some writing. You notice aberrant behavior that you have not carefully tracked, but one clear issue is that after a certain amount of time in any one session, drag and drop stops working. Indeed you cannot do any cut-and-paste operations until you reboot your computer, at which point everything seems normal. You periodically get a message from your Norton Software that it has found blaster.exe in a file and is unable to repair it. But if you run a system scan with Norton, it reports no infection found. Although rebooting periodically is a bit annoying, it is an annoyance you can live with while in vacation mode. Should you?

Conservative You might have a serious infection on your computer that you could transmit to others. You should figure out what is wrong with it either yourself, or by taking it to a computer service outfit.

Liberal Since the problems are not affecting you too seriously, it is probably okay to wait until you are home to deal with them. But at some point you need to figure out what is going on as computer issues do not usually go away on their own.

SUMMARY

As a recipient and sender of e-mail and worms, you are effectively part of the Web's immune system. It is possible in situations like this for your computer to catch a worm even if you have virus protection software. The blaster worm was able to penetrate any computer online operating Windows software that did not have the latest operating system software installed. A firewall would have blocked the worm, which enters through an open port, but not virus-protection software, which watches e-mail and incoming files. Norton could keep the worm from doing full damage, but it could effectively disable the copy function, used in drag-and-drop operations. The Norton and Microsoft Web sites each had extensive write ups about the problem and the steps to eliminate the worm. These could be found by searching with a standard search engine with descriptive words about what you found—in this case the "drag-

and-drop problems blaster." It would take some effort on your part, but it is a required action to be a good Web citizen.

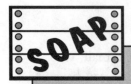

End-user Irresponsibility
Spoiling the Internet for the Rest of Us

The Internet is a shared environment that depends upon the responsible behavior of all participants. Years ago we occasionally suffered from actual computer viruses (usually spread by irresponsible end-user behavior). But true viruses are relatively difficult to write. It has been much easier in recent years to spread malicious software by simply e-mailing Trojan horse software to users and relying on their irresponsibility to ensure its spreading. Think about it. How many times have you received an e-mail "virus" or "worm" that wasn't the result of the sender acting irresponsibly by executing an unknown e-mail attachment? Then there is spam, accounting for more than half of all e-mail. Think about it. Would spam exist—and would we have to endure it—if end users refused to ever respond to the invitations? spam exists, and only exists, because end users finance spammers by responding and buying their products. We require drivers' licenses to drive a vehicle in public to make the roads safer for all of us. But we tolerate users on the Internet who do the equivalent of routinely running red lights and making the streets unsafe for everyone.

William H. Curd, Ph.D., Ltd.

The Microsoft Patch by E-mail – Should You Open It?

You receive an e-mail with the Microsoft logo that says "please update your Windows now by opening the attachment." You do so and a few screens go by that say something like "Windows is updating your files." Not much seems different until you go into e-mail and you have 500 messages in your Inbox. You are getting nine or ten copies of each e-mail you receive. Apparently you have received a virus. What should you do?

Conservative Reinstall Windows to clear the matter up, or take your computer to a service center that can take care of the situation.

Liberal If the virus is not doing more damage, you can delete the extra e-mails until you can determine what is going wrong. Whatever happened has happened.

SUMMARY

The basic rule holds: never open an attachment from anyone unless you are sure of its source. Microsoft does not send updates via e-mail attachments. Anyone can duplicate a company logo. It is unclear if you are passing this virus on, but you might well be, so you should refrain from going online until you get it removed. As with the previous example, you can learn a lot by going to the virus protection software vendors' sites, such as McAfee that maintains a full database of all known viruses, worms, and hoaxes. Using someone else's computer to do so, you will likely learn all you need to do to purge your system.

Web Site Browsing and Usage

Going to a company's or organization's Web site is one of the fastest ways to learn about them. However, some sites are not what they portray to be. For example, you may know of free software called VNC and go to vnc.org to download it, only to find you are at a competitor's site that charges money for a similar product. Using a search engine, you find what you want at realvnc.org. Similarly, some political sites and celebrity sites are run by others, sometimes in competition with the person you are seeking. Legitimate sites may use your information in ways you do not care for as in the following sections.

Personal Responsibility for Privacy – Taking Steps to Minimize Exposure

You have been led to an animal rescue Web site that promises to feed dogs in shelters with every visit to their Web site. However, it also solicits funds for contributions and exposes you to pop-up ads. Soon after the visit, you start receiving spam advertising all kinds of products. Apparently the animal shelter site has sold your e-mail address. What is an appropriate course of action?

Conservative It may be obvious that your e-mail address has been released to third-party marketers, but you are not able to prevent all of these types of actions. If you want to ensure your privacy you should not give out your e-mail address to Web sites, and contribute directly through traditional means.

Liberal You should accept the real possibility of your e-mail address being sold, and if you can verify that the site does indeed donate food to animal shelters, then whether you have an issue with it is merely a matter of your priority.

SUMMARY

You may need to accept a certain amount of e-mail address selling in order to use the full spectrum of benefits available on the Internet. But you can take measures to minimize exposure to unwanted marketing strategies. Web sites can learn your e-mail address just by your browsing to them, but it takes some fast work on their part, using an File Transfer Protocol (FTP) request to your Internet Service Provider (ISP). Your ISP can offer some protection against this behavior. However, when you enter your e-mail address into any kind of form on a commercial site you should suspect it will be sold, unless you can confirm otherwise through their privacy policy. A good safety measure is to use a separate e-mail account for just this kind of purpose, so if it gets sold and full of spam you can delete that account and start a new one.

The Relative Security of Online Sites – Should You Trust It?

You have decided to enroll in an online traffic school to avoid a permanent speeding citation on your driver's record. You learn all of the schools are regulated by the state. Each requires specific personal information to enroll. The one you choose states that all information is encrypted and totally secure. It uses a familiar logo and the name of VeriSign to assure security. Do you trust the traffic school with your driver's license information?

Conservative You are mildly interested in an online traffic school because of their flash cutting edge technology. You should avoid entering your personal details into an online form as a matter of personal policy.

Liberal You can trust in the VeriSign symbol and encryption the site offers. Besides, the worst that can happen is credit card fraud and either the merchant or the card company are the only ones that stand to lose.

SUMMARY

Research would explain what a VeriSign symbol is and its implications on entering information to this Web site. Anyone can buy a VeriSign certificate, but the fact that they took the trouble and say they are secure shows they are at least thinking about the issues. The enrollment is at least somewhat secure and much better than attending an eight-hour session in a bleak and empty room. Instead, you can do so in the comforts of your own home.

Conspicuous Consumption – Is It too Easy?

While shopping for replacement cartridges for your HP inkjet printer, you discover a new printer on sale for only slightly more than the cost of the two cartridges yours requires. Your printer is working fine, but maybe it will not for long. Should you buy a new one?

Conservative Why get rid of something that is working well? Instead, look for a better price on the cartridges.

Liberal Sure, go ahead and buy the new printer. You can always give your old one to a school or non-profit organization.

SUMMARY

One of the features of online shopping is you can find great bargains. And computers have become so cheap that many of us have extra parts and accessories from upgrades. Loads of these wind up in the dumpster and landfill because people do not know what to do with them. Non-profits will take some equipment, but it can be more trouble than it is worth for them. There are computer recycling centers that will resell used equipment such as your printer. But be aware that new printers do not come with nearly as much ink as do new replacement cartridges, so you may not be getting all the value you think you are. Also, some cartridges can be refilled, which is much cheaper than buying a new cartridge. You should assess how long you have had your printer and if it has some good life in it, see if you can find a home for it before buying a new one.

DIY Spyware – Will It Make You Paranoid?

You have seen ads for software monitoring your spouse's activity on the Internet, and it could detect if your wife has been having an affair. You have been happily married for eight years and have no reason to suspect her. But she did have an affair in her first marriage years ago. You are away from home a lot for work, including out-of-town business trips, while she pals around with her friends. Maybe you should install this software, just for your peace of mind, to eliminate any nagging doubts. Should you?

Conservative   No. You would be spying on her. Talk to your wife if you have any nagging doubts about her faithfulness. Installing spyware would be taking a negative approach to a situation that may not even exist. What if she is innocent of the slightest thought of an affair and somehow discovers the spying system? Maybe she would find a sales receipt. The trust in your marriage would be severely damaged.

Liberal   If indeed it would give you peace of mind it would be worth the cost. But it would only uncover any affair your wife may have if she does it over the Internet. You might get a false negative.

SUMMARY

Spy software was originally designed for parents to monitor the use of their computers by children and employers to watch over employees. It does that well, however, its sales have grown much faster to people looking for online cheating by their spouses. The software watches and records everything that happens on a computer. It captures the screen every 30 seconds, remembers the programs you open, keeps track of all the Web sites you look at, saves a picture of every chat conversation and e-mail, and knows how long you spent doing each of these things. And you can set up the program in "stealth mode" where no trace of it is visible to your spouse. It would do the job of uncovering any online affair ideas your wife may have. But is it the best idea for your marriage? If you start down this path you might increase your paranoia.

Cookies – Managing Your Privacy

Cookies are small files Web sites place in a known location on your computer. They contain identification cues enabling a Web site to recognize you when you return to it. Companies routinely place these items on our computers without our knowledge. When you go to a Web site like www.flowers.com that you regularly frequent, the system can identify you, reference their database, and know your preferences and contact information all without you typing a character. Many Web sites have the ability to read other Web site's cookies on your computer to learn where you have browsed, and adjust your advertising accordingly.

You have just added a firewall to your computer and instructed it to ask you before allowing a cookie. You start into your normal evening computer routine, checking e-mail in your hot mail account, reading cnn.com, checking sports scores, and doing a bit of shopping, but before you even get into your hot mail account you are asked to allow cookies from msn.com, a hot mail server, classmates.com and adbiz.com. Each click of your mouse brings up two or three cookie requests. What should you do?

Conservative Do not allow any cookies unless you have good reason to, such as when you want to make an online payment to a credit card provider and the credit card Web site needs to collect information about you.

Liberal Cookies have silently been on your computer since the time you first went on the Internet. Just because you now know they are there does not make them a problem. Set your firewall to allow all cookies and you will not see all of these intervening messages.

SUMMARY

Web sites have no fundamental mechanism for saving state; each action is atomic. They send a request, you send a reply. Cookies permit them to get around this limitation by maintaining a record about you on their computer and using a cookie on your computer to access it. In many instances this procedure is in your interest, such as when dealing with merchants and financial institutions. So generally allowing cookies is okay. If your computer has ever been used to go to a porn Web site you undoubtedly have many cookies on it that lead to unwanted ads and even spam e-mail.

A useful approach would be to erase all of your current cookies and, as you go through your normal routines, watch who wants to place cookies on your computer. Sites you are visiting such as MSN and CNN are fine to allow. Disallow anything that looks like advertising. After an evening or two of this level of scrutiny you will tire of it and want to set your cookie control on your browser and firewall. The firewall takes control first, and if a cookie is accepted at that level, it goes to the browser to decide. A good strategy is to have a moderate to low level of scrutiny on the firewall and then adjust your browser more often. You may want to leave your browser set to a fairly high level of privacy if you have kids going on the Internet. In Microsoft's Internet Explorer and Netscape browsers you need to go through a series of steps in the browser's menus to get to the appropriate privacy and cookie control. As a user it would be useful to have this control as an easy button to click on the toolbar, but until that day comes, you should become familiar with how to control cookie settings in your browser so that you can adjust it regularly.

Browsing Pornography on the Internet – Those Persistent Web Sites

Internet pornography is easy to access should you choose. Most of it is quite hard core, as it seems viewers get immune to light sexual stimulation and want to see more and more lewd content. Indeed, if you try to find soft core material you are led to sites with claims such as "soft core porn—nastiest live sex show." The issue with porn is not how to find it, but how to stay away from it as discussed in the following sections.

You are curious to see what pornography looks like on the Internet. Thinking maybe you will find a few playboy-like photos, you type in "sexy nude photos" in Google and follow some links. You find sites offering "xxx hard core movies," and photos of group sex inviting you to join their member's-only service. You have quickly had enough so you quit. Within a couple of days you are receiving e-mail messages in your Outlook account from people like Jennifer, asking you to click on the link to see what happens. Once you do, not even sure if it is sex-related, and before you know it, you have got several windows popping up with very explicit pictures. As you close one window, another opens in a seemingly unending chain. And you are getting more and more spam saying they are glad you joined their service with offensive sexual subject lines. What happened and what can you do?

Conservative You have gotten in over your head on this one and may need to reinstall your operating system to clear any trace of the material from your computer. At a minimum, you should run a trust worthy spy ware detection program such as spybot Search and Destroy or adaware. You have learned a hard lesson about frolicking around on the Web.

Liberal You have had a classic cyber-sexual experience, and now you know what it is all about. Just delete any e-mails you do not want; hopefully your e-mail junk filter will pick up most of them and avoid going to such sites if they bother you.

SUMMARY

Pornographic Web sites are set up so if you follow the first link a java script runs, which upon the close of one window triggers the opening of a new one on another site. They hope you will be titillated enough by what you see that you will join one of their clubs, conveniently setting up a monthly charge on your credit card. Porn sites want to get your e-mail address whatever way they can, and a visit to their site seems to have enabled them to. Do not respond to any such e-mail for any reason, even to unsubscribe; you will only encourage them by confirming you are alive and reading their messages. There is really no effective way to get off of spam e-mail lists as they are sold quickly. Finally, if you must visit such sites, Netscape is a safe browser than Internet Explorer.

While browsing, it is quite possible to accidentally encounter pornographic sites, though you will not stumble onto ones with illegal content such as child pornography. If you seek that out, you are subject to prosecution, so do not try even just for curiosity. (Many who are caught say they were just curious.) To avoid encountering pornographic sites you can use a filter, either through AOL if you use it, or a separate piece of purchased software. There are attempts underway to have a sex rating system and have all Web sites put rating information in their pages. But new porn sites crop up daily, all over the world, and most do not care to participate in the rating system. Internet Explorer has a filtering capability with a nice interface, but it is not very effective. It can be set to either block unrated sites, which means most sites, or it lets everything through. The purchased software filters and AOL's filter do better as they actually evaluate content. But any filter at some point limits what you want to do, for example, restricting a cooking site with chicken breasts in a recipe. As with firewalls, people can get so frustrated with the filters getting in their way they just bypass them.

The US government would like to regulate porn sites, but the pornographic companies First Amendment rights allows them to actively solicit adult access. A few years back it was proposed to give the sites a new top-level domain suffix so instead of being .com they would all be .xxx, for example. This seemed like a great solution as one could then easily set up computers to avoid any such domains. But again, sex on the Internet is very much an international affair, and there is no current way to regulate these sites in other countries. The sites migrate to wherever the rules are the most lenient. We as Internet users are left to our own ways to manage the situation.

eBay Shopping – Buyer Beware

eBay is the great garage sale in the sky. You can find everything you have ever wanted and more. You can sell your own junk and that of your kids. People have learned items they have had for years can be of surprising value. For example, the hardback first edition of Alcoholic Anonymous' book sells for over $500. eBay not only lasted through the major Internet shakeout, but it became a dominant player for new goods as well as used. Some of the reasons are the reasonable terms, the rules are strong and clear, and you can get great deals. Moreover it's an auction—it is like gambling, yet legal. Still there is ways to run into trouble.

Your friend Dayna has been buying rugs on eBay and shows you how great it is. The shipping can be expensive, but the rugs are reasonable. Per her advice, you go to auctions that are about to close and have 0 bids. You find a hallway rug you like for an opening bid of $9.95. It might look great in your hall. There is no time to consult your husband and you try to find the shipping price but do not see it listed. It says to contact the seller for any questions, but there is just an e-mail address and the auction closes in one minute. Dayna says she has paid $25 to $30 for shipping rugs this size. You place a bid, figuring you will see your total price with all taxes and shipping and handling charges before confirming. But the next thing you know your e-mail is coming up saying congratulations, you won the auction. Moments later you get an e-mail from the seller including the shipping and handling costs of $63 and total due of $73. You have major buyer's remorse—at this price suddenly you are not so sure about the colors and you should have talked to your husband. You want to get out of the deal. Can you?

Conservative No. By eBay rules you have made a commitment to purchase and you need to meet it. Chock it up to experience for the next time.

Liberal Contact the seller and see what they can do for you. Being a first-time buyer they may be lenient towards you.

SUMMARY

eBay has strict rules about the canceling of a sale to preserve their portion of the proceeds. It is only after the sale's buyers and sellers learn each other's identities that they could cancel the sale to avoid paying the eBay fees. If a sale is indeed canceled, the seller still owes the eBay fee. Sellers list a lot of standard information with their products such as warranty, their credentials, and how they handle and ship their merchandise. But the shipping cost is specific to that item and appears only with the item description. eBay is different than other online retailers in that you have to learn your own resultant costs, including price, taxes, and handling fees, and sum them up before placing a bid. By the time you place your bid you are committed.

Slow Fulfillment – Do You Have Recourse?

You buy some face cream on eBay and keep looking for it to arrive, but it does not come. You send an e-mail to the seller asking about the product, and she replies she shipped it already. Weeks go by. After repeatedly contacting the seller, you finally receive the package, postmarked from only six days ago. You ask the seller about it, and she replies it's the Post Office's fault. What are your recourses?

Conservative You received the product at the agreed-upon price so you could leave it at that. If you want to pursue the matter more you could leave negative feedback about the seller on eBay. In the future, read a seller's feedback before doing business with them.

Liberal   You could continue to engage in a dialog with the seller to understand what exactly happened at the Post Office to help her clear up the problem for the future.

SUMMARY

Your best course is to give negative feedback on the seller so other buyers will be advised as to what happened to you. Be aware that sellers dislike this, and can be quite snippy about it. The seller can in turn post negative feedback about you as a buyer, but you would have a chance to post a reply to her comments. eBay has a fraud protection policy covering up to $200 per item, with a $25 deductible. This policy applies when you do not receive the item at all or if it is clearly not as described, such as a brass item described as gold.

Fraudulent E-mail – Ignore It?

You receive an e-mail saying

"Dear eBay User, It has become very noticeable that another party has been corrupting your eBay account and has violated our User Agreement policy listed: 4. Bidding and Buying ….. eBay requires immediate verification for your account. Please verify your account or the account may become disabled. Click Here To Verify Your Account:

www.angelfire.com/ab7/ebay13"

What should you do?

Conservative   Ignore the message and delete it.

Liberal   The message seems suspicious and you should e-mail eBay before responding to see if indeed they sent it. They have a special address, spoof@ebay.com, just for e-mail messages like this.

SUMMARY

Companies like eBay are subject to fraudulent acts like this one. If you followed the link you would go to someone's server where you would be asked to give all of your account information, which they could in turn use to buy items in your name. eBay publishes a tutorial on spoofed mail. Check it out at http://pages.ebay.com/education/spooftutorial/. A reputable ISP will shut down such activity if you report it to them, sending all logs and the full e-mail headers of the message, but in the meantime be very leery of giving out your information, especially password-protected data.

Downloading Music – Try Before you Buy

It started with Napster, who made the practice famous until it was declared illegal. One can still find sites, legal or not, where you can download free music such as MP3 files and save them to a custom CD. This is an extremely common practice among younger folks and is not restricted to music only. One of the authors of this book found a .pdf of a book he helped write on intrusion detection available for downloading on a peer-to-peer network. Whatever your personal feelings are on this issue, it would be wise to be aware that if there is virtually no penalty for stealing intellectual property, that might serve to demotivate potential artists and authors in the future.

Your teenager and his friends download music regularly from Web sites that come and go with the wind. You have been missing an old Frank Sinatra tune, Fly me to the Moon. It is in your head and you would like to get it, but have not been by a store to pick up the CD. Your son offers to get you a copy from the Internet so you can see how you like the recording. Should you let him?

Conservative No. Music rights belong to the artist, or in this case to his estate. Violating them is a form of stealing and is illegal.

Liberal Since you are planning to buy a CD anyway, there is no harm in downloading the tune first. After all, music comes for free over the radio, why not over the Internet?

SUMMARY

The downloading of music is often illegal, depending on the site, as discussed in the chapter on System Administration. You should verify the legality of the site your son uses and if it is legal, then it should be okay to access the song in this case.

Sharing an Internet Connection – Is it Okay Not to Share with Others?

Having high-speed connections at work gives most of us a taste of what it is like, and makes it all the more painful to go to a dial-up connection at home. Plus, with kids using the Internet and the phone these days, there is hardly a time free where the line is available. More and more people have high-speed connections at home as well as in the office.

You have installed high-speed Internet at home using a cable modem service. Your neighbor is a freelance Web designer from home, who is having trouble finding enough work and struggling to make ends meet. He would like to have high-speed Internet also and offers to split the cost of your service if you run a wire to his house. Should you do so?

Conservative No. This is essentially stealing from the cable company. Also, you would be entering into a business arrangement with someone who is in financial trouble. You might be encouraging him in further over his head.

Liberal It is all right if your neighbor cannot afford to get the high-speed service anyway. In this way, you are not depriving the cable company from revenue as your neighbor was not planning to sign up for their service.

SUMMARY

Even though a high-speed modem has enough bandwidth to cover two houses, sharing the connection is not ethical without permission from the provider. You should check with the cable company to see what their view on the matter is, but expect them to reject the idea.

Chapter Summary

The ethics of personal use cover a wide range of topics depending on your habits and interests. Hopefully the ones we've shared here have given you some insight as to how others are using their computers and the issues they run into.

Frequently Asked Questions

The following Frequently Asked Questions, answered by the authors of this book help get you thinking about how we use computers in our personal lives. Unless legal issues are involved, then answers in the FAQ may not be the right answer for your organization.

Q: How many computers do families typically own nowadays?

A: American's have over one PC for every two people, including every man, woman, and child, and most of those are connected to the Internet. Most households have several computers, in various states of configuration, hooked to the Internet used primarily for e-mail, browsing, and games.

Q: How much of the information on the Internet is factual?

A: The Internet can give you answers to any question under the sun, including this one. The question is, how reliable is it? There are estimates that about a third of the information on the Internet is incorrect. If the veracity of the information is important, go to more trusted sources on the Web, such as universities, the government, and non-profit organizations. Which ones you trust vary according to your beliefs and values. Be aware that it is easy to find wrong information on the Internet that can look very accurate. For this reason, high school teachers will make it a research requirement that only a portion of a student's sources can come from the Web. People will cite Internet information as gospel and you may need to lightly inform them of its fallacies.

Q: What are the main uses of the Internet?

A: The Internet has three primary purposes: to publish information, to advertise goods and services, and as a forum for discussions.

Q: Is it safe to buy products over the Internet?

A: It is often scary and a little thrilling to make your first purchase over the Internet—it is so easy, so quick, and the product comes right to your door. The majority of Internet vendors are very reliable. Those that are not do not last long. You are certainly safe to buy from the big name outfits such as Amazon and companies that have a major store presence like Toys R Us. When you buy from the latter you have the advantage that if you want to return the product for any reason you can do so at the store. Smaller stores also care a lot about their reputation, and will help you if you have problems. In some ways, you can get the personal service of a neighborhood store but from a specialty store in Oklahoma.

Chapter 17

Penetration Testing

Ethical Dilemmas in this Chapter:

- **Misrepresenting the Penetration Test**
- **Undermining the Overall Security Picture**
- **Testing Non-clients**
- **Ulterior Motives Presenting Reports**

Introduction

The purpose of penetration testing is to determine whether a corporation's information technology (IT) system poses any level of security risk due to unwanted intrusion. Penetration testing checks applications, databases, networks, remote computing resources, and any other system connected to the business that is vulnerable. In addition to routinely checking existing systems, a business may require a penetration test when a new system goes live in production. For example, if the company rolls out a new e-commerce Web site and infrastructure, that system needs penetration testing. Penetration tests reveal whether unauthorized users can obtain access to the system. Once an unauthorized user obtains access, they can hack the system and wreak havoc by stealing credit card information or disrupting functionality.

There are many complex layers to penetration tests. The primary objective of penetration testing is to discover system vulnerabilities prior to when someone may utilize them outside of the organization for malicious purposes.

According to the ITSecurity.com dictionary, a penetration test is as follows.

> "Sometimes called 'pen testing', it is a security testing procedure that involves the legitimate attempt to penetrate a system's security under the authority of the system's owners. Its purpose is to locate and eliminate any vulnerabilities that could be exploited by hackers. Penetration testing can be used as a method of auditing a company's own security, or undertaken as part of a security certification process (such as TCSEC or Common Criteria). Testers are sometimes called Tiger Teams, and usually include the use of automated software packages such as SATAN and Crack. It is useful to employ penetration testing to check the implementation of a new firewall. Users should expect to receive detailed logs and reports following the test, and should receive help and advice on how to close any vulnerabilities located."

A penetration test involves testing and verifying all of the core technology services run by the company. The core services are firewall systems, electronic mail programs, Domain Name System (DNS), password programs, File Transfer Protocol (FTP), dial-up connections, file servers, database servers, wireless networks, Public Branch Exchange (PBX) systems, and Web servers. The penetration test also includes a check of the physical integrity of the system. This includes physical access to the server room, backup, and network facilities. All of these aspects of the information system require verification in a successful penetration test.

The ethical issues in this chapter include misrepresentation during penetration tests, undermining security through penetration test reporting and communications, testing non-clients, and ulterior financial motives when performing penetration tests.

Misrepresenting the Penetration Test

There are several different means that can be used to misrepresent a penetration test. You can misrepresent yourself and claim to possess adequate experience to perform the test, when in fact you do not. You can do a partial penetration test and pass it off as a complete test. Finally, using free tools to perform a penetration test that is questionable in its effectiveness and failing to check the facts is another form of misrepresentation. Misrepresentation occurs whenever you do not fulfill the obligations and expectations of the client. Your client is expecting the best from you to help protect their system from attack.

This section discusses the ethical issues of these misrepresentation scenarios. You decide if any of them have moral grounds.

Common Sense in Penetration Testing

In our current society, the lines between black and white are often so gray that it is hard to determine right from wrong. I am familiar with a few instances where a pen tester has taken the "freedom to do what they want to get in" a bit too far. I think common sense has to play a role in what we do and I think common sense is sometimes abandoned during penetration testing. As technology people, we can hide behind the technology with anonymity just like a malicious hacker. So during penetration testing, we may forget what role we are playing for the customer. Our number one goal is to HELP the customer, NOT HURT the customer. When a penetration test is underway, the pen tester has a tendency to put blinders on and forget their actions can do serious damage to the customer's systems and networks. It is good to think like a malicious hacker during penetration testing; it can be bad to act like a malicious hacker during the penetration testing. For example, you run across a vulnerability that appears to be exploitable. The only problem is the exploit will do one of two things: 1) give you root access, or 2) cause the system to crash with

Continued

potential permanent damage to the database it houses. What do you do? Of course the client has signed appropriate documentation letting you off the hook for system damage, unless you go outside the bounds of the agreement or screw up. You assume the customer has backups and are ready to go into action to repair the system if it does fail. What do you do? Is it ethical to knowingly and intentionally damage a client system? Will that customer ever want you to come back and do more work for them?

This is where common sense comes into play. My suggestion would be to take a step back for a moment and think. What do I gain from exploiting this vulnerability? Is it within the scope of the effort? What direction were we given from our customer contact? Should we contact the customer before we do this one? Do I need to ask legal counsel about this one since there is a high probability of system damage? Don't conduct penetration testing blindly. Generally, the customer will have a greater appreciation for your actions if you make intelligent decisions throughout the process.

The moral of the story is don't hurt the ones you are there to help.

Greg Miles, Ph.D., CISSP, CISM
Security Horizon

Misrepresenting Yourself – Is it Okay?

You have experience in information security but nothing as far as penetration testing. A former client of yours does not understand what a penetration test is and presumes that you would know how to do one. Is it ethically appropriate to agree to perform a penetration test even if you do not have the proper skills needed to successfully do the work?

Conservative It is never appropriate to perform any type of technical duty if you are not adequately qualified for the job. This is especially true for information security roles. Only qualified experts should conduct penetration tests. It is impossible to get away with performing an effective penetration test if you are not amply qualified. Eventually your lack of qualifications will become obvious.

Liberal Few people in the world possess the exact qualifications for all aspects of penetration testing. Since this example mentions that the person requested to perform the penetration test is an information security professional, they have a baseline of the necessary skills and a good head start above most individuals. If they communicate that they have never performed a penetration test in the past but feel they could adequately provide such a service, there is no ethical reason why they should not take the job.

SUMMARY

It is important that qualified personnel conduct penetration tests. This being said, it is up to the hiring company to determine the criteria for qualification, assuming that the applicants do not misrepresent themselves in any manner. If the hiring company wants to hire someone with very little experience, that is entirely their prerogative. Since this is a former client, you probably know why they are requesting an ethical hack and can determine whether you and possibly a better-educated contractor can meet their needs.

Vulnerability Scanners – In Place of Penetration Testing?

You do not have time to perform a full penetration test because your client changed the timeframes after you agreed to do the work, so you run a vulnerability scanner on your client's system instead. Is it ethical for you to charge the company for a full penetration test when all you are really doing is running a vulnerability scanner against their system?

Conservative It is not ethical to charge for services that you did not render. Running a vulnerability scanner is not the same as performing a full penetration test; scanners miss a lot of critical things such as resistance to social engineering and the effectiveness of your plant's physical security.

Liberal If the client shortens the timeframe required for a full penetration test but you are still required to present results quickly, you must be flexible to other options. In this circumstance, the client is setting the parameters for the test under nearly impossible circumstance. If those parameters only allow you to do a vulnerability scan, it's the company's fault, not yours. You should not reduce your payment due to their rush job requirements.

SUMMARY

The client often sets the timeframe, and for business reasons may reduce this period of time. It may or may not be ethical to still charge for a full penetration test, depending on the exact circumstances of the situation and the communications between the penetration tester and the client. However, if you have the time required to do a full penetration test and only perform a vulnerability scan, you have ventured out of reasonable ethical boundaries.

Using Free Tools – Should You Share the Knowledge?

When performing a penetration test, you utilize a suite of free tools that you downloaded from the Internet. You use these results as the end reporting mechanism you provide for your client. When you present the penetration test results, you fail to communicate the means by which you obtained the reports. Presuming you did not disclose how you obtained the results or did not offer to teach the client how to use the free tools, is it morally correct to give your client the results of a penetration test as if they are your own, when all you did was use free tools?

Conservative Performing a penetration test with free tools is not going to be effective enough. The client hired you to perform a thorough penetration test. In addition, using free tools to perform a penetration test without communicating that you did is completely unethical. Also, failing to teach the client how to use these tools is morally incorrect. Part of the penetration test is a transfer of knowledge. You failed in all aspects of this ethical scenario.

Liberal If the client does not decide in advance how you should conduct the penetration test, there is nothing morally wrong with utilizing free penetration testing tools. If you do not have a clue as to what you are doing and just use the tools, that is a different story. You are also not obligated to teach the client how to use free tools to perform their own penetration test. Just because there are tools on the market does not mean the average person can use them properly. These tools still require your expertise. An unqualified individual could not use them to the benefit of the company.

SUMMARY

Many consultants use software tools to perform their services. This may be a right or wrong choice; it depends on the circumstance. A really good penetration tester has access to the same tools that hackers do; such a tool set requires a more significant investment than the term "free tools" indicates. However, passing off the results of free tools as your own work may be questionable behavior morally, unless you are clear that it is the collection and use of them that you are calling your own work.

Penetration Testing Rules of Engagement

Before embarking on a penetration test, it is crucial that you establish and agree upon explicit rules of engagement with the owner of the target systems. These rules describe the nature of the testing activities and significantly help to minimize unpleasant surprises on the part of the tester and the target. Conducting a penetration test without firm rules of engagement could easily jeopardize the target network, as well as the penetration tester's job and reputation. Strong ethics require that the rules of engagement be agreed upon in writing, signed off by the head of the penetration testing team as well as the owner of the target environment. The rules should describe the testing approach on the following issues:

- Target systems and applications: Which network address ranges or system addresses are inside the scope of testing? Which are explicitly forbidden for testing?

- Denial of service: Will denial of service tests that could cause the target system to crash or otherwise be unavailable be included in the testing regimen?

- Time of day for testing: Should testing be conducted off-hours? What timeframes are allowed?

Continued

- Dates and days of week for testing: What is the schedule for testing?

- Contacts at the target environment: If the penetration testing team notices erratic behavior or a crash in a target system, whom should they contact? If in the course of testing, the penetration testing discovers evidence of a previous intrusion, whom should they contact? Include name, mobile phone number, and pager in all contact lists.

- Contacts on the penetration testing team: If the owners or operators of the target systems have questions or notice erratic behavior during a test, whom should they contact on the penetration testing team? Include name, mobile phone number, and pager in all contact lists.

- Daily debriefing: Will the penetration testing team report preliminary findings to the target owner on a daily or other regular basis?

- Informing administrators and other personnel of the testing: Will the system administrators and/or security team of the target environment be informed of the testing? Or, will their response be measured by the penetration testing team?

- Shunning: Will any traffic be automatically shunned during the test, potentially leading to invalid test results and/or a denial of service?

- Black box vs. Crystal box testing: Will the testing team be provided with a network and/or application architecture diagram (a crystal box test)? Or, will the team merely be given a target range, with everything in the range being in scope (a black box test)?

- Client-side systems: Will client-side systems be tested? Can the penetration testing team attack browsers by causing users to surf to the penetration testing team's own sites? Can the penetration testing team send e-mail to victim users to exploit their e-mail readers and/or test their response to executable attachments?

- Social engineering: Can the penetration testing team call administrators and/or users in the target environment on the telephone and use various manipulative

Ed Skoudis
SANS Instructor

Undermining the Overall Security Picture

The results of a penetration test must support the overall security picture for the business. The end product of the penetration test should not only reveal system insecurities but also include solutions to eliminate the security vulnerabilities. This is the primary factor that makes the penetration test different from a simple system audit. A penetration test verifies and solves. An audit simply reports as is. Part of a penetration test requires procedures that are designed to remediate the vulnerabilities revealed during the testing process. This means that the results of the penetration test must be fully released to the client. The penetration tester must expect that part of their job is to be involved in the system repair process to some degree.

In some circumstances, the problems lie in the enforcement of existing information security policy. If that is the case, this information belongs in the penetration test reports. Other required results include updating system patches and software releases. Regardless of the issues, they all require thorough documentation after the completion of the penetration test. With this kind of sensitive information, it is imperative that the report receives ample protection. It must be handled in a very sensitive manner. If this information fell into the hands of a dishonest penetration tester or even worse, a hacker, it would mean disaster for the company. Therefore, the penetration tester must represent the highest of ethical values. They must properly treat this data in a manner that secures its confidentiality and serves the customer.

Providing a False Sense of Security – Should You Ever?

You just completed a penetration test that was very positive. You could not find any way to compromise or gain access to your client's system. Because of these results, you joyfully communicate to your client that they are absolutely secure. Can you really tell a client that they are utterly secure after a penetration test? Is this morally acceptable on any terms?

> **Conservative** It is never appropriate to tell a client that due to penetration test results their systems are completely secure. There is no such thing as a completely secure information system. It does not exist. This is a sure sign that you do not know what you are talking about.

Liberal While you may have been overzealous in communicating to your client that their systems are secure, you have done nothing wrong ethically. To the best of your knowledge, they are secure. Maybe that would have been a better way to word your report to the client.

SUMMARY

Because all systems are vulnerable, communicating absolute security of information systems as a result of a penetration test is a mistake. Is it a moral mistake? It is if your client believes you. All penetration tests are only good for the exact configuration that was tested. New vulnerabilities are being discovered every week and there is also the problem of the "zero day" attack, where the exploit exists and the attacker knows how to use it, but it is not yet known to the security community.

Providing Limited Results – Never a Good Idea

When you perform a penetration test, you optimize the work so that you can later charge additional fees for more information on the test. Therefore, you only give the client the results of the penetration test. You do not provide enough detail that will enable them to reproduce the problem or fix it. You only provide that additional information if they pay you additional money. Is it ethically appropriate to withhold information from a penetration test to assume additional financial regards?

Conservative It is dangerous and unethical to withhold information from a penetration test. While you are withholding information, attackers have the precious time they need to penetrate the client's information system. This does not even take into account the ethics of setting up a penetration test to drain money out of a business for answers to that very test. All aspects of this issue are unethical.

Liberal You have the right to handle business anyway you like to maximize your profit as an IT professional. You do not breach any issues of ethics for profit by withholding additional information beyond the initial scope of the test. However, it is dangerous for the company to not be fully aware of how to remediate a problem as quickly as possible.

SUMMARY

Both points of view indicate that it is best to communicate penetration test results and remediation strategies as quickly as possible to protect your client from unnecessary attack. You should provide remediation information, if you have it, whether you charge extra money for such results or not. Keep in mind that almost anyone can acquire a recipe for a cake, but not everyone can bake the cake. Give them the remediation recipe and if their system administrators cannot fix the problems, your client can pay you to do the job. Be careful when bidding on the job; remediation is a manual process and can be complex and time consuming.

Failing to Provide the Full Picture – Not in Your Best Interest

When you perform a penetration test, you want the company to feel secure because they pay a lot of money for your services. At the completion of your services, you do not explain to the company that a penetration test is only a small view into certain aspects of the company's total security risk. Are you ethically required to communicate the scope of a penetration test within the big picture of corporate security risk?

Conservative You must communicate all aspects of the overall security picture to the client. Failing to do so is unethical. You should communicate that the penetration test is only part of the overall assessment when determining a secure corporate environment. Penetration testing is an important part of determining overall security, but not everything.

Liberal It is not your obligation as the penetration tester to address the overall corporate security of an organization. You must address the scope of the penetration test. Very few people are qualified to address all aspects of corporate security. This is an unrealistic expectation, not a moral one.

SUMMARY

It is a personal choice if you wish to go above and beyond the scope of the job you are there to perform. If the company does their homework prior to hiring you, they will know that your piece of the puzzle is one part of the overall perspective. Nevertheless, you may decide to make sure the company knows this and communicate how the penetration test fits into overall corporate security. This may bring in more work for you in the long run.

The Penetration Test Goes Bad – Are You Responsible?

You perform a penetration test and clearly identify system weaknesses in the company's IT infrastructure. Because you are performing a penetration test, you attempt to exploit those weaknesses with a third-party security penetration tool. You know there are risks involved when you exploit known system vulnerabilities however, you go ahead and do it as part of the test. Consequently, major damage occurs to the production network, which takes the business down for the day. Does the company have the right to hold you ethically accountable for this damage, or were you just performing your proper job function?

> **Conservative** You should be able to predict to some degree how third-party tools will interact with the known vulnerability. In addition, since these tools are also available to hackers, they can develop their attacks around the technology of the third-party tools. Alternatively, in some cases, you must use the tools to trigger problems or openings within the system. Since you did not pay attention to the potential consequences of using the tools, you are partially at fault ethically. You generated more damage to the system by running a third-party tool.

> **Liberal** You did your job to the best of your ability. You were hired to perform a penetration test. You did the test and the results were that the company has serious problems. This is not your fault and you should not be held responsible for these problems. It should be common knowledge that whatever issues arise during the penetration test are not the fault of the tester but the vulnerability of the system. Follow this philosophy for all relatively similar circumstances, unless there is gross negligence on the part of the penetration tester.

SUMMARY

This example illustrates the primary difference between a vulnerability test and a penetration test. The expectations on the part of the tester must be different because the penetration test seeks to exploit system weaknesses. The vulnerability test attempts to detect the presence of vulnerabilities, but not actually penetrate security openings. Either approach can break a system or a network, everyone in this field has a dozen, "I was running the test when the phone rang, it turned out I broke the ...." stories.

The client must expect that penetration testing is a highly intrusive process that has the potential to result in destruction to the system under the testing regiment. However, a qualified penetration tester must be able to control to some degree the flow of the test so that it is not overly destructive. This is not any easy job. When a tester utilizes third-party tools, there is always the risk of not being able to control those tools in a vulnerable penetration environment. You must use special care when using third-party tools in the production environment or on a system that directly affects the other clients or business partnerships. Before you ever put yourself in such a situation make sure the rules of engagement, what is permissible and what is not, are clearly stated.

Testing Non-clients

It is quite common for penetration testers and wannabes to perform penetration tests to varying degrees on potential clients. This occurs when the penetration tester pokes around a potential client's Web site looking for vulnerabilities. They then take the results of the modified penetration test and present them to the prospective client. This is a form of self-promotion and marketing that they hope will inspire the client to hire them to perform a full penetration test.

This section addresses the ethics of the different means testers use to obtain work. We address whether these means are appropriate. We discuss the information security equivalent of ambulance chasing, wireless network penetration, and detecting networks without the WEP/EAP/LEAP/802.11X enabled.

Chasing the Web Ambulance – Bad for Your Reputation?

Your penetration team finds a vulnerability on a Web site just by poking around the site. The company that owns this site is not a client of yours. Do you tell the Web site company who you are and that you have discovered a vulnerability? Do you offer to assist them with the vulnerability (for pay or free) by offering them a full penetration test?

Conservative You should definitely inform the company of the system vulnerability. You do not need to provide them with the full fix information, but give them a chance to address this weakness and tell them how you located it. Sign the e-mail with your name, title, and company name, but do not push your services onto the prospective client. If the client appreciates the information and does not feel you have been intrusive in your actions with checking out their Web site, they will call you for follow-up services. If you try to push your services on the company, they may suspect you of creating any existing problems they already possess. If you discovered the vulnerability in an innocent manner, offer to fix it for free. If you ask for money to fix the problem, you may, depending on the circumstances, be bordering on extortion or blackmail. You may not feel this is true but the potential client may read your actions this way.

Liberal Since you did not cause the security flaw but are helping them to discover problems, you have every right to offer your services for pay. Why not? This is an appropriate action under the circumstances. If the potential client misreads you, they are in the wrong ethically, not you. Just let them know who you are, what you do, and how much your services cost. They already know how good you are from what you discovered without formal access to their site. This is not chasing an ambulance. The only way that this situation falls into an unethical position is if you found the security vulnerability and then directly exploited it to bring the issue to their attention. Then you have crossed over the line and done something unethical.

SUMMARY

The key to this ethical issue is the difference between finding a vulnerability when using a Web site versus poking around technically to discover a vulnerability. If you find a problem when you are using a Web site, all of the actions you take after that point, whether to offer your services for a fee or for free, are ethical. However, if you directly invade the privacy of a potential client and hack to some degree into their Web site, all actions after that point are unethical, even if you offer to fix the problems for free. Using a site as a customer is completely legitimate. Hacking into a site to determine security weaknesses so that you can get a job is just plain wrong and aggressive behavior. Think about it from the site owner's point of view. Someone pokes a little too far into your site and can access customer credit card information. They write you and tell you they can fix this problem they found for a fee. Most Web site administrators will first focus on the fact that someone just obtained access to customer credit card numbers.

Wireless Security Breach Detection – Not the Best Advertising

You do a wardrive/walk around your city and find a gold mine of wireless networks without any encryption or access control. Their network is broadcasting a Secure Set Identifier (SSID) that is set as their business name. You take a look in the phone book or look them up on the Web to determine their office location, which matches up with where you were when you detected the network. Do you think it is unethical to approach them with your services based on those results?

Conservative Once you intentionally associate with a wireless access point that is not your own without the proper consent, you have performed a system penetration, which is not ethical. It does not matter whether you can see anything on the network or penetrate it any further. It is unethical for you to now attempt to sell your services to the potential client after you have violated their privacy.

Liberal This issue is an example of a passive vulnerability scan. With a more active vulnerability scan, you send traffic to the target specifically to find vulnerabilities. This traffic does not process through in the normal course of business. Therefore, just detecting wireless networks is not an ethical issue. Using this information to obtain work as a penetration tester is an asset to the community. It is like performing a level of free work for the client.

SUMMARY

The right ethical response to this issue really depends on the delivery. Whether or not you could gain clients in this manner is a different question. Some organizations will not hire someone regardless of the quality of their discovery if they go about obtaining work in this manner. Others may appreciate your initiative. Approaching a client for work based on an advance discovery of vulnerability due to their wireless connection is probably not the most effective advertising.

Detecting Networks without WEP Enabled – The Most Important Thing is Your Integrity

You detect a network that appears to not have Wireless Encryption Protocol (WEP or, in the future, 802.11X) enabled. The networks' SSID, however, reveals nothing about who they are. You could connect to their wireless local area network (WLAN) and snoop around for some information that would identify them to you, so that you can contact them and propose your services. Alternatively, you could connect to their networked printer and shock them with a printout prior to calling, so that they understand their system vulnerability. Is it appropriate to snoop around for identifying company information so that you can offer your services? Would it be ethically acceptable to add shock value by printing to a networked printer your offer of services, which illustrates the security vulnerability?

Conservative This issue is not acceptable to any degree of ethical standards. It may be fun for the techie but falls under the classification of a system break in. Then you may be the one to accept the blame for the very problem you discovered. There is not a single aspect of this issue that is ethical.

Liberal It is true and terribly unfortunate that so many businesses leave their systems wide open. However, that still does not make it right for you to access their network infrastructure and verify the SSID or use the WEP. On the extreme liberal side, the more radical techies may argue that potential clients will admire their audacity and still want to bring them in to perform penetration testing.

SUMMARY

Just because you can do something does not mean you should. It also does not make it ethically right. The primary thing to learn from this issue is that when a business is in the market for an information security professional, the most important characteristic of that person must be that they have moral integrity. You have demonstrated that you are not ethical in this issue. There is nothing more dangerous than an unethical information security professional. Therefore, if you demonstrate unethical behaviors to try to get the job, the odds are you will not be the one chosen.

Ulterior Motives Presenting Reports

On some occasions, penetration testers will provide limited results of the penetration test because they intend to charge additional monies for each set of results. When it comes to information security, how much of a role should marketing play in the ethics of penetration testing work. This section determines whether the penetration tester can ethically structure their services in a manner that optimizes the financial return they receive, or if it is simply morally wrong to exclude any information from a penetration test for financial reasons. This section also includes overstating problems to obtain future work, marketing services based on test results, retaining information from a penetration test, and exploiting the client based on the results of a penetration test.

Overstating Problems – It is Best to Be Accurate

In order to provide additional work for yourself at a client site, you overstate or over emphasize (making a problem worse that it really is) security risks in your final penetration reports to the client. This will require them to keep you on longer to further assess and potentially fix these problems. Since there is a valid risk that needs your immediate attention even if it is not a severe risk as you have indicated, does it matter if you exaggerate that risk to give the client a sense of urgency so that they will fix the problem immediately with your help?

Conservative It is never appropriate to provide inaccurate results to a penetration test. This is especially true if you communicate a lie for marketing purposes. You are providing false information on matters of information security, which need to be exact. You are morally wrong in this matter.

Liberal Since there are problems and you are just exaggerating the problems, it is forgivable. It is always best to be as accurate as possible when dealing with matters of information security. However, sometimes it is necessary to drive the point home so that matters are addressed in a timely manner. Since you performed the penetration test, you are the most qualified to perform additional tests and remediate the security vulnerabilities.

SUMMARY

Ethics are always a question when you do not provide exact information in response to a penetration test. The only marginally acceptable time to exaggerate information is if the client requires that type of communication to address the vulnerability at all. If you communicate that it is a minor security problem, they may not address the issue. However, a minor vulnerability can quickly turn into a major one.

Using Results to Sell Services – Is this a Trick?

You perform a penetration test for a well-known company. Later, you use the results and information in the test reports to sell additional services to the client. In addition, when you initially performed the penetration test, you failed to leverage the information to help them understand the problems. Is it morally acceptable to fail to explain the results of a test because you want to come back and offer more services?

Conservative In this circumstance it would be better to make it known that you possess the skills to help the client remediate the problems and vulnerabilities discovered during the penetration test. Do not wait and then come back later with information from the test. It almost sounds like blackmail if you state that you know the company's vulnerabilities therefore they better hire you to fix them.

Liberal It is not within the scope of the services of a penetration tester to help the client fix all of the system vulnerabilities discovered. There is nothing wrong with using information gathered from the penetration test to market your services back to the client for the next phase of the information security process.

SUMMARY

It is true that the penetration tester does not have to explain to the company how to fix all of their system vulnerabilities. However, that may be the most effective way to obtain additional employment. Withholding information and then asking money for that data even though it was not part of the scope of your job sounds more like a trick than someone who sincerely has an interest in supporting the client. The straight and narrow is always the smartest road to take.

Holding Back Information – Handle with Care

You know that a potential client has a serious vulnerability. Since you perform penetration tests for a living, you do not tell them about the vulnerability because you want to perform a penetration test for your normal fees and use the information you already know about the company. Is having inside information about a client but not telling them because you are trying to sell them on a vulnerability assessment ethical?

Conservative If you have information about a potential client's vulnerabilities, it is ethically inappropriate to withhold that information. Telling the client about the system weaknesses will inspire them to get a penetration test, because there are endless possibilities of other problems besides the one you made them aware of.

Liberal You are not morally required to communicate system vulnerabilities to potential clients. Your job is to make money from performing accurate vulnerability tests. Whether you are aware of the system weaknesses prior to the penetration test is irrelevant. The client will still receive excellent services from you.

SUMMARY

When you possess inside information about a potential client's information security profile, you must handle this data in a sensitive manner. In some cases, it may be wise to wait until you perform a penetration test to disclose the information. In other circumstances, this may be dishonest. For example, if you do not actually perform the penetration test when hired, and receive payment for what you already knew, that is morally wrong.

Exploiting the Company – Honesty is the Best Policy

Your best friend works at a bank and you ask him to convince his boss that the company needs a penetration test. They really do not need one since they just had one, but you convince your friend to explain that the earlier penetration test was incomplete. Is taking advantage of relationships or friendships that you built through other means ethically acceptable? In the same light, is invalidating a previous penetration test morally right?

Conservative You should never have someone invalidate a penetration test for marketing purposes. If we presume you get the job to perform another penetration test and you conclude the same results as the first, you may be tempted to create a system vulnerability so that you do not end up looking like a fool. There is no room for marketing schemes in the arena of information security.

Liberal The way you obtain the penetration-testing job may be questionable, but in reality it is useful to have a second party perform a penetration test. This type of redundancy is smart. Therefore, in the long run your marketing strategy will help the company be more secure.

SUMMARY

When it comes to information security, lying never pays off even if your intentions are good. This is also true if you have someone else lie for you. Regardless of the end results, honesty is a necessity for penetration testers.

Chapter Summary

This chapter defined the purpose of penetration testing and the ethical pitfalls of marketing, performing, and communicating about penetration tests.

We learned that the purpose of penetration testing is to determine whether information systems are at risk. You discovered that the penetration test checks applications, databases, networks, remote computing, and any other system connected to the business for vulnerabilities.

An unethical penetration test can take advantage of several means to obtain the job or make more money from performing the test. In the section on misrepresenting the penetration test, we discussed how testers misrepresent themselves or how they test using free tools.

The overall security picture can be undermined by the penetration test, because information security professionals may feel required to make blanket comments such as, "Due to the results of this penetration test, your system is 100 percent secure." These types of communications are completely false and undermine information security.

Next, we discussed the ploys used to obtain clients and how far is too far to go when testing non-clients and communicating the results. We determined that the number one quality a penetration tester must have is integrity and strong ethics.

Finally, the chapter closes with a consideration on ulterior motives when presenting penetration test results. Some testers will hold onto information in order to gain future employment with their client. We reviewed the ethics of these marketing strategies and determined the limits of moral acceptability.

Frequently Asked Questions

The following Frequently Asked Questions, answered by the authors of this book, are designed to get you thinking about the ethical considerations of penetration testing. Unless legal issues are involved, then answers in the FAQ may not be the right answer for your organization.

Q: What are the different means by which someone can misrepresent a penetration test?

A: A penetration test can be misrepresented in several different ways. The tester may misrepresent their qualifications and skills. They can misrepresent the information gathered or the means by which they collected data. This means that a penetration tester may perform only one part of the penetration test and try to pass it off as the entire test, or they may use free tools to perform the test and fail to communicate that information to the client.

Q: Is it ever appropriate for a penetration tester to communicate to their client that the company's information systems are 100 percent secure?

A: One hundred percent information security is a myth. No system at any point in time, past, present, or future is completely secure. It is never appropriate to communicate absolute security. In fact, systems never pass penetration tests. There is always a weakness. No one who performs a penetration test and communicates that the system passed or that the company is secure performed an adequate penetration test.

Q: In the realm of penetration testing, how do some people describe ambulance chasing?

A: You "poke around" a non-client's Web site to find vulnerabilities. When you find them, you reveal these vulnerabilities to the potential client and hope to get a job performing a penetration test.

Q: What are the different ways that penetration testers display ulterior motives?

A: Penetration testers display ulterior motives by overstating system vulnerabilities in order to obtain additional work, marketing their services based on test results, holding back specific information from a penetration test in order to perform later marketing, and exploiting the client based on the results of a penetration test.

Chapter 18

Content Providing

Ethical Dilemmas in this Chapter:

- **Research: Sifting Through Data to Find the Facts and Due Diligence**

- **Taking an Unethical Technical Writing Job**

- **Writing with Accuracy**

- **Performing Product Reviews**

- **Concerns of System Documentation**

- **Information Integrity with Web Content**

- **The Rules of Fair Use**

- **Work for Hire and Authorship**

Introduction

Providing content falls under several different categories. The most well known form of content providing is Web content. Companies hire a contractor or employee to provide marketing and informational data for their Web sites. This information or content is encoded with Hypertext Markup Language (HTML) tags and displayed on the Internet. Have you ever played an elaborate online game that has text? A Web content provider wrote those scripts.

However, content providing is much more vast than just information for Web sites. Technical documentation, courseware, and books also fall under the umbrella of content providing. When performing technical writing of any type, there are many key ethical issues such as accuracy, integrity, and authorship.

This chapter discusses the ethical dilemmas content providers may find themselves in when accepting a new project and in daily writing activities. The topics include research, writing content for unethical businesses, accuracy, product reviews, system documentation, writing and reproducing Web content, and authorship.

Research: Sifting Through Data to Find the Facts and Due Diligence

An integral first step when producing any type of material, be it Web content or a complex technical book, is research. A good writer may spend more time researching than writing. In this section, we review the importance of research. In addition, this section reviews how ethics come into play when writing training papers, professional research papers, articles, and white papers. The key ethical concerns when performing research are plagiarism and distinguishing facts from personal opinions.

Due diligence is performing the research and fact-checking activities that a reasonably competent person would do to ensure that all information is correct. In the area of technical writing and content providing, due diligence includes making sure the writing you provide is correct and meets your clients needs and expectations.

In other words, a technical writer or content provider must meet with the appropriate and knowledgeable subject matter experts and perform the necessary background subject research in order to produce quality material. Writers must adhere to a set of due diligence standards. The writer must take the appropriate steps to ensure that the proper review, edit, and revisions occur. They should check copyright laws concerning their material and be certain there are no violations. They should also check for inclusion of acknowledgement of necessary trademarks, if necessary, in their written material.

Finally, in some cases, complete due diligence requires the writer to follow up with a lawyer when writing about sensitive material that may infringe on legal issues to avoid legal liability for themselves and their clients. This section addresses due diligence when interviewing experts for writing assignments, distinguishing facts from personal opinions, and issues of accuracy.

Assuming the Expert Knows Best – What if you Take Material You are Given at Face Value?

You wrote an article about an information security device based on an interview you had with an expert in the information security industry. It turns that out all of his information was wrong and the company who builds the device received unnecessary negative press. Are you ethically at fault for slandering this company?

Conservative Do not assume that just because you are speaking with an expert that they know best. Experts can make mistakes and even have prejudice again certain companies. This situation was your fault for relying on one source and not checking all of the information yourself.

Liberal You are not at fault. The so-called expert you interviewed is the one who made a huge mistake. Write a follow-up article with the correct facts and interview as many experts as possible as well as performing your own independent research on the matter. Give the vendor a voice in the follow-up article.

SUMMARY

It is important to keep in mind that an expert can be wrong. Sometimes they get so used to being the one called upon for questions that they venture out of their area of expertise and provide advice in areas they know little or nothing about. Relying on experts is imperative when writing effective articles, make no mistake there. Nevertheless, make sure you perform due diligence and question the expert about their area of expertise.

GIAC Training Papers and Research Ethics – What Price Should the Guilty Pay?

Plagiarism is rampant; it is a major problem at every college and university. The thought that someone would take another's work and pass it off as their own seems strange, but it happens a lot. When someone taking the Global Information Assurance Certification (GIAC) training courses plagiarizes, intentional or not, the SANS (SysAdmin, Audit, Network, Security) Institute terminates their attempt at that particular GIAC certification for one year. They are not removed from their courseware access because they have paid for that. This plagiarism is on the certification side, so that is where the student loses their access rights. That student is welcome to attempt any other GIAC certification in that year, but they cannot attempt the same certification where they produced plagiarized papers. After one year is up, they can attempt that certification again. This has happened to 95 students taking the GIAC training courses so far, which indicates that there is a real problem with plagiarism among information technology (IT) professionals. Information security officers must hold themselves to the highest standards of ethical and professional conduct. Do you think it is appropriate to terminate a student's technical information security training in an area for one year because of plagiarism or other ethical breaches?

Conservative Expectations of ethical integrity and corresponding consequences of temporary termination are necessary. They hold students to a higher standard, which is absolutely necessary in an industry where the information security officer or system administrator maintains a great deal of power over the corporation. This type of consequence may even be too lenient. A more conservative choice would be to disallow the student to perform any type of certification for a year.

Liberal This may be a little strong since it appears many students plagiarize unknowingly because they do not know all of the rules of writing. They may be expert administrators but not knowledgeable about how to use other people's material in their own writing. A better choice for the one-year course expulsion may be to allow them to retake the course after they complete a course on IT ethics. This would provide them with the education they need to create original papers. They could then take the certification training after the ethics course to demonstrate that they understand the reprimand and will not repeat the same mistake.

SUMMARY

Standards for information security professionals requires them to adhere to a more profound level of integrity due to the power they control at their fingertips. Letting a student continue with a course would not benefit the student. Maybe they chose to plagiarize because they do not know the material well. Strict disciplinary consequences are necessary when there is a breach of ethics. Educational institutions should set a standard for businesses to follow. In addition, this type of discipline should include stalwart education on IT ethics.

Checking the Facts – What if You Do Not Research Results You Did Not Acquire?

You receive a set of survey results from your boss and immediately write an article about vendor tools based on those results. You describe which ones are the best solutions. Is it your ethical responsibility to check the accuracy of the statistics personally prior to writing a conclusive article?

Conservative Determine whether to perform accuracy checks on statistical information based on the source of the data. If your boss is an expert, there is no need to research his findings. However, if your boss just pulled some data from the Internet and handed it to you, research the source of that data and determine if it is in fact accurate. Your boss will appreciate the protection of both of your reputations.

Liberal Your job is to write, not fact-check every bit of data that comes across your desk. It would be a different story if you were in charge of the company or magazine. Do not question your boss in this circumstance. When he provides you with statistics write them up without question.

SUMMARY

It is perfectly acceptable to spot check statistics from your boss. If you feel that you must perform a detailed follow up on the statistics provided, formally ask your boss for permission.

Distinguishing Between Facts and Personal Opinions – Should You Use Both?

You are responsible for writing a book about how certain compilers perform in different operating systems, comparing their performance in UNIX and Microsoft Windows. During your research, you come across several different points of view. Some of them are factual and others are opinions from people who are biased because they have a personal favorite operating system. Is it appropriate to use personal opinions when writing an assessment or is it better to stick with the facts?

Conservative Writing comparisons of a tools' performance within different operating systems should be the result of ardent facts, not personal opinions. Back up your material with accurate statistics and true product testing in a realistic environment. If there is limited factual material, do not resort to opinions, even that of experts. Sift out the opinions from the hard facts when performing research.

Liberal It is perfectly appropriate to include the personal opinions of experts in the industry when writing a book comparing operating systems. Provide quotes from those individuals. Try to include personal opinions on both sides of the argument, which will bring fairness to the consideration.

SUMMARY

If you decide to use opinions, make sure they represent experts, not just anyone with an opinion. This brings credibility to them. Some writers may choose to stick with the facts when performing research, whereas others will opt for opinions, critics, and facts. You jeopardize your personal ethics when you base your writing strictly on opinions. Researching opinions as well as facts is part of the content-providing process when obtaining material for a book or article.

Determining the Accuracy of Technical Details – Know What You are Buying

Unfortunately, marketing hype has gone a little too far in the technology industry. In many cases, the inaccuracies in marketing material are not intentional. A disconnect often exists between the marketing team and the technical team who actually build the product. When there are glaring discrepancies in the marketing material it is because the promotional writing department does not understand the technicalities of the system they must promote. However, there are also many circumstances of blatant vendor hype of a vendor tool for marketing purposes. For example, do you consider it acceptable to say that a personal firewall will protect you from any type of attack when it will not?

Conservative False promises are wrong for two reasons. One, you are misleading and lying to the buyer, which is morally wrong, and two, those lies will come back to haunt you with negative product feedback that cancels out the hype. Even worse, your company may face legal ramifications if a problem occurs at a company because your tool was promising something it failed to deliver.

Liberal People know that marketing information is always full of hype. They should know this when they purchase a product and do so in a responsible manner by requesting a trial version first, which will determine if that vendor tool will meet their specific needs. Anyone with the purchasing power to buy a firewall solution must know that no single tool on the market can guarantee protection from all types of attacks.

SUMMARY

Tool hype has gone too far. There is not much to do about it besides performing research prior to purchasing. Blatant lying is not acceptable but is common practice in marketing, whether it is intentional or not. Before you buy, know exactly what you are getting.

Taking an Unethical Technical Writing Job

How important is making money to you compared to personal ethics and beliefs? Is there an industry you will not work for because of the nature of the business? The following issues address this very question for technical writers and content providers. We discuss writing for unethical industries such as an online gambling sites or snooper ware. This section also covers personal ethics conflicting with writing assignments such as advocating a business practice you find personally offensive. And finally, we address the writer's duty to warn and whether this is a code of honor or unethical in and of itself.

Working in Unethical Industries – Are You Willing to Compromise?

You are a highly skilled technical writer in the market for a new job. Would you consider it ethical to write system administration documentation for a server or network environment knowing that it was for one or more of the following industries: gambling, pornography, weapons, hackers, or snooper ware?

Conservative In order to maintain personal integrity you cannot work for a company that goes against your belief system. Working for the gambling or pornography industries just feeds those industries and you are as guilty as they are if you support and receive payment for writing administrative documentation for them. Even worse is working for illegal weapons, hacker, or snooper ware businesses, which gain money from destruction and malicious attacks.

Liberal When the job market is lean, sometimes you have to do work for a company you would not necessarily personally support. This does not make you like them. It is just an unfortunate reality of life. Regardless of the industry, you will always find yourself in a position where there are tasks you must perform that are contrary to your personal beliefs and ethics. This is part of being an adult. However, you do need to know when you must put up personal boundaries; otherwise, you may quickly find yourself beyond the ethical issues and in trouble with the law. Do not perform work that is beyond the ethical limitations you set for yourself.

SUMMARY

The most important issue to consider when accepting a job at a company you find unethical is the legal issue. Whether you are willing to compromise your personal ethics or not, always be aware of any legal ramifications that may result from your employment at a questionable company. In addition, consider the effect that company will have on your reputation as a writer. If you know the company is a risky one, do some research and make sure they avoid illegal activity. For example, if you document system administration information for a weapons Web site that posts information on how to build a nuclear bomb, you might want to stay away from that job. Not only might you get in trouble legally, but the people you are working with may be dangerous.

Personal Ethics Conflicting with Job Assignments – Should You Refuse?

Your boss asks you to write an article for a popular IT magazine that is highly respected in your industry. The article states the financial benefits of hiring overseas programmers versus people within the U.S. This point of view is against your personal beliefs of supporting the people in your own country even if it is more expensive. Do you write the article or refuse on ethical principle?

Conservative Never put your name on an article that is against your personal beliefs and ethics. This undermines the integrity of the article anyway, because it requires you to lie. The article is useless to you and your boss, because there is no foundation for its validity since you disagree with the argument. Writing material that is in direct opposition to your personal beliefs will wear you down as a person. You may make a lot of money but you will not like who you are in the end.

Liberal Management hires technical writers or content providers because of their writing skills and pays them accordingly. In most cases, pushing your personal beliefs on others in the industry is not part of the job description. Whether you agree or disagree with the subject matter is irrelevant. The only case where personal beliefs play a significant role in technical writing is with senior level auditors and skilled vendor assessors. They received payment for their personal opinions and not necessarily for their writing ability.

SUMMARY

Use caution when writing a public article that targets a particular business or point of view. In some cases, you may damage your reputation. However, part of writing is producing quality work and not necessarily pushing your own point of view. If you strongly disagree with the stance you must take to perform you job duties when writing an article, consider requesting that your name be left off or ghost write the article and request someone else's name be used that agrees with the point of view of the article.

@#&!?!

Sometimes You Have to Jump

In teaching ethics (in security) to mid-level managers, almost inevitably someone in every class raises the issue of what to do when you find something unethical going on. Each particular situation has a different answer, of course, but I always conclude by stating that sometimes you cannot resolve the ethics of a situation. Sometimes you have to leave.

This is not a facile observation for me to make. I have been in these situations, and have had to walk away from jobs, contracts, time and work invested, and money.

Most recently, I was asked to provide a course on software forensics for a university college. During the development of the course, the question of providing source code for malware programs arose. Pedagogically, analyzing malware itself doesn't teach the introductory student anything that couldn't be demonstrated by examination of a basic utility program. More importantly, in ethical terms, the code of conduct of the international virus research community has very strict standards in regard to distribution of source code for malware. Before I agreed to prepare and teach the course, I made sure that the institution covenanted to abide by those standards.

Unfortunately, that agreement was broken shortly after the beginning of the course: malware source code was distributed to the students in my course by another party within the program in clear violation of the compact. And, despite negotiations and representations to successively higher levels of the institution, we were unable to resolve the agreement. Therefore, I had to abandon six months of work, a fully prepared course,

Continued

multiple contracts with the college itself, and ancillary contracts with other bodies. The loss of the contract fees hurt quite a bit, but continuing with the course would have put me in an untenable position with colleagues and other researchers.

Ethical considerations are seldom cut and dry. Having signed a contract, I did have a responsibility to fulfill that arrangement. On the other hand, generally it would be held that the institution, in violating the bargain, had voided it. On the third hand, what of the students? They had no say in the matter, but the course was cancelled anyway, although soon enough that they had not invested much effort in study or assignments. I very much regret not having been able to complete the course for them, but could not, in all conscience, have continued.

Robert M. Slade
Author of "Software Forensics"

Writing with Accuracy

Writing accurately may appear to be a simple task, but it is much harder than you might imagine, especially in the IT industry. First, a writer must be able to sift through the hype and marketing promises. To find the reality of any given product, writers should be required to personally test every tool prior to writing a word about them. This is the only truly accurate way to determine the facts of a product's effectiveness. As you can image, this type of fact checking is impossible; therefore, professional opinions are required. Product and personal bias is common when utilizing professional opinions. So, how does a writer know what is accurate information?

In this section we discuss several examples of accuracy in writing that address the ethics of hype, puffery, distorting facts, and logical fallacies. You will see that finding 100 percent accurate information is like finding a needle in a haystack.

Puffery: Making a Product Sound Better Than it Is – Is This a Good Idea?

Many companies advertise that their product is the best, such as "The world's best information security solution on the market," when there is no proof to back it up. Is puffery ethical in this day and age of information overload?

Conservative Inflating a product without backing it up with survey results, trial results, or other statistics is unethical. It does not add any additional credibility to the product. Stick to the truth when creating marketing material and your company will maintain a reputation of integrity that alone will sell your product better than any marketing hype.

Liberal When a prospective buyer sees the words "The world's best information security solution on the market," they will be more apt to purchase the product because everyone wants the best that their money can buy. This is an effective marketing technique even if the claim does not prove true.

SUMMARY

Writing advertising that calls a vendor solution the "The world's best information security solution on the market," is misleading and, for the most part, is not taken seriously in the technology industry by skilled technologists. This may work in other industries, but in technology you are dealing with a specific group of individuals who often know how to write the code for the product itself, so they know what works and what does not. This is the wrong industry in which to puff up the facts.

Distorting the Facts – Will it Come Back to Haunt You?

You work at a high tech company as a technical writer, and your primary job is to create brochures that promote the company's products. You have deliberately distorted the facts in a marketing brochure to make your company look better than the competition. You did this by using "loaded" words such as the competitor "admitted" that your product is better than theirs, when they only "said" one small aspect of your product was better than theirs. Is this out of line ethically?

Conservative It never pays to exaggerate the truth or use loaded words to make things sound different than they really are. Just tell it like it is; if the product you are marketing is a good one it will shine through. Poor tools, for the most part, do not succeed in the competitive market for IT solutions.

Liberal Business is war and marketing materials are the tools you use against your competition. Make sure they are strong and effective. The creative use of writing can make the difference between massive sales and failure. Just look at how Microsoft markets. They are the industry leaders because of their aggressive marketing, not necessarily because they have the best tools on the market.

SUMMARY

Marketing is all about making your company look good and the competition pale by comparison. As a content provider, you need to use your arsenal of words to succeed at business warfare. However, avoid writing yourself into a corner with fallacies about a product that may come back to haunt you. You may simply make yourself look bad by writing an adolescent article, which simply bashes another business.

Using Logical Fallacies – Is This Misleading?

Writers often use logical fallacies to validate points, which may be misleading. An example of a logical fallacy is as follows:

If John strongly advocates product XYZ and Sally approves of John's purchasing decisions, Sally must advocate product XYZ.

The technical writer presents this material as proof that Sally recommends product XYZ, when it is only a deduction. The example in this issue is a very basic one, which can become extremely complex in the IT arena. Did you make a mistake by doing this?

Conservative Evidence of a result does not equal the result. Deducing a result from other factors does not produce correct information. Using logical fallacies is just another name for lying or forcing results to turn in your favor. Strong technical writers avoid these childish tactics to prove their points. You should be able to prove your points with research and creditable information, not mind games and word tricks.

Liberal Using words and drawing the reader into your point of view is part of the skill of writing. Providing content that molds the point of view of the reader is the power of effective written work. Using logical fallacies is part of the job of a content provider and is ethical.

SUMMARY

Logical fallacies are common tricks used in the technical writing industry. They are just that, tricks, and it is up to you as the content provider to decide what type of reputation you want to have. Do you want to be known as a factual and straightforward writer, or a manipulative but persuasive writer? The choice is up to you.

Performing Product Reviews

Documentation specialists often receive a call to duty that requires them to perform slanted product reviews. This process involves determining the effectiveness of a given vendor solution. Product reviews are powerful tools that can make or break a tool depending on whom the review comes from.

In this section, we discuss the power of product reviews including negative reviews, positive reviews, controlling statistics, and personal attacks through product reviews. We start out with the issue of writing a positive product review in a magazine for a poor vendor solution because they pay for advertisement within the magazine.

Negative Product, Positive Review – How Do You Communicate the Truth?

You are a content provider for a technical magazine. One of the companies that purchases advertising in the magazine you write for has come out with a new networking product that is terrible. You are required to write a positive review of the product because of the revenue generated from their advertising (part of the agreement.) Is it ethical to write a good review for a bad product because of the profits gained from the company that produced the tool?

Conservative There is no excuse for misleading the public. Money governs a lot in the world of business, but it is every writer's responsibility to keep it honest. A magazine company's drive should not be for just monetary goals but also for quality work, because a magazine based purely on profit will soon collapse. Other industries may get away with it, but it is not as easy in an IT magazine. Out of respect for the relationship between your company and the company who developed the new tool, you may decide not to write anything rather than write a negative review, since you cannot in good conscience write a positive review of the product. Explain to them that you cannot lie to your readers and support a tool that will not fulfill their needs.

Liberal   In the world of business, corporations need to make alliances. You also have an ethical responsibility to those business partnerships. Sometimes you will have to sacrifice your personal beliefs for the relationships you maintain. It is not wise to alienate your own clients. Write the review in a positive manner without being misleading and hope that they will improve the networking tool as quickly as possible.

SUMMARY

Business is a very complicated matter and sometimes you have to bend the rules to stay in the game. Try not to misinform the public to the best of your ability when writing positive product reviews for poor vendor solutions. There is always a way to communicate the truth without sounding negative, such as damning them with faint praise. Aspire to the highest possible ethic here, to be a thought a leader requires the respect and trust of the public.

Controlling Statistical Results – Communication is Key

You wrote an article comparing different vendor products for networking solutions. The statistics you utilized are from one area of the market and not cross-sectional. This area has certain specific needs that do not address the products as a whole. Is this unethical since your article may determine whether others in all industries buy the products or not?

Conservative   When writing an article that will affect the purchasing choices of vendor products, it is best to provide a well-rounded approach and include the totality of product use, not just one market that utilizes the tool. If you only have statistics for one section of the market, consider collecting additional data to cover all of the areas that the products support. It is not appropriate to misrepresent products in this manner and may alienate you from the vendors that provide those solutions.

Liberal You may use the statistics for the specific area; just indicate in your article the source of the statistics and that you are assessing the product for a specific market segment only. Indicate that the tools may be useful in many other ways that you are not communicating in your article. It is fine to write about one area of a given market.

SUMMARY

Communication is a key factor in the issue of representing vendor tools accurately. You may judge products according to a specific market that does not encompass the full spectrum of the products, which you should communicate clearly in your article. If you feel it is simply unfair, perform additional statistical gathering until you have a well-rounded sampling of data that can address the products as a whole. This may be impossible if you are assessing a specific industry niche; many products may have different functions and comparison is not effective except within a specific market segment. Consider all of the ramifications of your article and try not to misrepresent any vendor solutions.

Personal Attacks in a Product Review – Should You Keep Your Emotions Out of It?

Many people in the database industry respect you as an authority on database information systems within the data warehousing industry. You accept a new job that involves writing and collecting reviews for a new data warehousing tool on the market. You do not like the Chief Executive Officer (CEO) of the database tool company for personal reasons: when you first started out in the industry, over 15 years ago, you worked for him and he fired you for personal reasons. Now that you are the expert, you decide to write a very negative review to put this man in his place. Is it ethical to write a negative review about a company and product for the purpose of personal retaliation?

Conservative Business and technical writing is not the place to settle personal scores. Do not stoop to that level; it will only tarnish your reputation as a writer and make you appear petty. If the database solution is bad and will not adequately address the market's needs, fine, write the truth, but never slander a company or product because of one individual, even if he is the CEO of the company. Many others who are innocent will fall with him if you succeed in ruining the reputation and sales of the business.

Liberal   In reality, business is hardball and sometimes you have to show your strength. Do not directly say the product is junk. Be more calculating. Perform due diligence to accurately find all of the weaknesses of the database tool and carefully describe them. All products have strengths and weaknesses, so focus your article on the weak points of the tool exclusively. Keep it true but focus that truth carefully.

SUMMARY

It is always better to keep personal feelings out of business. However, in reality that rarely occurs. Try your best to avoid attacking a company or product because of a personal gripe with the CEO or others at the company. If you must write a negative review for your own reasons, do not lie or get personal in the review. You would be amazed how many people can see right through such emotionally driven writing.

Concerns of System Documentation

You may not think of system documentation as an area with many ethical issues, however, all areas of business have their ethics to contend with. System documentation is a straightforward and highly technical business. On the other hand, what about the ethical responsibility for document maintenance issues and documenting open-source systems?

   This section addresses the responsibilities of technical writers when it comes to maintaining system documentation and documenting open-source systems that may be used for malicious purposes.

Completing System Documentation – Make Sure you Do the Updates

You are systems technical writer and must document all of the systems for the organization. You have completed the documentation for a segment of the system, and your manager has signed off on it. Later that day a programmer informs you that one small piece of the system you just finished documenting has been changed in a minute way. Do you go back and rewrite that document or decide that it is not your responsibility?

Conservative If you do not rewrite the documentation for the altered system it will return to haunt you later, so do it now while it is still fresh in your mind. Your purpose at the company is to document the systems accurately, not just at a given point in time. Do your job with pride and make it a point to keep all documentation current to the best of your ability. Updating documentation you wrote earlier will not take much time or energy, but will make all of the difference in the world if there is a system failure and they need to use your documentation to restore everything and quickly bring it back online.

Liberal Wait on the updates to the documentation. If you went back and fixed every document as things change, you would never get past the first segment of the system. Complete all documentation and then do a round of updates and versions. You are not accountable for the recent changes because your boss signed off on your work already. Therefore, there are no ethical repercussions for you.

SUMMARY

Whatever method you choose, make sure you do the updates. System documentation is only useful if it addresses the current system. Keep all of the data on it current and take pride that your work may one day help the system recover.

Open Source Systems – Should You Provide Documentation?

You accept an offer for a new job creating system documentation for open-source technologies. You know that the users of open-source technology vary from conscious users to questionable ones. Most technologist use open-source tools for positive means, however 5 percent of the programmers who use open-source tools do so for malicious purposes such as using freeware tools to create viruses, worms, hoaxes, and spam. Do you refrain from documenting open-source systems because a small percentage of people use them for negative means?

Conservative Since there are always a certain percentage of users of open-source tools that take advantage of them for malicious means, do not make their job easier by providing documentation. Stay out of it completely. Unfortunately, the 95 percent will not benefit from your skills, but this is better then aiding known attackers.

Liberal A 5 percent ratio is very small. Provide the documentation for open-source technologies. If a malicious programmer wants to use open source for destructive means, your documentation will not change that.

SUMMARY

This issue brings into focus the dilemma of performing technical writing that may result in negative consequences. There are many strengths of open-source technology, which is an entire subject within itself; however, making open-source easier to use through extensive documentation, also makes it easier for abuse. Determine your personal ethics in this manner. Do you feel okay about it since 95 percent of the people use it for good? On the other hand, do you veto this type of documentation work altogether since 5 percent use it for malicious means of which you may fall victim to someday?

The Myth of "Security Through Obscurity"

There is an ongoing debate relating to both open-source and commercial software, regarding how each can be used for less-than-ethical purposes. This can be as simple as using a network monitoring package to sniff user passwords rather than for its "intended" purpose of network troubleshooting and traffic analysis. Recently, the debate has also included the question of when it's "alright" for a software vendor to release information regarding security holes or bugs in their products. If a vendor releases information about a security hole in their product before they have a patch ready, are they actually doing anything more than providing a roadmap for hackers? For that matter, should vendors even release this information at *all*? Maybe if malicious users don't find out about these security vulnerabilities, they won't be able to use them to attack personal and corporate machines. Unfortunately, withholding information in this

Continued

manner will only help legitimate users a very little, while it is helping potential attackers quite a bit. True, by releasing information about security vulnerabilities, a technical writer is running the risk of pointing out to a hacker what they need to do to write the next killer Internet worm. However, you really need to work under the assumption that *someone* is going to find out about the vulnerability you're writing about whether you write about it or not. By informing network administrators and security personnel about the potential for attack, you're helping them to defend themselves and their networks. Assuming that you aren't releasing step-by-step instructions on how to use a vulnerability to attack a system, the information that an attacker could glean from a security release is far outweighed by the good it will do for the legitimate users of the affected pieces of software.

Laura E. Hunter
Network Engineer and Technical Trainer

Information Integrity with Web Content

The Internet brought a new market to the technical writer and research analyst. Web content is a huge industry with its own ethical questions. This section addresses the concerns of the Web content provider, which include the content review process, ethical criteria of Web content, maintenance of Web content, and authorized versus fake Web sites. One of the tendencies of online publishing is to be a bit more lax about accuracy, since you can always change it. That is fine, even reasonable when you are trying to write about events in near real time, but always think about the way the customer is likely to use the information you give them and make sure the quality assurance process meets the "smell test."

Web Content Review Process – Is it an Effective Business Tool?

Your business prepares electronic brochures in .PDF format to advertise upcoming events. The posting of these brochures occurs on the corporate Web site in advance of the events. The success of any event is directly related to how much time in advance that event was advertised. Therefore, the more quickly you can post the brochures, the better the event turnout. However, the lengthy review process is holding them up as always. What can you ethically do to resolve this circumstance?

Conservative   A review process is in place for a reason and circumventing that process will have a negative impact on the business. The review process ensures that all material is legal and appropriately aligned to the corporate mission. Be patient and wait until you have formal approval from the formal review process. After they add their edits to your work and you update everything accordingly, upload the brochures.

Liberal   The dreaded review process! A quick review process is an effective business tool. A lengthy review process equals disaster for a corporation. You must make a decision when it comes to the point of the review process negatively affecting business and marketing. In this case, the slow review process directly affects sales and will eventually take down the business. Take an educated risk and post the electronic .PDF files prior to completion of the review process to attract new business. Then update the files once they return edited.

SUMMARY

Determining what to do with a slow review process is a tricky matter. If you decide to wait it out, you may not have a business left and thus no use for the advertising material. However, if you opt to post the material anyway, make sure you check it for obvious legal issues such as copyright symbols and properly quoted material. Purchase a book on the basics of content-providing legalities. At the very least, try to weed out major problems in your advertising material prior to posting it on the Internet. Since you are using .PDF files, you have a layer of protection because the text is not easily copied.

Ethical Criteria in Preparation of Posted Information - Should You Enforce these Rules?

The company you write technical documentation for has a Web site that posts information on best business practices. Associated with the best practices site is a link for a Web forum. You are responsible for monitoring this forum, which allows others to express their opinions of the best business practices. The corporate standard for posting information on the site and in the Web forum is that the preparation of information for posting must meet a specific set of posted ethical criteria. Is it appropriate to remove information from the best practices listing if it does not meet the prearranged criteria? Would your response be the same in reference to removing threads from the Web forum if they do not match the criteria?

Conservative   Strictly abide by the rules for preparation of material so that it is within the ethical guidelines without exception. Remove any material listed under the best practices that does not comply with the ethical writing rules posted. Immediately delete any new threads that breach the ethical boundaries. Since posting of the ethical rules occurred in advance, you provided fair warning. At this point, you must appropriately follow through with the necessary disciplinary action.

Liberal   In terms of best practices, that information was set up in advance. If it does not strictly adhere to the rules of ethical preparation, it is not your place to remove it. The material may be intentional and you are misunderstanding the rules. However, it is your responsibility to delete discussion threads in the Web forum that do not adhere to these rules of corporate ethics. You may decide to add a warning at the top of the forum that states that threads failing to comply with the corporate ethics policy will result in the deletion of such files.

SUMMARY

Adhering to corporate ethical standards is important in maintaining integrity, especially in the case of issuing business best practices. Enforcing these rules both internally and externally sets a standard for the future of your corporation. Use strength when enforcing corporate ethics.

Maintenance of Posted Material – What is Expected of You?

You just started a new job as manager of Web content posting at a new insurance company. The Web site for this business already has a significant amount of material posted, including insurance policy data for the clients to read. Is it your ethical responsibility to review all of the material and provide maintenance for the information currently posted?

Conservative A solid Web content manager would review all of the existing material on the company's Web site for two primary reasons. One, reviewing the current material will provide you with a sense of the corporate voice, which you then must match for future work to maintain continuity for the company. The second reason to review existing content is to verify that it is quality work and correctly represents the company and the client's insurance policies. You should not presume that all previous work lies out of your area of responsibility.

Liberal As the Web content manager you may want to review what currently exists on the corporate Web site, but do not duplicate it or presume to change the material. Bogging yourself down in the past will not demonstrate your skills. After a quick review of existing material, start your first new project and wow senior management with your style and ingenuity. Over time, you will replace most of the old content with the new content your team writes.

SUMMARY

Most people do not like maintenance work, especially clean-up maintenance work. The average writer will probably avoid the old material and try to improve on it in new projects. Always review the old material if it contains information important to the business. If time permits, propose rewriting weak content to senior management. Whichever way you choose to handle this problem, consider your job description and what the Web content should provide. Make sure you know what senior management is expecting from you and adhere to those expectations.

Authorized vs. "Fake" Web Sites – Everyone Should Understand the Difference

You are a Web master and must educate the company about the difference between authorized and fake and underground Web sites. You never bothered to do this in the past because the fake or underground Web sites were not dangerous. Initially, fake Web sites mimicked official Web sites making fun of celebrities or political leaders. Today, cyber criminals who mimic well-known banking institutions run fake Web sites or electronic fund transfer sites such as

Paypal; their goal is to steal money from people. How do you propose to explain to the employees of your company about the difference between authorized and fake Web sites? Are fake or underground Web sites ethical?

Conservative You should compose some examples of fake Web sites and forget the non-hazardous ones. Focus on the ones that intend to steal your money and scare everyone at the company into avoiding these sites at all costs. They are completely unethical and illegal. Make sure the employees understand the danger at hand.

Liberal Some fake Web sites are harmless and often very entertaining. Your job is not to utterly suppress everyone on the Internet, but to ensure they do not fall victim to identity fraud or put the business at risk. Explain the difference between authorized Web sites and fake Web sites. Warn them of the dangers of fake Web sites. Show some funny examples of harmless false Web sites and then the results of more dangerous fake online banking sites. Only the criminal fake sites are unethical. People have the freedom of speech and can make fun of celebrities if they wish. Do not suppress this type of activity, just the more dangerous versions of fake Web sites. There is nothing ethically wrong with fake Web sites unless they perform the illegal activities mentioned in this issue.

SUMMARY

When addressing a group about the difference between authorized and fake Web sites, the only important thing to do is make sure they know about the dangerous underground and fake Web sites so that they can protect themselves and their computer systems. Whether they choose to visit other fake sites is up to their personal ethics.

The Rules of Fair Use

The rules of Fair Use indicate that it is acceptable to utilize some Web material for other original works. The purpose for this use must include works of criticism, comment, news reporting, teaching, scholarship, or research. In these special cases, using this material is not an infringement of copyright. It is dependant on the nature of the copyrighted material and the amount of it that is used. This section discusses printing materials from the Internet, material merging, and the reproduction of material.

Printing Materials from the Web – Do You Have the Authority?

You are a senior systems administrator at a brokerage house. For your own purposes, you have created a large binder consisting of printouts from various networking Web sites. You have all of the material on the Web in your line of work available to you in printed form, because it is easier to reference than continually looking up the Web sites. Is it ethically acceptable to print material from the Web and create your own reference book from this material? What about if you make a photocopy of this material for the junior network administrator? What if you made copies for your friends who are also system administrators, and charge them a nominal fee for your time?

Conservative Creating your own reference manual from various Web sites saves time, but is in a sense stealing when you compile it into your own form of book. The Digital Millenium Copyright Act (DMCA) gives Internet publishers the authority to prevent you from printing a Web page, or in some cases, reading it aloud. For example, if you purchase and download an electronic book from the Internet and figure out how to circumvent the reader software so that you can print it out to utilize it on the job, the DMCA deems what you have done as a federal crime. If you take it a step further and tell anyone how you did it, you will face a fine of up to $500,000 and five years in prison. In your binder, you probably have a mix of material that is appropriate to print such as notes on the operating system that grant you printing access, and material forbidden from reproduction. Some sites protect their material with electronic .PDF files and lock it so that you cannot copy, paste, or print it unless you perform a complex workaround. You do not own the material and are not at liberty to compile it for your own personal reference book. Making photocopies of the material for the junior system administrator is not only ethically wrong but also blatantly illegal. Charging a fee for this material, on top of everything else, is completely inappropriate and you may find yourself in jail for doing so.

Liberal Printing material from the Web for your own personal use as a systems administrator is illegal in most cases, unless fair use applies. However, most people do not presume they will be caught and find the laws suppressive. Some may not be aware of the DMCA law and are breaking it unknowingly. Making a copy of your administrator binder of Web material for the junior system administrator or selling the material is also illegal. Just because you compiled it, does not give you the right to reproduce it for a profit. The key point here is that some people may not choose to acknowledge the laws in place, presuming that it is too difficult to monitor them.

SUMMARY

It is common for people to print pages from the Web for their own reference, and most believe they can get away with it because everyone does it. However, this is completely illegal and there are severe penalties in place to protect Web content. The only case where this type of activity is acceptable is if you have the legal right to download and print the material given to you by the content providers. If you are not breaching any legal issues, making yourself a book of reference material is a smart thing to do. User manuals are not often current in technology and other system administrators may have posted useful insight on the Web that you can use on the job. Never reproduce Web material even if you have the right to print it yourself.

Web Material Merging vs. Actual Authoring – There are Good Points and Bad Points

There is so much material on the Web available for research papers. It is difficult and costly for content providers to protect Web content, because finding all of the culprits is nearly impossible. With this in mind, do you feel that material merging (taking Web content from different sites and forming your own document based on this content) is acceptable, and is this the same as actual authoring?

Conservative Material merging is not unique authorship; it is an easy way out of creating original content. From an ethical point of view, stay away from pulling materials from different Web sites and compiling it together to place your name on the top. Material merging is not a wise ethical choice as a content provider. In addition, this type of activity in many cases is an illegal infringement on copyright law.

Liberal   There is nothing wrong with quoting material from various Web sites as long as you properly provide credit, utilizing footnotes and quotes to indicate where you obtained the information. Perform a word-by-word check to ensure that you have quoted the material exactly. If you distort an author's original idea in your own way, it is better not to quote them because your interpretation may cause offense. This is no different than using books for research. Few people can manifest a completely unique piece of work without performing research and integrating information from different sources. Legally speaking, the Copyright Act specifies that certain uses of copyrighted works lie outside the control of the initial copyright owner. This act invokes many new exceptions to the "exclusive" rights of the copyright owners.

SUMMARY

Merging material from the Internet has its good points and negative ones. On the positive side, the Web allows researchers and writers to obtain access to much more information from the comfort of their home or office than ever existed before. The Internet also links us globally, thus catapulting knowledge and various points of view. The negative impact of this much information at your finger tips is that anyone can publish their points of view on the Internet with little or no regulation, unlike in a book. Therefore, you must be extremely cautious when utilizing Web material, because it may not be accurate. Question the integrity of all Web material prior to using and merging it into your own writings. In addition, be certain you are not in breach of copyright law by remaining in the boundaries of the Copyright Act, which allows a controlled level of "fair use" to Web material.

Reproduction of Materials from the Web – Be Cautious

You are writing course material for a localized information security standard, which is already in existence on an international level. Is it appropriate for you to reproduce materials from the Internet to create this course?

Conservative All content you create must be unique. Do not reproduce material from other sources on the Web, even if there are no legal ramifications. A lot of Web material comes from secondary sources that are not reliable. Make it a point to come up with your own standards that do not reflect existing material on the Internet. If you absolutely must create similar standards, properly reference the resources from which you obtained the ideas.

Liberal When creating an information security standard based on an international standard, this job requires that you encompass all that exists prior to your standard and build on that. Do not directly copy material from the Web, but do incorporate it into your work. Otherwise, your work will not be complete and comprehensive.

SUMMARY

In some cases, incorporating material from the Web is required. Do so in a cautious manner only including what you must, and provide detailed footnotes when necessary to allocate credit where credit is due. Do not violate copyright laws or over indulge in fair use.

Work for Hire and Authorship

This section attempts to determine the ethical issues of authorship. It addresses where responsibility lies for the material within an article or book.

Topics include one person taking credit for the work of two when work for hire was not established at the start of the project, providing material for an author, and writing a critical product review that results in legal action.

Two Authors Producing One Article – Who Gets the Credit?

You and a coworker jointly wrote a book on the secrets of java scripting for the World Wide Web (WWW). During the process of writing the book, there was an unspoken understanding that both of you would be listed as the authors. When the project neared completion, your boss communicated to you that you were performing work for hire, or ghosting writing, and your coworker's name would be the only one listed with the book. Is exclusion of an authors name for marketing purposes ethical?

Conservative Assuming you receive fair financial compensation for the book, expect no more than that. The marketing of a book is as important as the writing of it. It is common practice to place only the names of well-known authors on the cover of a book to give it credibility. Of course, they must be involved in the creation of the book but may not necessarily be the primary writers. This is an industry standard and is by no means unethical or unfair. Ghost writing is a common industry practice. For example, everyone knows that there are speechwriters for politicians and public relations experts for celebrities.

Liberal Although being notified at the project's completion that you were performing your writing on a work-for-hire basis is unethical on the part of your boss, you must accept the end result. Most writers' work in a ghost-writing fashion; this is a perfectly acceptable career path. Ghost writing is the authorized use of another's thoughts and ideas. It is honorable paid work. Therefore, there is nothing illegal or unethical about it. You receive payment for the writing you perform. If you felt strongly about having your name as an author, you should have set that up in advance.

SUMMARY

Work-for-hire in the writing industry is more common than authorship. Work-for-hire means that the author understands that any material they produce as part of their writing assignment, whether it is original work or derives from another, is "work made for hire" and the initial copyright ownership of the material belongs to the hiring company, publisher, or educational institution. The only ethical mistake possibly made was your boss's failure to notify you at the start of the project that your writing was being done on a work-for-hire basis.

@#&!?!

Work for Hire

I have a friend who is a preacher in a fast growing church. He begins to prepare his sermon on Monday every week to be delivered the following Sunday. He tells me that without fail, whatever he is preaching on goes sideways in his life that week. The good news is that it provides him lots of war stories for his sermon. The bad news is that he has to go through a lot of crazy stuff. He told me, "I go through a lot of pain, but I believe God really wants me to understand this text and that is the reason for the pain." When he told me this, I nodded, but I thought he was over exaggerating. During the writing of this book, one of the people involved suddenly wanted to change the agreement midstream to something other than work for hire, and ceased working on the project. As I stayed up late at night fixing their work in addition to doing my work, I remembered my preacher friend and I understood exactly what he meant. Writing a book is a major effort. I have seen it go wrong in every possible way. All I know is that the ethical and wise writer will make sure they understand the deal before beginning and then finish the job to the best of their ability.

Stephen Northcutt

Assuming Responsibility for Authorship – Consider the Ramifications When Under Agreement

You work for an educational Web company and independently wrote a magazine article criticizing a vendor solution. You listed your title and the Web company name on the article. The vendor company decided to sue your company because of this article, and targeted the Web business because they have more money than you do personally. Because of your employment agreement with the Web company, they technically own all of your work and are legally liable, even if they did not approve the article. Should you assume any responsibility or let your company take the heat?

> **Conservative** Since you wrote the article knowing that the Web company did not review it and would probably not approve of it, and you still

listed your title and the company name, you are at fault and should assume appropriate responsibility. You should make a statement that you are solely responsible for the negative article. There is no reason why the company you work for should take the heat for your personal negligence. Do whatever you can to clear their name.

Liberal You really did not think that what you wrote was that damaging and could result in this type of outcome. You have a right to your opinion. The magazine company required you to add your title and place of employment to the article, which is standard practice, and there is nothing you can do about it. You made a mistake by not thinking this through completely, but should not personally absorb the heat. Your company has insurance if there is prosecution. You did not do anything ethically wrong; you exercised your freedom of speech.

SUMMARY

When you work for a known company, you must be careful because what you do independently will reflect on the business that employs you. You may have also breached your employment agreement or contract with the Web company, by writing an article without their direct consent. Be sure you consider all of the ramifications prior to doing independent work when you are under an agreement with another business. Whether you decide to take the heat or let it fall on the publishing company, you will most likely face unemployment once this fiasco passes.

Knowledge Hoarding – Keeping it to Yourself

We've all worked with a knowledge hoarder. You know, that person who thinks it is necessary for them to keep certain facts about a system or technology to themselves. In every IT job I've had, there has been at least one of these people who believe that they become more valuable if they know something and no one else does. I've actually had people admit it to me. "I can't train others on how to support this system, because then my job is more at risk," or, "If someone cheaper than me knows how to work it, then I'm the first to get laid off."

Statements like this can be very dangerous for an IT environment. The people who act this way are putting everyone's job at risk by creating a single point of failure, and they are also not letting others do their jobs. More importantly, it is as unethical as you can get. In the security field, we as professionals need to be held to a higher ethical standard. There is no room for this type of behavior.

There is a great push in certain corners of the IT field for "open" communication, and security professionals need to be a part of this movement, if not lead it. I don't mean that source code for every operating system should be released on the Internet; but how to support it could. News groups, Web sites, mailing lists; all of these things allow us to share information with people around the world. Why can't we talk to the admin in the next cubicle? Open communication creates improved skill sets of others on the team, which can lead to new ideas for an improved environment. If nothing else, people will stop calling you while you are on vacation.

With a job in IT security comes a certain level of responsibility. This includes leading by example and sharing what you know, whether it be a company policy, best practice, or how to run the mission critical systems in your environment.

Jerry Patterson, Senior Security Engineer
Tarpat Network Consulting

Chapter Summary

In this chapter, we discussed the ethical considerations of content providing. You discovered the issues you may face when performing research prior to writing such as determining what the real facts are.

Next, we delved into finding and accepting a technical writing job. You learned where your personal boundaries are in relation to what type of unethical industries you are willing to write for to make a buck. Everyone has a price, now you know yours.

We thoroughly covered the subject of accuracy in writing, especially when writing marketing material and brochures. You learned about the power of media hype and the necessity to keep it to a minimum.

In the section on performing product reviews, we investigated the power of product reviews and the pressure to create positive reviews for poor products if your business has an alliance with the product's company. We also discussed personal retaliation with product reviews and the need to keep a balanced point of view whenever possible.

Following product reviews, you learned that surprisingly enough system documenters face their own set of ethical challenges when documenting systems. The primary concerns in this area are the responsibility to maintain system documentation as changes occur on the systems and writing documentation for open-source systems, which may be used by a very small percentage of people for malicious purposes.

Information integrity plays a key role with Web content developers. You learned the dangers of fake and underground Web sites. We discussed how to prevent and educate others of identity fraud. You learned the value of being aware of the intentions of fake Web sites.

Finally, we discussed the ethical issues of authorship. We touched upon concerns of ghost writing and reasons for adding additional authors or removing the names of the original authors.

At this point, you know where you stand on the ethical concerns of technical writers and content providers. You know your personal boundaries and limits after considering the various ethical dilemmas content providers face.

Frequently Asked Questions

The following Frequently Asked Questions, answered by the authors of this book, are designed to get you thinking about the ethical circumstances you may face when performing content providing or technical documentation services. Unless legal issues are involved, then answers in the FAQ may not be the right answer for your organization.

Q: Is it ever appropriate to plagiarize someone else's writing?

A: Plagiarism is never an acceptable option for content providers. It is illegal, even though charges are rarely filed. Avoid direct copying of someone else's work.

Q: Do writers have a duty to warn prospective buyers or users of significant system problems?

A: This question is up to the writer and their personal ethics. Ethically, it is not appropriate to hide a serious system problem in your writing; however, you may feel an obligation to your employer to protect them as well.

Q: How far should you go to ensure accuracy of your writing?

A: Ensuring accuracy can be a painstaking task. You would never complete a project if you fact-checked every bit of information obtained from industry experts or statistical results. Attempt to ensure a reasonable degree of accuracy in your work.

Q: If you have a personal grievance with an executive of a company, are you then justified in giving their products a negative review?

A: You are never justified in bashing someone else's products for personal reasons. Business warfare is one thing, but taking the childish playground mentality out on someone is just plain bad business.

Q: When writing system documentation, is it your responsibility as a writer to keep it current because if the system changes your earlier documentation is misleading?

A: The answer to this question depends upon the agreement you have with the department or business that employed you. If part of your agreement is to keep the data current, then you must.

Q: What is the difference between authorized Web sites and fake Web sites?

A: Authorized Web sites are official sites for a celebrity, corporation, or other organization that represent them and what they do. Fake Web sites range from unofficial sites about people or businesses to fraudulent sites designed to steal identities and finances.

Q: Is it ever appropriate to list someone else as the author of an article you wrote?

A: If you are performing ghost writing for another person who is providing you with information and ideas for the book, it is ethically appropriate to list them as the author and remove your name from authorship of the book.

Chapter 19

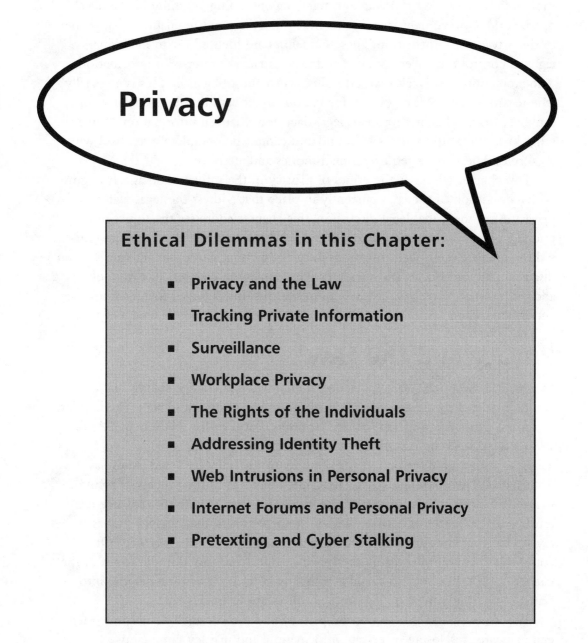

Privacy

Ethical Dilemmas in this Chapter:

- Privacy and the Law
- Tracking Private Information
- Surveillance
- Workplace Privacy
- The Rights of the Individuals
- Addressing Identity Theft
- Web Intrusions in Personal Privacy
- Internet Forums and Personal Privacy
- Pretexting and Cyber Stalking

Introduction

One of the most important ethical issues in information technology (IT) is privacy, because IT makes it possible to track anyone doing anything in the developed world. Government is racing to issue guidelines and regulations that pertain to the privacy of information. These guidelines are focused on an individual's right to control the collection, use, and dissemination of personal information. The protection of privacy is an ethical concern and obligation. This is especially true regarding personal medical information, credit card numbers, social security numbers, driver's license numbers, legal data, and financial information. However, ethical issues regarding privacy abound and cannot be completely resolved with legal rules. These issues require human morals and attention.

This chapter addresses the ethics of privacy in the information age. It begins with a discussion of the laws currently in place that address the legal matters of privacy. After the initial legal discussion, this chapter addresses the topics of tracking private information, surveillance, workplace privacy, the rights of individuals, identity theft, Web intrusions, Internet forums, and cyber stalking. It then discusses privacy policies and standards. The remaining chapters of this book address Internet privacy issues such as Web intrusions, Internet forums, cookies, and cyber stalking.

Privacy and the Law

In 2003, the American Bar Association implemented a change stating that lawyers could disclose their clients' secrets under a number of circumstances. The first law to address privacy was the Electronic Communications Privacy Act (ECPA) of 1986. Privacy and the law are still somewhat plastic.

Due to threats of terrorism, a reassessment of privacy laws and issues has occurred over the past few years. The United States is in the process of trying to strike a balance between privacy and national security. Where that balance currently lies, is a matter of debate. One of the newest acts, the Patriot Act, has revised existing laws to address the pressing matters of national security. One could write volumes discussing the specific ethical and moral implications of the Patriot Act. One could also spend a comparative amount of time delving into criticism and the potential "big brother" implications of this law.

The issues within this section on privacy and the law include unfunded federal mandates, disclosure of private information, and privacy complaints.

Privacy Bits

Privacy is a rapidly evolving field and if you are a manager or decision maker, you have an ethical responsibility for the good of your organization to keep up. As an example, it is clearly obvious to all of us that we need to protect any private information our organization collects about children. However, a number of organizations did not formally assess and strictly follow their privacy policy and implementation and then suddenly found themselves the target of Children's Online Protection Act (COPA) lawsuit. One of the best ways to keep up is to sign up for PrivacyBits, a free, weekly report on privacy news worldwide available from: www.sans.org/newsletters/

Stephen Northcutt

Unfunded Federal Mandates – What if You Cannot Comply Even if You Wanted To?

You lead an IT development team for a financial institution. You realize that to comply with the number of new laws and regulations to privacy, such as the Patriot Act and anti-terrorism mandates, you require a staff of programmers ten times your current size. Everyone knows it is mathematically impossible to comply with these new and changing regulations. To what extent is it appropriate for you to inform your senior management that not only is the business non-compliant but it cannot become compliant?

> **Conservative** Failing to comply with legal mandates such as the Patriot Act is not acceptable. You must inform senior management that they need to find the funding to hire the additional staff necessary for compliance with these legal issues.

> **Liberal** It is unrealistic for most businesses to hire the staff necessary for exact alignment to government mandates. Very few organizations can afford the staff necessary to comply with all of the new privacy acts. Senior management knows this reality. If they ask, you must answer them honestly. However, if they do not ask, it is not your ethical responsibility to bring this matter to their attention.

SUMMARY

One of the struggles facing businesses today is having the financial and human resources to comply with the privacy regulations set by the government. If you are an IT manager, you must decide whether to disclose this fact to senior management or not. The ethics of this matter are many-fold. Disclosing the information will build stress into your job, but you must stand firm on the resources necessary to get the job done.

Disclosure of Private Information – What's Your Responsibility?

You are a new IT manager for a company, which historically fails to disclose the existence of systems containing private information and the way it is used. Should you now disclose this information or keep to the existing practices?

Conservative It is your responsibility as the IT manager to comply with government regulations. Just because the business has not previously disclosed systems containing private information does not mean that you should stick to that policy.

Liberal Even though there are laws in place that require the disclosure of systems containing private information, big businesses are fighting this matter. You must respect the privacy of your business and their customers.

SUMMARY

There are contradictory rules regulating such disclosure of information. Some businesses opt toward right alignment with the newest privacy laws, whereas others are fighting to protect the system with private customer information.

Privacy Complaints – What's if it's a Matter of National Security?

The Electronic Privacy Information Center (EPIC) filed a privacy grievance with the U.S. Department of Transportation against an airline company. The grievance stated that the airline business allegedly engaged in unmerited and misleading practices by disclosing millions of passenger records to the federal government. Imagine you are the decision maker at Jetblue. It is a cold hard fact that Islamic extremist terrorists intend to utilize jet aircraft as weapons of destruction. Representatives of the U.S. government Transportation Security Administration are in your office asking for customer data that you know should be protected. How do you weigh the protection of individuals against your own personal privacy?

Conservative Matters of national security must override individual privacy. This is especially true with airlines, which are a primary means for terrorism.

Liberal There should never be a sacrifice of individual privacy at any expense. The federal government broke the spirit if not the letter of their own privacy laws. If businesses and the government strip away all personal privacy, we will all be living in a world where the individual is not valued.

SUMMARY

This is a huge topic of debate right now. A satisfactory common ground is nowhere in sight at this point. Determining which is more important, national security or individual privacy, an impossible. The only right answer is that they both are critical. That being the case, we must determine how to balance the two so that neither is compromised.

Jetblue's Privacy Policy

Needless to say, the whole TSA Jetblue event was a black eye for the company and for TSA and that always leads to soul searching. And soul searching combined with decisive action leads to a more ethically grounded company. If you were to visit Jetblue's Web page today and read their privacy policy, you would be quite impressed, the January 2004 edition is one of the best written and most comprehensive policies on the Internet.

Stephen Northcutt

Tracking Private Information

The privacy of customer information and activities contains loaded ethical issues. This section addresses customer privacy in relation to such ethical matters as the use of radio frequency ID's for marketing, using private information about customers, respect for customer privacy, and default cookies.. As a general rule, all technology related to communication leads to the exposure of private information. In general, as consumers we cannot avoid the use of communications technology, so the ethical responsibility falls on the shoulders of the collector of the information.

Radio Frequency ID's for Marketing – Is it Okay to Track a Consumer?

You run a store that embeds radio frequency ID's (RFIDs) into shopping carts, which are small inexpensive chips used to track the shopping habits of the user. In order for this to happen, the user must pay with a credit card or utilize a loyalty card to reduce their bill. Is tracking the shopping habits of consumers through radio frequency ID's an ethical practice?

Conservative Embedding RFIDs into shopping carts is a direct invasion of personal privacy. Not many people would want their shopping habits stored in a database, which later may be sold to other stores. These actions result in a bombardment of aggressive advertising directed towards the consumer.

Liberal Tracking consumers' shopping habits already occurs with on-line shopping e-commerce sites such as amazon.com or any on-line catalog. Many consumers find this type of data collection useful because the sites make recommendations based on your shopping history. You are always presented with fresh ideas for books and music you would not ordinarily discover.

SUMMARY

Feelings about personal privacy and the consumer vary greatly depending on whom you speak with. Some people could care less; others are very passionate about the privacy of their personal shopping habits.

Privacy in a Technological World

It's pretty obvious that privacy is a big concern in this day and age. The question that remains is whether anything is really private at this point anyway. Not to take too paranoid of a view on things, but almost any activity performed by an American citizen is recorded or logged somewhere. The only privacy available is the restrictions on who can collate and view **all** of your activity as compared to just the portion that a specific group is watching.

For example, your credit card company keeps track of every purchase you make. Your grocery store tracks your purchases by credit card or 'discount card.' Your vehicle locations are tracked by where you fill up for gas, traffic cameras, or GPS systems. Your home security company tracks the times that you arrive or leave your home. All of this is somewhat innocuous if taken individually, but just imagine what someone could find out about you if they had access to the information that all of these sources maintain.

Paranoia and fear of 'big brother' is a bad thing, but it's probably a good idea to be aware of what could happen if people stopped fighting for privacy rights and all of this information was available to the highest bidder.

Jeremy Faircloth
Systems Engineer and Author

Private Information about Customers – What about Reselling their Information?

You work for an e-commerce Internet business. A customer places an order and you fail to inform them that your company sells customer information to third parties. This results in the disclosure of their private information to a third party for marketing purposes. Is it morally appropriate to use a customer's information for marketing purposes without their knowledge?

Conservative Using and selling customer information for marketing purposes is not ethical. This is doubly true when you do not disclose to the customer that their private information, entrusted to your e-commerce Web site, will receive this type of exposure.

Liberal Marketing has been in existence ever since the beginning of business. This is not a new practice. The only thing different is the new technology. This issue describes the foundation of marketing principles that have been in existence a very long time.

SUMMARY

While it is true that marketing strategies such as the method mentioned in this issue have been in existence a very long time, the speed by which this information disseminates is dramatically different. In the early days of marketing, businesses utilized customer information. However, this procedure was by word of mouth in a much smaller product market. Today, when customer information transfers to a third-party vendor, that data could end up in the hands of thousands of business worldwide. Some of these businesses are reputable whereas others have malicious intent. Even in the case of a reputable business, the sheer volume of advertisement unleashed on the customer as a result is overwhelming.

Respecting Customer Privacy – Sneaky Businesses

You work for an intrusion detection company and signed up for a three-month account with anonymizer.com to do some analysis of competitors' products under the veil of anonymity. When the three months ended, you received an e-mail message that your subscription would be renewed automatically if you do not unsubscribe. You are so busy you forget to cancel the subscription, which is precisely what the company hoped you would do. After receiving the notice for the second three months, you take immediate action. Unfortunately, they would not allow you to send a simple unsubscribe response. You had to go to their Web site and enter a bunch of information. Again, the ploy was to make it more involved for the user. The Web site requested all of your identifying information, including name and the credit card you used to subscribe. Are these types of ploys ethical?

Conservative This type of business ploy is tacky and unethical. If you come across something like this cancel the service via telephone and directly inform them of their security gaffe.

Liberal Although this ploy is tasteless, it can be effective. However, the effectiveness is negative. The company may retain customers in this manner but they will not be happy ones.

SUMMARY

Some e-commerce sites push the limit in terms of keeping those monthly charges piling in. These tactics may work. Nevertheless, this type of trapping borders on coercion and overall is not a positive ethical practice.

Default Cookies – What about those Silent Trackers?

Cookies are a major concern for Internet users. World Wide Web (WWW) sites collect personal data from users through online transactions, registration forms, logs of user interest, and information from various other Web pages. This information is often stored in "cookies." Cookies are silent tracking devices that do not request the permission of the user to track data about them. Most users do not delete the massive amount of cookies stored on their computers because there are one or two cookies that store passwords for their favorite on-line shopping sites. In addition, managing cookies is simply too complex for the average user. Many of the Web sites utilizing cookies do so on a default basis. This means that they create and enable cookies on your personal computer, which collects and tracks information about you. Do you feel it is ethical for Web sites to gather information about you in the form of cookies and store that information on your personal computer? What if you have cookies on your machine that keep logs of every page you view on the Web?

Conservative Default cookies cross a few too many boundaries of personal privacy. Even though almost every site inserts some type of cookie on your computer, it is still wrong. The worst types are the ones that track every Web site you visit. This is a complete invasion of personal privacy.

Liberal Most cookies have a logical and practical purpose and are a functional requirement for the Internet. Without cookies, you could not store products in shopping carts while shopping on-line. In addition, without cookies customers would be required to remember all of the hundreds of user ID'S and passwords for all of their subscriptions to on-line merchants. Cookies are a necessity for the e-commerce function of the WWW.

SUMMARY

Determining whether cookies are an invasion of personal privacy or a necessity for Internet shopping is all in the use. Cookies that gather information about people unrelated to their services, border on attacks of personal privacy. Cookies that have a simple function are positive. It all depends on their purpose.

Surveillance

Cameras and other types of recording and monitoring devices are found nearly everywhere in the public and in private homes. They are in almost all stores to detect shoplifting. You will find them in elevators, police cars, traffic lights, parking lots, ATM's, personal security systems to name just a few. There are even Webcams setup in public parks and landmarks for Web sites. Everyone is under the surveillance monitor when going into town. Many people have home surveillance systems as well, which monitor their driveways, child-care providers, and even their children.

Living under surveillance brings up many different types of ethical issues. One of which is who monitors these cameras? Maybe the monitoring in itself is necessary but who are the individuals behind the cameras. Another aspect of surveillance is the use of Global Position Systems. Companies like GM and AT&T utilize these technologies in their products.

This section will address the issues of surveillance including: if video surveillance ethical, third party monitoring, GPS, the GM OnStar program, parental surveillance, and activity monitoring.

Video Surveillance – Is It Ethical?

Whether shopping or at the bank, you are guaranteed to be under video surveillance. Do you feel this is an invasion of your personal privacy?

Conservative The only reason a person would need to concern themselves with security video surveillance is if they were a criminal. Otherwise, they are irrelevant. Businesses have the right to monitor activities to protect themselves from theft.

Liberal No one should be taking a video of you unless you authorize it. Everyone has a right to privacy. In addition, you have no way to protect the video of you. What if someone keeps it for personal reasons that you do not know about?

SUMMARY

There is a necessity for some level of security surveillance where theft and violence may occur. However, personal privacy is important and the rules governing the use and storage of such video need to be taken into account.

Monitoring by Third Parties – What if Others are Just Watching?

Third parties often monitor surveillance systems. This means that the information surveillance cameras and equipment gather may not be secure. It all depends on the person who is running and monitoring the system. Of course, this does not include cameras run by police officers or military. For example, the night security team at a five-star hotel often watches the hot tubs to check out the girls. In most cases, a woman would feel extremely uncomfortable if she knew that others were watching her for this specific reason via security cameras. In this case, an underpaid security officer or nightshift person was watching the surveillance cameras. Is this right ethically? Can minimum wage night staff be trusted?

Conservative Surveillance is an important part of security. However, senior management often overlooks the qualifications of staff running surveillance in terms of the security risk and privacy imposition they represent. It is inappropriate for staff monitoring surveillance systems to be underqualified in any way. They should be security professionals. Just hiring someone off the street without a thorough background check is dangerous.

Liberal In reality, there are not enough qualified people to operate all of the surveillance systems in existence; therefore; businesses need to take what they can get. There is nothing immoral about someone monitoring cameras and watching others.

SUMMARY

Workers are often hired at minimum wage to monitor the vast amount of surveillance equipment used in stores, banks, hotels, parking lots, and so on. Some people may consider this an invasion of privacy depending on the person monitoring their activity; not all security personnel that watch people on camera practice good ethics. In the worst-case scenario, there have been incidents where cameras were placed in women's dressing rooms. However, this is not the likely result of hiring unqualified individuals to monitor surveillance.

GPS – Tracking Where You Are and Go

Recently, cell phone companies such as AT&T began offering a new service that allows customers with the same AT&T cell phone program to locate each other utilizing the company's global position systems. Is this a direct invasion of personal privacy?

Conservative Information made available for anyone to find you via your cell phone and Global Positioning Systems (GPS) tracking is just plain scary. Fortunately, this type of service does not appear to be popular yet with cell phone users.

Liberal   The advancement of technology is amazing. Some individuals may find this type of technology useful. Anyway, you do not have to purchase the service if you do not want it.

SUMMARY

We have already entered the age where technology can identify people wherever they are. For example, people who use debit cards and credit cards leave a trail behind them. Cellular technology utilizing GPS is simply real-time trails. Many people may not like it, but we have gone too far to stop it.

The General Motors OnStar Program – GPS for Security Reasons?

Most General Motors advertising contains huge plugs for their OnStar program, which offers a variety of services utilizing GPS satellites. Many of the services are useful to the customer. According to GM's OnStar advertising, their services have saved lives by sending help immediately when there is an emergency. They also provide useful information such as directions or unlock locked doors for clients who have left their keys in the car. Do you feel that this type of GPS product use is an invasion of your personal privacy?

Conservative   Even though the services are useful at times, it is dangerous to start tracking everyone through GPS. There is absolutely no privacy. Once this information is available to General Motors, it is possible that hackers can get it.

Liberal   Utilizing GPS in a manner that potentially saves lives is an example of how to use technology to improve the quality of life. If you lock yourself out of your car with your child in it and the car running, you will find this type of service a blessing. This is the correct use of technology.

SUMMARY

On one side of the argument you will find those who feel that even if used for positive means, using GPS systems to track individuals or automobiles is unethical. In fact, these people may feel that technology has opened Pandora's Box and that we are in for trouble. The other side of this argument believes that the use of technology to save lives or make life easier is positive and morally correct, even if it affects personal privacy to some degree.

Parental Surveillance – What if Tracking is for Your Child's Safety?

A specialty market has opened up in terms of parental surveillance. Parents can now purchase surveillance systems that monitor their children in the home. Children these days can potentially grow up under constant surveillance similar to the *Truman Show*. When a child is old enough, the parents may or may not tell them that they are constantly under surveillance. They can also track their children while they are on the road with global tracking systems. In addition, they can take their children to daycare centers that utilize cameras to monitor the children. Is all of this really necessary and healthy for the children? Do you feel performing around the clock surveillance on children is ethical?

Conservative   There is something definitely wrong with this picture. Children have the right to privacy. The only case where surveillance may be useful is if the parent suspects a daycare center to be questionable. You cannot argue that it is for the child's safety in any of the other circumstances because even if you saw your child in a dangerous situation, you are viewing it after the fact and the safety of the child was still jeopardized whether you were monitoring them or not.

Liberal   Utilizing surveillance technology to protect your children is an intelligent choice. What if you suspect your teenager is doing drugs or the babysitter is not taking proper care of the child. You have the right to know.

SUMMARY

Performing surveillance on children and teenagers may help you find out if they are up to something that may be dangerous to themselves or others. However, having open communications with your children will usually provide this same information.

Activity Monitoring – No Privacy in the Office?

A trusted 1099 contractor with access to critical projects suddenly starts producing inferior work. When this is pointed out to her, she becomes very emotional and then claims that she is medically disabled. She then advises the company that she is filing a civil law suit against them. The senior management directs systems to terminate her access to corporate systems and a note is sent to all employees of the company that legal action was probable and to have no work-related discussions with the former contractor. Since this is a high security company, all communications are recorded and monitored according to the company security policy. The terminated contractor's name is added to the "dirty word search" in the monitoring system. A day later, an e-mail message is sent by an employee from a corporate e-mail to a number of employees for a night out at a bar, and the contractor is included in the invitation. This message is detected by the security systems and brought to management's attention. A note is sent from management reminding all employees that received the list that while their personal time is their own, since the intended venue was a bar, be very careful not to drink too much and disclose company business. One of the employees expresses anger at the infringement of her privacy and begins to probe as to the exact nature of the monitoring systems. Does she have an ethical right to complain about an invasion of personal privacy?

> **Conservative** Management has the right to monitor their intellectual, financial, and physical property and personnel in the workplace. The monitoring policy has been communicated to all employees. This is not a violation of personal privacy. The notion that a night out with someone is enacting a frivolous law suit against the organization shows incredibly bad judgment. The employee not only does not have an ethical right to complain, she should probably be terminated as well.

> **Liberal** It is not necessary to constantly spy on employees. This breaks down trust and teamwork. Very few people would be willing to work in this type of distrustful environment. The employee is absolutely right; her personal privacy has been violated and she would be wise to find a more trusting work environment.

SUMMARY

The strength of communication monitors and Webcams in the workplace is that they can determine whether employees are performing illegal activities or putting the organization at risk. In certain industries, such as the financial industry, this is absolutely necessary. Communications and visual monitoring may also motivate personnel to work harder knowing that they are under surveillance. However, as we see in this example, close monitoring of employees complicates the work environment. Senior management probably made the best ethical decision they could under the circumstances. Alcohol and corporate secrets do not mix well. The angry employee should probably watch her step for a while.

Workplace Privacy

This section addresses how far is too far when it comes to workplace privacy. Workers today face drug tests, video monitoring, e-mail monitoring, Internet usage tracking, Internet filtering, chat monitoring, personality tests, and keystroke logging. This section attempts to define fairness in the information age in terms of the relationship between employers and employees.

Topics in this section include accuracy and privacy, private information on computer and communication systems, searching personal affects, processing confidentiality and security, private information from job seekers, and information given to the individual.

Accuracy and Privacy – Controlling Your Assumptions

You are the senior IT manager at a bank and receive monitoring statistics on one of your best employees. The stats indicate that he was visiting gambling Web sites on the job. When you confront him, he honestly states that they were just pop-up windows and he does not even gamble. What if you fired him based on the data you received? Is this type of information collection useful and accurate or just an invasion of personal privacy?

Conservative   Collecting extensive data about employees destroys their dignity and pride and significantly affects moral at a company. There must be a modicum of human esteem remaining in business where there is mutual respect and trust. Aside from being an invasion of privacy, constantly monitoring employees is stressful for everyone. There is also the risk of coming to the wrong conclusion about someone simply based on data.

Liberal Employers have an interest in monitoring in order to address security risks and sexual harassment, and to ensure the acceptable performance of employees. Similarly, background checks are often appropriate for positions of trust, such as a police officer, but not appropriate for jobs unrelated to public safety or the handling of very large sums of money.

SUMMARY

Constantly monitoring everything an employee does is a direct invasion of their privacy unless you have good reason to monitor their activities, such as you suspect them of committing a crime. If a business decides they must monitor their employees, they should implement a process whereby the employees have a chance to defend themselves against the data collected against them. Do not presume the data is correct and draw conclusions from there.

Private Information on Computer and Communication Systems – Who Owns It?

All e-mail messages sent over the company networks belong to the company, not you personally. They fall under the ownership of the business. You feel that your personal e-mail should be private even if it originates from within the office. Is this ethical determination correct?

Conservative Sending personal e-mail from the office is an inappropriate use of company resources. It is an obvious presumption that these communications belong to the company, because the company pays for them and they occur during working hours. The business pays for the ISP connection, computers, everything. You own nothing at work except the photos on your desk.

Liberal Even though writing personal e-mail while at work is inappropriate, this does not give the company the right to own your personal communications.

SUMMARY

Most people would agree that it is morally wrong to use company resources for personal means. However, ownership and review of personal communications remains a point in disagreement between liberal and conservative types.

Searching Personal Effects – A Necessary Evil?

Many businesses in downtown New York City instituted a new employee search policy after September 11th. This policy allows employee personal effects to be subject to search without notice in the workplace. Do you find search without notice in the workplace to be ethical in terms of personal privacy?

Conservative Although physical searches are invasive and time consuming, their intention is to protect the people within the offices. They are necessary to save lives and therefore are ethical.

Liberal Searching everyone is a violation of personal privacy. Between the video surveillance and bodily searches, a person at work has zero privacy. In addition, these searches cost the companies more money and take up valuable time.

SUMMARY

Some business may deem it necessary to perform searches of employee's personal affects. This is strictly for protection and is in response to terrorism. It is also an active deterrent for protecting the company from theft. Some employees may find this activity to be an invasion of personal privacy, whereas others will appreciate the added protection from terrorism.

Processing Confidentiality and Security – Should it be Encrypted?

The senior manager of the IT team possesses very sensitive personal medical information that he must send to one of his employees. He fails to take the proper technical measures to protect this personal medical data, and sends the file via unencrypted e-mail. Is this type of disrespect toward personal information a violation of privacy?

Conservative The IT manager should know better. Sending personal medical information through e-mail without encrypting it is needlessly making that data vulnerable. For one thing, e-mail is easy for a hacker to intercept. In addition, system administrators and postmasters have access to e-mail logs and can see the medical information.

Liberal The senior manager made a common mistake. Many people forget to encrypt sensitive information. He did not make a moral mistake but rather a human error.

SUMMARY

In either case, failing to encrypt sensitive medical information is an error on the part of the senior IT manager. Whether it is a human error or a moral one is up to you to decide.

Private Information from Job Seekers – Is this Discriminatory?

You have the task of hiring a new executive assistant for the Director of Finance for a fast moving, rapidly growing IT company. He would prefer an older, more experienced female assistant with classic secretary training, including a fast typing speed. Therefore, you lower the interview priority for all male and straight-out-of-college female resumes. Is this an appropriate means of handling job seekers if you know their gender, age, and experience?

Conservative   You should keep yourself out of his decisions. If he wants a female assistant of a particular type or age, let him select one from the resumes, not you. Your actions are immoral.

Liberal   You know the Director of Finance personally. He is concerned that he would be working long hours with his assistant and that he did not want any complications with his marriage. You also know that he does not want to invest in training a new assistant. He has been very clear that he wants someone with a stable job history and proven skills, so you carefully screen resumes and calculate the number of years of experience the applicants have, avoiding the youngest ones. You realize that he is motivated by a stereotype, but you are pretty certain that in the end he will gladly accept the most qualified candidate.

SUMMARY

At first glance, selecting a job applicant based on their age or gender is unethical and illegal behavior. However, in five years of hiring in IT, you have learned that there is no substitute for experience. In this particular circumstance you are not the one with the preference, the Director of Finance is. His request is reasonable, and if a qualified applicant meets his vision for the position, you should be able to staff the position without jeopardizing your sense of higher principles.

Information Given to the Individuals – Should You Sue?

During a work survey of personnel, the Human Resource department released personal medical data about an employee who recently found out she had cancer. They did not have the consent of this employee. This consequently resulted in the loss of the employee's health insurance. Due to the employee's recent discovery of cancer, she feels obligated to sue her employer for releasing her personal data without consent. Does she have the moral right to sue company for releasing personal medical information about her without her permission?

Conservative The employee absolutely has a moral right to bring her company to court for releasing her personal medical information, which resulted in the loss of medical coverage. This action is an atrocity .

Liberal While the company was wrong to release her medical information, they must have done so for a good reason. They obviously did not consider the matter thoroughly. It is a terrible mistake. Maybe they can personally compensate her out of court by providing new medical coverage for her.

SUMMARY

Under all conditions, releasing personal medical information about an employee without their consent is morally and probably legally wrong. The only thing that comes into question is the intent. The liberal point of view feels that intent should play a role in the consequences of this action. On the flip side, the conservative point of view dictates that regardless of intent, the employee has the right to sue since great wrong was done to her. In every case, an immediate review of the process and refresher training for all employees with access to sensitive personnel data is clearly called for.

The Rights of Individuals

One of the most important aspects of handling private information is the individual's right to information about themselves. Individuals must have the right to inspect this information and debate any inaccuracies. This is to protect the individual from walking blindly into circumstances of erroneous information collection. Another positive point of making personal information available to the individual is to identify how that information is obtained and be certain all means utilized are ethical.

Web Sites and Availability of Information – Should You Have Access?

Most Web sites do not allow users to access all of their own information. They can input it, but not access it. Would you consider it unethical if you could not access your own personal data within a Web site database?

Conservative   Anyone who collects information about you, especially financial information, should allow users to access and update their own data, or delete it altogether. Web sites that do not allow proper access of personal information are unethical.

Liberal   One of the reasons why some Web sites opt to prevent access to personal information is to protect that information. More Web access to personal data increases its vulnerability.

SUMMARY

For the most part, people should be able to access their personal data. If this is not available online, you should be able to call the company and have your information updated or deleted.

Accessing Human Resource Data – Should You See All of It?

You work in the Human Resources department and over ear your boss denying access to another employee regarding reviewing their personnel file. Is this a violation of employee/management ethics?

Conservative   Failing to allow an employee access to their personnel file is a direct violation of employee rights. All employees should have access to their personnel file.

Liberal   There are instances when information about an employee must remain private. If this information contains the opinions of another, it does not necessarily warrant you the right to access it. For example, if someone writes in their diary about you, that does not give you the moral right to read their diary.

SUMMARY

Having access to information about you is an important human right. However, some information in personnel files may not be appropriate to give to employees. It may contain performance reviews, which the manager must go over in relationship with the employee. It would be insensitive to just throw that information at them in an impersonal manner.

Individual's Right to Object – Do You Help Them?

An employee objects to the use of their personal data for marketing purposes. Knowing that the owner of the company has fired employees in the past for the same objection, you want to help the new employee keep their job and blatantly fail to remove the personal data from the marketing list. Did you make the right ethical choice?

Conservative You made the wrong ethical choice in failing to delete personal data of an employee. Now you are entwined in this conflict. You knowingly went against the wishes of the employee, which makes you more at fault than the manager that did not know how the employee felt.

Liberal Your intention was to protect the employee from a quick termination. Intention dictates morals in circumstances such as this one.

SUMMARY

Going against the privacy wishes of another in most cases is a moral violation of privacy. This circumstance is unique because you were attempting to protect the employee. Your intention is good, however, your actions may still be considered inappropriate.

Disclosure of Personal Data to Third Parties – It's All About the Facts

You are in the process of firing an incompetent employee in the IT systems group, and have major historical documentation of many grievances. Another employer who is also a close friend of yours, calls for a reference on this same person. You share personnel data with this employer but fail to notify the employee that have released this personal data to the third party. Is your failure to communicate the release of information about the employee unethical?

Conservative It is unethical to communicate work-related information about an employee without disclosing that information to them and giving them a chance to explain or defend themselves. Being forced to communicate grievances directly with the employee forces you out of any prejudice you may have. Back talking will have the effect of discrediting you rather than the employee.

Liberal When someone calls for a reference, a manager has the right to provide his point of view. If they had a bad experience and have serious grievances, it is morally acceptable to communicate such issues. However, the manager must be careful that they can back up that information with hard facts, not just opinions. If an employee does not get a job because of a reference, they have the right to prosecute the manager if they cannot back themselves up with valid information.

SUMMARY

In general, as long as what you disclose is the truth your organization is legally protected. It would be far better not to disclose anything until the termination process is complete. However, there is a high cost to hiring and firing and if you can help your friend avoid a loser then it probably makes sense. Also, employees with IT systems access can do a tremendous amount of damage, which has to be factored in to your decision. You probably made the right choice.

Foreigner Traveler Data Collection – Does it Inhibit Tourism?

A new system is in place that tracks an incredible amount of information about foreigners traveling within the United States. This information includes fingerprints, personal history, and personal travel information. Is it ethical to track and fingerprint everyone who enters the United States as a protective measure against terrorism?

Conservative A balance needs to be struck between national security and personal privacy. Fingerprinting people who enter the United States as if they were criminals is going too far. This type of security mechanism breeds prejudice.

Liberal New systems to track foreign visitors in the United States are necessary to counter terrorism. Therefore, they are morally correct.

SUMMARY

The positive aspect of tracking foreigners is that it makes it more difficult for potential terrorists to enter the United States. It also makes it easier for law enforcement personnel or military personal to find these suspected terrorists. However, often terrorists use alias or simply enter the country by illegal means, which this system will not catch. Therefore, innocent foreign travelers are tracked, which costs the government a great deal of time and money for nothing. It also may inhibit tourism to the United States, because people do not want to give up their right to privacy.

Addressing Identity Theft

Identity theft is a rampant crime in the age of IT. Imposters simply obtain the social security number, credit card number, or a combination of the two of an innocent victim and assume their identity. These imposters then obtain credit in the name of the stolen identity and make purchases, which end up being the responsibility of the victim. This consequently ruins the victim's credit history and requires an incredible amount of energy to battle the fraudulent charges and repair their credit. In some cases, the imposter commits illegal crimes under the name of the identity theft victim, which has horrible consequences. Identity theft is one of the fastest growing crimes in the United States today.

This section discusses the morals and means by which imposters steal the identity of others. Among them are illegal transfers of personal information, credit card phone scams, sign-in sheets and rosters, identity theft disguised as charity organizations, and "Do Not Call" list scams.

Illegal Transfer of Personal Information – Who is at Fault?

Some employees possess high levels of access to sensitive customer information in the workplace. This is especially true of insurance company personnel. There have been instances where an employee obtained personal information of a customer and then transferred that data to a third party, usually for a commission. This third party then commits credit card and/or identity fraud. Since the employee did not commit the fraud but simply divulged the information to other parties outside of the insurance company, should they be held morally accountable for the act? What if they did not know that the third party had malicious intent?

Conservative The insurance company employee possesses greater moral responsibility than the imposter because they are trusted with sensitive information such as social security numbers, bank account information, credit card numbers, and driver's license numbers. Therefore, the moral obligations of the insurance company employee are higher.

Liberal Since there is a chance that the insurance company employee did not know this information would be used for fraud, they are somewhat innocent in the moral results of the circumstance. They are still at fault for passing this information on to a third party.

SUMMARY

Information that empowers an impostor to perform illegal fraud is available in the world of business. All it takes is one crooked employee or one very desperate employee. We have determined that from both the conservative and liberal points of view that this action is unethical.

Credit Card Phone Scam – Never Divulge Personal Information

Some con artists use the telephone to execute well thought out identity theft scams. For example, you receive a call from someone stating that they are an employee of your VISA or MasterCard Company. They say they are from the fraud division and are checking on a warning flag in the system, which indicates an unusual spending pattern in regard to your account. They ask for the three-digit secret code from the back of your card and your credit card number. Since they sound very professional and creditable, you provide the information. It turns out you have just been scammed. Were you at fault at all in this circumstance?

Conservative You are not at fault. You should contact your credit card company immediately upon discovery of the fraud and have them cancel the card and begin tracking the imposter.

Liberal You are at fault to a certain degree. When a company calls you for sensitive information, you should always ask the caller their name and employee number even if the caller feels annoyed by the request. Then call them back on the 800 number listed on the back of your credit card. Never give your credit card number and secret code out over the phone.

SUMMARY

You have some blame to carry for providing the information. You must never provide secret codes over the telephone, especially when you are the call recipient.

Sign-in Sheets and Rosters – Should You Sign Them?

Some businesses, universities, and government agencies request that you place your name and social security number on a sign-in sheet or roster. People who make a living from stealing other identities will often attend these events and sign in at the end of list. They then copy all of the other names and social security numbers from the sheet and commit identity theft with the information gathered. If you come across this type of roster and the owner of the roster requires you to put your name and social security number down, what should you do?

Conservative If you come across a roster where you are required to put something down, simply write that you will provide your social security number in person. Alternatively, write 000-00-000 as your number. Even if there is significant pressure from the roster owner, try not to provide the information. This is an extremely dangerous form of information gathering and you have every right to protect yourself. If the social security number is an absolute requirement then do not put your name on the roster.

Liberal It is always good to be safe with your social security number. However, if you are at a government building you can hardly tell them "no." There are some instances when you must provide the information. At colleges, it is often required to obtain credit for a class. When there is significant personal loss at stake, you must provide the information in the roster.

www.syngress.com

SUMMARY

If you opt for the conservative approach and fail to put your social security number on the roster, make sure you do not make up a number as this may harm another innocent person. However, if you decide you must put down your own social security number on a college or government roster, you may want to communicate the dangers of this type of information gathering and the associated risk to the administrations office.

Identity Theft Disguised as Charity Organizations – Always Check Them Out

You are at work and receive a call from a known charity, which requests a small donation from you. The dollar amount is so small that you decide to go ahead and make the donation; after all, it is tax deductible. Have you made a mistake?

Conservative You just made a huge mistake. Never give your credit card number over the phone. You should know that random callers are not necessarily reputable charities. They are probably just scammers in the market for identities to steal.

Liberal Refraining from making charity donations because of potential scams has a horrible impact on non-profit organizations. There is no way you could have known that the charity was fraudulent.

SUMMARY

When you receive a call from a charity and you want to make a donation, always ask for a call back number and detailed information about that charity. Perform some research and find a secure means by which you can make the payment. Also, be very careful about any questions you answer about your organization; they may be fronting for a legitimate charity, but in fact are more interested in any information they can collect than your donation.

www.fundrace.org

There are circumstances where your personal decisions affect your privacy and potentially the privacy and security of your employer. Who would imagine that the money you give in a political campaign would affect anything? Well, before you open up that checkbook, be certain to visit www.fundrace.org. Your name, address, the candidate you funded, and your title and organization will all be listed along with the amount you contributed. It certainly is not unethical to make a campaign contribution, but it might be unwise.

Stephen Northcutt

"Do Not Call" Telemarketing Scams – Do Not be Intimidated

With the advent of the "Do Not Call" list, a new breed of identity theft is surfacing. Scammers call people explaining that they are from the state or federal government and request social security numbers, bank account numbers, and credit card information from unsuspecting people, which will add or verify their names on the "Do Not Call" list. You fall prey to this scam. Is there a way you could have better protected yourself?

Conservative You should know that the government would never allocate the resources to call everyone in the state or country and ask them if they would like to be on the "Do Not Call" list. Social security numbers have nothing to do with the "Do Not Call" list anyway. Therefore, this is an obvious giveaway that the call is from an identity thief.

Liberal There is no way you could know that identity thieves would get this creative. Posing as federal employees is very dangerous so it is easy to presume that imposters would not take the risk. In addition, it may be intimidating for some people to refuse someone who claims to be an official government representative. This is an easy mistake to make.

SUMMARY

Never provide sensitive information such as your social security number, credit card number, bank account numbers, or anything else that an imposter my use to steal your identity over the phone. Do not let the caller intimidate you by using official government titles. The government would never request this information from you over the telephone.

Web Intrusions in Personal Privacy

With the advent of the WWW comes the intrusion of personal privacy through Web sites. Interference of personal privacy comes in the form of hostile Web sites, questionable Web links, misleading Web sites, java trapping, and pop-up windows. This section addresses the ethical concerns of these issues.

Hostile Web Sites – Protect Your Computer

You are conducting Internet research and one of the Web sites you visit downloads spyware onto your computer. This means that others can potentially view the information on your machine as well as monitor your Web use. Is it ethical for a Web site to download software on your computer without your knowledge when you visit their Web page?

Conservative It is completely unethical to download spyware onto another's computer. This is a direct breach of privacy.

Liberal If you are dumb enough to not use a firewall or other protective measure to protect your computer from spyware, it is your own fault that this happened.

SUMMARY

Most people would consider installing spyware on another's machine to be unethical. However, this does not change the fact that people need to adequately protect their computers from malicious attack.

The Maze of Web Site Links – Are You Offended?

You are visiting a Web site that offers links to other sites. Once you click onto a link and go to another site, you find no way back to the original site. Is this type of linking procedure, which traps you in another site so that you cannot return to the place of origin, ethical?

Conservative Manipulating Web users is inappropriate Internet use. Trapping a user on your site so that they cannot return to the previous site is not ethical use of the Internet.

Liberal There is nothing wrong with using strategy to keep users locked into your Web site. If the user wants to get around it, they simply need go to the browser history and select the page they were at previously. They will immediately be back to where they were before getting stuck at the link site.

SUMMARY

Although being caught in a maze of links is not as malicious as the other issues we have discussed in this chapter; it can be quite annoying and disruptive. Some people may opt to simply work around this by going back to their browser's history, and not find it to be a moral problem. Others may be deeply offended by these controlling actions.

Misleading Web Sites – Freedom of Speech?

You are surfing various Web sites, gathering information for an article you are writing. During your research, you click on a link that turns out to be a hostile Web site. Is it ethical to mislead people on subject matter, which will bring them to a hostile Web site?

Conservative It is unethical to mislead Internet users to a site that is negative. People do not want to be bombarded with other's prejudice or negativity.

Liberal Everyone has the right to freedom of speech. Taking away this right is unethical. The Web is a non-political means for communicating personal beliefs and should not be suppressed.

SUMMARY

This is an interesting consideration on the freedom of speech versus the destruction it may cause and in this case, the disturbance to work. Some feel that anything can be written on the Web because people have the freedom of speech, whereas others feel there needs to be regulations on this matter.

Java Trapping – Intrusive Advertising?

You are leading a military response meeting and are sitting in front of a 19-inch screen with military generals. A coworker mistypes a Web site address. To her embarrassment, she finds herself in a porn site and scrambles to close out of the site. Instead, she finds herself locked into Java Trapping where additional nudity pages continue to pop up. Was this type of trapping ethical?

Conservative   Java trapping is unethical use of Internet technology. No one likes to be locked into an endless array of Web pop-up pages that are of no interest to them. This eats up system resources and time. This is especially true with pornography Web sites.

Liberal   Java trapping can be annoying but it is hardly unethical. It is simply a means to advertise.

SUMMARY

Java trapping is an obnoxious technology. You would be hard pressed to find someone who would disagree with this statement. However, deeming whether it is unethical is another matter. Advertising in all forms can be quite intrusive. Is the Web any different? Some may say yes, others no. That is up to you to decide.

Pop-ups – Do They Cross the Line?

You sign into your e-mail service provider and quickly find that they bombard you with a ton of annoying pop-up advertising messages. You see a pattern in these messages, informing you that they offer the perfect software to kill these exact messages. Is this type of marketing ethical?

Conservative This issue goes beyond advertising ethics to downright lying and coercion. A company creates a problem and then wants money from you to solve the problem. This is highly unethical and will hopefully be illegal in the near future.

Liberal Marketing in this manner is very shady. The best thing to do is ignore it. Offering solutions to problems the company has created is really pushing the limits of marketing. Through the system administration functions of your computer, you can prohibit pop-ups from occurring. If you do not know how to set these properties, ask someone who does.

SUMMARY

Pop-ups annoy everyone, especially if a company trying to sell you a product that will stop pop-ups generates them. Most would consider this manner of marketing unethical. There is a line that should not be crossed in advertising. This issue crosses it.

Internet Forums and Personal Privacy

The creation of Internet forums has generated additional privacy concerns for users of the WWW. Internet forums are on-line communities where Web users can post questions or communications about a subject. Forums are used to facilitate discussions online. The down side of Internet forums is misuse. Sometimes forums are used for self-promotion, advertising, or petty arguments. This section addresses the ethical misuse of Internet forums such as Web forums as marketing tools, forums and privacy risk, and hacker forums that provide keys to software codes.

Web Forums as Marketing Tools – Is this Acceptable?

You have a technical question about a software product you are using at work. You post your question on a Web forum. Shortly thereafter, sales representatives wanting to sell you a similar product hound you. Is it ethical to use information from Web forums for marketing purposes?

> **Conservative** It is unethical for sales representatives to scan discussion forums for leads and then aggressively pursue them. If you were sincerely looking for a new product, this type of behavior would be acceptable. Since you are not looking for something new and communicated that you already have a solution, this type of aggressive marketing is an invasion of personal privacy.
>
> **Liberal** If you post a question to a public Web forum, you must expect a variety of responses. You may end up dealing with obnoxious people who just want to argue with you, or sales representatives that will bombard you. This is the chance you take when posting on an open Web forum.

> ### SUMMARY
>
> There are inherent risks you take when you post a question on a public Web forum. First time posters may not be aware of the consequences of posting their e-mail on a public forum. Even worse is providing any other information about yourself. This does not, however, make it right for marketers to hound you.

Forums and Privacy Risk – Limit the Information?

You post a technical question about the architecture of the new UNIX system you are building for your company on a Web forum. Are you putting the company's technology privacy at risk by doing this?

> **Conservative** You should never post details of your company's IT systems on the Internet. You are morally incorrect for supplying this informa-

tion to a forum of unknown people. This will put the security of your company at risk.

Liberal In reality, when seeking technical advice, you must provide some details about the system in question. If the forum you utilized is a private one for a specialized product you utilize at work, you have a chance of not placing your company at risk. However, if you posted sensitive technical information on a public forum, you may be at serious risk.

SUMMARY

It is never a good idea to post technical information on a Web forum about your company. This is true even if it is a secure forum. This information can easily be used against the business in the form of a malicious attack. In some instances, it may be necessary to post your question on a Web forum, when using a particular tool that does not have phone technical support. If you must post sensitive information, be certain it is on a secure forum, which requires a password and grants access only to users of the product. Even then, limit the information you provide.

Hackers Forum Sites – Is this Code Really Free?

There are some Internet Web site forums that provide the most recent software key codes. This enables people to use software without purchasing it. Are forums providing key codes to software ethical?

Conservative Forums providing key codes for software allowing the user to access the software free is essentially hacking and stealing. This type of software abuse is morally unacceptable. Using something you did not pay for is stealing. There is no denying that.

Liberal International laws differ for the use of software. For example, in some Asian countries, copyright laws do not even exist. Within the U.S., posting and using software codes is unethical. However, outside of the U.S., people may have different ethical beliefs, which should not be quickly brought to judgment.

SUMMARY

There is no arguing that posting and using codes to access software for free that you would otherwise have to purchase is morally wrong. However, those morals may differ from country to country.

Pretexting and Cyber Stalking

"It's actually obscene [sic] what you can find out about people on the Internet."

—Liam Youens, the man who used an online information brokerage/pretexting agency to locate and kill Amy Boyer.

Pretexting is the process of collecting data about a person using false pretenses. The way it works is that an investigator calls the family members or coworkers of a person under the umbrella of some official purpose such as job screening for security or to say that they are a sweepstakes winner or are due an insurance payment. The coworkers and family of the victim are fooled and provide the personal data requested about the victim.

There are some types of pretexting that are against the law. In 1999, the Gramm-Leach-Bliley Act prohibited pretext calls targeting financial, insurance, and brokerage organizations. This act does not protect the average person from pretexting. These calls are under false pretenses and their goal is to collect personal data on the soon to be victim.

This section addresses methods of pretexting and how the WHOIS database plays a part in cyber stalking.

Pretexting Calls – Never Divulge Other's Personal Information

You receive a call about your brother in New York. The caller states that he just applied for work at a brokerage business and they are simply performing a minimal background check on him. The say they are from the SEC. You supply them with his unlisted phone number and home address. Since this information seemed harmless because you did not provide social security information, did you make the right choice by providing it?

Conservative This has been stated many times in this chapter but it is worth stating again, never provide any personal information about yourself or anyone else on the telephone regardless of who you believe you are speaking with. You made a huge mistake by providing this information. This investigator now has enough information to sell to someone who wants to go to your brother's house and steal from him or harm him.

Liberal Providing phone numbers and address information is hardly useful. It is easy enough to find if someone really wants it. You have done nothing wrong ethically.

SUMMARY

You may not have provided enough information to do serious damage, but any information is power in the hands of a cyber stalker.

The WHOIS Database – Should it be Accessible to the Public?

The initial intention of the WHOIS database was to provide network administrators the information they need to locate and remediate problems in a simple manner in order to keep the Internet stable. However, the WHOIS database now poses a risk to privacy because it exposes the registrants of domain names personal information to cyber stalkers, spammers, criminal investigators, and other legal organizations such as copyright enforcers. This information consists of mailing addresses, e-mail addresses, telephone numbers, fax numbers, domain information, and domain server information. Is it ethical for this Internet database to be accessible to the public?

Conservative Having this type of information available to anyone on the Internet is completely unethical in terms of personal privacy. The wealth of information that can be gathered makes it easy for stalkers and malicious attackers to victimize individuals.

Liberal The WHOIS database has both positive and negative values. It simply depends on who uses it. The information on the WHOIS database is necessary for administrators and the maintenance of Web stability.

SUMMARY

While the information on the WHOIS database is valuable, it is a risk to personal privacy to have it accessible on the Internet. Some registrants use this information to perform cyber stalking; others need to protect their identity and personal information. In this case, it seems the bad outweighs the good.

Chapter Summary

Privacy in the age of technology is a bigger issue then most people think. This chapter illustrated all of the various ethical dilemmas concerning personal privacy. It began with a consideration of privacy and the law determining where the law stops and where human ethics must begin.

The next section discussed tracking private information such as customer purchasing patterns at grocery stores and online using cookies.

Surveillance is a very hot issue, which most people do not think about much because it is not as obviously intrusive as the other privacy topics. We have gone from a culture of general personal privacy to one under almost constant surveillance by security video cameras and GPSs.

We discussed workplace privacy in relationship to e-mail monitoring and the privacy of personnel records.

In the section on the rights of individuals, you learned that you have the right to know the details of what information about you is in the possession of others. You have the right to debate and dispute this information.

We covered at length the different scams used to steal identity. We discussed the means by which imposters utilize stolen identities to conduct credit card fraud and criminal activities.

The sections on Web intrusions and Internet forums reviewed how technology procedures and mechanisms could be an invasion to personal privacy. The epitome of this type of intrusion is cyber stalking where we concluded this chapter.

Frequently Asked Questions

The following Frequently Asked Questions, answered by the authors of this book, are meant to get you thinking about the ethical considerations of personal privacy. Unless legal issues are involved, then answers in the FAQ may not be the right answer for your organization.

Q: Do you feel it is appropriate for big business to disclose information about their customers to the government?

A: In most cases, it is inappropriate to disclose private customer information to anyone.

Q: In what ways do businesses track private customer information (i.e. shopping habits) for the purposes of marketing and advertising?

A: Businesses use physical radio frequency ID's and electronic cookies to track private customer information.

Q: In what ways are you under constant surveillance?

A: Video surveillance exists at ATM machines, corner stores, malls, home security systems, hotel pools, and most other places that you can imagine.

Q: In what ways do employers monitor their employees?

A: Employers track employee e-mail, keystrokes, personnel employment records and history, medical information, and much more.

Q: Do individuals have the right to know all of the information about themselves, which is stored by employers, businesses, Web sites, and any others?

A: In most cases, individuals should have the right to know and defend the information gathered about them.

Q: What is identity theft and how can you protect yourself from it? What are the signs?

A: Identity theft is a crime in which imposters obtain the social security number, credit card number, or a combination of the two of an innocent victim and assume their identity. These imposters then obtain credit in the name of the stolen identity and make purchases, which end up being the responsibility of the victim. Signs of identity theft include any phone calls or e-mails requesting your personal information from any organization.

Q: How far is too far when it comes to Internet marketing tactics, including using technology to lock you into Web sites or send endless pop-ups to your browser?

A: Forcing pornography or illegal Web sites on individuals through pop-ups is going too far.

Q: Are you looking for trouble when you post a message on an Internet forum?

A: You must be very careful when you post a message on an Internet forum. If it is not a secure forum, meaning that it requires registration with a creditable organization, then you may receive unwanted marketing calls or end up interfacing with people who would like to argue with you.

Q: What is pretexting and how can you protect yourself from it?

A: Pretexting is the process of collecting data about a person using false pretenses. It is hard to protect yourself from pretexting because, although you will be the victim, the ones providing the information about you are friends, family, coworkers, previous employers, and so forth.

Chapter 20

Management/ Employer Ethics

Ethical Dilemmas in this Chapter:

- Diversity and Ethics

- Fair Treatment for All Employees

- Thinking of Employees as Human Beings

- How Far Will You Go to Make the Extra Buck

- Personal Employee Issues

- Hiring, Firing, and Quitting

Introduction

When management thinks of ethics, they usually consider guidelines and policies for the employees they manage. However, the effectiveness of ethics in the workplace is completely dependant on the example set by senior management and the commitment management places on enforcing ethical standards. Management is ultimately responsible for the overall ethics of the organization, which requires them to be held at a higher standard than the employees. Management's ethics determine the resulting employee moral boundaries. Therefore, the success of ethical standards for an organization depends on how well management leads by example.

There are many benefits of instituting an ethics program in the workplace. Ethics is part of management. Ideally, corporate ethics cultivates teamwork, supports employee growth, helps prevent criminal acts that result in corporate fines, improves the quality of management, and provides the company with a strong public image. The management of ethics must be integrated with other management practices for lasting success.

This chapter discusses the moral dilemmas that manager's face. It begins with issues of diversity in the workplace. It then discusses the fair treatment of employees; treating them like human beings rather than commodities. After discussing the employee manager relationship, we probe how far a manager should go to make that extra buck. What are the ethical limits of ambition? We then take this consideration out of the direct workplace and review the role of ethics when management interacts with vendors and business partnerships. This chapter then considers employee's personal problems and whether there is a place for personal issues in the workplace and how to ethically handle them. This chapter concludes with the complex issues of hiring, firing, and quitting that manager's face.

Diversity and Ethics

Handling diversity in an ethical manner is critical in today's workplace. It is a very sensitive matter that requires careful consideration. Managers often find themselves dealing with conflicts of religion and business or language barriers. This section discusses how the manager rightly aligns their morals to the dilemmas of diversity.

Language Barriers - Should Language be Considered when Hiring?

Your company has a strong program of diversity in the workplace. You, as the Senior Vice President, take pride in your aggressiveness with hiring minorities. You are performing interviews for a new job opening and meet an Asian candidate who is a perfect match with the job description. However, you have a concern that your customers will not be able to understand her because she is still in the process of learning the English language. Her accent and use of the English language is difficult to understand. What is the appropriate ethical response to this circumstance?

Conservative Since the candidate is a perfect match for the job technically and academically you should hire her. That was the posted criteria for employment. You must not add additional criteria that you consider after the fact. You have found yourself an excellent employee. All new hires have some limitations.

Liberal Although the candidate is an excellent match for the job, it is important that she be able to communicate effectively with customers. You are not being prejudice by any means. It is simply that communication is an important aspect of the job that must be taken into account when hiring someone for the position.

SUMMARY

Handling diversity is a sensitive matter. The manager must hire the best person for the job, and that means balancing a number of factors. To avoid any misunderstandings it is best to provide a detailed job description from the start. One of the lessons managers must take to heart is to know when to put the effort into the planning and requirements phase of a project, which is as true of hiring as it is of software development. If you decide on other factors beyond the scope of the job description, you may be heading into a gray area in terms of diversity ethics.

Managing Conflicts of Religious Beliefs – What Happens with Conflicts of Interest?

Your top application developer suddenly refuses to use the corporate e-mail system. He explains to you that, as a strict Catholic, he cannot possibly use a product built by a company that provides benefits to the partners of homosexual employees. Your employee is making a big scene out of this issue, trying to draw others in, which is hindering the product development life cycle. How should you properly handle this sensitive circumstance?

Conservative Simply provide an alternate e-mail solution for any employee that feels the e-mail product used by the company is in direct offense with their religious beliefs. Creating any type of direct confrontation would be disastrous. Do not make a big deal out of it; just offer an alternative and move forward. If the employee is still offended that the company is using this tool, then this matter needs to be dealt with in another manner.

Liberal This is hardly a religious issue. For that matter, anyone who uses condoms is going against the man's religious beliefs. Does he want to veto every product and the company itself? You should not give in to this type of radical who simply wants to stir up trouble.

SUMMARY

Dealing with matters of personal religion is extremely complicated, both humanly and ethically. For diverse groups of people to work together requires some level of generic compromise. This does not mean that people have to compromise their personal actions, but they do not have the right to force their beliefs on an entire company. It is impossible to make a company completely adhere to one religion without violating the beliefs of others. We live in a diverse world that requires an incredible amount of cooperation and tolerance.

Fair Treatment for All Employees

In every work environment there is a star employee. In some cases, this person may simply play up to the boss a little more than the others. However, in other circumstances they are the employee's that put the extra time in and therefore shine uniquely. Not everyone under a manager's responsibility deserves equal privileges and pay.

This section addresses the ethical handling of star employees and distributing special privileges.

Rewarding Star Employees – How Much is Enough?

You are a senior manager at a company that prides itself on its merit-based pay system. One of your employees has done a tremendous job all year, so she deserves strong recognition. However, she is already paid at the top of the salary range for her job grade and your company has too many people in the grade above her, so you cannot promote her. How should you handle this circumstance?

> **Conservative** Explain to the employee that they did a phenomenal job and as soon as there is an opening for her to be promoted to the next job grade it will be hers. She will be happy to receive the recognition.

> **Liberal** This is a circumstance where you need to challenge bureaucracy. Simply promote her regardless of how many people are in the job grade above her. If you absolutely must, bump someone down who is not pulling their weight. Do not let bureaucracy hinder the right treatment of a star employee.

SUMMARY

The conservative and liberal responses to this issue represent two different types of managers. The first type is by the book and fair according to the company rules. The second type of manager gets in there and fights for their team. Neither is more ethical then the other. It is also crucial to remember that financial compensation is only one type of reward. If you have a star employee, be sure to use praise as part of the reward package; no company can regulate that.

Special Privileges and Management Decisions – Who Gets to Do What?

Everyone wants to telecommute rather than coming into the office every day. You as the manager allow one or two individuals that you know you can trust completely to work from home. With some of your other employees you do not know if they will be effective working from home. Is it ethical for you to allow only the individuals you select to work from home rather than providing the entire department with this opportunity?

Conservative Privileges should be offered to everyone in your department equally on a trial basis. You will know relatively quickly if someone is going to be effective working from home. If you allow everyone the opportunity to work from home dependent on their performance, you do not end up being the bad guy. Individuals will disqualify themselves by the corresponding results.

Liberal Most people on the team will view your decision as allowing your favorites or personal friends to work from home. They will not see the management decisions you are making in regard to performance and specific employee attributes and abilities to work from home. As the manager, it is up to you, regardless of what others say. If you deem some people can work from home effectively, then allow only them to work from home. A manager is not always the most popular person. A good manager effectively utilizes the team to the best of their abilities.

SUMMARY

Working from home can be the demise of an employee, so blindly treating everyone equally can lead to problems with a less disciplined employee. A manager may choose to utilize either of the these strategies to deal with special privileges in the workplace. Management is not done by consensus if it is effective management.

Managers: The Ethics Beacons in the Organization

Sometimes I look around and try to find out how ethical the IT people I know are. "No rocket science," you might think, "if you are ethical, you are ethical." Well, let me disagree with you. In real life, ethics are not black and white but grey-scale. And even worse, every different person understands ethics in a different way.

In a society where making money is the primary (and sometimes only) goal of every organization, managers are seen as those individuals who can make the most of the human and material resources they manage. However, when a major security incident is caused by an insider (sometimes maliciously, sometimes not), we should stop and think how it is related to a management failure, to a wrong perception of the ethics in the organization.

Managers, and IT managers in particular, should be the ethics beacons that every employee should follow. They should be living proof of the ethics of the organization, and responsible for creating its ethics culture. A manager that shows lax, improper or errant behavior in ethics-related subjects doesn't make a good manager; the costs in terms of risk for the whole organization can prove prohibitive.

Jess Garcia - Security Engineer
National Institute for Aerospace Technology (INTA) - Spain

Thinking of Employees as Human Beings

In the large impersonal workplace of today's metropolitan environment, it has become easy to objectify the human being as a commodity. Out of necessity, managers have learned to divorce themselves from relationships with their employees. For example, if you were a manager that has a sincere love and appreciation for everyone on your staff and due to downsizing are forced to fire half of them, it would be very painful. What people have opted to do instead is treat individuals as commodities rather then human beings. In some instances, human relationships are in direct opposition to the business, and a manager who cares too much does not last long. How have we gotten so off base? With the advent of the computer age there was a lot of talk initially of computers developing personalities and becoming similar to humans. Well, in some instances, the opposite has occurred. Some managers have become more like the computers. They are calculating, efficient, logical, strategic, and cold.

This section addresses how to bring human nature back into the workplace. We discuss the moral responsibility of managers when they must perform staff layoffs, the management obligation to new employees, and the overworked software development team.

Warning Employees of Layoffs – Should You Keep it Quiet?

You are a project manager for a new web development team. Your boss informs you that one of your employees will be one of many to be laid off from the company very soon. Your boss tells you that you cannot tell your employee yet because the employee may forewarn others in the organization that layoffs are about to happen. This would create a huge disturbance. Meanwhile, you heard that your employee about to be laid off is just closing on purchasing his first home. What is the morally correct thing to do?

> **Conservative** You must follow the orders of your boss and not forewarn the employee, even though this will result in the employee making a choice he would not otherwise make and will significantly impact his life. This circumstance is unfortunate but it is not your problem.
>
> **Liberal** This is one order you should not follow if you want to live with yourself afterward. You must forewarn your employee that he is about to be laid off so that he does not put himself in a compromising position financially. Since you have proven he can trust you, ask him for his confidence in return. Communicate to him that he cannot breathe a word of this layoff to anyone else. Hopefully he will appreciate the risk you are taking and keep this matter to himself.

SUMMARY

This is a very difficult circumstance to handle ethically. The odds are pretty good that if you forewarn your employee he will be very upset and even though you put yourself out on a limb to help him, he will be too caught up in his own emotions to see that as help. He will not have anything to lose after you tell him he is being laid off, whereas you have everything to lose. However, if you fail to give him fair warning he will go ahead and buy the house and end up in significant financial danger. The higher principle here is to keep privileged information to yourself, otherwise you violate the trust your boss has in you.

Moral Obligations to New Employees – How Long is Long Enough?

You are developing a sophisticated biotechnology product and have hired someone who appears to be a good match for the position you require filled. This person is selling his house in Texas and moving his family to New York to begin working at your company. After his first month of work you realize that he is not everything you thought he would be. Simultaneously, you get a very impressive resume from a new candidate whom you interview and know would be a better fit for the job. Do you have a moral obligation to the first employee because he sold his home and moved his family to New York just for this employment opportunity?

Conservative It is your job as the manager to select the best team possible to get the job done. You gave the employee from Texas a wonderful opportunity but he did not make the best of it. It is not your responsibility to make sure his life works out for him. This is an unfortunate circumstance, but you must keep in mind what is best for the company.

Liberal Since the man from Texas moved his family, sold his house, and changed his life based on a job proposal from you, you do owe him some time in the job. One month does not determine much. It is irresponsible and unethical to offer a job to someone and then change your mind because you receive a new resume that looks better on paper. You owe the new employee some level of respect for the investment he has made with your company.

SUMMARY

You have to choose between doing whatever is best for the business and honoring the offer made to the new employee, especially because of the sacrifices the new employee made to take the job. Both points of view have their strong points. This is tough, because if an employee does not shine in their first two pay periods, they usually never shine. If you show mercy here, you will question that decision again and again. Is it more ethical to keep a team member that is not performing for another month? Another quarter? Strong expectations of performance build strong companies.

The Software Development Team – What About Quality of Life?

You are a project manager for a team of software developers. It seems that the team is always under aggressive deadlines because management sets impossible timelines for the completion of projects. Your team works around the clock. They eat their dinner out of the vending machine every night. They are all beginning to look a little pale from so much time under fluorescent lighting and their eyes are buggy from staring at their computer screens non-stop. They get very little time with their families and friends. All of the members of your team are doing whatever it takes because they cannot afford to lose their jobs. Is it your responsibility as the project manager to go to senior management and communicate that these timelines are destroying the quality of life for your employees?

Conservative The software industry is a very competitive business. Many software companies have work environments such as the one mentioned in this issue. If job demands conflict with the employees' personal lives, it is not the right job for them and they need to find something more conducive to their personality. It is not your problem as the manager.

Liberal Even if the software industry has turned into a business that keeps crazy hours, this does not mean that you as the manager should support this type of morally destructive work environment. You need to go to bat for your team and speak with senior management. Explain that this pace will only burn people out and produce mistakes. Regardless of the job demands, people need to have a life outside of work.

SUMMARY

The information technology (IT) industry has become extremely competitive. Startup companies often require individuals to live at the office. In some organizations this has become the norm rather than the exception. If you work for this type of company, you need to determine whether you need to speak up and try to influence a positive change in the environment. Realistically, working lots and lots of hours is not the same thing as being productive; speak up and get some rest.

Unbridled Change is a Sign of Lax Ethics

It is unethical as an executive to manage a business that depends on IT, and not manage IT changes effectively.

I have been in countless enterprise IT operations and heard the "yeah, we've got that" claim when IT managers are asked about change management. My experience has been that much of the time what they have in place amounts to change miss-management. The word manage can be used as a noun or a verb. I prefer the verb usage. Webster defines manage this way:

"To handle or direct with a degree of skill: to make and keep compliant."

To effectively and ethically manage change one must do the following:

1. Intend to manage all change as an organization.

2. Communicate the intention and the requirement to all stakeholders

3. Provide a structure to do change the right way (process, education)

4. Create measurement tools that objectively express actual effort in relation to the pre-established goals

5. Use the measurement tools regularly

6. Implement a system of controls that can instrument success or failure of the process (IE detective controls that detect change-does it match a change request?)

Continued

7. Reward people for the correct behavior.

8. For all other behavior - training.

Kevin Behr
CTO IP Services
President ITPI

How Far Will You Go to Make the Extra Buck

Management always faces the temptation to cut costs through unethical means. These means are within the law, but affect the quality of life for individuals or the amount of work allocated to the local community. Most professionals fall victim to the desire to make an additional buck through questionable morals.

This section addresses the ethical issues managers may face when choosing between what is morally right and what will make them or their company more money. The first issue discusses sources of cheap labor such as the practice of sponsoring visa's for non-citizens and then capitalizing on this practice. The next issue addresses business decisions that result in personal financial gains. Finally, we discuss the ethics of business partnerships and whether the moral standards of a business partner are reflections upon the company.

Cheap Labor – Should You Hire Them?

You are a senior manager in IT for a telecommunications company in midtown New York City. Average independent Oracle database consultants bill between $60 and $150 an hour. You have the option of hiring consultants from India through a contracting company that sponsors their work visas. The consultants from India only cost $12 an hour. You know that these $12-an-hour imported consultants live in horrible conditions, separated from their families, and are treated unfairly. Since they are so desperate for work so they can send money home to their families, they will tolerate almost anything. In addition, these imported consultants take work away from U.S. citizens. The work done by the people from India is comparable to the work generated by the independent consultants. Do you do hire the $12 an hour consultants to save money?

Corporate Responsibility for Information Security

Have you ever noticed that many individuals fail to see the inherent value that information security provides until it's simply too late? When cost-conscious organizations start to consider an investment in security one of the first terms that consistently pops up is 'return on investment.' So tell me, how do you show someone a return on their investment when they don't understand the real risks that are involved to begin with?

The answer is usually "You can't." Unfortunately, many organizations ignore security as a by-product of paranoid minds and it seems nearly impossible to convince them until that one fateful day that they, too, become a victim. Yes folks, it happens everyday. New organizations are jumping on the security bandwagon every day because they now understand what the return on investment can be.

There is an ethical obligation by all organizations that have customers to protect any information about that customer. It shouldn't always come down to whether we buy a new server or implement a firewall. Customers are the key to business. Without them, businesses would never make it past the initial business plan. Let's totally ignore the fact that poor security can result in down time, lost resources and revenue, or a total loss of competitive advantage. Simple consider the fact that when our customers are let down, they move on to a more reliable source. When customers move on, we have no business.

Russ Rogers, CISSP
Security Horizon

Conservative Hiring someone just to save money regardless of the circumstances of that hire is inappropriate. You need to take into account the whole picture. If you know someone is being grossly taken advantage of and their quality of life is terrible, you cannot in good conscience use them for your personal gain.

Liberal Your job as the senior manager of the telecommunications company is to get the best person for the job and to economize wherever possible. Independent consultants are simply over priced. Since the resulting work is comparable, the intelligent thing to do is hire the workers from India. The $12 an hour is better than what they would make in India, so you are doing nothing wrong.

SUMMARY

The conservative point of view made a statement that is useful for overall consideration of this issue. Look at the big picture. This issue is much more complex than it first appears. Once you have taken all aspects of this dilemma into account, you can make the right ethical choice. Some management decisions require careful consideration before action. There are several moral issues to consider:

1. The process of hiring individuals that are severely underpaid and mistreated because they have no say in the matter due to their visa status is a serious moral consideration.

2. The act of hiring individuals imported from other countries rather than supporting the U.S. economy addresses the moral issues of a corporation's support of the local economy.

3. Trying to prevent a waste of corporate money and resources by not hiring overpriced independent consultants, counters the previous two moral issues and is a valid argument in and of itself.

It would seem that the reasonable choice would be to pay them $15 dollars an hour and insist they are treated humanely.

Acquisitions for Personal Reasons – Should You Challenge It?

You work in marketing as a product manager for a line of inkjet printers for a major computer company. The Senior Vice President of Marketing has heavily promoted the acquisition of a small inkjet printer company. As you look at the company's business, it makes no sense to you because it has no added value to what you already provide. In your evaluation process you discover the Chief Executive Officer (CEO) is a very close friend of your marketing VP. In company meetings, people challenge the strategic value of acquiring the inkjet printer company and your VP defends it strongly without revealing that he has what you believe to be a personal stake. What should you do?

Conservative Since you are the product manager and are junior to the Senior Vice President of Marketing, it is not your place to question him or his motives. This will only backfire on you and your career with the company. You must presume that there are reasons other than personal motives for acquiring the inkjet company. A senior VP would not make this type of decision just to help out a close friend.

Liberal Stockholders and additional senior management have the right to know the reality of the decision to acquire the inkjet company. All of the facts need to be laid on the table. It is decisions like this that make or break a company. Take the chance and lay it all on the line. You may be saving the company by displaying the courage to challenge an unethical senior manager.

SUMMARY

In the role of manager you often see a lot more corporate politics in play. You need to pick your battles. If there is a gross dramatization of failing morals, you must step forward. However, not every battle can be won. If your goal is to align the company to the right ethics, it is better for you to stay with the company as long as you can. If you decide that this battle is one that you should fight, make sure you know the facts. Research all of the details of the acquisition and provide evidence to support your point of view. Just throwing a gut feeling out there will do nothing except create a formidable enemy or quickly get you fired.

Ethics in Business Partnerships – What About Human Rights?

You are a senior vice president at a clothing company responsible for monitoring the production operations of vendors and strategic partnerships. Your business designs the clothing line in the U.S. and then farms out the production process to companies outside of the U.S. because the labor is cheap. You know that the vendors you use violate human rights by utilizing child labor for very little money. Does your corporation have any responsibility for the continuity of child labor? In addition, you have the power to change how your company does business. Do you propose to find other vendors who can produce the clothing line at a greater cost, but that do not violate human rights?

Conservative When dealing with matters as stark as child labor, you cannot overlook the practices of your strategic partners even if the laws are different in their country of business. If you know for certain that the vendors you utilize use child labor, you must find better alternatives even if those alternatives cost the company more money.

Liberal   You cannot be held accountable for the ethics of every business partner, vendor, or product you utilize. This is absurd. Would you check the business ethics of the company that makes your staplers or paper clips to make sure they follow proper ethical guidelines? You are responsible for the ethics and moral values of your company. You cannot possibly control anyone else or presume to avoid doing business with other companies because you question their moral values.

SUMMARY

There is truth to both points of view regarding the issue of child labor and strategic partners or vendors. The way to sift through the arguments and find out which point of view is true is to feel the answer with your heart rather than analyze the facts. It is up to you to decide if it is obsessive to consider every single vendor and veto any that potentially have some part of their product made in an ethically questionable manner. Everyone inherently knows the difference between right and wrong. Managers get stumped because they let all of the data and arguments cloud their initial gut feeling about right behavior.

Doing Business with a Non-reputable Company – Should You ask for References?

You need to find a software product for your payroll system. One company you come across has an excellent product that will not put much of a dent in your budget. The only problem is they have a poor reputation in the industry. Do you go with them anyway?

Conservative   Industry reputation is a key factor when considering a vendor solution. If a vendor does not possess a good reputation it is a risk to purchase from them, even if you can save money by doing so. The price may be attractive but remember, you get what you pay for. If a company lacks morals, they cannot be trusted with your sensitive payroll system.

Liberal You need to find out for yourself if the product is good or not and if the company is responsible. If possible, perform a trial and meet with company representatives yourself. It is not ethical to listen to gossip without finding out the facts.

SUMMARY

IT professionals and businesses are trusted with highly sensitive information such as payroll data, credit card data, corporate strategies, and so on. Because of this, technology leaders must adhere to a high code of ethics. Reputation should not be under estimated. If the potential vendor has a reputation of selling sensitive customer information to third-party marketing companies and this can be proven, by no means should you do business with them. However, if they have a reputation for weak customer service, phone calls to company references will quickly help you determine if this is gossip created by a competitor or truth.

Personal Employee Issues

At some point in time, managers find themselves listening to the personal problems of one of their employees. The circumstances of these instances may vary from a long time employee who confides in you because you have developed a friendship over the years, to a new hire with serious personal problems. This section addresses whether personal issues belong in the workplace. We consider how much, if any, a manager should listen to or address employee personal issues. At first glance you might think that personal matters do not belong in the workplace. However, in reality, most people prioritize their families and relationships above their careers. In order for both to work there needs to be some level of compromise. Some workplace environments are supportive of the personal needs of employees, whereas others leave personal matters out of the office.

We begin this section with a discussion on promiscuous dress in the workplace and how management must handle these matters. Next, we delve into affairs in the workplace, especially when they are known to or with senior management. The next topic regarding lewd or inappropriate comments made by coworkers brings to light the referee role management must play at times with employee interactions. Finally, we summarize this section with a consideration of exactly how much time management should spend on personal employee dilemmas.

Dress in the Work Place – What is Appropriate?

A new hire comes to work in extremely tight and somewhat promiscuous attire. Although your company is pretty liberal, there is a dress policy. Her attire is not exactly fitting to the corporate environment. You notice that the way she dresses causes minor daily disruptions in the workplace. Her attire is also creating quite a stir with the women at the office who stand around gossiping about how she looks. Your female coworkers ask you to speak with her. However, as her male boss you are actually attracted to her style of dress. Do you have to reprimand her?

> **Conservative** If an employee's attire is distracting others from working, it is time to talk with them. This should not be part of the manager's job but in reality, management is a lot more than structuring workflow. No human being is perfect and to get a combination of different types of people to work together effectively, a good manager is required to have excellent interpersonal skills. You need to speak with the new hire and explain the dress code. Keep the conversation light and simple.

> **Liberal** This is not high school and employees are entitled to dress as they please within reason. It is not your place to tell the new hire how to dress. It is not the place of other employees to determine that either. This is not a management issue.

SUMMARY

If you decide you must address this issue, to avoid additional problems you may want to ask a female manager or female coworker to speak with the woman. This may be a better way to deal with the problem, especially if you are attracted to her style of dress. If you decide to confront the employee, have a female manager present.

Travel Expenses for Affairs – Should You Intervene?

One of your employee's is having an affair with an employee from another office and frequently requests to travel for business to that office. You know of this affair. Do you confront them or utilize it for the business?

Conservative Stay out of personal matters. If you require your employee to travel, request that they do so. If travel is unnecessary, deny the request. Ignore the affair completely.

Liberal Depending on how well you know your employee and the other person in question, you may want to speak to them about the affair since, in a sense you are funding these trysts. The primary issue to communicate is that their personal choices are their own but they need to consider how this affects the work they do for the company and how it may reflect on the company.

SUMMARY

Affairs in the workplace are sensitive matters both for the individuals involved and the coworkers who are aware of the affair. Some people may find it morally wrong to keep it a secret since they themselves would want to know if their partner was fooling around on them. As more employees become aware of the affair, it will become more of a complex matter in the workplace. Is it more ethical to ignore it for another week? Another month? Until it blows up into a big mess?

Lewd Comments in the Workplace – Is this Harassment?

You are a male senior manager for a Wall Street brokerage business. The trading floor is a pretty rambunctious environment. The men make lewd comments to each other. One of the male traders has not been performing well on the job. The other men make comments to him such as asking him if it is that time of the month or call him names such as "girly" or "pansy." All of the men in question are heterosexual. The employee complains to you that he is being harassed by the other men. The laws against sexual harassment protect women and men from unwanted advances by the opposite sex. In this circumstance the man is not being singled out because of his sex; he is being picked on because of his lack of guts or skill on the trading floor. Addressing this matter will alienate you from the rest of the macho team who are the ones that bring the money into the business. Should you as the senior manager address this ethical dilemma as if it is sexual harassment?

Conservative Lewd comments in the workplace need to be addressed. No one should have to work in an environment where they are being harassed, whether it is by someone of the same sex or the opposite sex. It is part of your job as a manager to enforce a professional work environment. Meet with the team and set up a formal policy against these types of comments.

Liberal There is no reason you should "deal" with your star performers because someone who cannot pull his weight is being sensitive. Ignore this matter completely.

SUMMARY

Addressing lewd comments and behavior in the work environment is not an easy thing for a manager to do. It is almost always a mistake to take action when you have only heard one side of the story. Talk to more of the team. Consider the intent of the comments before making a final judgment as to how it should be handled.

@#&!?!

Hostile Work Environments

A large company noticed that the entire network was slowing down considerably over a few days. The slowdown became markedly worse one day for a two-hour period. In checking network usage, the IT administrator saw a peak of Internet usage from one machine in the mailroom. It turned out that an employee was spending his lunch hour e-mailing a CD of pornographic photographs to his friend. Aside from the copyright violation and possible creation of a hostile work environment for the women in the mailroom, the employee was misusing company resources and

Continued

slowing down the entire system. The employee saw nothing wrong with using "his" computer for this activity, and was surprised when given a stern warning.

Barbara Weil Laff
Director
Ireland, Stapleton, Pryor & Pascoe, P.C.

Personal Matters and Work – How do You Maintain a Balance?

You are a director for a large hotel chain and perform an assessment of the management of the hotel. You asked them how much time they spend helping employees with personal issues. You find out that a significant amount of the manager's time goes into the personal problems of their employees. You have determined that lower paid employees such as the cleaning staff and the security staff need some sort of support to do their jobs, such as childcare at the workplace and financial counseling. Is it the manager's responsibility to spend their time helping employees with personal problems? Do you feel that a program needs to be set up to help paid employees with these problems or do you think that the company is wasting its money paying management to help employees sort out their personal problems, which have no place in the workplace?

Conservative   Since it is unrealistic to expect that a worker live solely for the company, a realistic approach to the needs of the employees may potentially create a more effective work environment. Management will always have to deal with employee personal problems to some degree. An ideal circumstance that has proven to be effective in the workplace is to have the human resources department set up programs for employees that enable them to work and handle personal matters such as childcare, exercise programs, and continuing education.

Liberal   Management cannot try to fix all of the needs of their employees. This theory is simply unrealistic. Corporate resources need to go into the company not into coddling employees.

Summary

A balance needs to be struck between humanizing the workplace and meeting the goals of the corporation. Every work environment is unique. It is worth considering the benefits versus the cost to look into work environments that support the employee without taking anything away from the corporation.

Hiring, Firing, and Quitting

Hiring, firing, and quitting are some of the most difficult matters for management to handle. This section deals with the issues of management promotions, pulling resources from other departments, downsizing, and going into business for yourself.

Being Passed Up for Promotion – Should You Tell Your Manager?

A fellow project manager tells you that she plans to quit the company in one month because she received a great opportunity elsewhere. She is waiting a month because her new assignment does not start until then and she wants to be able to work until her new job starts. That same day, you meet with your boss who informs you that you will not be promoted to director because he will be promoting your fellow project manager (the one who accepted a new job). Should you tell your boss that the other project manager is leaving the company in one month?

Conservative It is not your place to communicate to your boss that a coworker is leaving the company. This is true even if that communication may promote your career.

Liberal By all means tell your boss what you know. You will not be hurting anyone. Your coworker already has something better lined up.

SUMMARY

This issue is a matter of personal ethics. You are hungry for the promotion to director. Your coworker can hardly blame you for spilling the beans when this type of promotion is on the line. Any choice you make could result in unintended consequences. The liberal point of view seems to make the most sense for you and for your organization as long as you understand telling the boss what you know will by no means secure the promotion for you.

@#&!?!

Ethics (or Lack Thereof) in the Use of Company Computers

I am an attorney specializing in the law of workplace technology, including employment and intellectual property.

A very angry Chief Executive Officer asked me if she could fire her top-producing employee for disloyalty. The employee, angry that she had not received the raise she thought was due for her services as an outsourced IT consultant, vented her anger in a series of increasingly vitriolic e-mails to a friend who was a former employee of the same company. To bolster her claims that she was underpaid and under-appreciated, she included examples of recent work she had performed, replete with client names, specific issues, and billing amounts. Of course, the disgruntled employee had used the company e-mail account, and somehow forgotten that the company's system administrator had access to all e-mail accounts. The company had informed its employees that it had the right to review all company computers and the data stored on those computers. The employee was fired for disclosing company trade secrets and customer confidential information to someone outside the company.

Barbara Weil Laff
Director
Ireland, Stapleton, Pryor & Pascoe, P.C.

Acquiring Personnel from Other Departments – Should You Make an Offer?

You need a new trusted assistant because your management workload has doubled. You have not been able to find someone that can keep up with you. You need someone really talented and special. There is a woman in accounting who is an excellent trusted assistant. You know she is not happy with her current boss. Do you make her an offer better then her current salary to come work for you?

Conservative   No matter how bad you need a qualified trusted assistant, stealing one away from someone else will not fill that void for you. If she is loyal to her boss she will probably tell him about your offer and you will look bad in the end.

Liberal   A talented worker receives a lot of offers. There is nothing wrong with making an offer to someone who can fit the job position you need filled. It is a compliment to make her an offer even if she refuses.

SUMMARY

An excellent worker is good not only for their skills but because of their work ethic. When someone is really good at what they do, they are not motivated by money alone. They may be motivated by the chemistry with their boss or by potential advancement. Or they are the type of person who takes a great deal of pride in their work. These types of people cannot be bought with money. If you really want her to be your trusted assistant find out what motivates her and speak with her boss directly.

Downsizing and Age Discrimination – Where is the Loyalty?

Your company must downsize immediately. Historically there is an unspoken policy that the individuals closest to retirement should be downsized first because they make the most money. This means that you will have to downsize some of the employees who have been with you the longest rather than the new recruits. They will receive a retirement package but not one equivalent to what they would obtain if they stayed on until their full retirement age. Is this strategy ethical?

Conservative Downsizing the individuals closest to retirement is a common practice in business. This strategy requires the fewest layoffs because the longest employees tend to make the most money and therefore you will only have to retire half of the amount of people.

Liberal Something is just not right about the strategy of letting the long time loyal employees go right before they qualify for full retirement benefits. It is wrong and does not display loyalty to those who showed the company tremendous loyalty.

SUMMARY

Maybe an optimum response to addressing this strategy is to offer early retirement to individuals who have demonstrated company loyalty. Do not reduce their benefits. This will still cut the money expended on employees down significantly without punishing those who have demonstrated years of loyalty. However, be aware that the next rank of employees, the ones 5 to 10 years from retirement, will bitterly question your decision because they will want the same benefits.

Breaking Out on Your Own – Should You Compete with Your Previous Employer?

You have been a senior manager for a networking consulting company for 15 years. Your pay has not increased significantly through the years. You decide to start your own network consulting business that will be in direct competition with the company you used to work for. Is it ethical to break out on your own and be in direct competition with a company you worked for?

Conservative If you need to make more money simply request a raise, do not go in direct competition with the hand that has fed you for years. You may end up with nothing in the end.

Liberal Today, the IT industry is filled with independents and small corporations for the very reason addressed in this issue. Big business takes as much as it can from the individual employee, keeping as much profit as possible.

This is just a business principle. The larger the business the more money it requires to sustain it. The entrepreneur is the answer to the employee limitations of big business.

Summary

Deciding to start up your own business after managing in someone else's for years is a brave move. If you decide to do this make sure it is not on impulse but based on a well-considered plan. Do not count on being able to hit the ground running. Most new businesses lose money the first year. Above all, if you are considering unethical force multipliers such as stealing contact lists, remember that you may not just be breaking trust, you may also be violating the law and your former employer can probably afford to sue you in court.

Chapter Summary

The information age has not just affected our privacy, communications, and global business, it has most directly affected our humanity. This chapter addressed a wide range of dilemmas faced by the management team. We began with diversity. Managing diversity requires sensitivity and strength when dealing with conflicts of religion and business or minority barriers.

Following the discussion on diversity we addressed management's responsibility for fair treatment of all employees. You learned that not everyone under a manager's care deserves equal privileges and pay.

Our next topic seriously responded to the need to remember we are all human beings first and workers second. We discussed how managers sometimes objectify the human being as a commodity and separate themselves from feeling and relationship with their employees out of necessity.

We then delved into pushing the ethics limits to make more money. We answered the question of how far is too far. Management frequently faces the temptation to cut costs through unethical means. This means may be through underpaying individuals or working a side deal that brings them more money personally.

A common management problem is dealing with personal employee issues. We addressed whether personal issues belong in the workplace and considered how much time a manager should allocate to employee personal issues.

This chapter concluded with a consideration on hiring, firing, and quitting and the ethics of appropriately handling promotions, downsizing, and going into business for yourself.

Frequently Asked Questions

The following Frequently Asked Questions, answered by the authors of this book, are designed to get you thinking about the ethical considerations of diversity and relationships in the workplace. Unless legal issues are involved, then answers in the FAQ may not be the right answer for your organization.

Q: What are potential ethical issues of diversity in the workplace?

A: Diversity issues in the workplace include religious beliefs that conflict with work practices, cultural differences that affect employment, hiring based on gender or race, and prejudice from other employees because of any of these differences.

Q: Is it acceptable to treat some employees differently then others?

A: If an employee is your friend and that is the only reason they receive differential treatment, then that is unethical. However, if an employee stands out from the rest because of exceptional job performance, it is morally acceptable to give them benefits that the others do not receive based on their job performance.

Q: What are some of the ways in which management dehumanizes employees?

A: There is a tendency in big business to think of the staff as commodities rather than as human beings with families and feelings. Sometimes not enough consideration is made when hiring or firing employees and how it will affect their lives.

Q: What is the bottom line when it comes to determining if your morals are correct when going for the extra buck?

A: Everyone inherently knows the difference between right and wrong. You can feel it. As a manager you must let go of the data and arguments that cloud your initial gut knowing.

Q: What are common personal issues that you as a manger may have to face with your employees?

A: A manager may relate to employees about personal issues ranging from mild issues such as inappropriate dress, lewd comments at work, vulgarity, and so forth to more serious issues of affairs in the workplace, a death in the family, and serious illness.

Q: If you decide to start your own business after managing at a company for many years, what should you seriously consider?

A: Start your business on facts and realism. Speak to an accountant, lawyer, and others who have done it. Most new businesses lose money the first year.

Chapter 21

Conclusion

We hope that you have enjoyed reading the ethical issues, Anecdotes and Soapboxes in this book. This has been a fun project for us. Now, as we conclude this book, we need to consider the application of what you have read. In the movie the Matrix, the sign above the door in the Oracle's kitchen said, *Tenet Nosce*, "Know Thyself." Each and every one of us has a choice to make, whether to pursue a regulated life or to act in a willy-nilly fashion. We encourage you to make that choice for your life right now. After all, how many times does an adult stop to consider right and wrong? In the workplace, the disciplined individual often rises to the positions of promotion and authority. Sure, we can all cite exceptions where someone with no principles, no vision, and no sense of human dignity somehow became the boss, but they never become a leader and usually are only in charge for a brief spell.

As we close, we consider the role of the human conscience in ethics as well as the two primary futures for Information Technology (IT) and Information Technology Security (ITSEC) workers. As professionals, we can choose to adopt standards for behavior and performance and set our feet on a path to professionalism, or not. Finally, we consider a code of ethics for our profession and end with a call to action.

The conscience is our compass of right and wrong; it rewards and it punishes. When we do something good, we often feel very pleased, and when we do something wrong we feel guilty. We can choose to sharpen our attention to that voice. As we face business decisions, we can to choose to ask ourselves, "Is this ethical, is there even a hint of something shameful in what we are considering?" We can also choose to keep our conscience silent. If we do the wrong thing again and again, ignoring our moral compass, soon we do not feel guilty, at least about that particular aspect of our life.

This is what happened with Andersen and Enron; they ignored their moral compass. Turning a deaf ear to the conscience is part and parcel of every great moral lapse. It is what the U.S. cellblock 1A workers in Iraq, the Nazis, the Klu Klux Klan, and extremist religious factions all have in common. Each of these groups must construct an elaborate belief system to make something obviously wrong seem okay. As you read through the issues in this book, you often immediately knew whether something was right or wrong. The odds are high that while you were reading this book you saw an issue where past or present you realized you might be making the wrong choice. If you felt an ethical pang, be thankful; you still have a working conscience. You still have a conscience left. However, you need to choose the right course of action and decide to live the principled life. If you do not, soon you will feel no ethical pangs. Of course, if you are stealing time, products, or resources from your employer, the odds are higher that the elaborate belief system you have constructed will allow you to see that you are going to get caught. Then you will be embarrassed before your peers and will likely face stiff discipline. This is the most important thing that we have learned while doing the research for this book. Choose wisely.

Though we would assert that the role of the conscience applies to all of life, the scope of this book is ethics in IT. We are a fairly new and immature job discipline as IT or ITSEC workers. As time progresses, the world will begin to render judgment on the status and trust level our profession has. Will we be viewed more as auto mechanics or as doctors? Currently, we have no ethical code, no expectations for performance, training, or behavior to govern our profession. As a community, we are at a fork in the road, there are two futures for IT; do we want to be known as principled, which requires both discipline and disciplining our own? When you set standards for a profession, when you draw a line in the sand between acceptable and unacceptable, that sets the stage for greater respect and higher compensation. We invite you choose the higher standard.

The Ten Commandments of Computer Ethics by the Computer Ethics Institute

1. Thou shalt not use a computer to harm other people.
2. Thou shalt not interfere with other people's computer work.
3. Thou shalt not snoop around in other people's computer files.
4. Thou shalt not use a computer to steal.
5. Thou shalt not use a computer to bear false witness.
6. Thou shalt not copy or use proprietary software for which you have not paid.
7. Thou shalt not use other people's computer resources without authorization or proper compensation.
8. Thou shalt not appropriate other people's intellectual output.
9. Thou shalt think about the social consequences of the program you are writing or the system you are designing.
10. Thou shalt always use a computer in ways that insure consideration and respect for your fellow humans.

Copyright 1991 Computer Ethics Institute
Author: Dr. Ramon C. Barquin
www.cpsr.org/program/ethics/cei.html

For the IT profession to choose to be viewed as professionals, there must be a standard of measurement. A Code of Ethics is the classical non-technical standard of measurement. To create the code shown in the following, we evaluated a number of existing and proposed codes giving particular attention to the Association for Computing Machinery (ACM), Brookings Computer Ethics Institute and Institute of Electrical and Electronic Engineers (IEEE). The following Code of Ethics is well suited for the IT and ITSEC professions and has been subjected to extensive public scrutiny.

IT Professional Code of Ethics

- I will strive to know myself and be honest about my capability.
- I will strive for technical excellence in the IT profession by maintaining and enhancing my own knowledge and skills. I acknowledge that there are many free resources available on the Internet and affordable books and that the lack of my employer's training budget is not an excuse nor limits my ability to stay current in IT.
- When possible, I will demonstrate my performance capability with my skills via projects, leadership, and/or accredited educational programs and will encourage others to do so as well.
- I will not hesitate to seek assistance or guidance when faced with a task beyond my abilities or experience. I will embrace other professionals' advice and learn from their experiences and mistakes. I will treat this as an opportunity to learn new techniques and approaches. When the situation arises that my assistance is called upon, I will respond willingly to share my knowledge with others.
- I will strive to convey any knowledge (specialist or otherwise) that I have gained to others so that everyone gains the benefit of each other's knowledge.
- I will teach the willing and empower others with Industry Best Practices (IBP). I will offer my knowledge to show others how to become security professionals in their own right.
- I will strive to be perceived as and be an honest and trustworthy employee.
- I will not advance private interests at the expense of end users, colleagues, or my employer.
- I will not abuse my power. I will use my technical knowledge, user rights, and permissions only to fulfill my responsibilities to my employer.
- I will avoid and be alert to any circumstances or actions that might lead to conflicts of interest or the perception of conflicts of interest. If such circumstance occurs, I will notify my employer or business partners.
- I will not steal property, time, or resources.
- I will reject bribery or kickbacks and will report such illegal activity.

- I will report on the illegal activities of myself and others without respect to the punishments involved. I will not tolerate those who lie, steal, or cheat as a means of success in IT.
- I will conduct my business in a manner that assures the IT profession is considered one of integrity and professionalism.
- I will not injure others, their property, reputation, or employment by false or malicious action.
- I will not use availability and access to information for personal gains through corporate espionage.
- I distinguish between advocacy and engineering. I will not present analysis and opinion as fact.
- I will adhere to IBP for system design, rollout, hardening and testing.
- I am obligated to report all system vulnerabilities that might result in significant damage.
- I respect intellectual property and will be careful to give credit for other's work. I will never steal or misuse copyrighted, patented material, trade secrets, or any other intangible asset.
- I will accurately document my setup procedures and any modifications I have done to equipment. This will ensure that others will be informed of procedures and changes I have made.
- I respect privacy and confidentiality.
- I respect the privacy of my coworkers' information. I will not peruse or examine their information including data, files, records, or network traffic except as defined by the appointed roles, the organization's acceptable use policy as approved by Human Resources, and without the permission of the end user.
- I will obtain permission before probing systems on a network for vulnerabilities.
- I respect the right to confidentiality with my employers, clients, and users except has dictated by applicable law.
- I respect human dignity.
- I treasure and will defend equality, justice, and respect for others.
- I will not participate in any form of discrimination, whether due to race, color, national origin, ancestry, sex, sexual orientation, gender/sexual identity or expression, martial status, creed, religion, age, disability, veteran's status, or political ideology.

The wise professional always strives to improve and is grateful for constructive criticism. If you feel there are tenets that are missing in the code, please let us know what they are. If you feel something is misstated, we would be eager to hear from you. If you feel one of the tenets is culturally inappropriate, we would love to give consideration to your impressions.

In this chapter, we considered the role of the conscience in ethics. We discussed the two primary futures for IT/ITSEC workers, one where we do whatever we think is right and the other a future of professional discipline. We realize that to live a regulated life, there must be standards of discipline. We have discussed a code of ethics designed for our profession. We have one last bit of work ahead of us in the book; we need to issue a call to action. As an IT professional, are you willing to agree to live by a published code of conduct?

We invite you to print out the code of conduct , sign it, and hang it on your wall for all to see and judge your actions by. It is available here at www.sans.org/resources/ethics.php

If you choose to join those of us in the community who seek higher standards of professionalism in IT, you are truly welcome. You will fail from time to time, that is part of the human condition. Do not think you can reach perfection through a path of discipline; that is not part of the human condition. However, we can strive to be professionals, we can strive not to extinguish the quiet voice of our conscience in a given area, and that is exactly what we challenge you to do.

About The SANS Institute

SANS is the most trusted and by far the largest source for information security training and certification in the world. It also develops, maintains, and makes available at no cost, the largest collection of research documents about various aspects of information security, and it operates the Internet's early warning system - Internet Storm Center. The SANS (SysAdmin, Audit, Network, Security) Institute was established in 1989 as a cooperative research and education organization. Its programs now reach more than 165,000 security professionals, auditors, system administrators, network administrators, chief information security officers, and CIOs who share the lessons they are learning and jointly find solutions to the challenges they face. At the heart of SANS are the many security practitioners in government agencies, corporations, and universities around the world who invest hundreds of hours each year in research and teaching to help the entire information security community.

Many SANS resources, such as the weekly vulnerability digest (@RISK), the weekly news digest (NewsBites), the Internet's early warning system (Internet Storm Center), flash security alerts and more than 1,200 award-winning, original research papers are free to all who ask.

Programs of the SANS Institute:

- Information Security Training (more than 400 multi-day courses in 90 cities around the world)

- The GIAC Certification Program (technical certification for people you trust to protect your systems)

- Consensus Security Awareness Training (for all the people who use computers)

- SANS Weekly Bulletins and Alerts (definitive updates on security news and vulnerabilities)

- SANS Information Security Reading Room (more than 1,200 original research papers in 75 important categories of security)

- SANS Step-by-Step Guides (booklets providing guidance on protecting popular operating systems and applications)

- SANS Security Policy Project (free security policy templates - proven in the real world)

- Vendor Related Resources (highlighting the vendors that can help make security more effective)

- Information Security Glossary (words, acronyms, more)

- Internet Storm Center (the Internet's Early Warning System)

- SCORE (helping the security community reach agreement on how to secure common software and systems)

- SANS/FBI Annual Top Twenty Internet Security Vulnerabilities List

- Intrusion Detection FAQ (Frequently asked questions and answers about intrusion detection)

- SANS Press Room (Our press room is designed to assist the media in coverage of the information assurance industry.)

SANS Computer & Information Security Training—(www.sans.org)

SANS provides intensive, immersion training designed to help you and your staff master the practical steps necessary for defending systems and networks against the most dangerous threats - the ones being actively exploited. The courses are full of important and immediately useful techniques that you can put to work as soon as you return to your offices. They were developed through a consensus process involving hundreds of administrators, security managers, and information security professionals, and address both security fundamentals and the in-depth technical aspects of the most crucial areas of information security. SANS training can be taken in a classroom setting from SANS-certified instructors, self-paced over the Internet, or in mentored settings in cities around the world. Each year, SANS programs educate more than 12,000 people in the US and internationally. To find the best teachers in each topic in the world, SANS runs a continuous competition for instructors. Last year more than 90 people tried out for the SANS faculty, but only five new people were selected.

SANS also offers a Volunteer Program through which, in return for acting as an important extension of SANS' conference staff, volunteers may attend classes at no cost. Volunteers are most definitely expected to pull their weight and the educational rewards for their doing so are substantial.

The GIAC Certification Program—(www.giac.org)

In 1999, SANS founded GIAC, the Global Information Assurance Certification, which has allowed thousands of security professionals to prove their skills and knowledge meet challenging standards. GIAC offers certifications that address multiple specialty areas: security essentials, intrusion detection, incident handling, firewalls and perimeter protection, operating system security, and more. GIAC is unique in the field of information security certifications by not only testing a candidate's knowledge, but also testing a candidate's ability to put that knowledge into practice in the real world. Because of GIAC's practical focus, a Gartner Group study named GIAC "the preferred credential" for individuals who have technical security responsibilities

SANS Security Awareness Training—(www.sans.org/awareness/)

Even when every computer system is tightly secured, users can accidentally open back doors that allow malicious code to enter the network and hackers to steal critical information. Most security awareness programs miss the most important threats and focus on the unimportant ones. SANS has forged an online program that gets at the heart of the threat. You can use it to train a few dozen or a hundred thousand employees or any number in between.

SANS Weekly Security Bulletins and Alerts—(www.sans.org/newsletters/)

Every Wednesday, a dozen security managers in large organizations around the world take time out to share what they are doing to protect their organizations against the specific critical vulnerabilities that have been discovered that week. On Monday morning, more than 190,000 people receive an email listing the critical new vulnerabilities and a summary of what those leading organizations are doing for self-protection. That vulnerability consensus report, called @RISK, is one of three weekly bulletins that SANS prepares for the community. Another one, NewsBites, summarizes the top twenty news stories in security and allows six of the most respected security guru's to offer commentary on those stories. More than 160,000 people get NewsBites every Wednesday. SANS also publishes PrivacyBits, a summary of privacy news and AuditBits, and NetworkBits.

To subscribe, use the portal, http://portal.sans.org or to access our archive, http://www.sans.org/newsletters

Information Security Reading Room—(www.sans.org/rr/)

More than three thousand five hundred people who have earned GIAC GSEC certification each invested dozens of hours creating original, peer-reviewed research reports on up-to-date topics of interest to security professionals. You can find more than 1,300 of the most recent papers in the Information Security Reading Room. On average, 14,000 people use the reports every day.

SANS Step-by-Step Guides—(https://store.sans.org/store_category.php?category=stepxstep)

Hundreds of security professionals working together have crafted step-by-step guides for hardening operating systems and applications. Among the most popular SANS guides are Windows 2000, Solaris, Linux, Cisco Routers, and Oracle. Step-by-Step guides are also available for Incident Handling, Business Law, Intrusion Detection and more.

SANS Security Policy Project— (www.sans.org/resources/policies/)

Security policies are difficult to write well and remarkably similar to one another in their key elements. SANS has gathered a set of field-proven policies to help you get started on creating a workable set for your organization.

Vendor Related Resources— (www.sans.org/vendor/)

Effective cyber defense requires tools and often requires outside support. Deciding among the myriad choices is very challenging. To help, SANS publishes a semi-annual Roadmap to Security Tools poster that is mailed to 350,000 people, and we also offer web broadcasts that allow you to hear and see what key tools can do. At the larger training programs, we allow vendors to demonstrate their latest and most important tools. We also maintain a library of white papers developed by vendors. Some are too promotional, but many of the white papers contain excellent analysis done by independent third parties.

Information Security Glossary— (www.sans.org/resources/glossary.php)

With enormous help from the National Security Agency, SANS makes available a glossary of common terms.

Internet Storm Center—(http://isc.sans.org/)

In 1999, SANS created the Internet Storm Center, a powerful tool for detecting rising Internet threats. The Storm Center uses advanced data correlation and visualization techniques to analyze data collected from more than 3,000 firewalls and intrusion detection systems in over sixty countries. Experienced analysts constantly monitor the Storm Center data feeds and search for trends and anomalies in order to identify potential threats. When a potential threat is detected, the team immediately begins an intensive investigation to gauge the threat's severity and impact. The Storm Center may request correlating data from an extensive network of security experts from across the globe, and possesses the in-house expertise to analyze captured attack tools quickly and thoroughly. Critical information is disseminated to the public in the form of alerts and postings.

SCORE—(www.sans.org/score/)

SCORE is a community of security professionals from a wide range of organizations and backgrounds working to develop consensus regarding minimum standards and best practice information. It provides its findings as input to the global security benchmarks consensus project being run by the Center for Internet Security (CIS) (www.cisecurity.org). CIS is widely regarded as the standard setter for safe configuration of systems connected o the Internet. The SANS Institute is a Founding Charter Member of The Center for Internet Security, a cooperative initiative through which industry, government, and research leaders are establishing basic operational security benchmarks and keeping them up-to-date.

SANS Top Twenty List—(www.sans.org/top20)

The "Top Ten" list was first released by the SANS Institute and the National Infrastructure Protection Center (NIPC) in 2000. Today, though it is now called the Top Twenty, it covers over 230 well-known, often-exploited vulnerabilities. Thousands of organizations use the list to prioritize their efforts so they can close the most dangerous holes first. The majority of successful attacks on computer systems via the Internet can be traced to the exploitation of security flaws on this list. A number of well-known vulnerability scanners test for the items on the Top Twenty. The SANS/FBI Top Twenty includes step-by-step instructions and pointers to additional information useful for correcting the flaws. SANS updates the list and the instructions as more critical threats and more current or convenient methods are identified. This is a community consensus document and SANS welcomes input.

SANS Press Room—(www.sans.org/press)

Our press room is designed to assist the media in coverage of the information assurance industry by providing:

- Latest Announcements from SANS Institute
- Information Security in the News
- Invitations to Upcoming Media Events
- Interviews with SANS faculty
- Resources and Soundbites for Articles
- Downloadable Resources and Bios

The articles, press releases and other information in the SANS Press Room are available for reproduction without prior permission as long as you cite the individual, source, and the SANS Institute.

GIAC (Global Information Assurance Certification)

The SANS Institute founded GIAC (Global Information Assurance Certification) in 1999 in response to the need to validate the skills of security professionals. GIAC's purpose is to provide assurance that a certified individual holds the appropriate level of knowledge and skill necessary for a practitioner in key areas of information security. We are pleased to announce that SANS' Security Essentials is now certified and 100% compliant with NSTISSI's 4013 training standards.

SANS training and GIAC certifications address a range of skill sets including entry level Information Security Officer and broad based Security Essentials, as well as advanced subject areas like Audit, Intrusion Detection, Incident Handling, Firewalls and Perimeter Protection, Forensics, Hacker Techniques, Windows and Unix Operating System Security. GIAC is unique in measuring knowledge and testing the ability to apply that knowledge in the real world.

GIAC certifications expire in a period of 2-4 years, depending on the certification. Students must review the information and retake the exams in order to remain certified. Realize that while there are competing certifications at the entry level, GIAC is the only information security certification for advanced technical subject areas.

Individual GIAC Certifications

Each GIAC certification is designed to stand on its own, and represents a certified individual's mastery of a particular set of knowledge and skills. There is no particular "order" in which GIAC certifications must be earned; though we recommend that candidates master fundamentals before moving on to more advanced topics.

- GIAC Security Essentials Certification (GSEC)
- GIAC Certified Firewall Analyst (GCFW)
- GIAC Certified Intrusion Analyst (GCIA)
- GIAC Certified Incident Handler (GCIH)
- GIAC Certified Windows Security Administrator (GCWN)
- GIAC Certified UNIX Security Administrator (GCUX)
- GIAC Systems and Network Auditor (GSNA)
- GIAC Certified Forensic Analyst (GCFA)
- GIAC Information Security Fundamentals (GISF)
- GIAC IT Security Audit Essentials (GSAE)
- GIAC Certified ISO-17799 Specialist (G7799)
- GIAC Security Leadership Certification (GSLC)
- GIAC Certified Security Consultant (GCSC)

GIAC Certificate Programs

Each GIAC certificate is designed to stand on its own, and represents a certified individual's mastery of a particular set of knowledge and skills.

Candidates may wish to earn a single certificate that is most suited to their individual needs and/or job responsibilities. GIAC currently offers the following individual certificate programs:

- GIAC HIPAA Security Certificate (GHSC)
- GIAC Windows 2000 Gold Standard Certificate (GGSC-0100)
- GIAC Solaris Gold Standard Certificate (GGSC-0200)

For more information: **www.sans.org** / **www.giac.org**

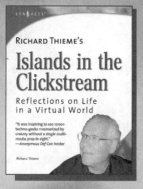
SYNGRESS®